D1502822

WELCOME no. 4 | TOMO TAKEUCHI
TO THE BALLROOM

# Contents

**Heat 12**

Gaju Akagi

003

**Heat 13**

Voltage

041

**Heat 14**

Radiation

077

**Heat 15**

Special Variation

115

**Heat 16**

Judgment

157

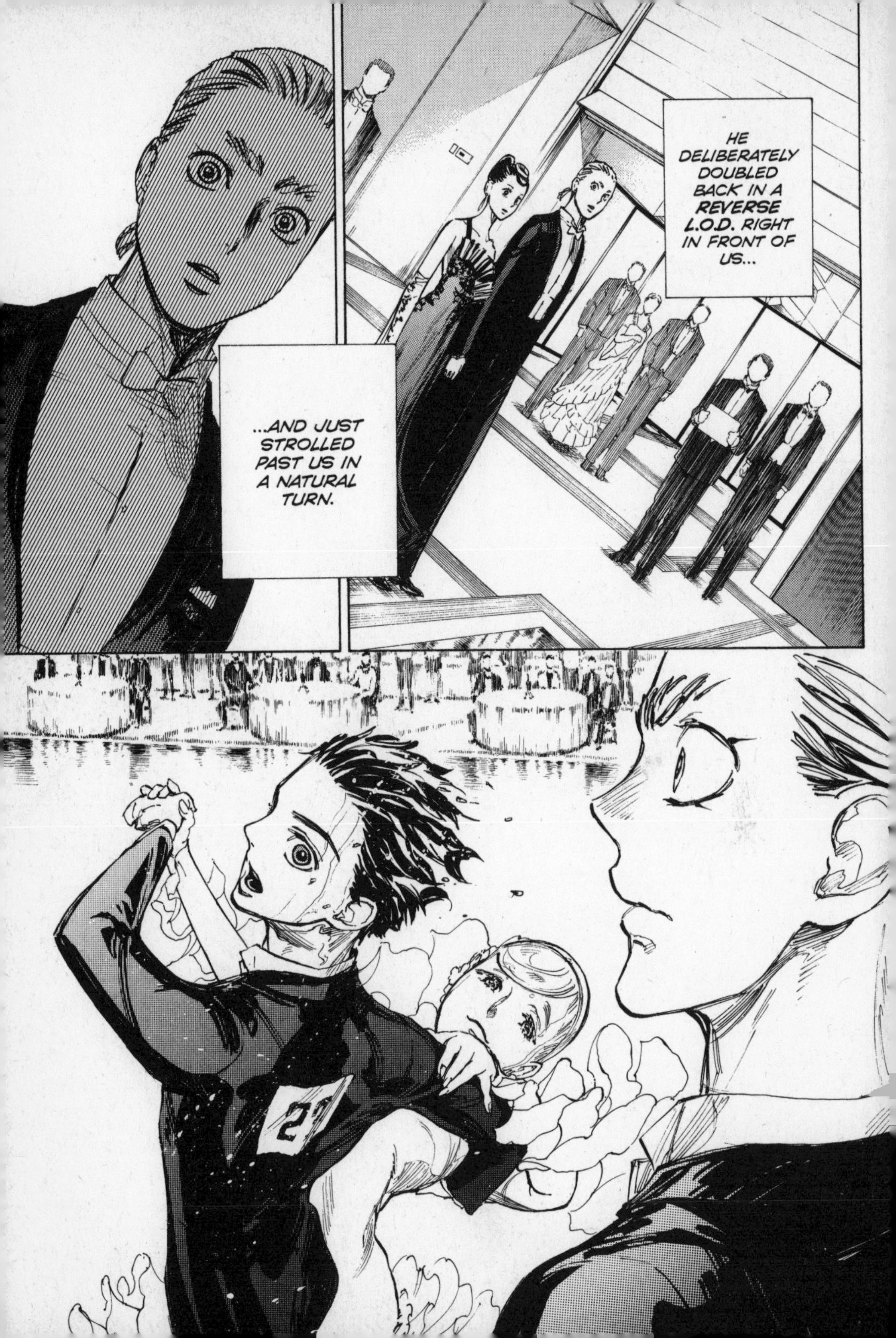
HE DELIBERATELY DOUBLED BACK IN A REVERSE L.O.D. RIGHT IN FRONT OF US...
...AND JUST STROLLED PAST US IN A NATURAL TURN.

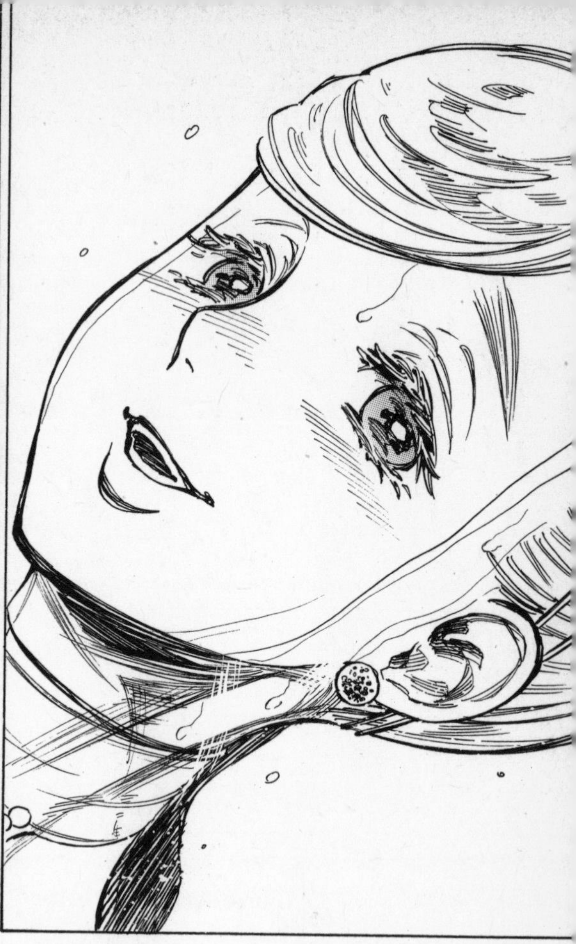

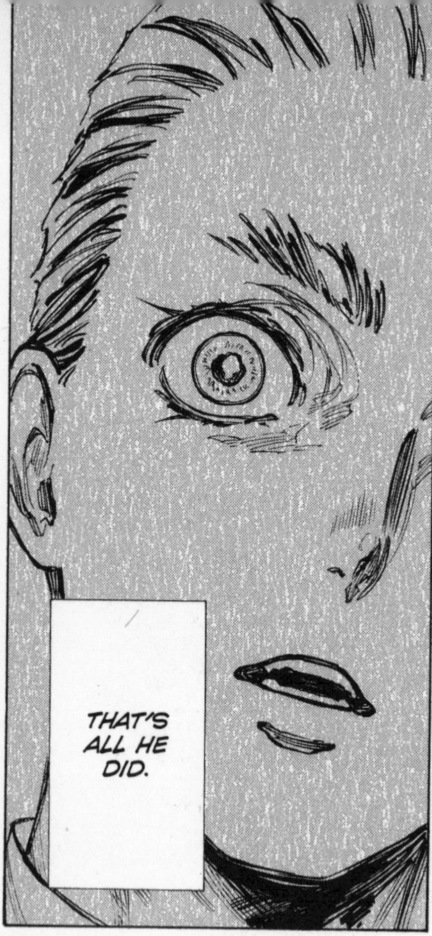
THAT'S ALL HE DID.

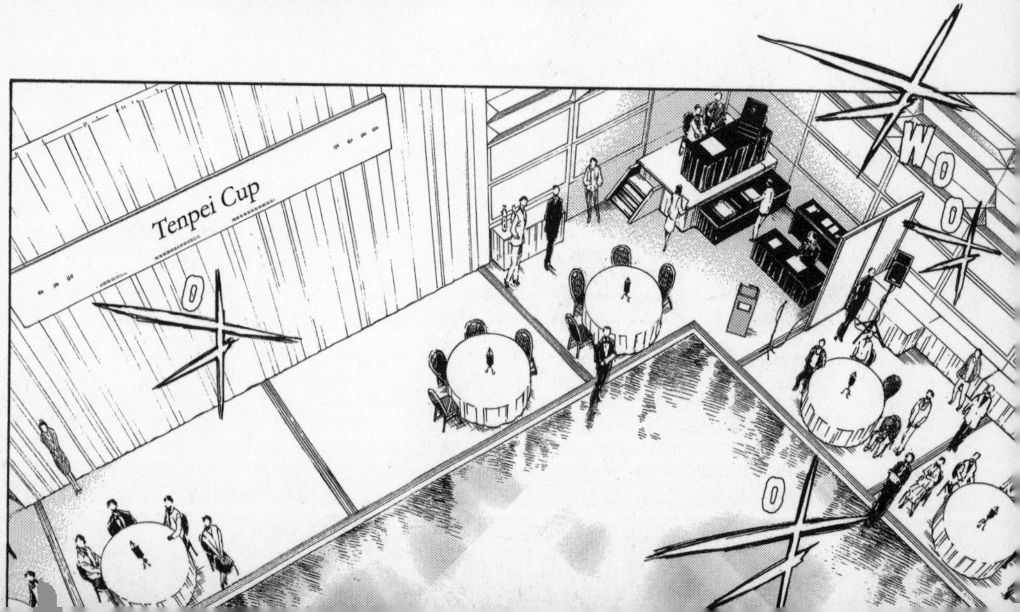
Tenpei Cup
WOOOO

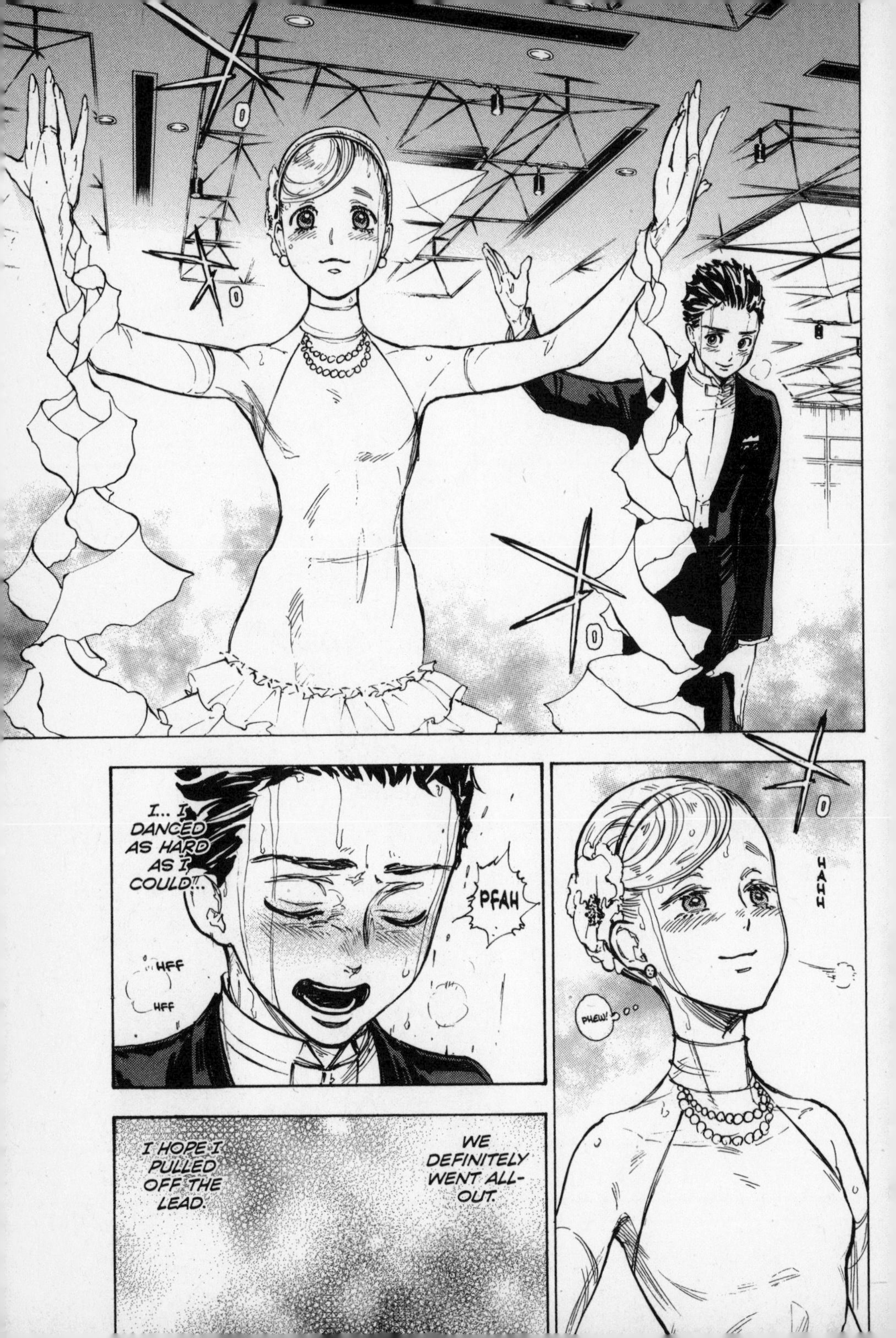
HAHH
PHEW!
I... I DANCED AS HARD AS I COULD!!
PFAH
HFF
HFF
WE DEFINITELY WENT ALL-OUT.
I HOPE I PULLED OFF THE LEAD.

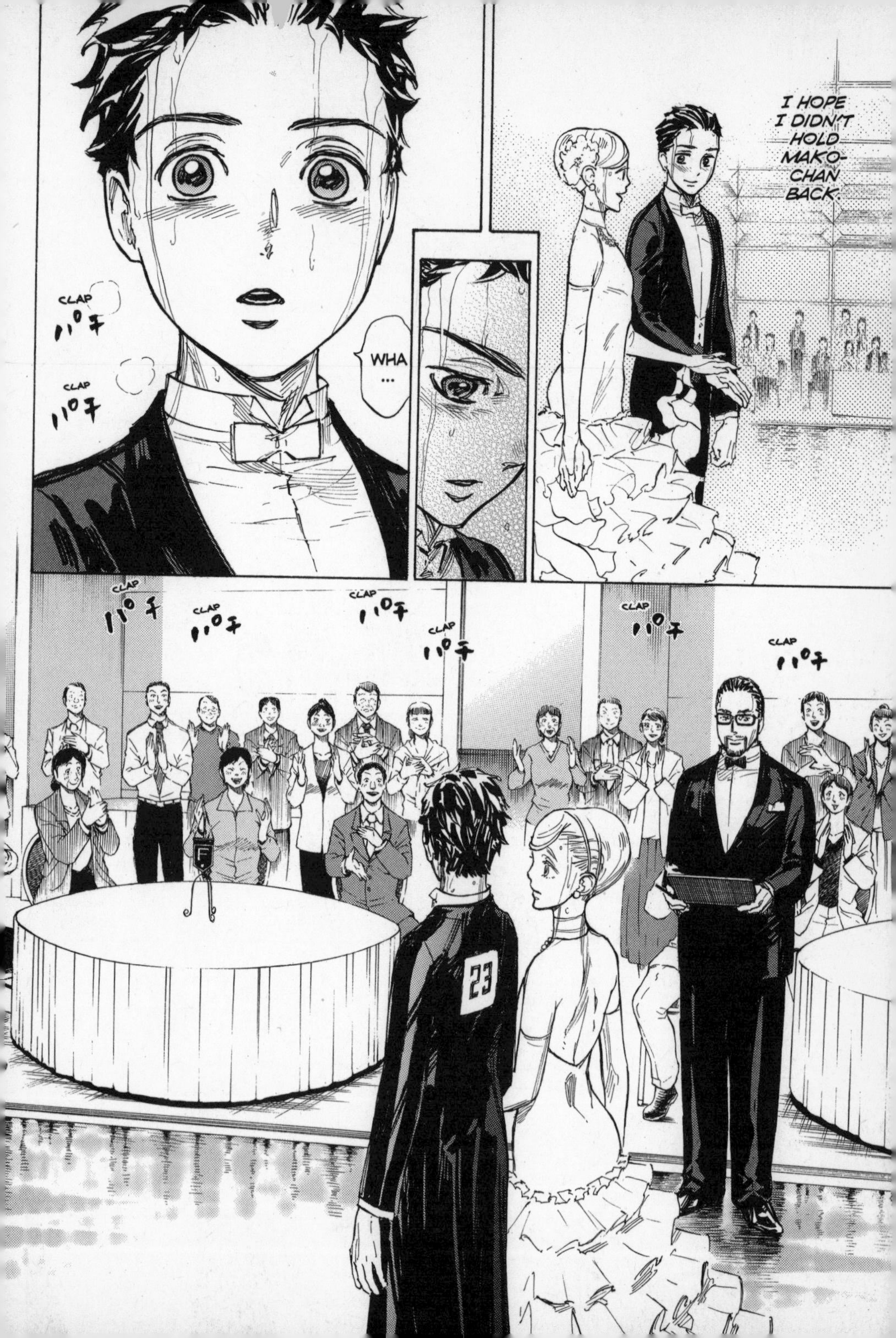

I HOPE I DIDN'T HOLD MAKO-CHAN BACK.
WHA...
CLAP パチ
CLAP パチ
CLAP パチ
CLAP パチ
CLAP パチ
CLAP パチ
CLAP パチ
CLAP パチ

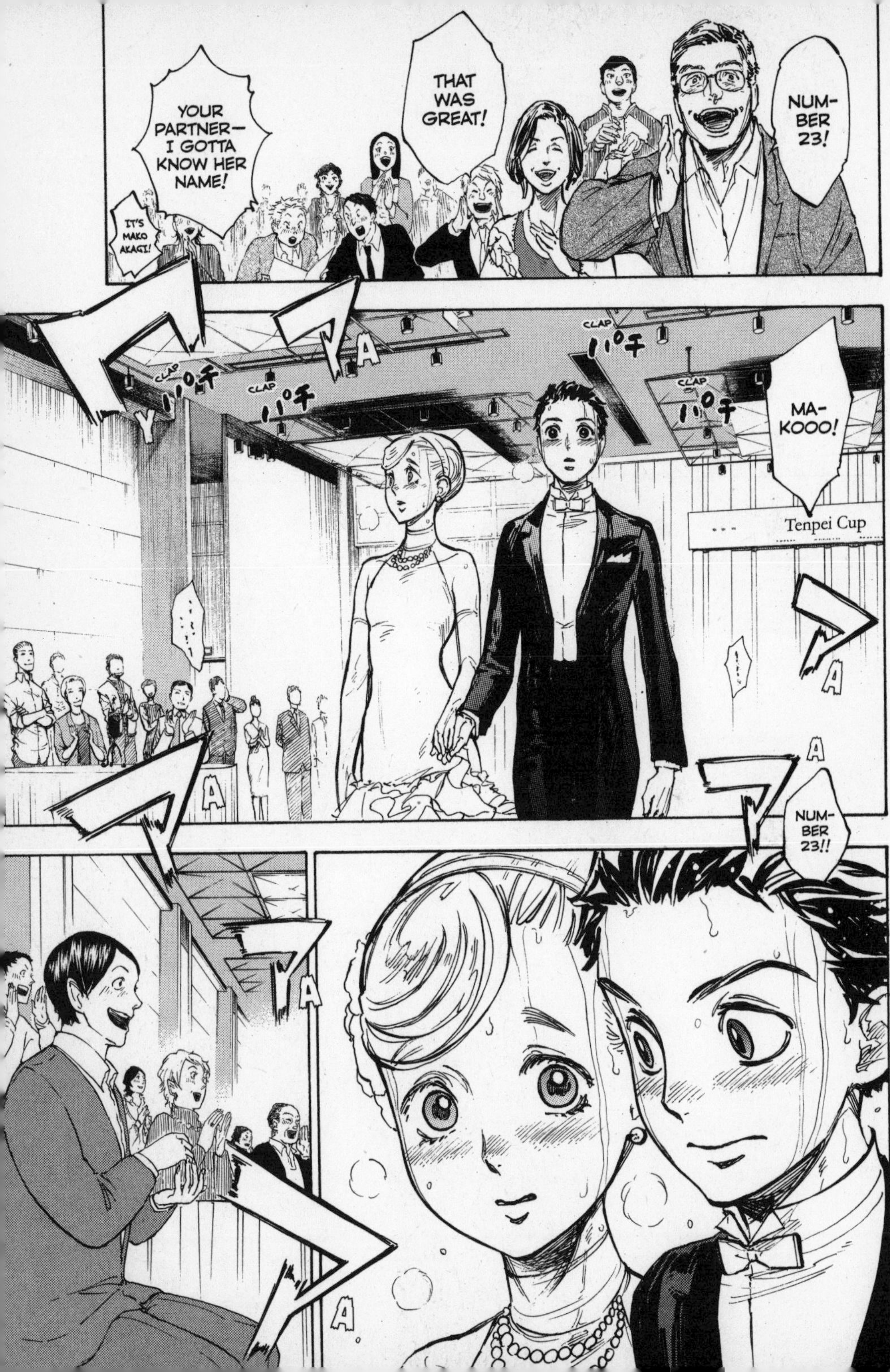
NUM-BER 23!
THAT WAS GREAT!
YOUR PARTNER— I GOTTA KNOW HER NAME!
IT'S MAKO AKAGI!
CLAP
CLAP
MA-KOOO!
Tenpei Cup
CLAP
CLAP
A
A
A
A
NUM-BER 23!!
A
A

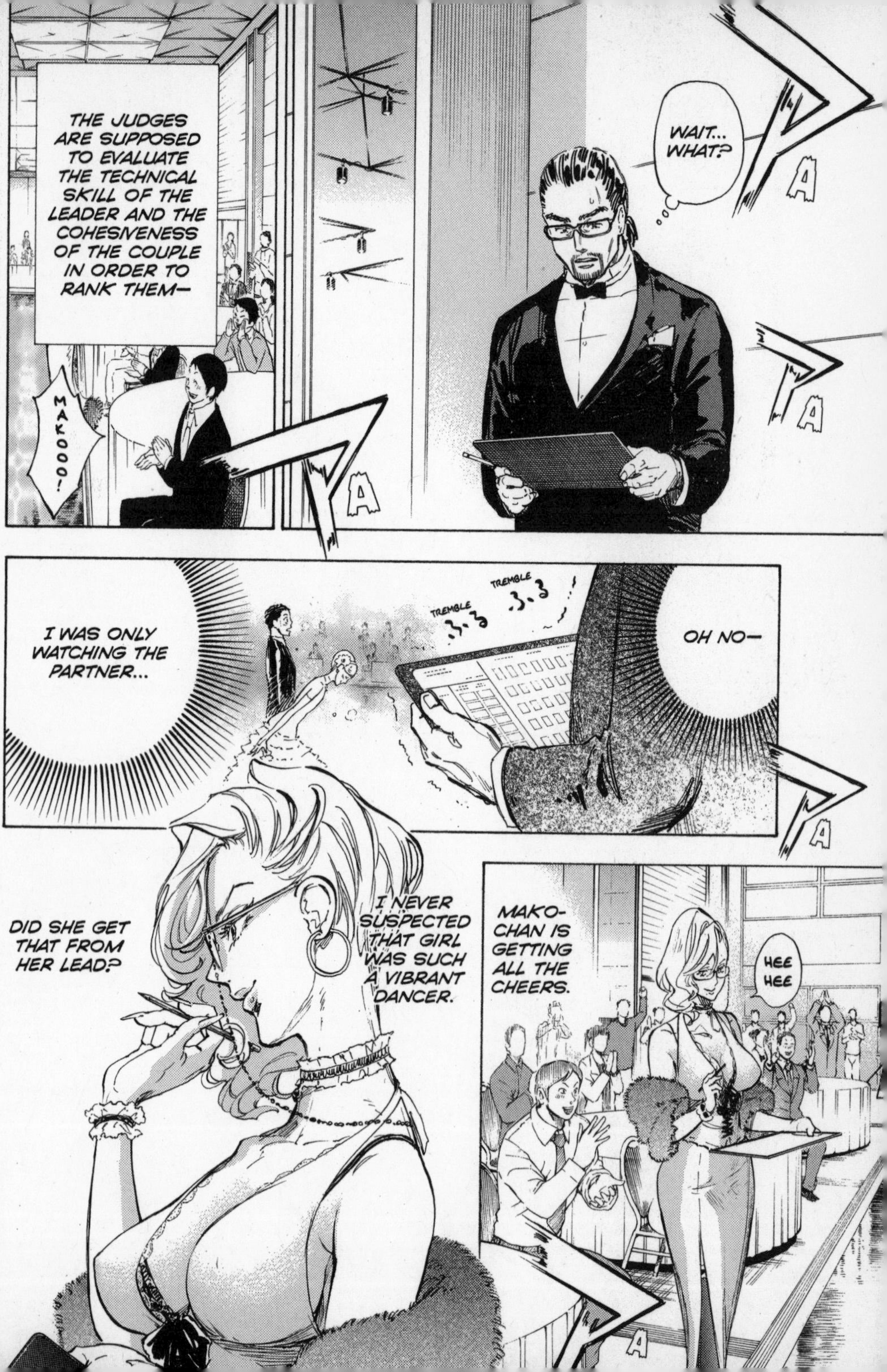
WAIT... WHAT?
THE JUDGES ARE SUPPOSED TO EVALUATE THE TECHNICAL SKILL OF THE LEADER AND THE COHESIVENESS OF THE COUPLE IN ORDER TO RANK THEM—
MAKOOOO!
OH NO—
TREMBLE
TREMBLE
I WAS ONLY WATCHING THE PARTNER...
HEE HEE
MAKO-CHAN IS GETTING ALL THE CHEERS.
I NEVER SUSPECTED THAT GIRL WAS SUCH A VIBRANT DANCER.
DID SHE GET THAT FROM HER LEAD?

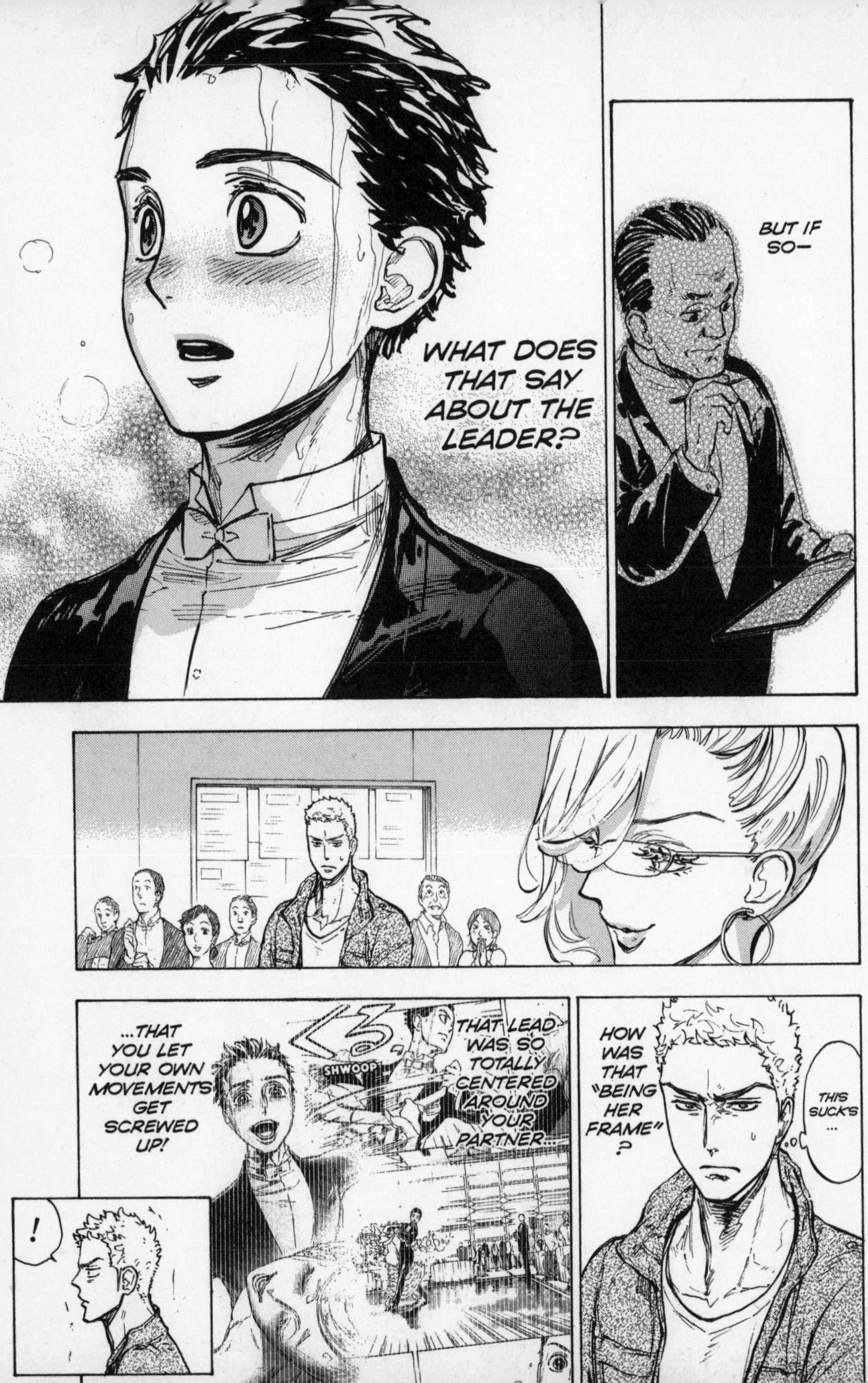
BUT IF SO—
WHAT DOES THAT SAY ABOUT THE LEADER?
HOW WAS THAT "BEING HER FRAME"?
THIS SUCKS...
SHWOOP
THAT LEAD WAS SO TOTALLY CENTERED AROUND YOUR PARTNER...
...THAT YOU LET YOUR OWN MOVEMENTS GET SCREWED UP!
!

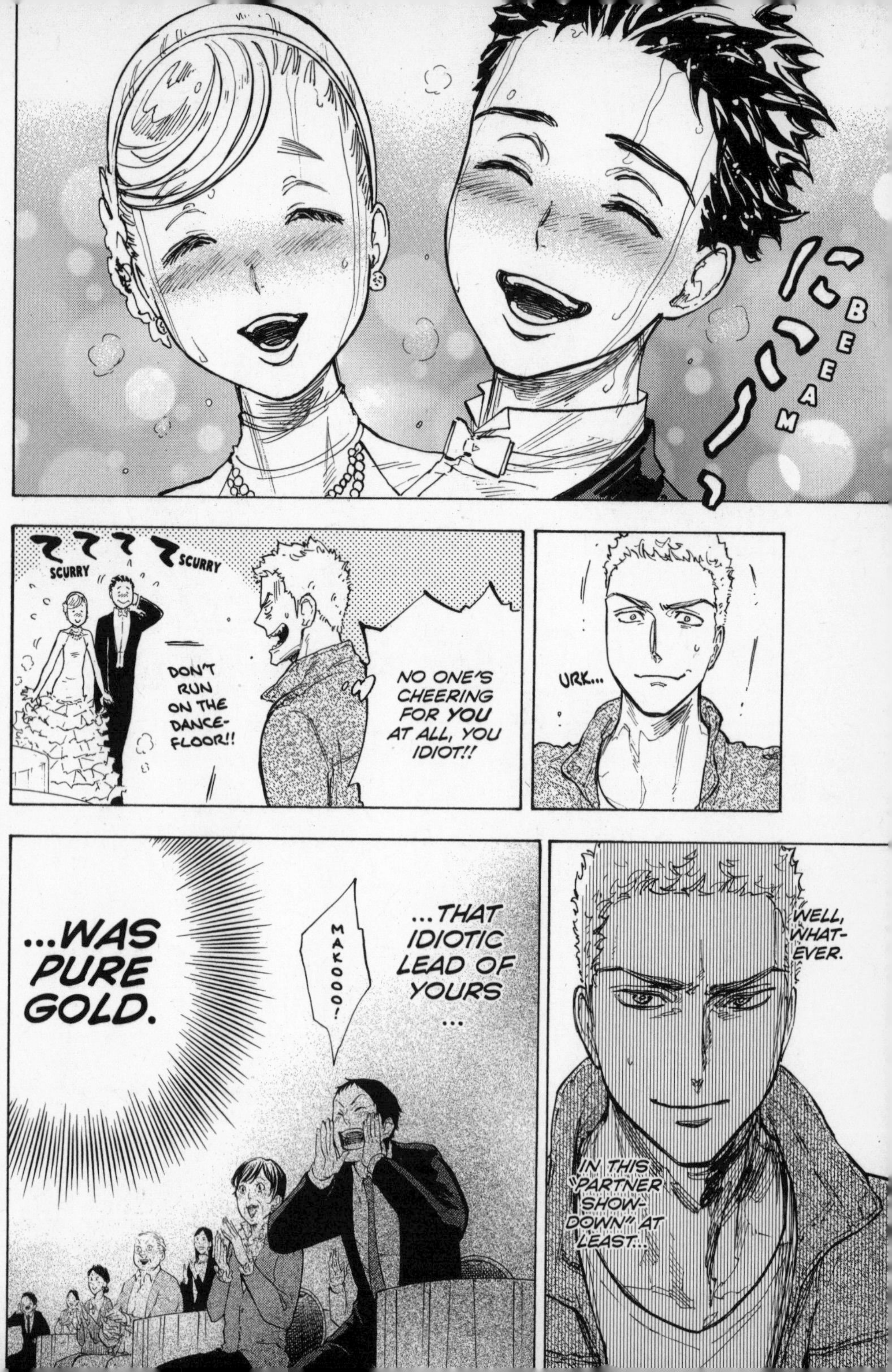
BEEEAM
URK...
SCURRY SCURRY
NO ONE'S CHEERING FOR YOU AT ALL, YOU IDIOT!!
DON'T RUN ON THE DANCE-FLOOR!!
WELL, WHATEVER.
IN THIS "PARTNER SHOW-DOWN" AT LEAST...
...THAT IDIOTIC LEAD OF YOURS...
MAKOOO!
...WAS PURE GOLD.

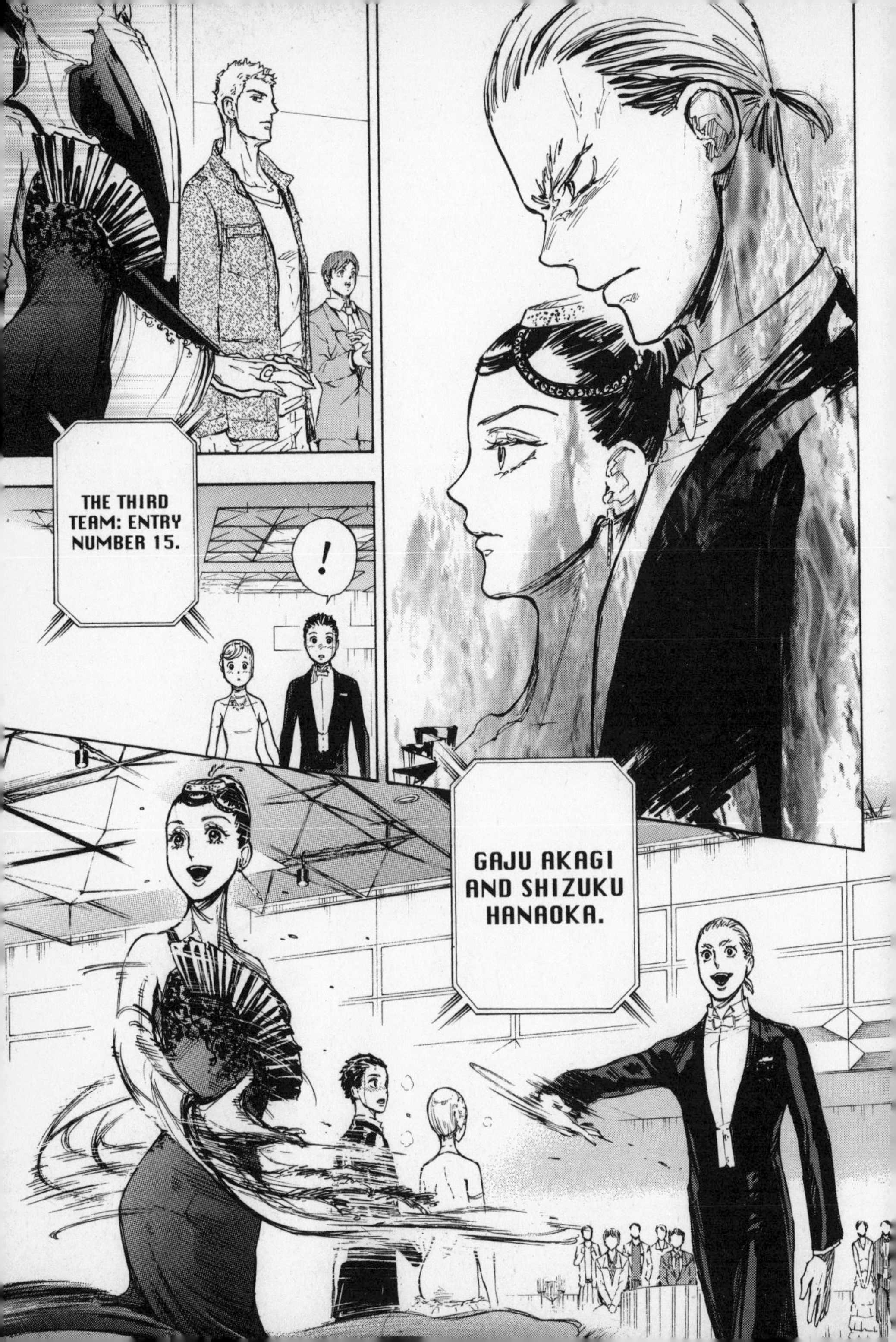
THE THIRD TEAM: ENTRY NUMBER 15.
!
GAJU AKAGI AND SHIZUKU HANAOKA.

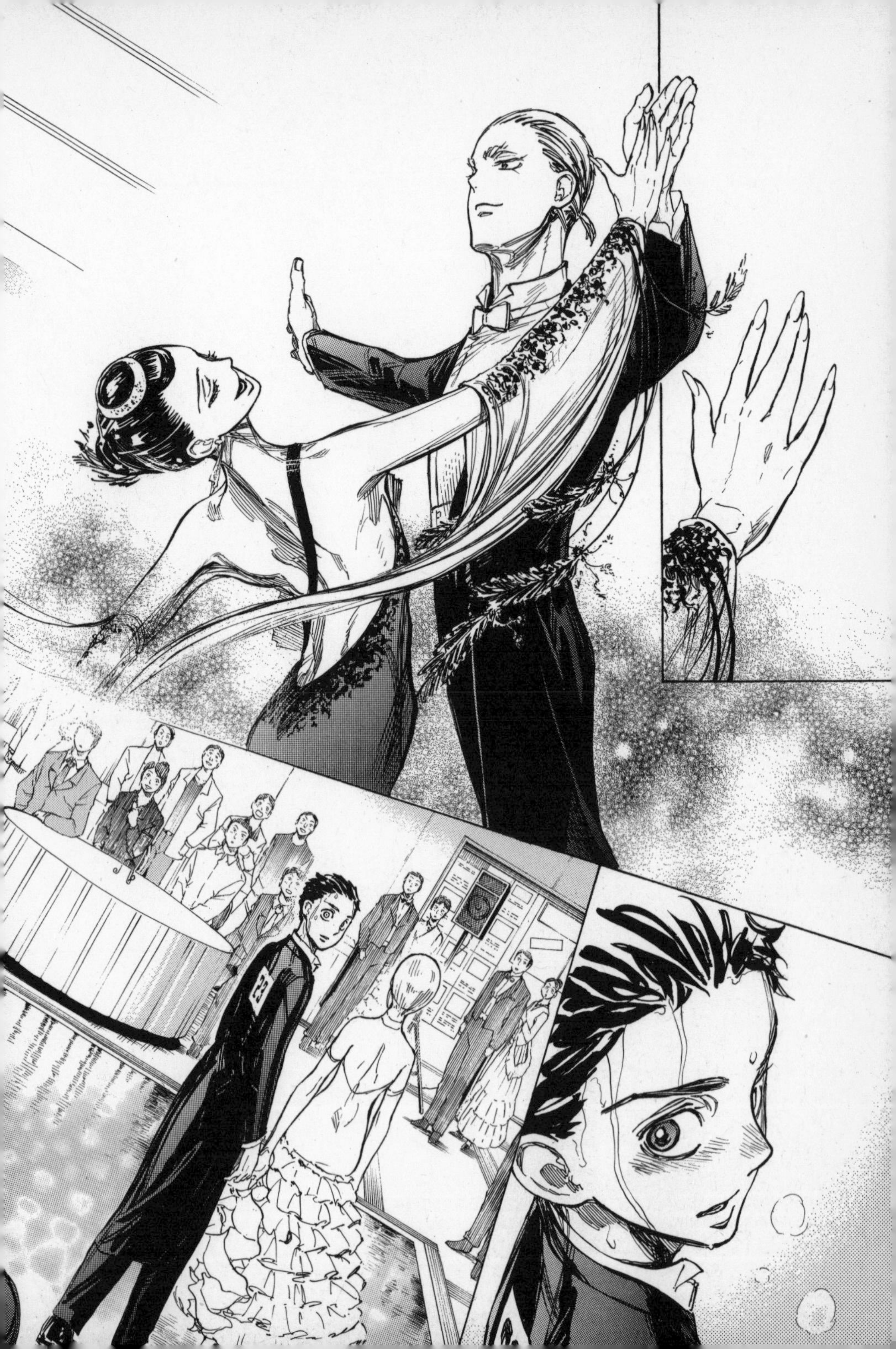

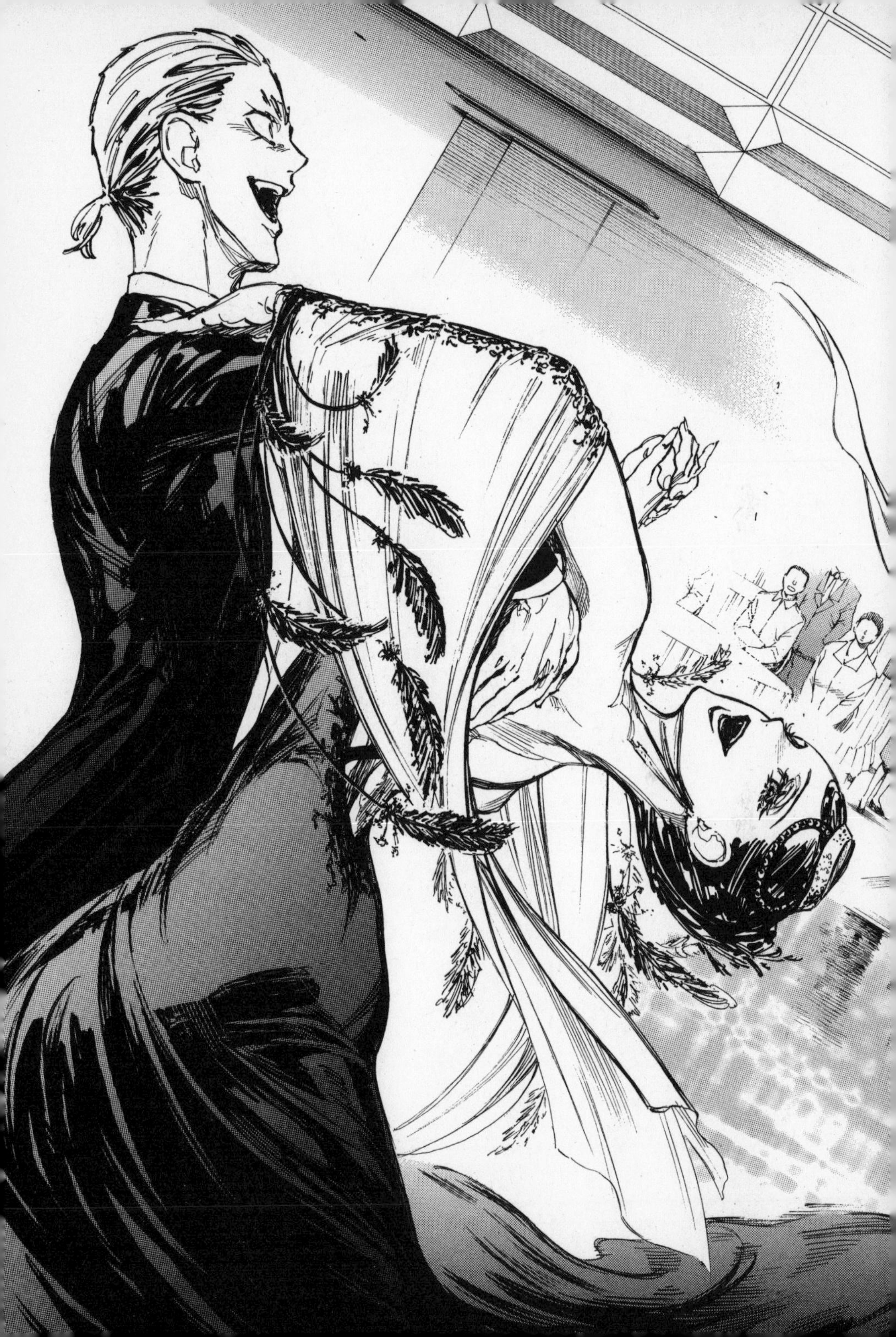

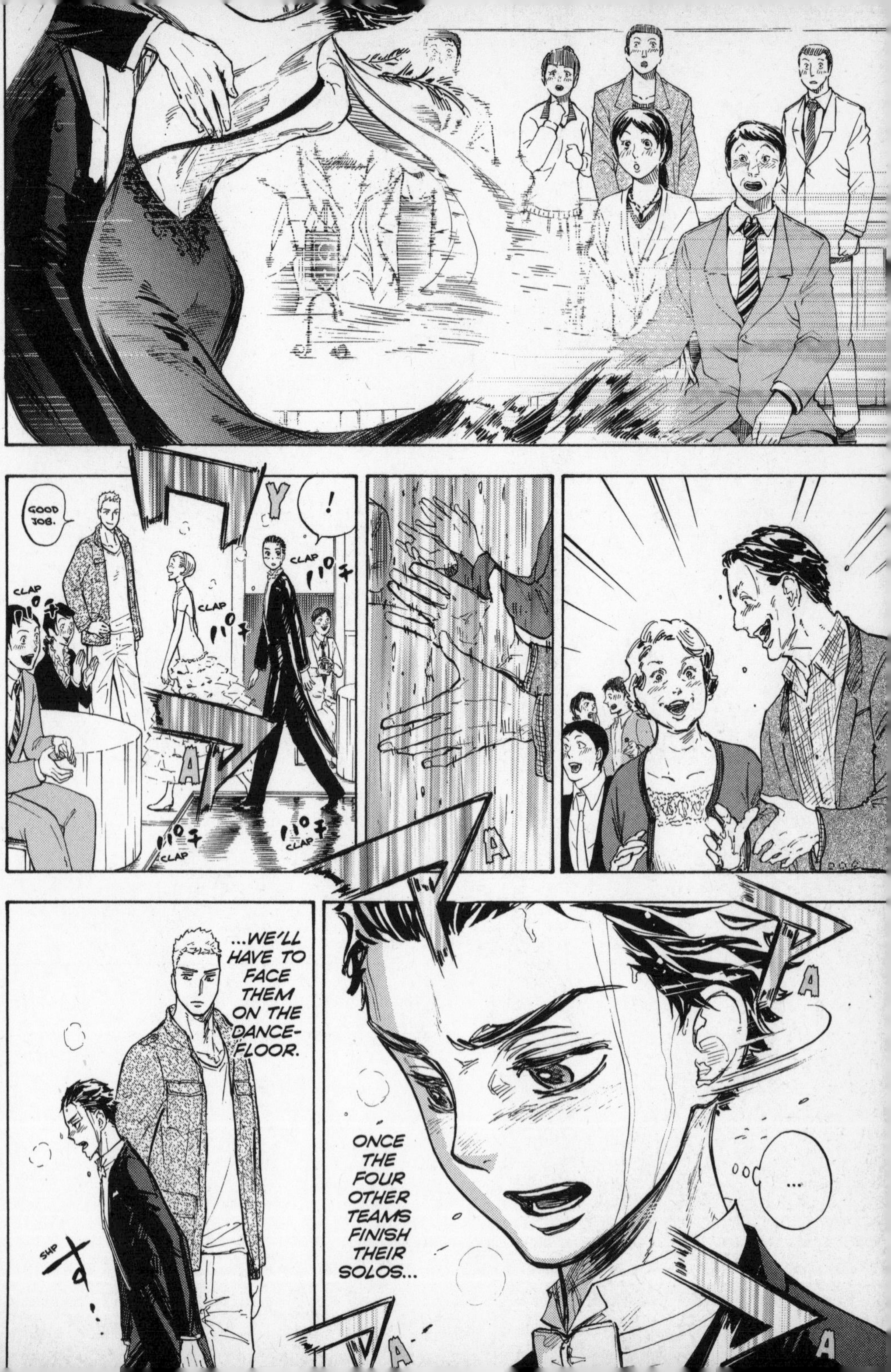

A
!
Y
CLAP
CLAP
GOOD JOB.
CLAP
CLAP
CLAP
A
A
...
ONCE THE FOUR OTHER TEAMS FINISH THEIR SOLOS...
A
...WE'LL HAVE TO FACE THEM ON THE DANCE-FLOOR.
SHP
A

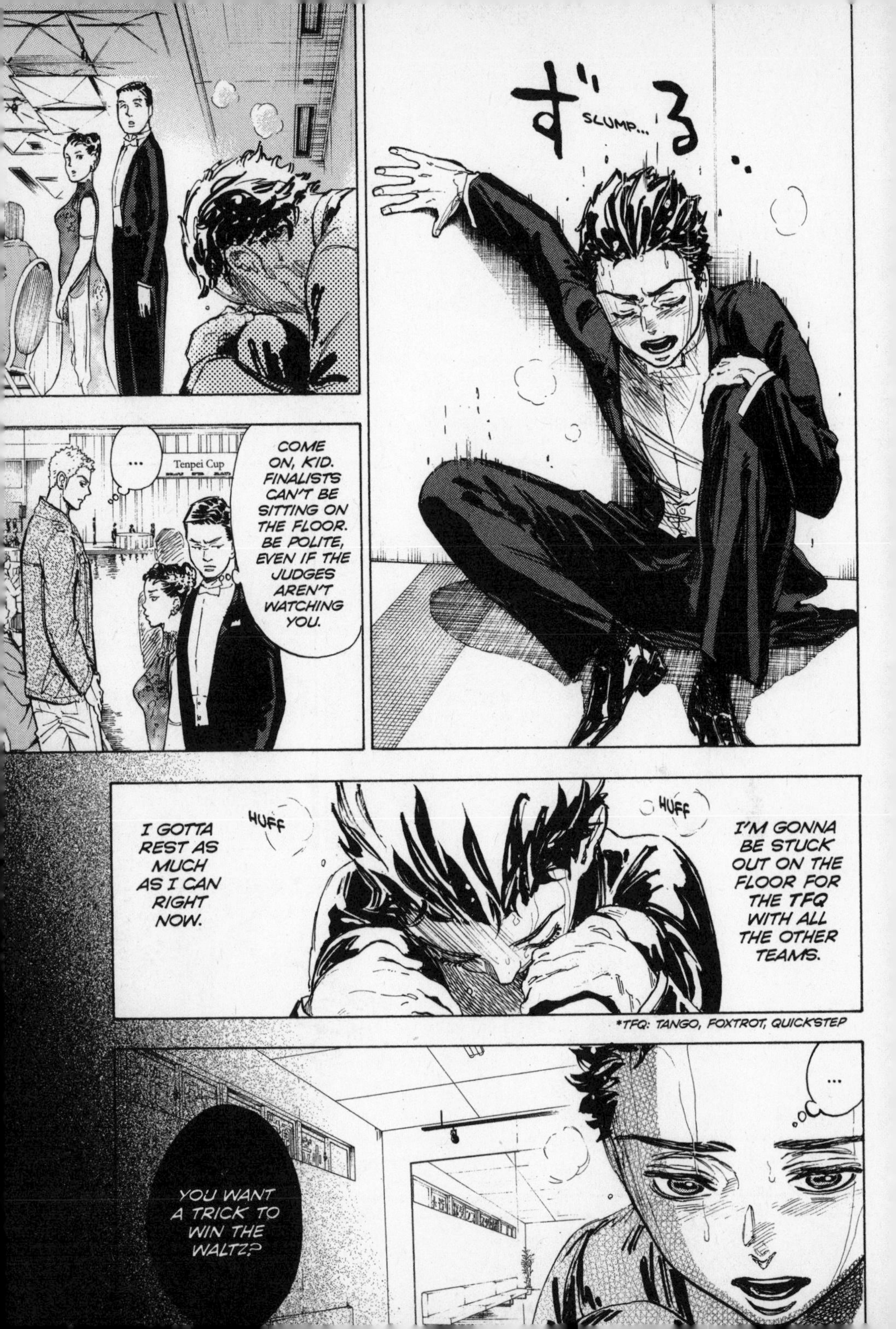
ずる
SLUMP...
...
Tenpei Cup
COME ON, KID. FINALISTS CAN'T BE SITTING ON THE FLOOR. BE POLITE, EVEN IF THE JUDGES AREN'T WATCHING YOU.
HUFF
I'M GONNA BE STUCK OUT ON THE FLOOR FOR THE TFQ WITH ALL THE OTHER TEAMS.
HUFF
I GOTTA REST AS MUCH AS I CAN RIGHT NOW.
*TFQ: TANGO, FOXTROT, QUICKSTEP
...
YOU WANT A TRICK TO WIN THE WALTZ?

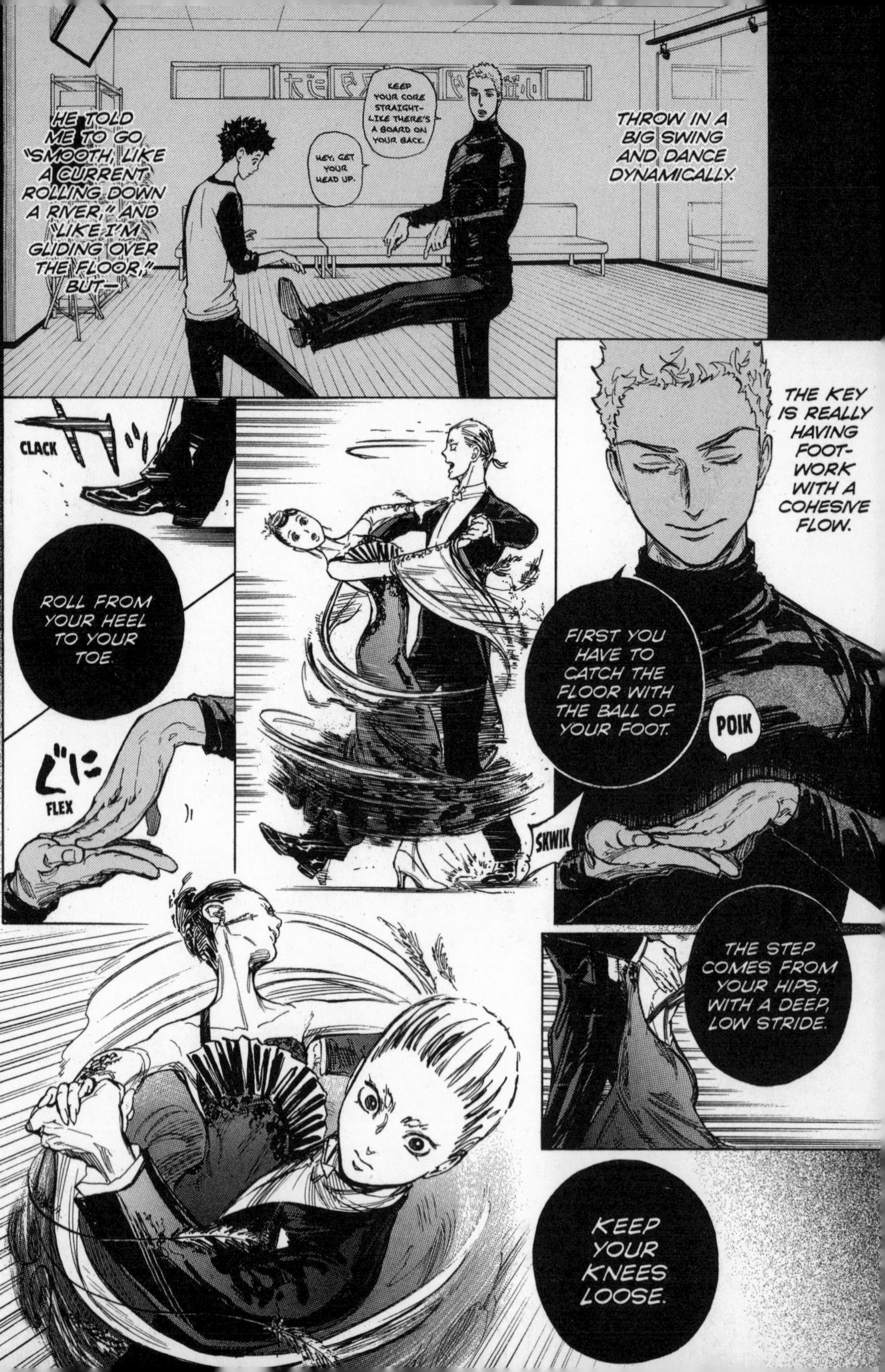
THROW IN A BIG SWING AND DANCE DYNAMICALLY.
KEEP YOUR CORE STRAIGHT—LIKE THERE'S A BOARD ON YOUR BACK.
HEY, GET YOUR HEAD UP.
HE TOLD ME TO GO "SMOOTH, LIKE A CURRENT ROLLING DOWN A RIVER," AND "LIKE I'M GLIDING OVER THE FLOOR," BUT—
THE KEY IS REALLY HAVING FOOT-WORK WITH A COHESIVE FLOW.
FIRST YOU HAVE TO CATCH THE FLOOR WITH THE BALL OF YOUR FOOT.
POIK
SKWIK
CLACK
ROLL FROM YOUR HEEL TO YOUR TOE.
ぐに
FLEX
THE STEP COMES FROM YOUR HIPS, WITH A DEEP, LOW STRIDE.
KEEP YOUR KNEES LOOSE.

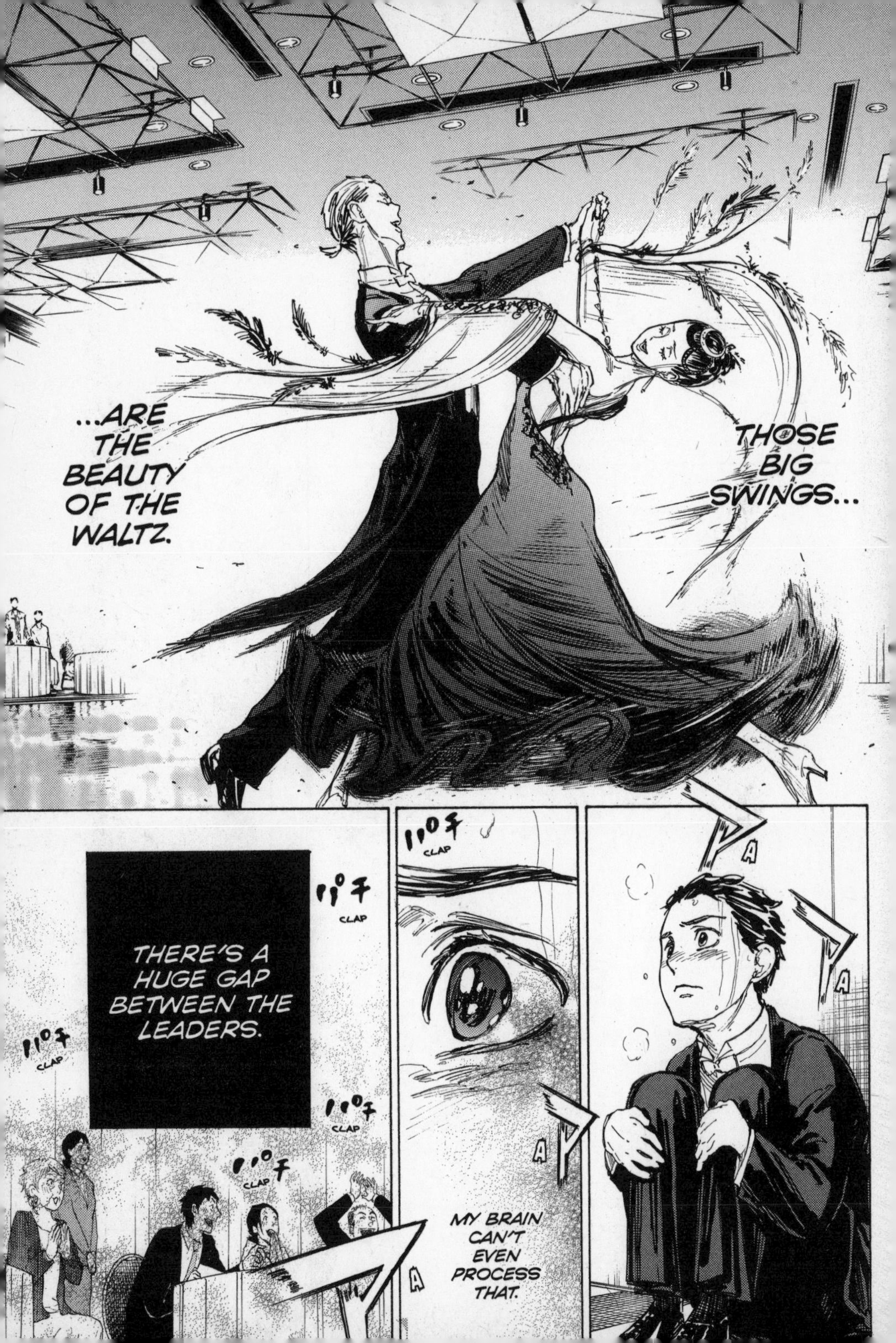
THOSE BIG SWINGS...
...ARE THE BEAUTY OF THE WALTZ.
A
A
A
A
MY BRAIN CAN'T EVEN PROCESS THAT.
パチ
CLAP
パチ
CLAP
THERE'S A HUGE GAP BETWEEN THE LEADERS.
パチ
CLAP
パチ
CLAP
パチ
CLAP

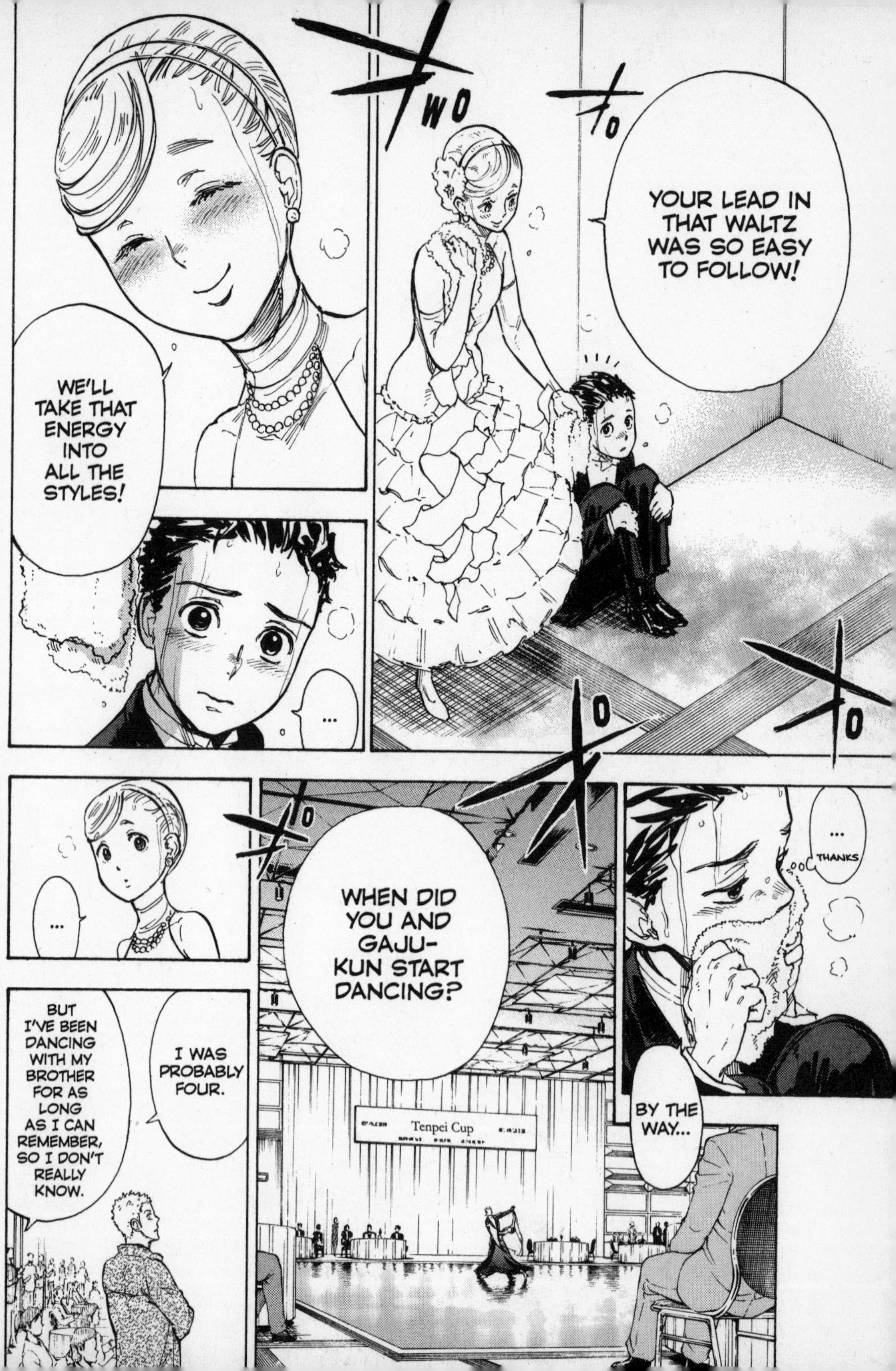
TWO
TO
YOUR LEAD IN THAT WALTZ WAS SO EASY TO FOLLOW!
WE'LL TAKE THAT ENERGY INTO ALL THE STYLES!
...
TO
TO
TO
... THANKS
BY THE WAY...
WHEN DID YOU AND GAJU-KUN START DANCING?
TO
...
Tenpei Cup
I WAS PROBABLY FOUR.
BUT I'VE BEEN DANCING WITH MY BROTHER FOR AS LONG AS I CAN REMEMBER, SO I DON'T REALLY KNOW.

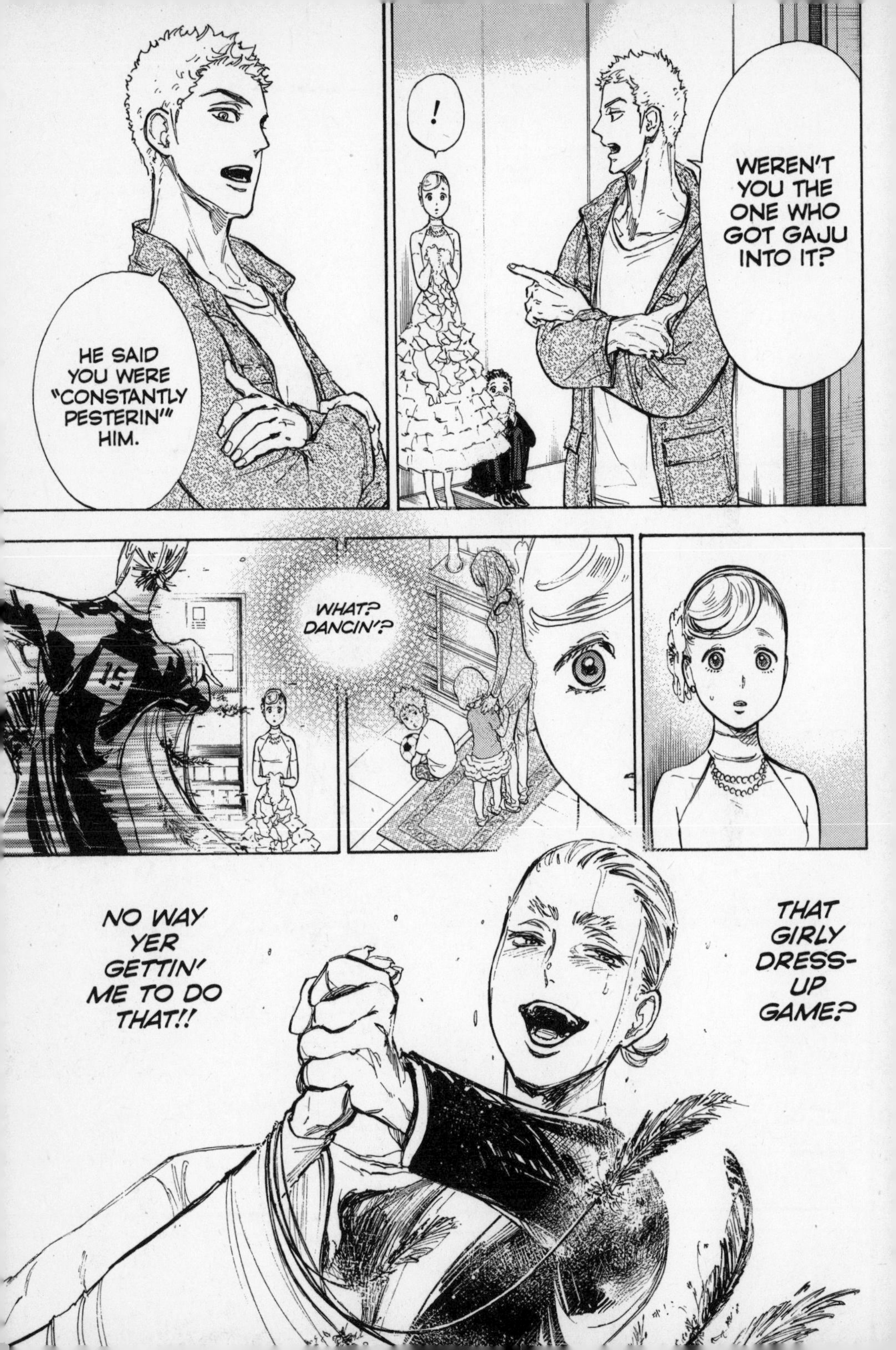
WEREN'T YOU THE ONE WHO GOT GAJU INTO IT?
!
HE SAID YOU WERE "CONSTANTLY PESTERIN'" HIM.
WHAT? DANCIN'?
THAT GIRLY DRESS-UP GAME?
NO WAY YER GETTIN' ME TO DO THAT!!

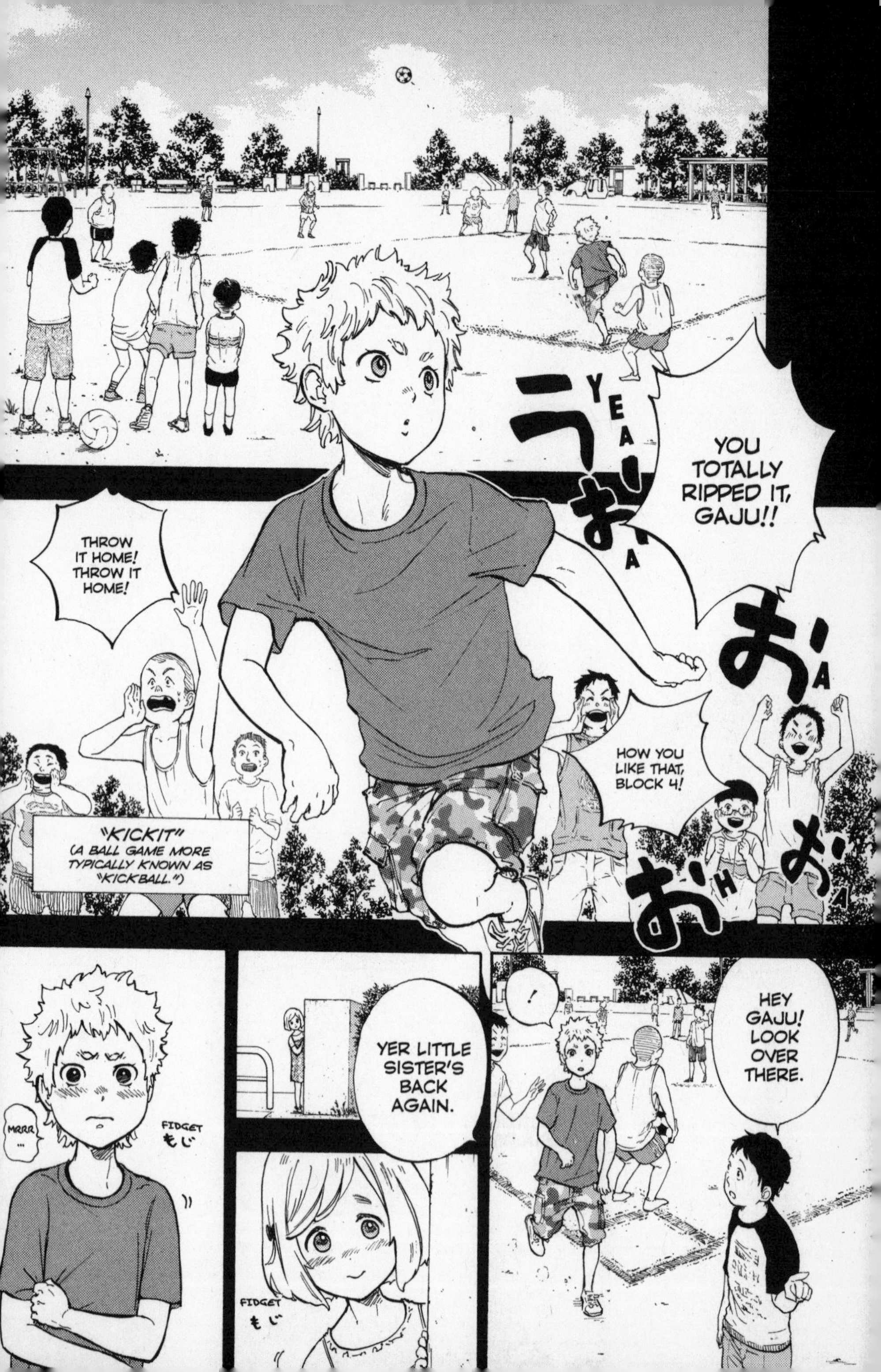
うお YEAA
YOU TOTALLY RIPPED IT, GAJU!!
おおお
HOW YOU LIKE THAT, BLOCK 4!
THROW IT HOME! THROW IT HOME!
"KICKIT" (A BALL GAME MORE TYPICALLY KNOWN AS "KICKBALL.")
HEY GAJU! LOOK OVER THERE.
!
YER LITTLE SISTER'S BACK AGAIN.
FIDGET もじ
FIDGET もじ
MRRR ...

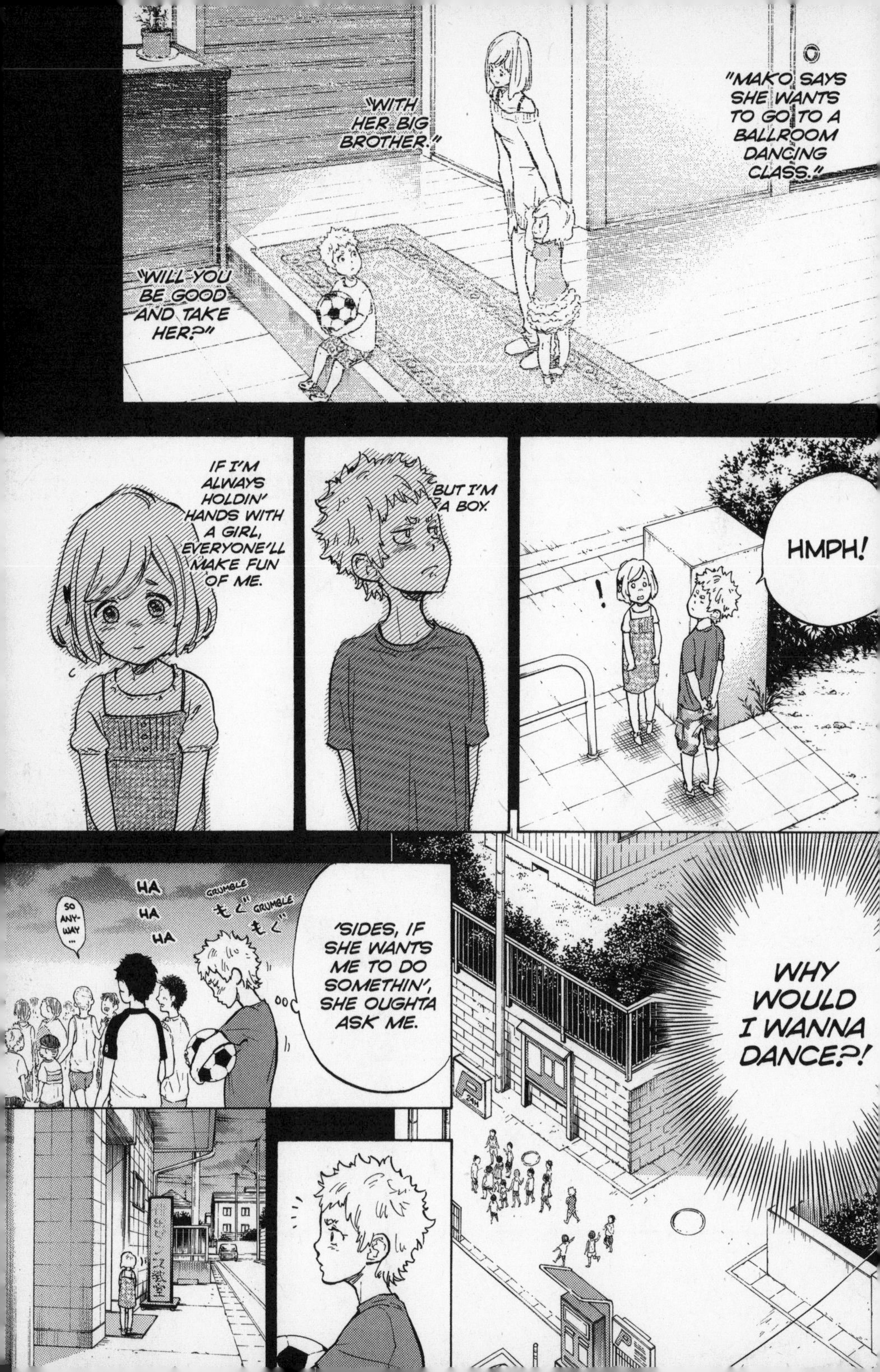
"MAKO SAYS SHE WANTS TO GO TO A BALLROOM DANCING CLASS."
"WITH HER BIG BROTHER."
"WILL YOU BE GOOD AND TAKE HER?"
HMPH!
!
BUT I'M A BOY.
IF I'M ALWAYS HOLDIN' HANDS WITH A GIRL, EVERYONE'LL MAKE FUN OF ME.
WHY WOULD I WANNA DANCE?!
'SIDES, IF SHE WANTS ME TO DO SOMETHIN', SHE OUGHTA ASK ME.
GRUMBLE GRUMBLE
HA HA HA
SO ANY-WAY ...
24H

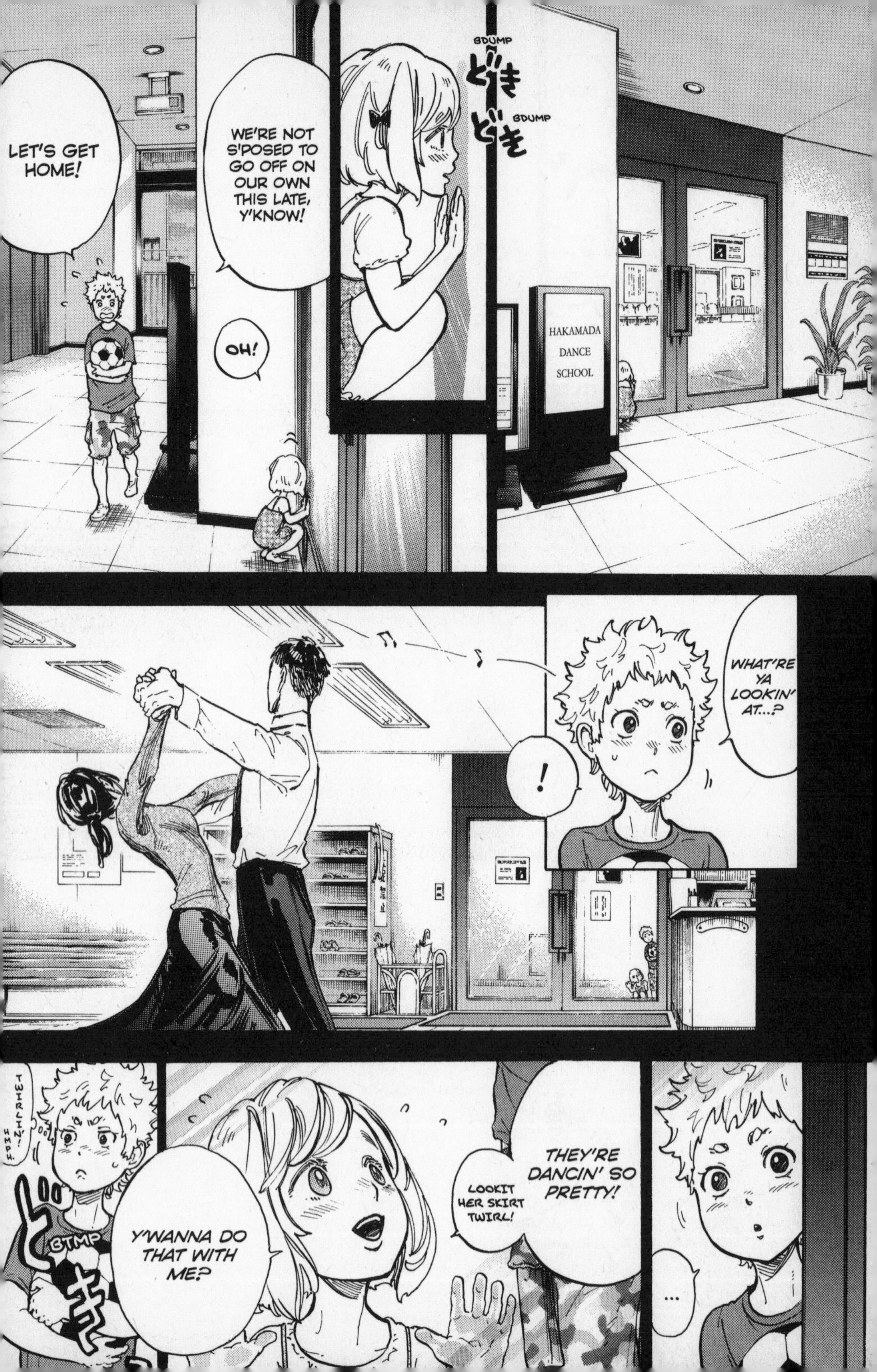

BDUMP
どき
BDUMP
どき
WE'RE NOT S'POSED TO GO OFF ON OUR OWN THIS LATE, Y'KNOW!
LET'S GET HOME!
OH!
HAKAMADA DANCE SCHOOL
WHAT'RE YA LOOKIN' AT...?
!
...
THEY'RE DANCIN' SO PRETTY!
LOOKIT HER SKIRT TWIRL!
Y'WANNA DO THAT WITH ME?
TWIRLIN'. HMPH.
BTMP
どき

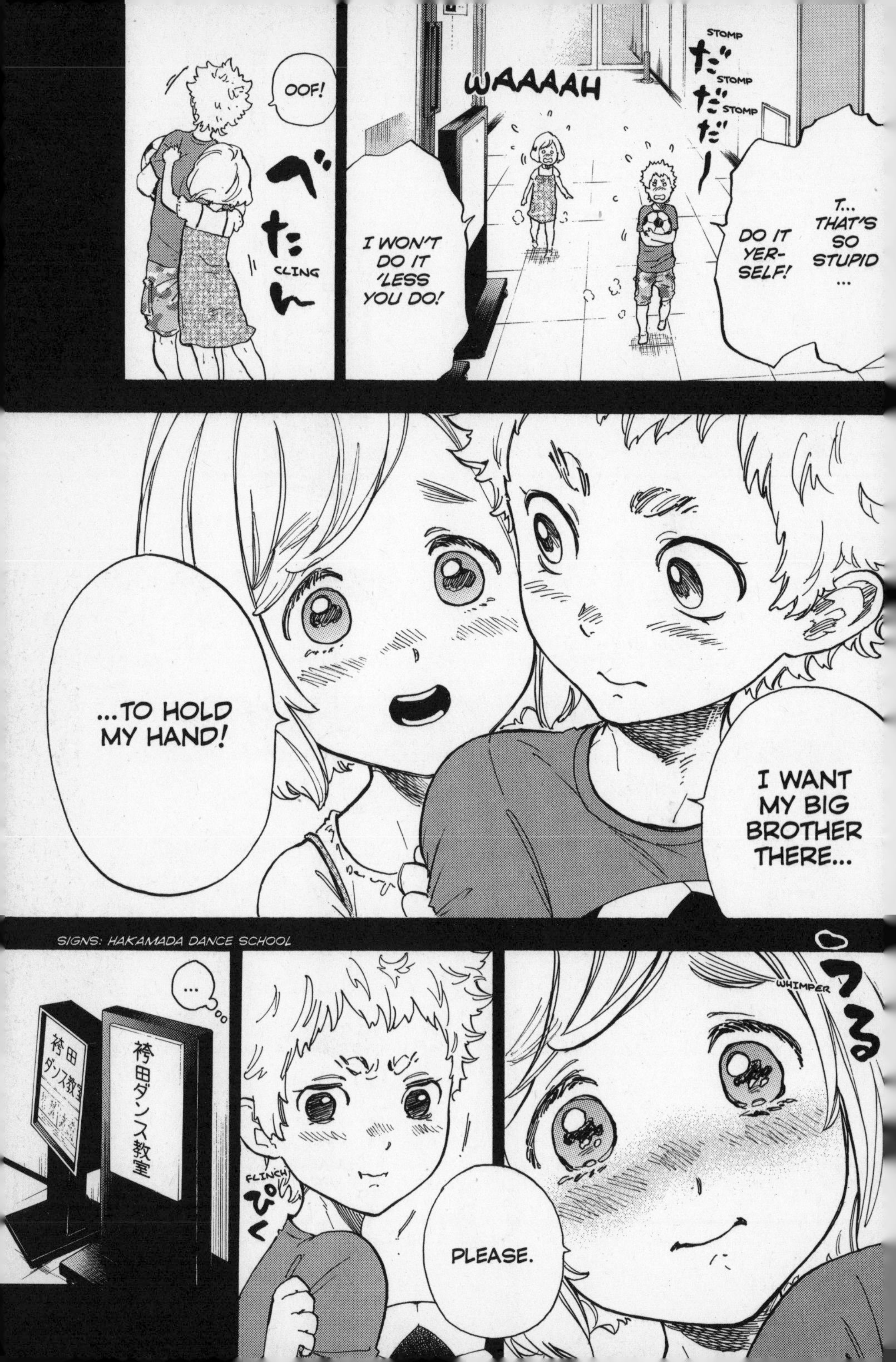
WAAAAH
だだだー
STOMP
STOMP
STOMP
T... THAT'S SO STUPID ...
DO IT YER-SELF!
I WON'T DO IT 'LESS YOU DO!
OOF!
べたん
CLING
I WANT MY BIG BROTHER THERE...
...TO HOLD MY HAND!
SIGNS: HAKAMADA DANCE SCHOOL
うる
WHIMPER
PLEASE.
ぴく
FLINCH
...
袴田ダンス教室
袴田ダンス教室

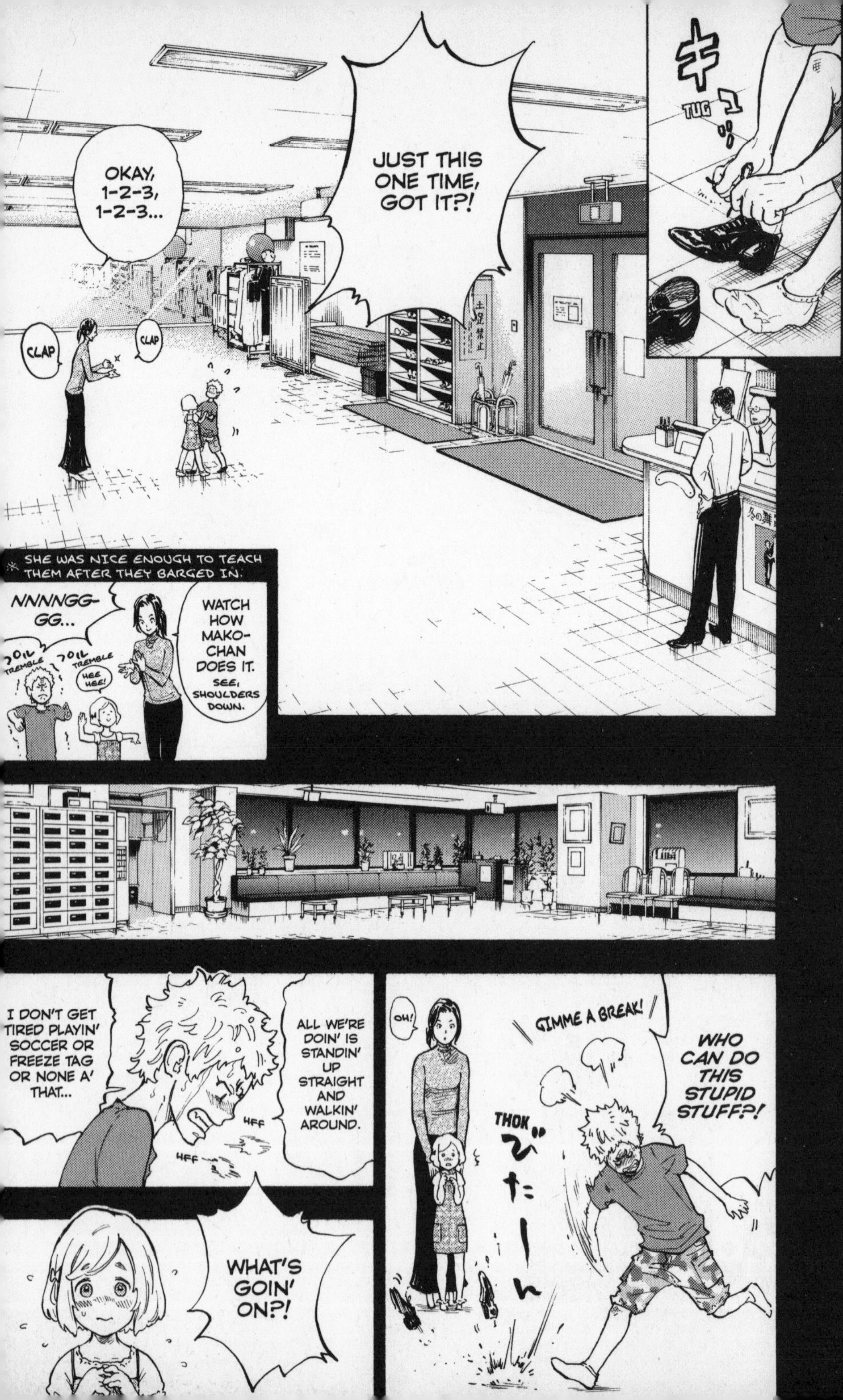
TUG
JUST THIS ONE TIME, GOT IT?!
OKAY, 1-2-3, 1-2-3...
CLAP
CLAP
※ SHE WAS NICE ENOUGH TO TEACH THEM AFTER THEY BARGED IN.
WATCH HOW MAKO-CHAN DOES IT. SEE, SHOULDERS DOWN.
NNNNGG-GG...
TREMBLE
TREMBLE
HEE HEE!
GIMME A BREAK!
WHO CAN DO THIS STUPID STUFF?!
OH!
THOK
ALL WE'RE DOIN' IS STANDIN' UP STRAIGHT AND WALKIN' AROUND.
I DON'T GET TIRED PLAYIN' SOCCER OR FREEZE TAG OR NONE A' THAT...
HFF
HFF
WHAT'S GOIN' ON?!

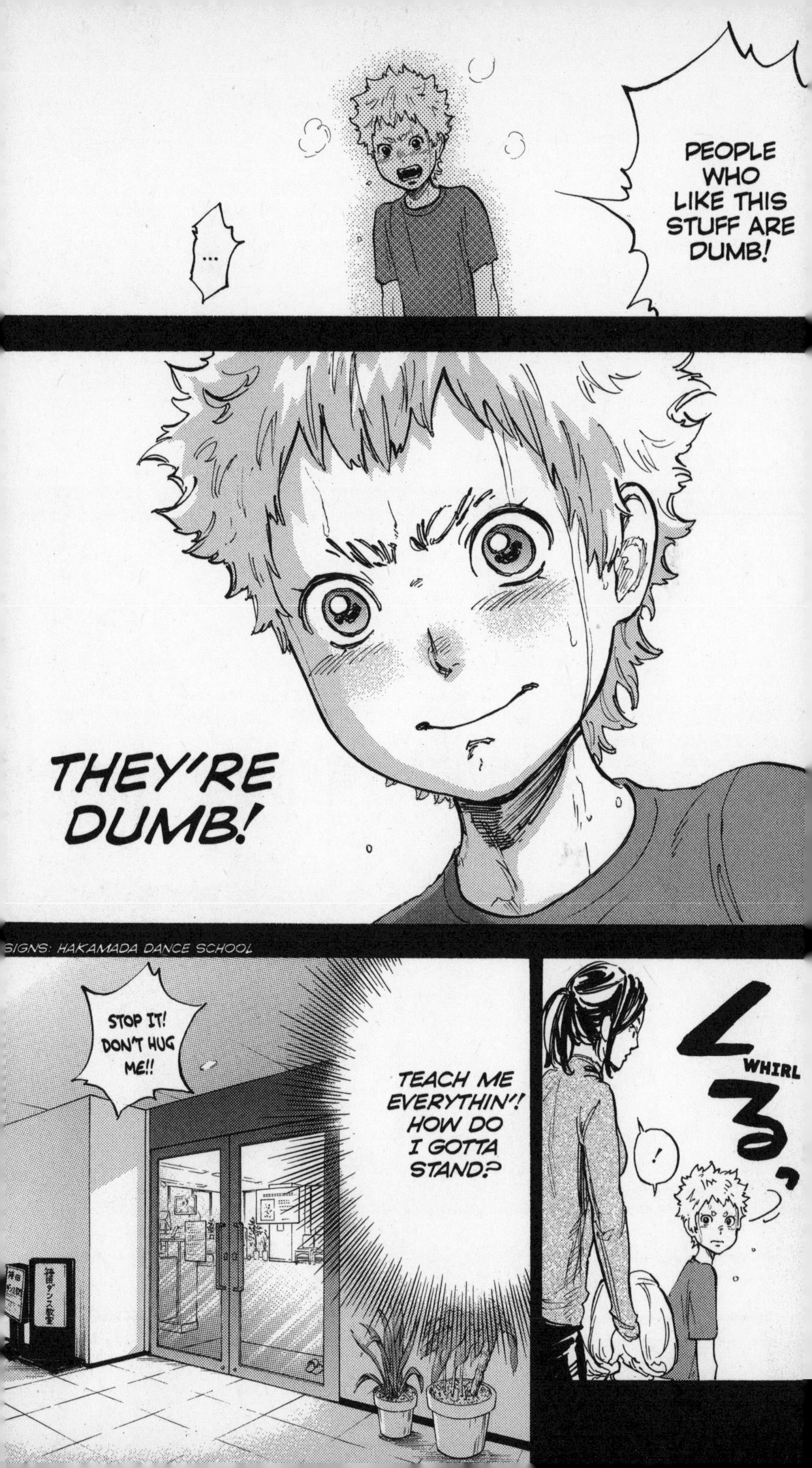
PEOPLE WHO LIKE THIS STUFF ARE DUMB!
...
THEY'RE DUMB!
WHIRL
!
TEACH ME EVERYTHIN'! HOW DO I GOTTA STAND?
STOP IT! DON'T HUG ME!!
SIGNS: HAKAMADA DANCE SCHOOL

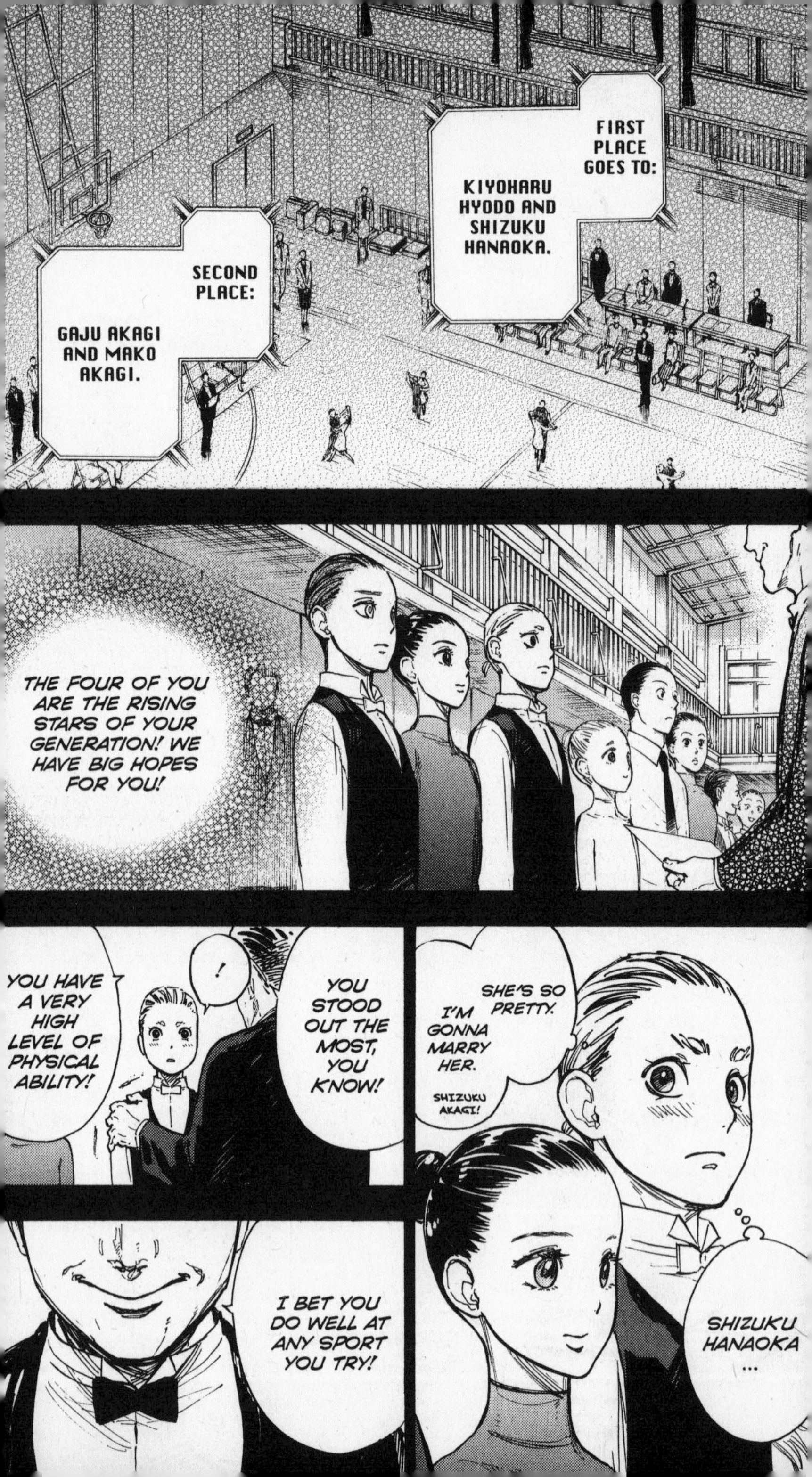
FIRST PLACE GOES TO:
KIYOHARU HYODO AND SHIZUKU HANAOKA.
SECOND PLACE:
GAJU AKAGI AND MAKO AKAGI.
THE FOUR OF YOU ARE THE RISING STARS OF YOUR GENERATION! WE HAVE BIG HOPES FOR YOU!
SHE'S SO PRETTY.
I'M GONNA MARRY HER.
SHIZUKU AKAGI!
SHIZUKU HANAOKA ...
YOU STOOD OUT THE MOST, YOU KNOW!
!
YOU HAVE A VERY HIGH LEVEL OF PHYSICAL ABILITY!
I BET YOU DO WELL AT ANY SPORT YOU TRY!

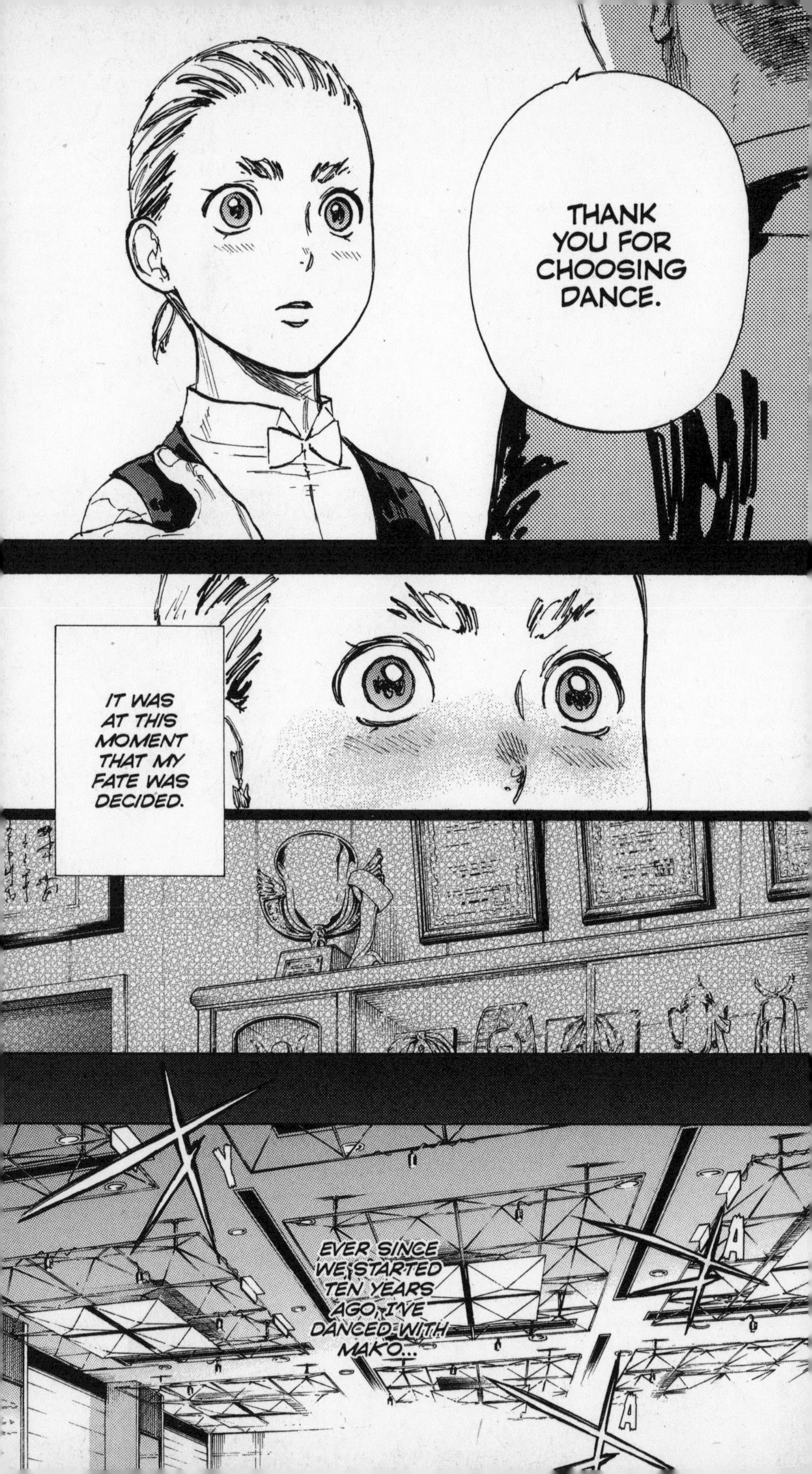
THANK YOU FOR CHOOSING DANCE.
IT WAS AT THIS MOMENT THAT MY FATE WAS DECIDED.
EVER SINCE WE STARTED TEN YEARS AGO, I'VE DANCED WITH MAKO...
Y
A
A

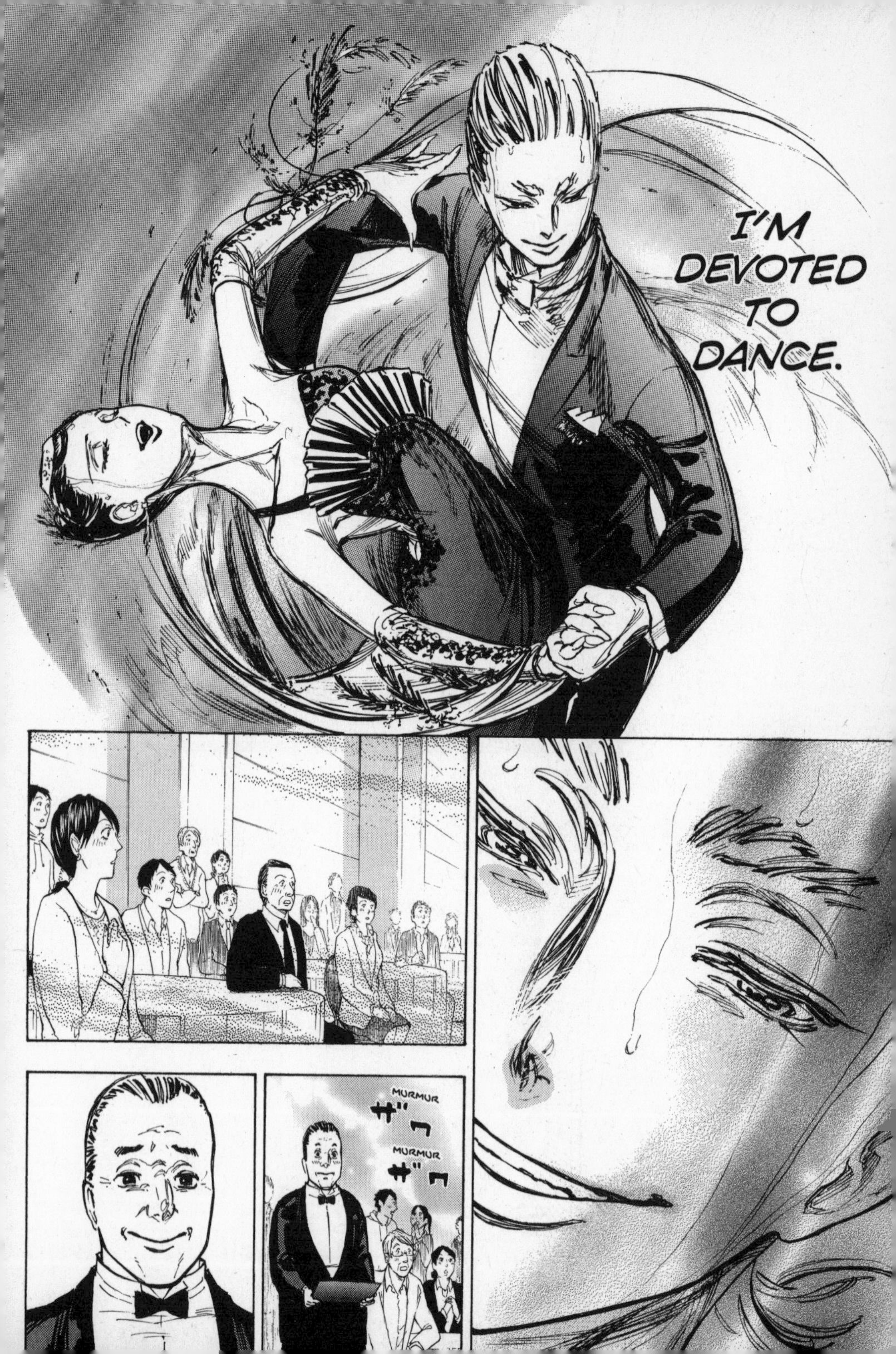
I'M DEVOTED TO DANCE.
MURMUR
ザワ
MURMUR
ザワ

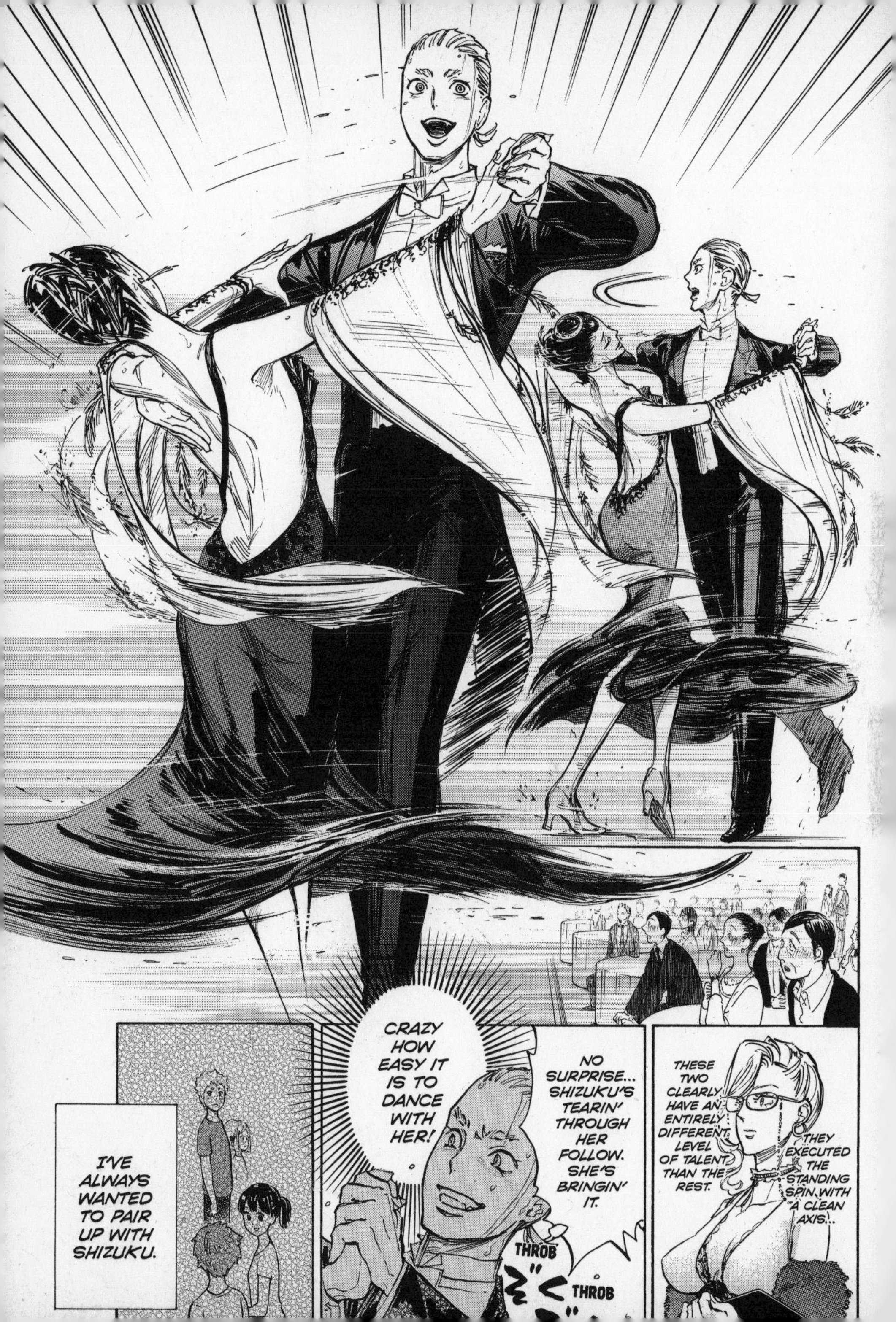
THESE TWO CLEARLY HAVE AN ENTIRELY DIFFERENT LEVEL OF TALENT THAN THE REST.
THEY EXECUTED THE STANDING SPIN WITH A CLEAN AXIS...
NO SURPRISE... SHIZUKU'S TEARIN' THROUGH HER FOLLOW. SHE'S BRINGIN' IT.
CRAZY HOW EASY IT IS TO DANCE WITH HER!
THROB
THROB
I'VE ALWAYS WANTED TO PAIR UP WITH SHIZUKU.

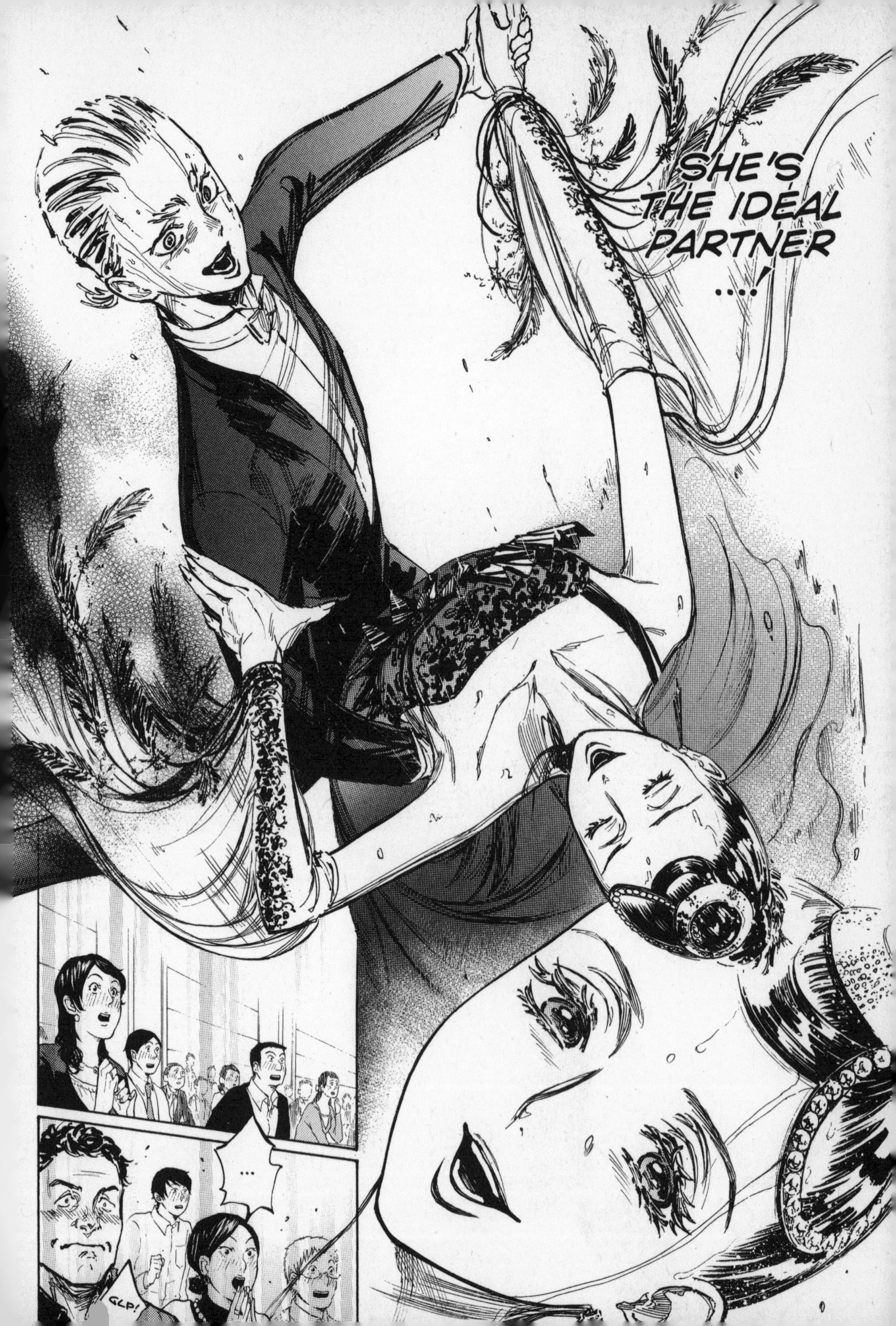
SHE'S THE IDEAL PARTNER ...!
...
GLP!

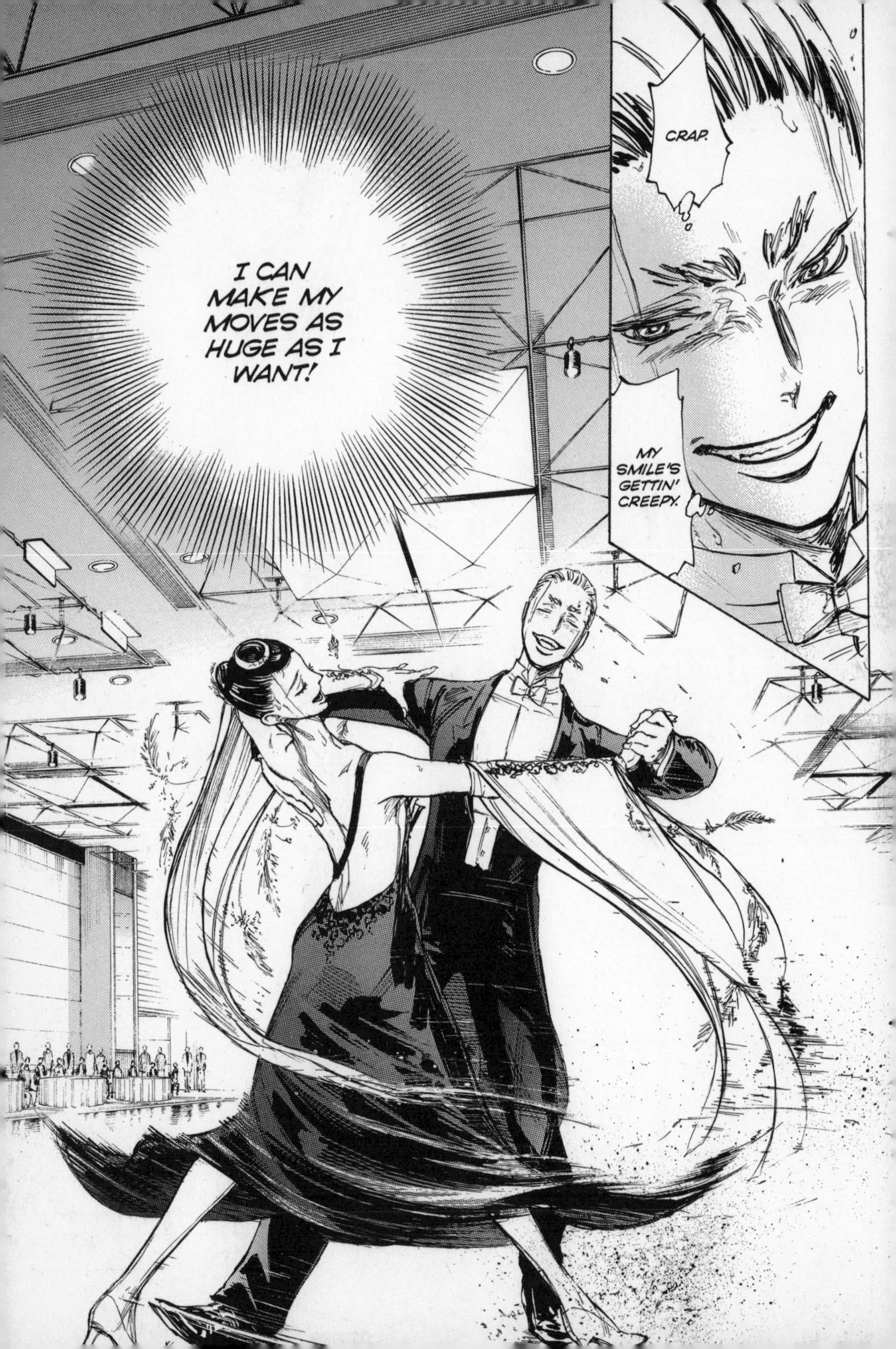
CRAP.
MY SMILE'S GETTIN' CREEPY.
I CAN MAKE MY MOVES AS HUGE AS I WANT!

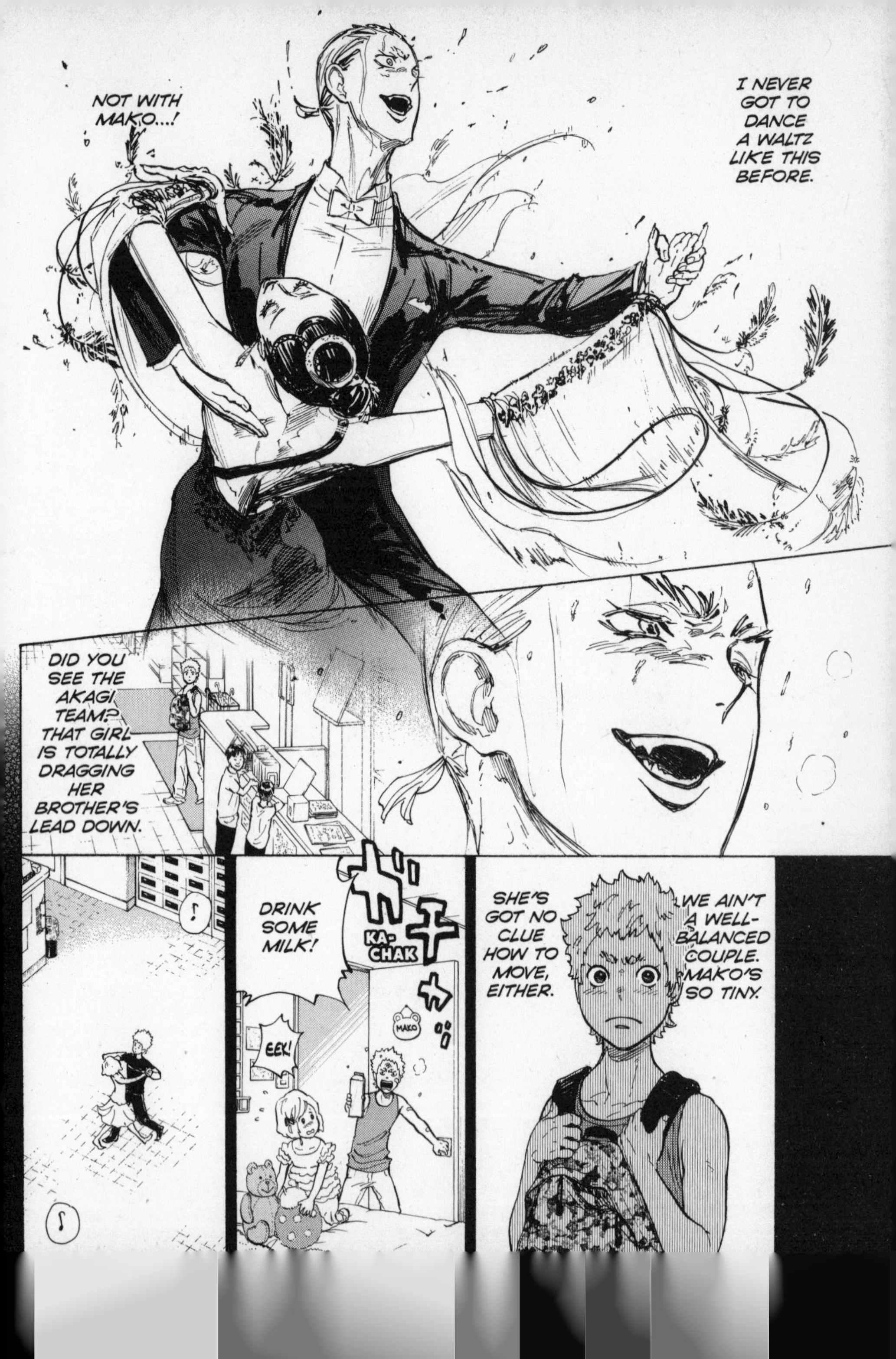
I NEVER GOT TO DANCE A WALTZ LIKE THIS BEFORE.
NOT WITH MAKO...!
DID YOU SEE THE AKAGI TEAM? THAT GIRL IS TOTALLY DRAGGING HER BROTHER'S LEAD DOWN.
WE AIN'T A WELL-BALANCED COUPLE. MAKO'S SO TINY.
SHE'S GOT NO CLUE HOW TO MOVE, EITHER.
KA-CHAK
DRINK SOME MILK!
MAKO
EEK!

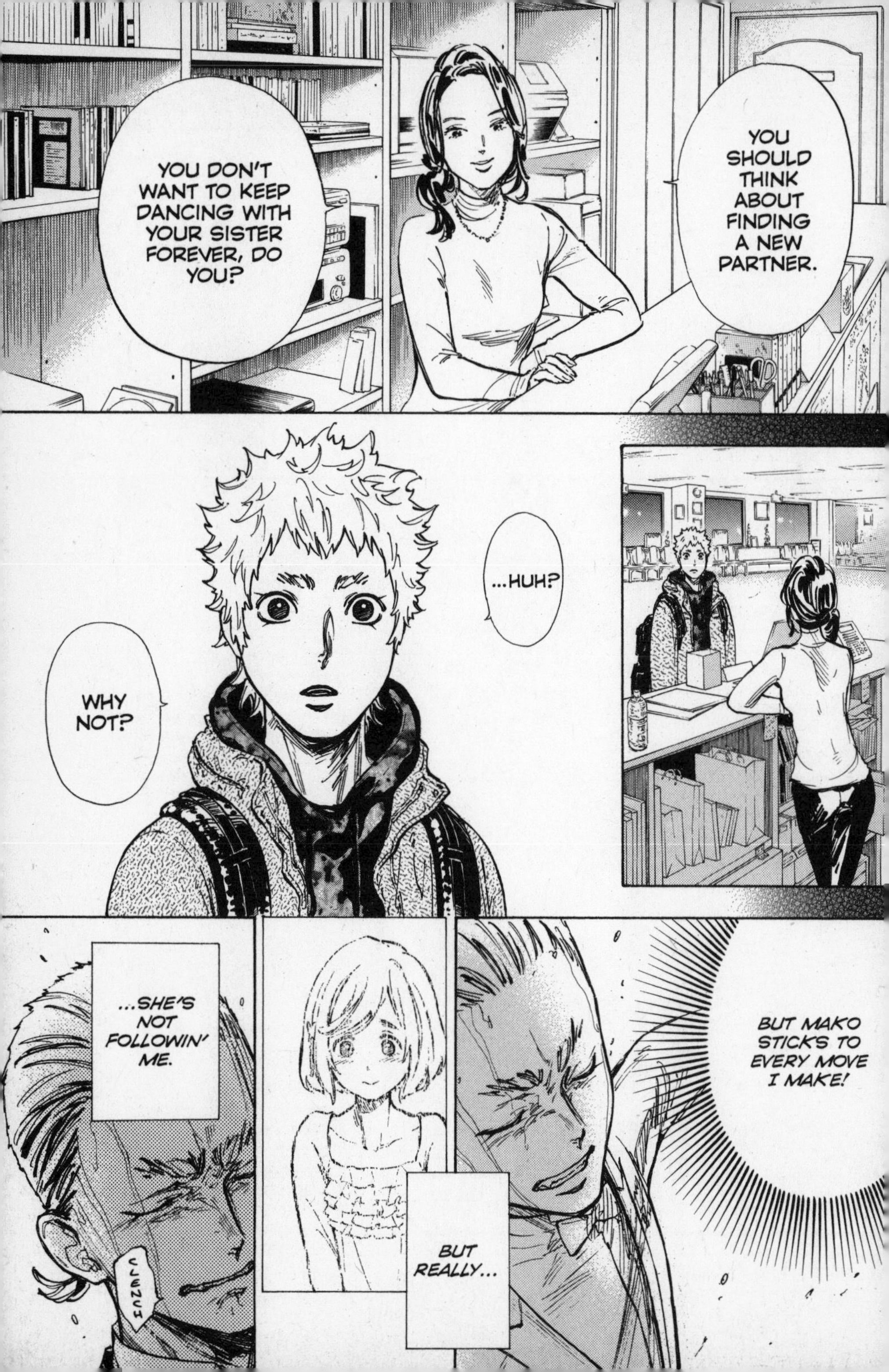
YOU SHOULD THINK ABOUT FINDING A NEW PARTNER.
YOU DON'T WANT TO KEEP DANCING WITH YOUR SISTER FOREVER, DO YOU?
...HUH?
WHY NOT?
BUT MAKO STICKS TO EVERY MOVE I MAKE!
BUT REALLY...
...SHE'S NOT FOLLOWIN' ME.
CLENCH

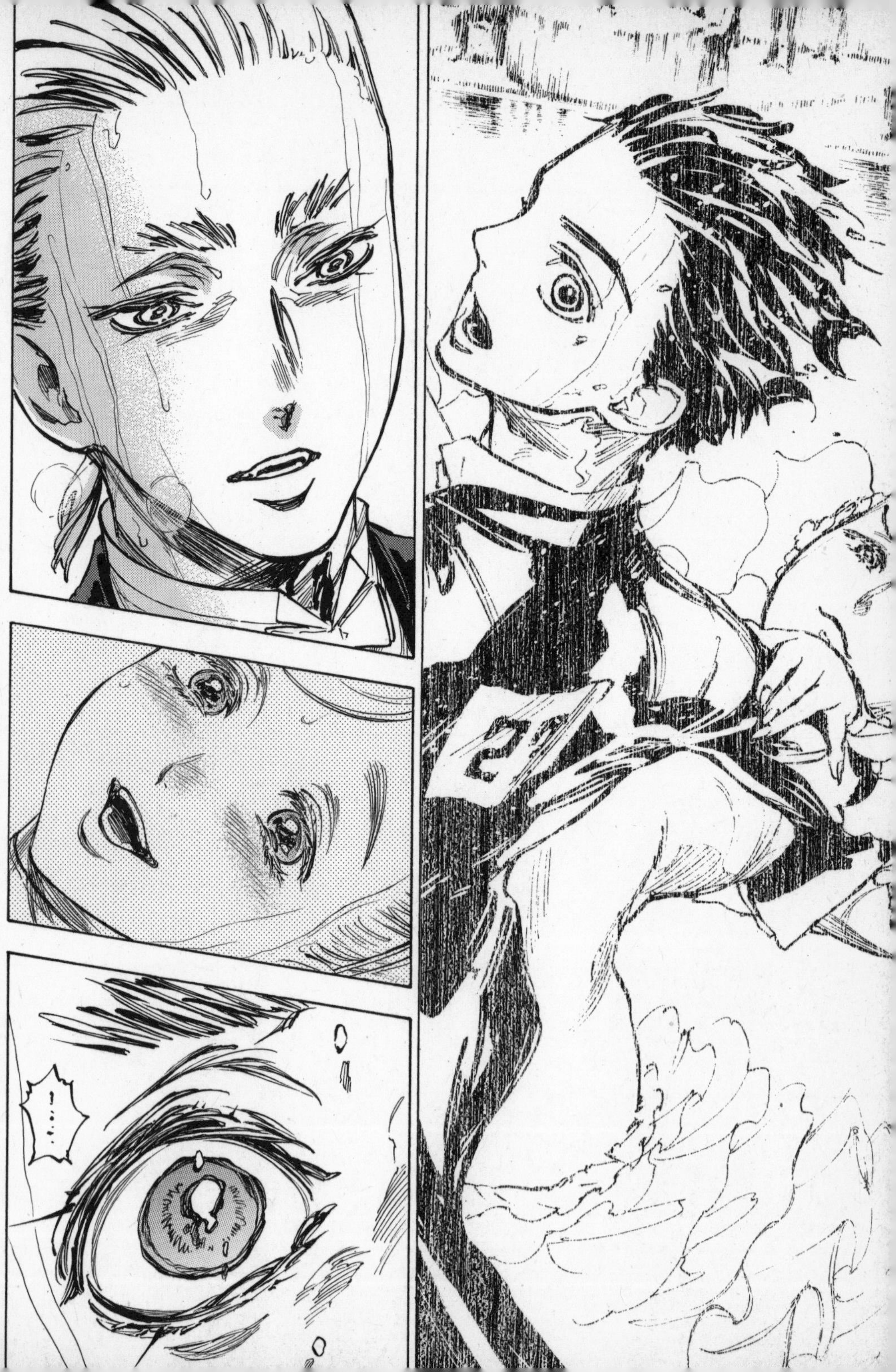
...!

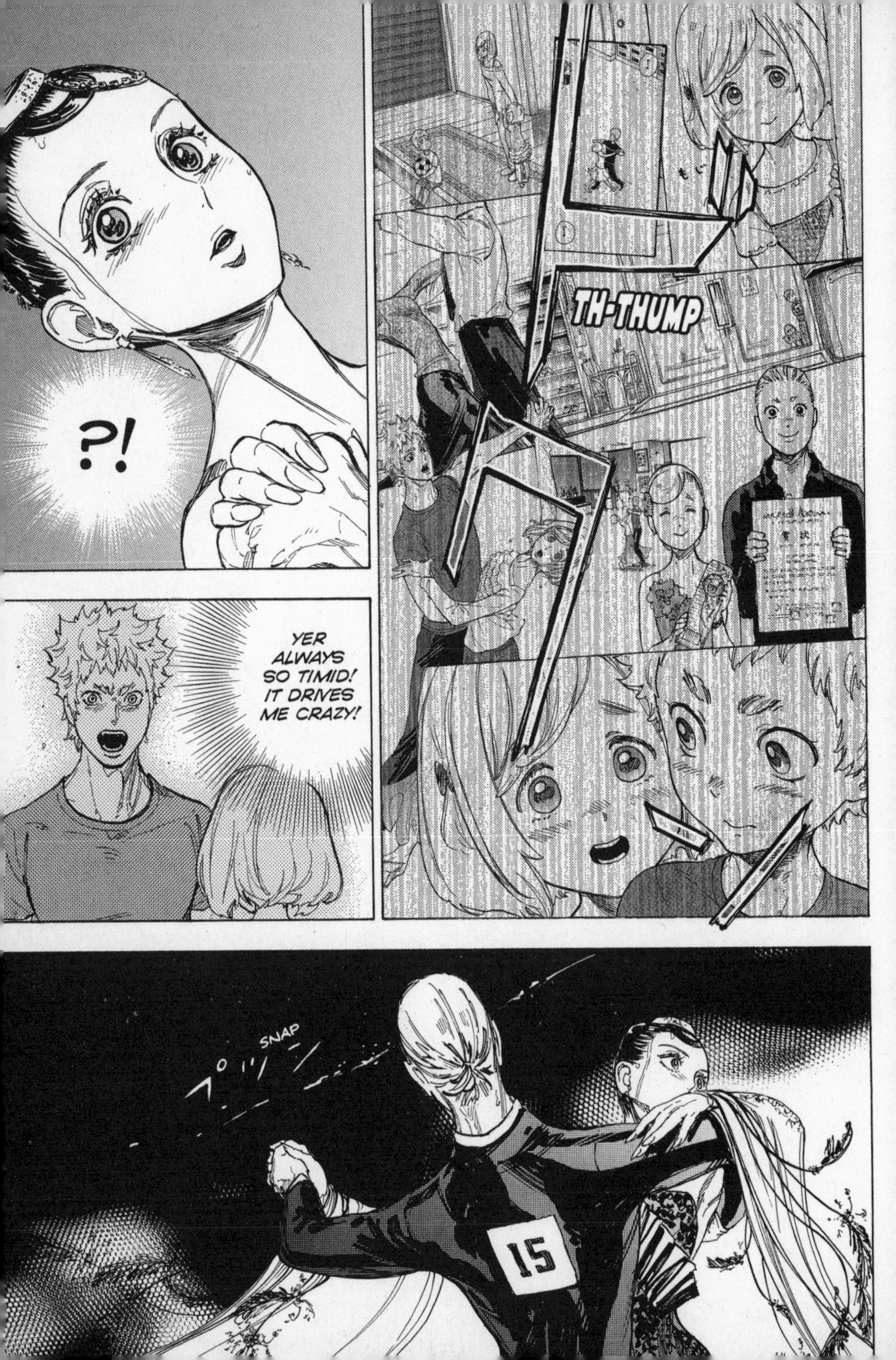
TH-THUMP
?!
YER ALWAYS SO TIMID! IT DRIVES ME CRAZY!
SNAP

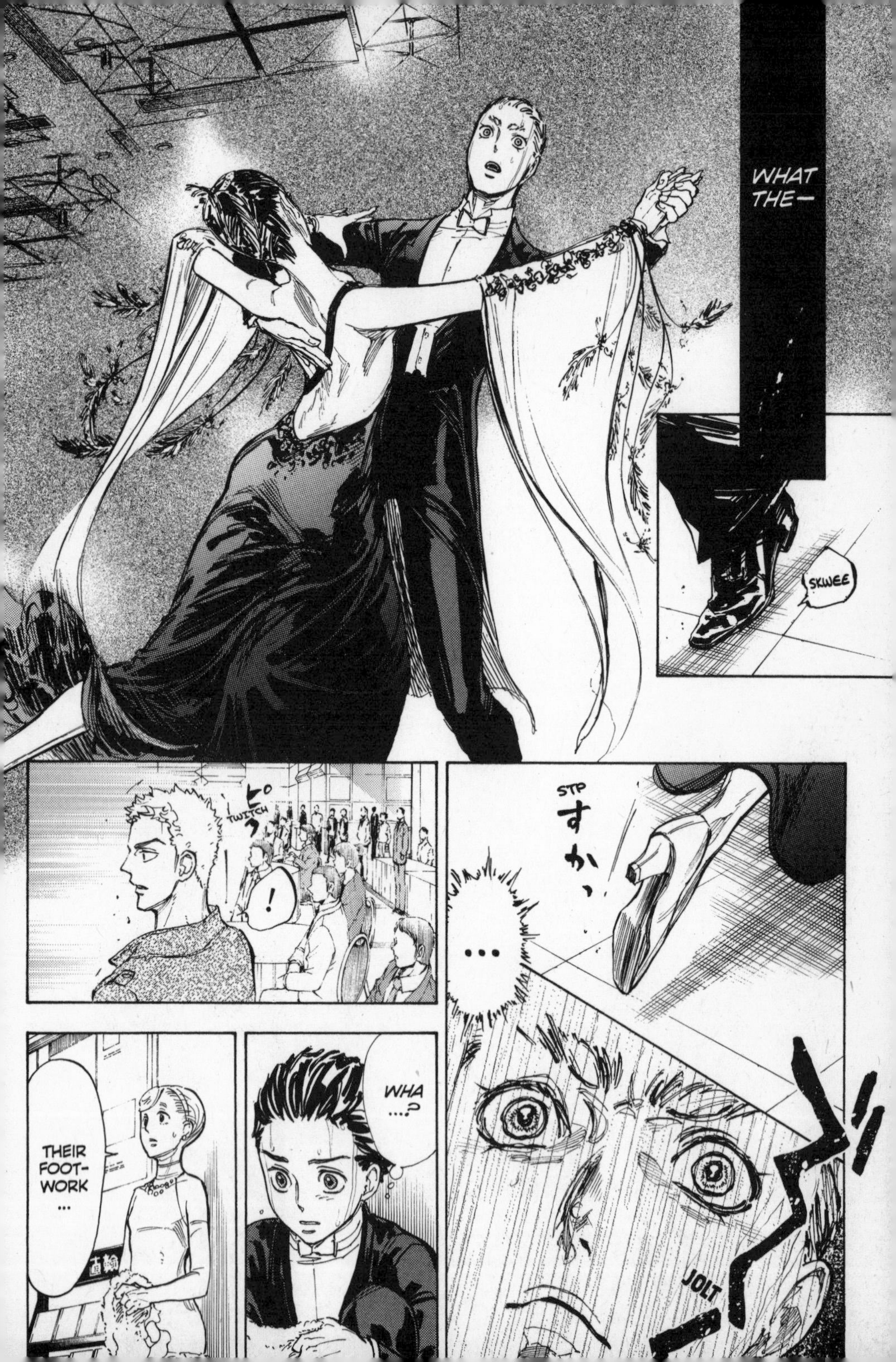
WHAT THE—
SKWEE
STP
すか
...
JOLT
ヒク
TWITCH
!
WHA ....?
THEIR FOOT-WORK ...

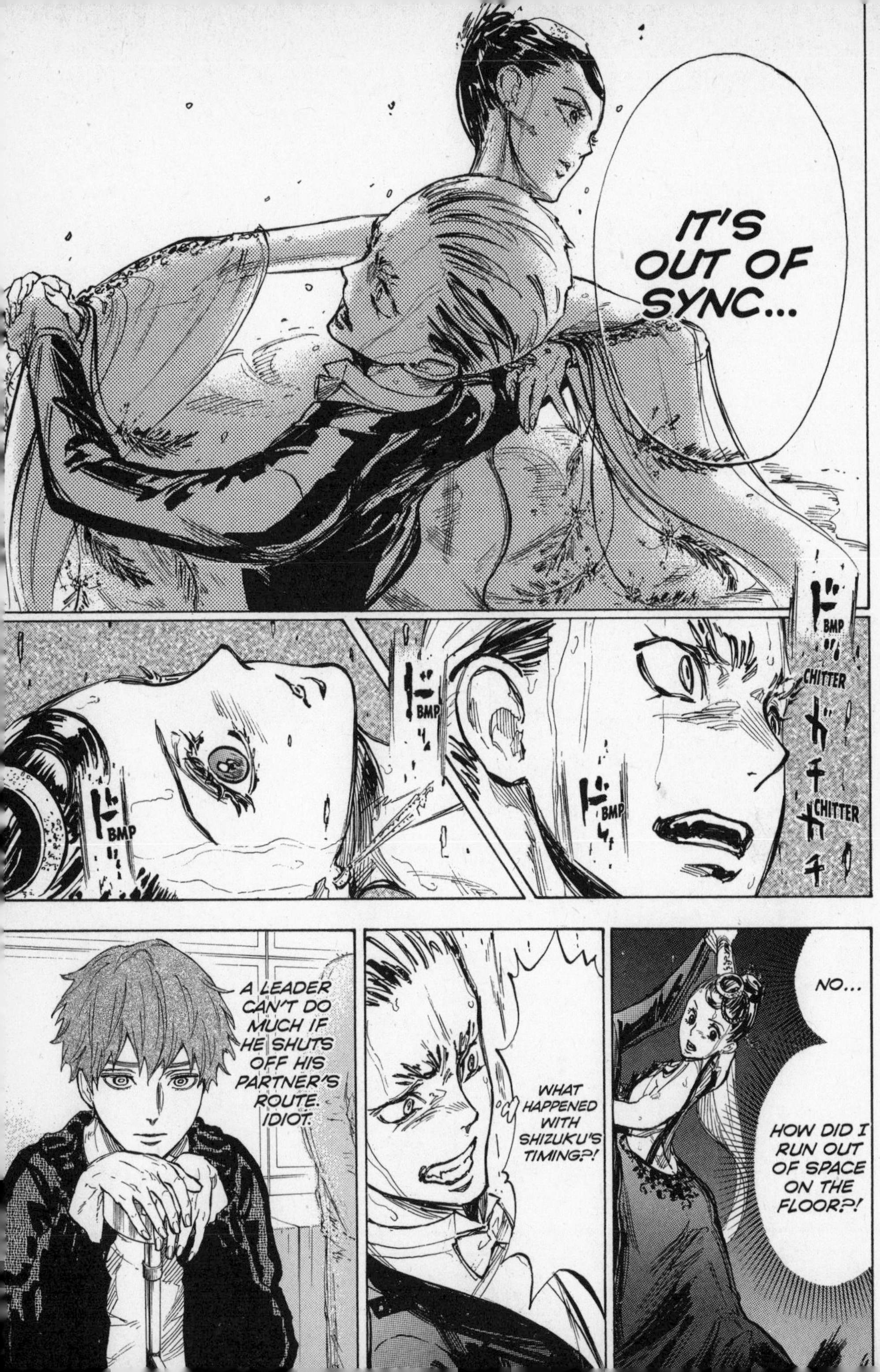

IT'S OUT OF SYNC...
BMP
CHITTER
CHITTER
BMP
BMP
BMP
NO...
HOW DID I RUN OUT OF SPACE ON THE FLOOR?!
WHAT HAPPENED WITH SHIZUKU'S TIMING?!
A LEADER CAN'T DO MUCH IF HE SHUTS OFF HIS PARTNER'S ROUTE. IDIOT.

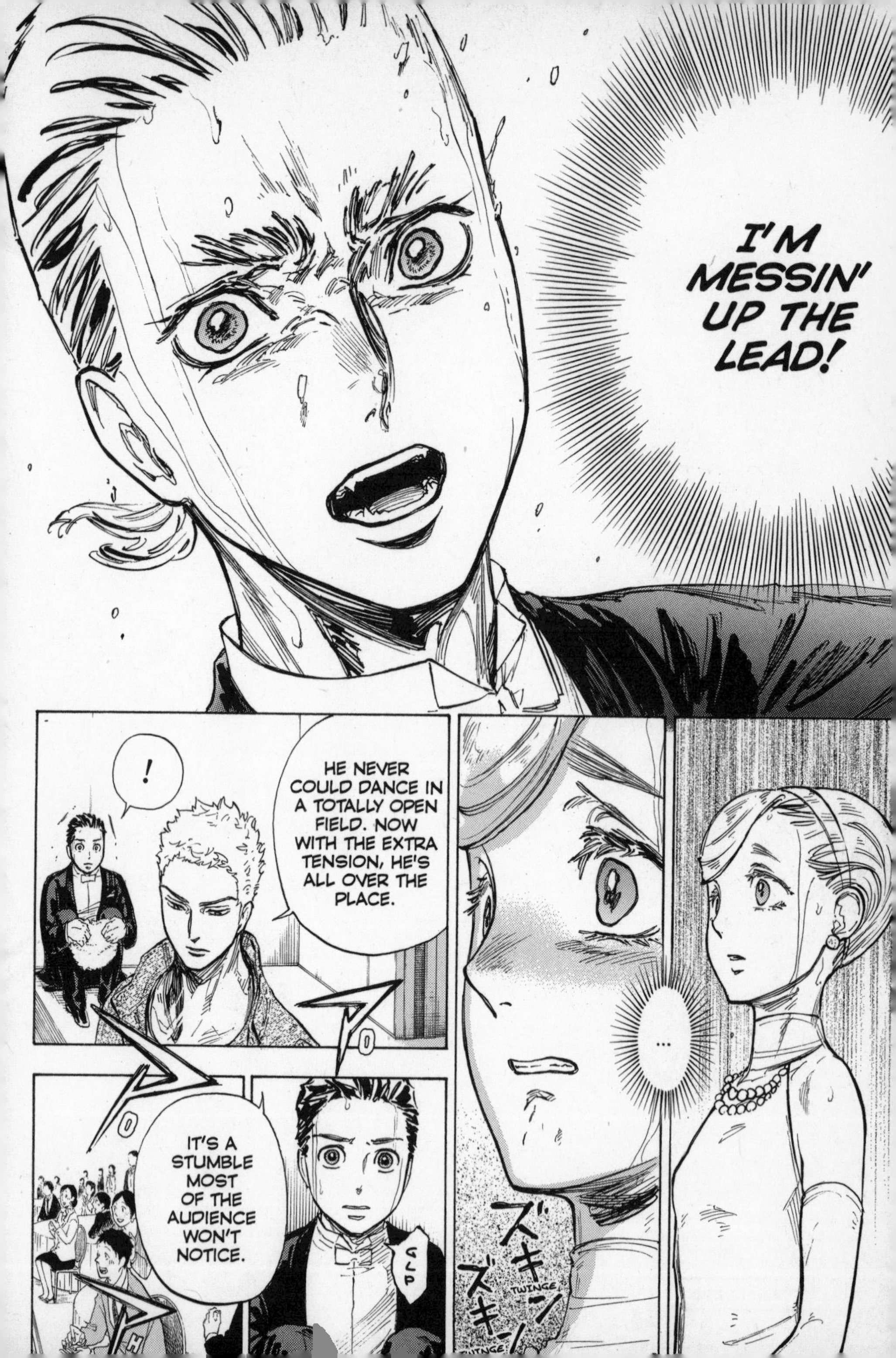
I'M MESSIN' UP THE LEAD!
...
ズキン
TWINGE
ズキン
TWINGE
HE NEVER COULD DANCE IN A TOTALLY OPEN FIELD. NOW WITH THE EXTRA TENSION, HE'S ALL OVER THE PLACE.
!
GLP
IT'S A STUMBLE MOST OF THE AUDIENCE WON'T NOTICE.

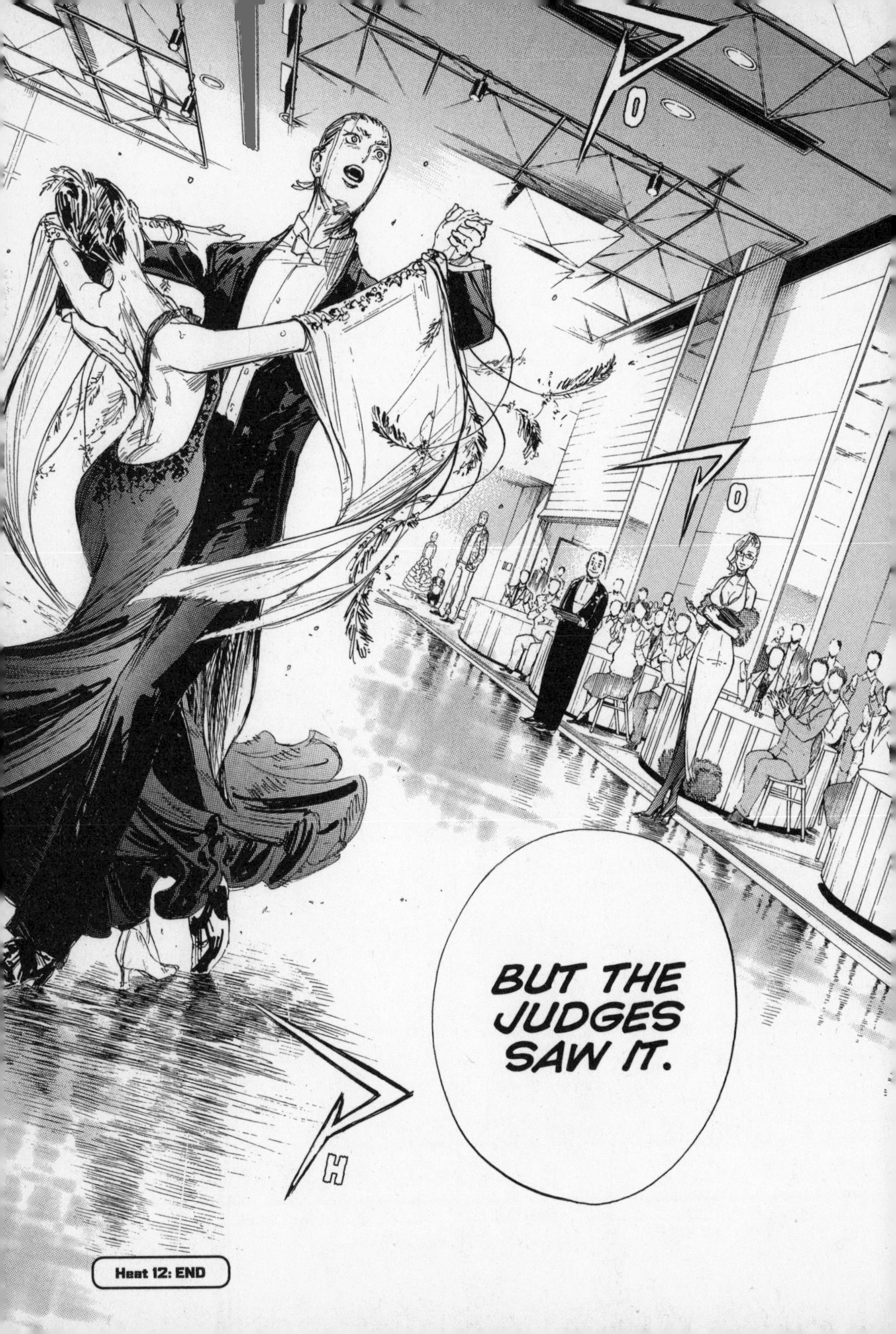
PO
PO
BUT THE JUDGES SAW IT.
PH
Heat 12: END

WELCOME TO THE BALLROOM

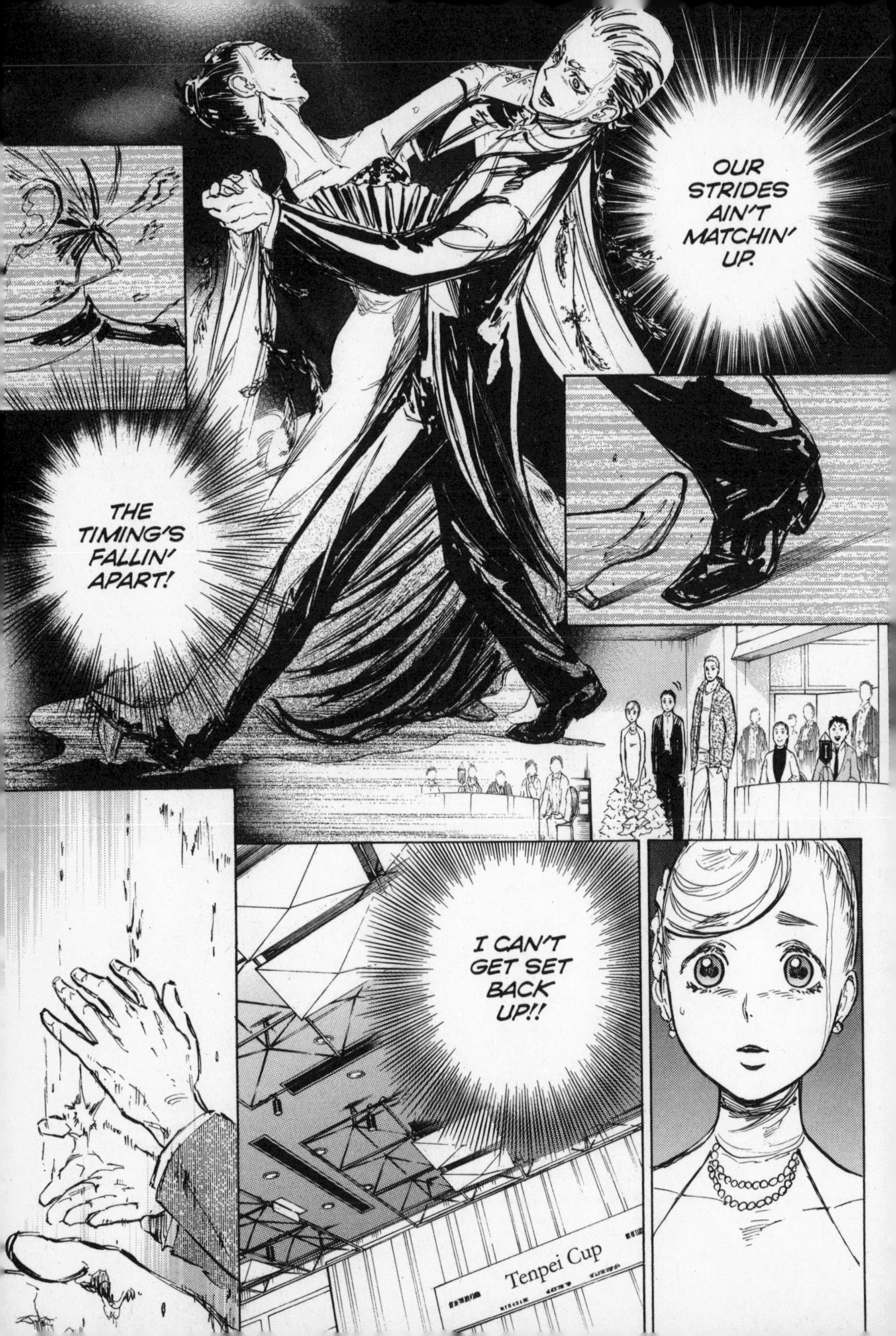
OUR STRIDES AIN'T MATCHIN' UP.
THE TIMING'S FALLIN' APART!
I CAN'T GET SET BACK UP!!
Tenpei Cup

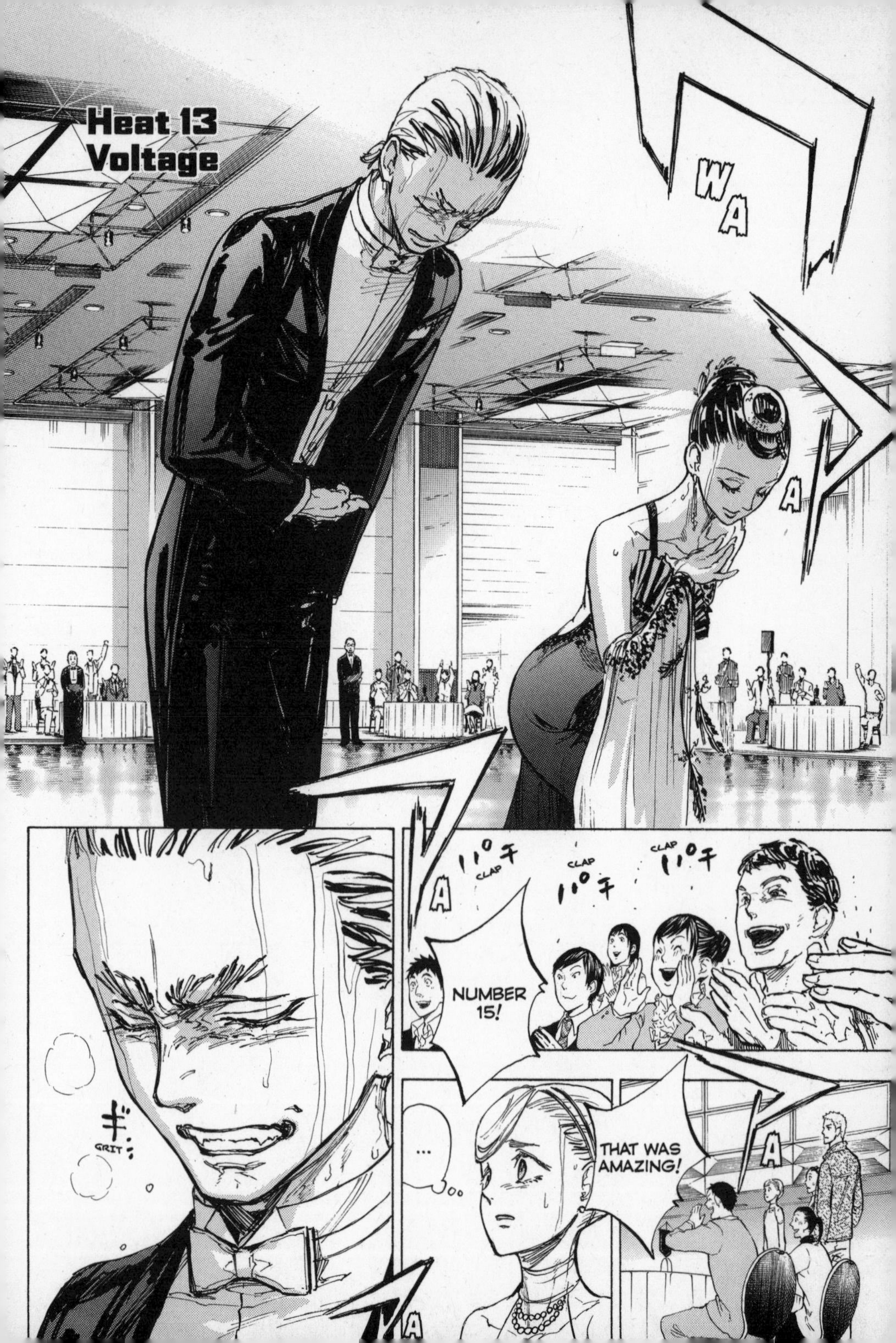
Heat 13
Voltage
WA
A
A
パチ CLAP
パチ CLAP
パチ CLAP
A
NUMBER 15!
A
THAT WAS AMAZING!
...
ギ GRIT
A

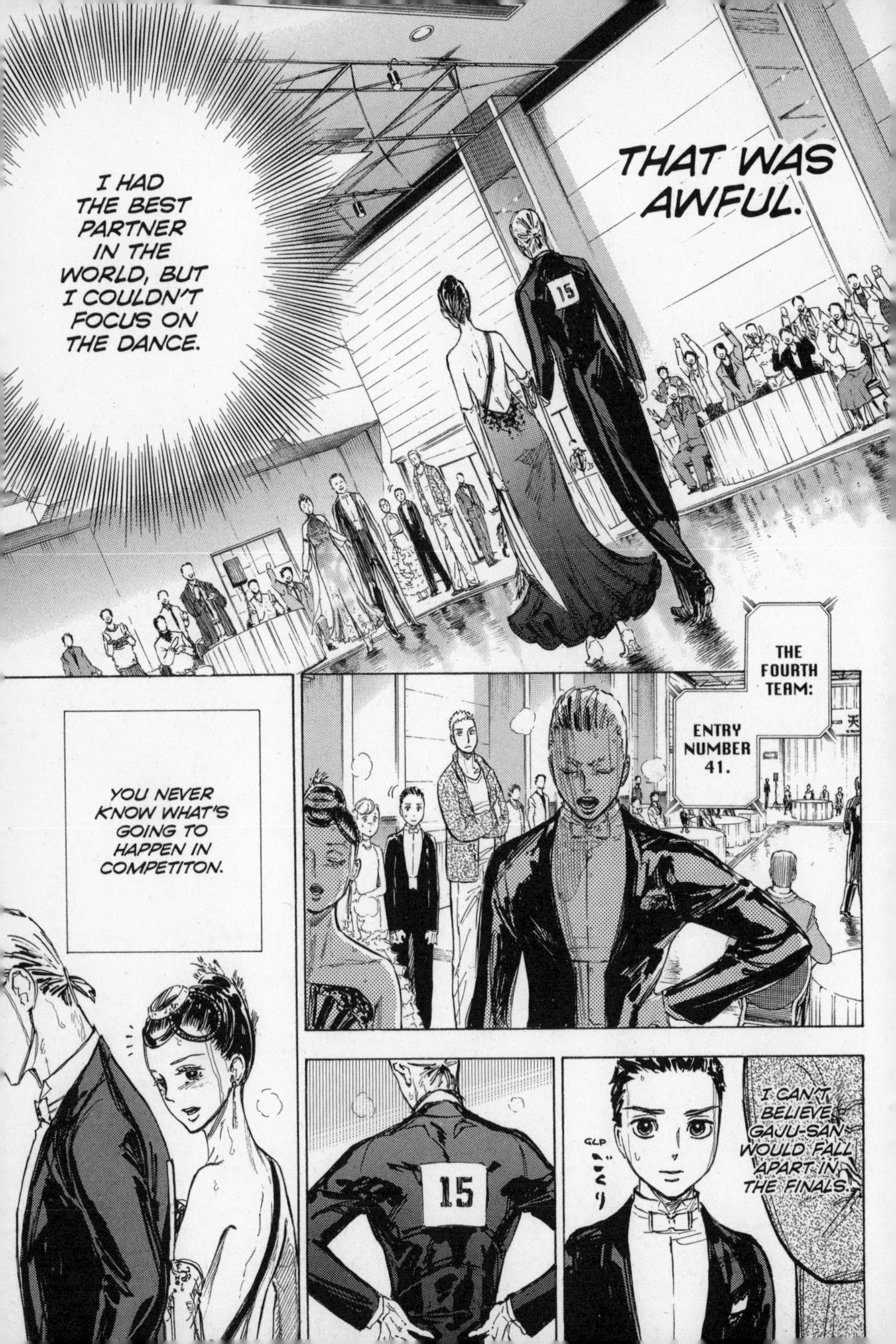
THAT WAS AWFUL.
I HAD THE BEST PARTNER IN THE WORLD, BUT I COULDN'T FOCUS ON THE DANCE.
THE FOURTH TEAM:
ENTRY NUMBER 41.
I CAN'T BELIEVE GAJU-SAN WOULD FALL APART IN THE FINALS.
GLP
15
15
YOU NEVER KNOW WHAT'S GOING TO HAPPEN IN COMPETITON.

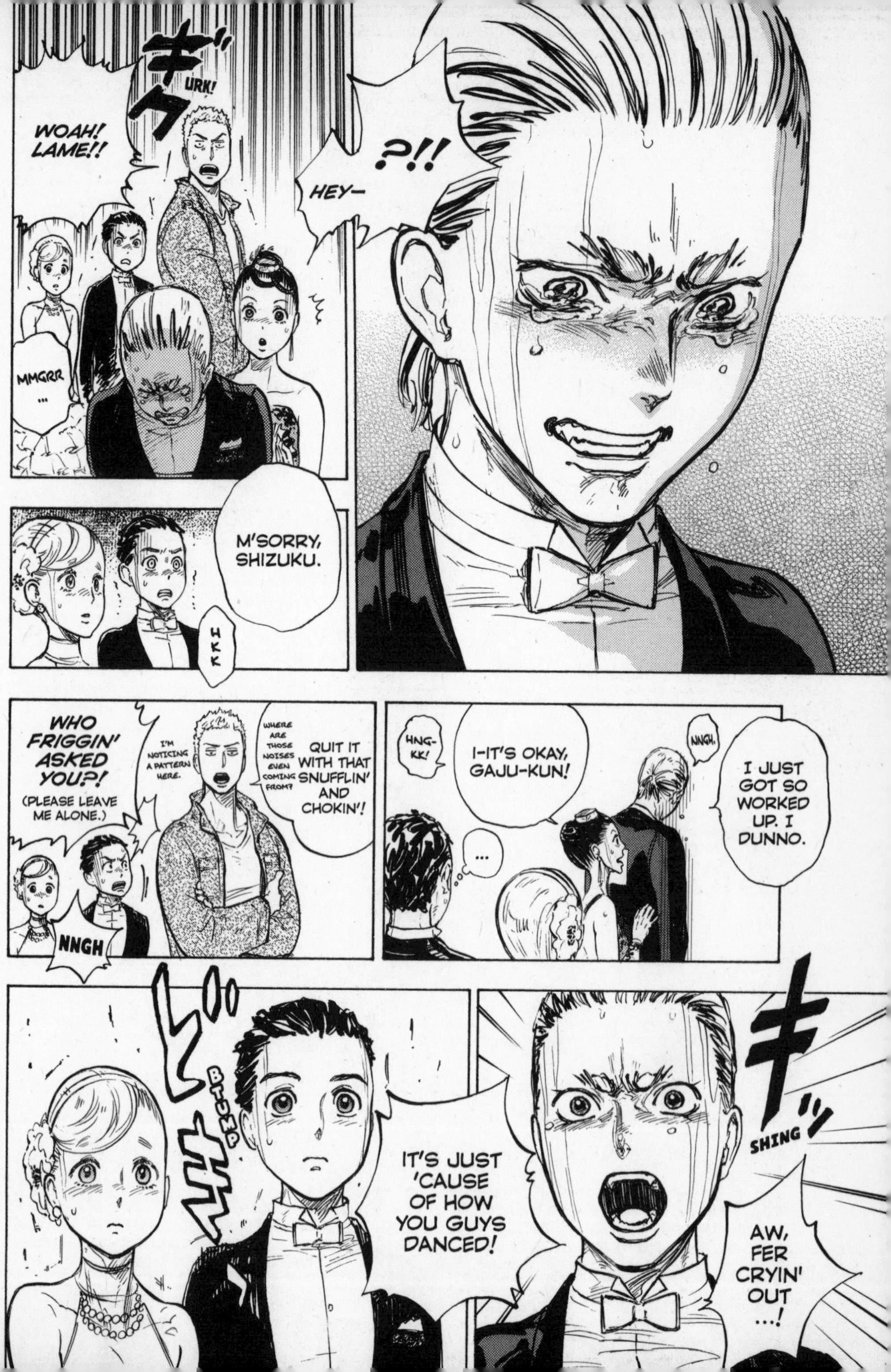
?!!
HEY—
M'SORRY, SHIZUKU.
ギク
URK!
WOAH! LAME!!
MMGRR ...
HKK
NNGH.
I JUST GOT SO WORKED UP. I DUNNO.
HNG-KK!
I-IT'S OKAY, GAJU-KUN!
...
QUIT IT WITH THAT SNUFFLIN' AND CHOKIN'!
WHERE ARE THOSE NOISES EVEN COMING FROM?
I'M NOTICING A PATTERN HERE.
WHO FRIGGIN' ASKED YOU?!
(PLEASE LEAVE ME ALONE.)
NNGH
キッ
SHING
AW, FER CRYIN' OUT ...!
IT'S JUST 'CAUSE OF HOW YOU GUYS DANCED!
BTUMP

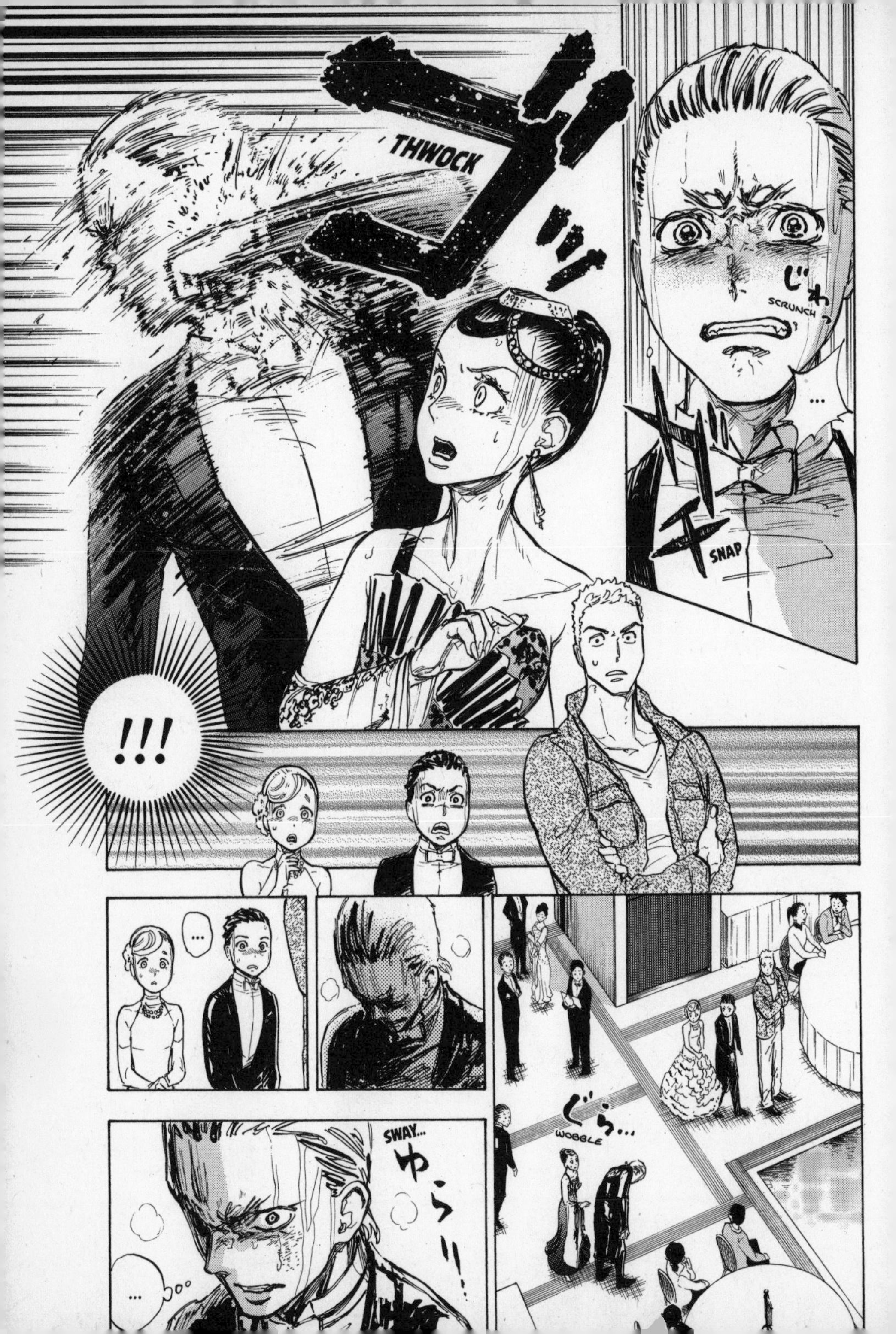
じわ
SCRUNCH
...
SNAP
THWOCK
!!!
ぐら...
WOBBLE
...
SWAY...
ゆらーり...
...

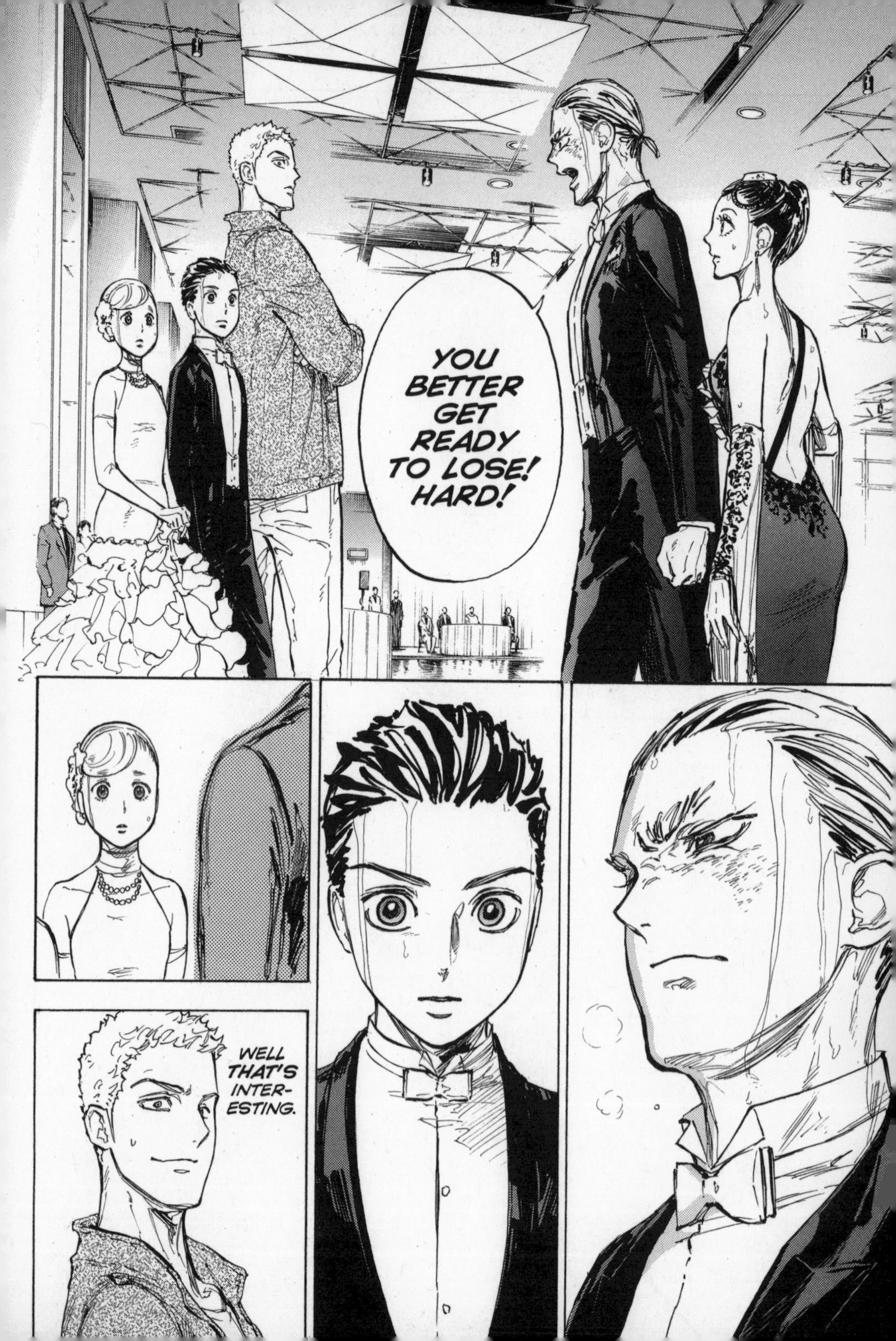
YOU BETTER GET READY TO LOSE! HARD!
WELL THAT'S INTER-ESTING.

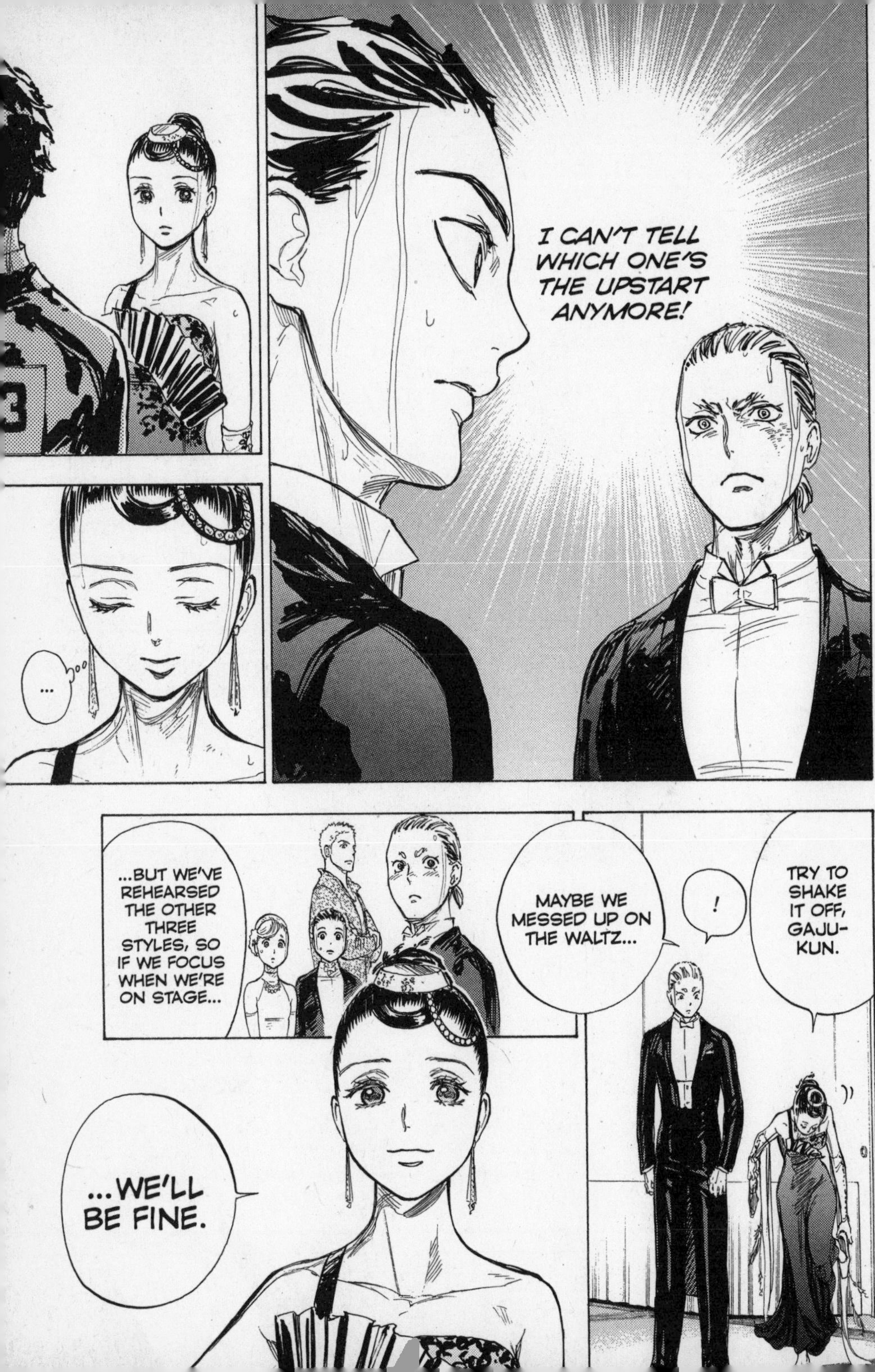
I CAN'T TELL WHICH ONE'S THE UPSTART ANYMORE!
...
TRY TO SHAKE IT OFF, GAJU-KUN.
!
MAYBE WE MESSED UP ON THE WALTZ...
...BUT WE'VE REHEARSED THE OTHER THREE STYLES, SO IF WE FOCUS WHEN WE'RE ON STAGE...
...WE'LL BE FINE.

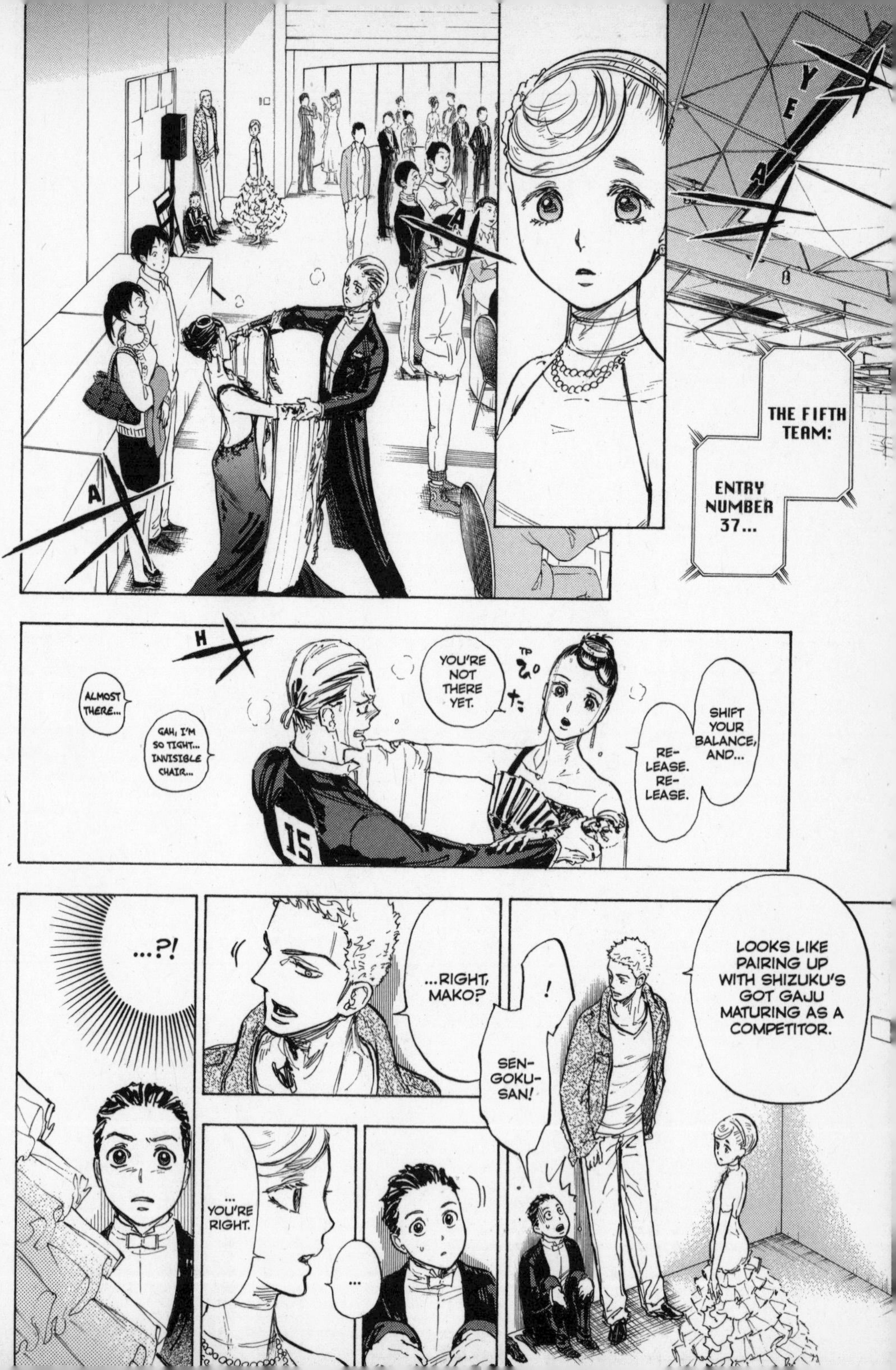
YEA
A
THE FIFTH TEAM:
ENTRY NUMBER 37...
A
A
SHIFT YOUR BALANCE, AND...
RE-LEASE. RE-LEASE.
YOU'RE NOT THERE YET.
TP
GAH, I'M SO TIGHT... INVISIBLE CHAIR...
ALMOST THERE...
H
LOOKS LIKE PAIRING UP WITH SHIZUKU'S GOT GAJU MATURING AS A COMPETITOR.
!
SEN-GOKU-SAN!
...RIGHT, MAKO?
...?!
...
... YOU'RE RIGHT.

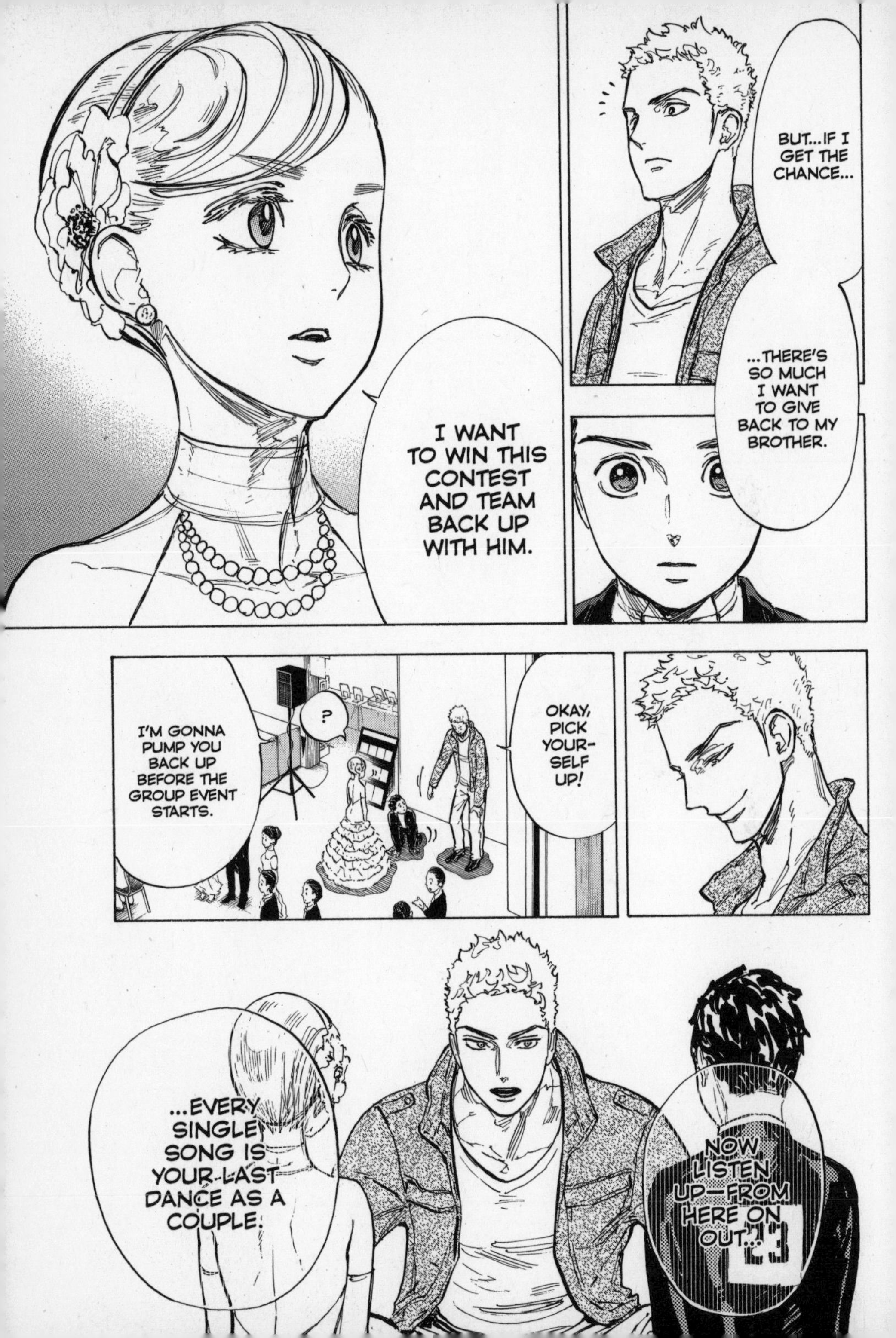
BUT...IF I GET THE CHANCE...
...THERE'S SO MUCH I WANT TO GIVE BACK TO MY BROTHER.
I WANT TO WIN THIS CONTEST AND TEAM BACK UP WITH HIM.
OKAY, PICK YOUR-SELF UP!
?
I'M GONNA PUMP YOU BACK UP BEFORE THE GROUP EVENT STARTS.
NOW LISTEN UP—FROM HERE ON OUT...
...EVERY SINGLE SONG IS YOUR LAST DANCE AS A COUPLE.

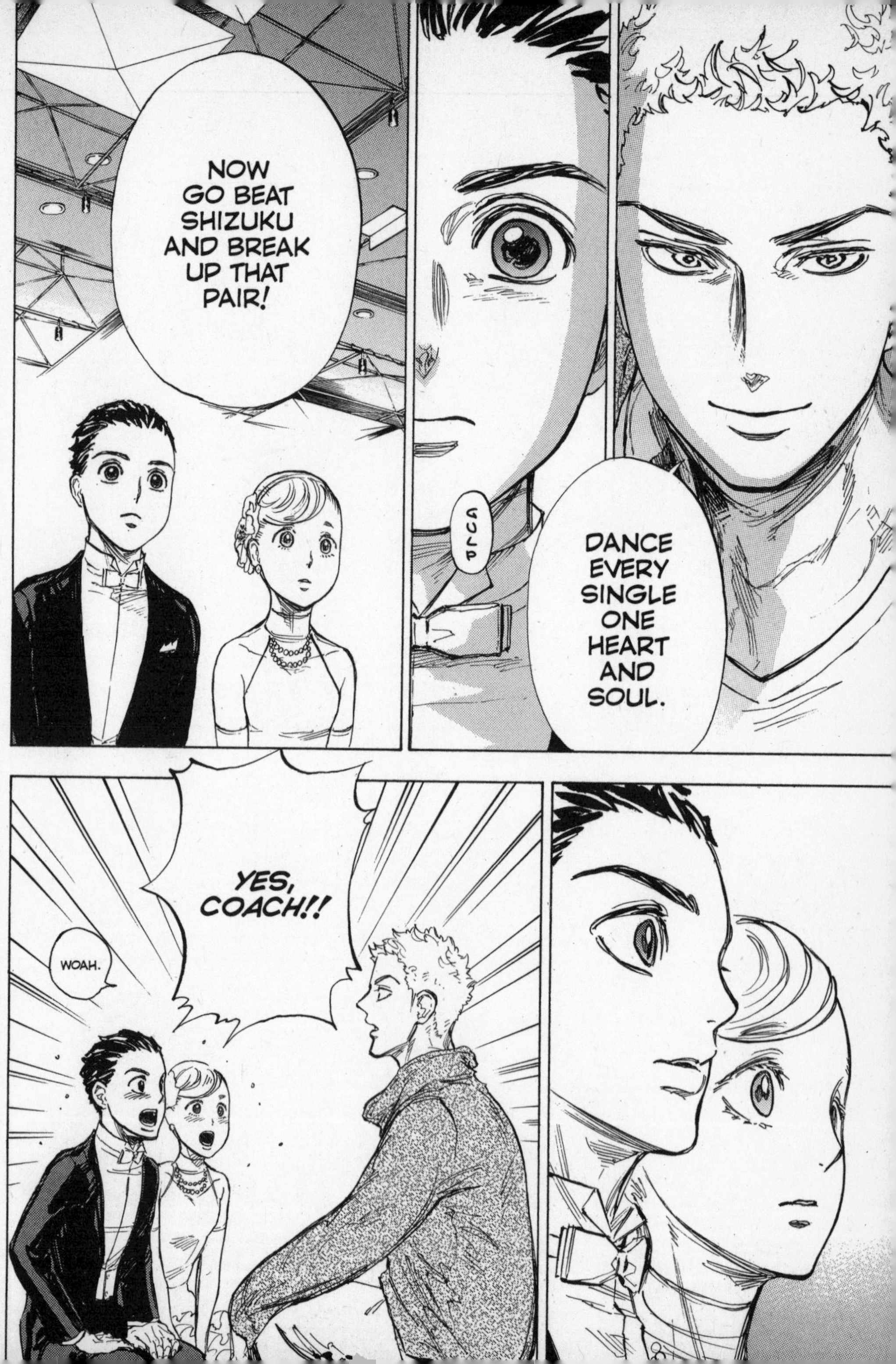
DANCE EVERY SINGLE ONE HEART AND SOUL.
GULP
NOW GO BEAT SHIZUKU AND BREAK UP THAT PAIR!
YES, COACH!!
WOAH.

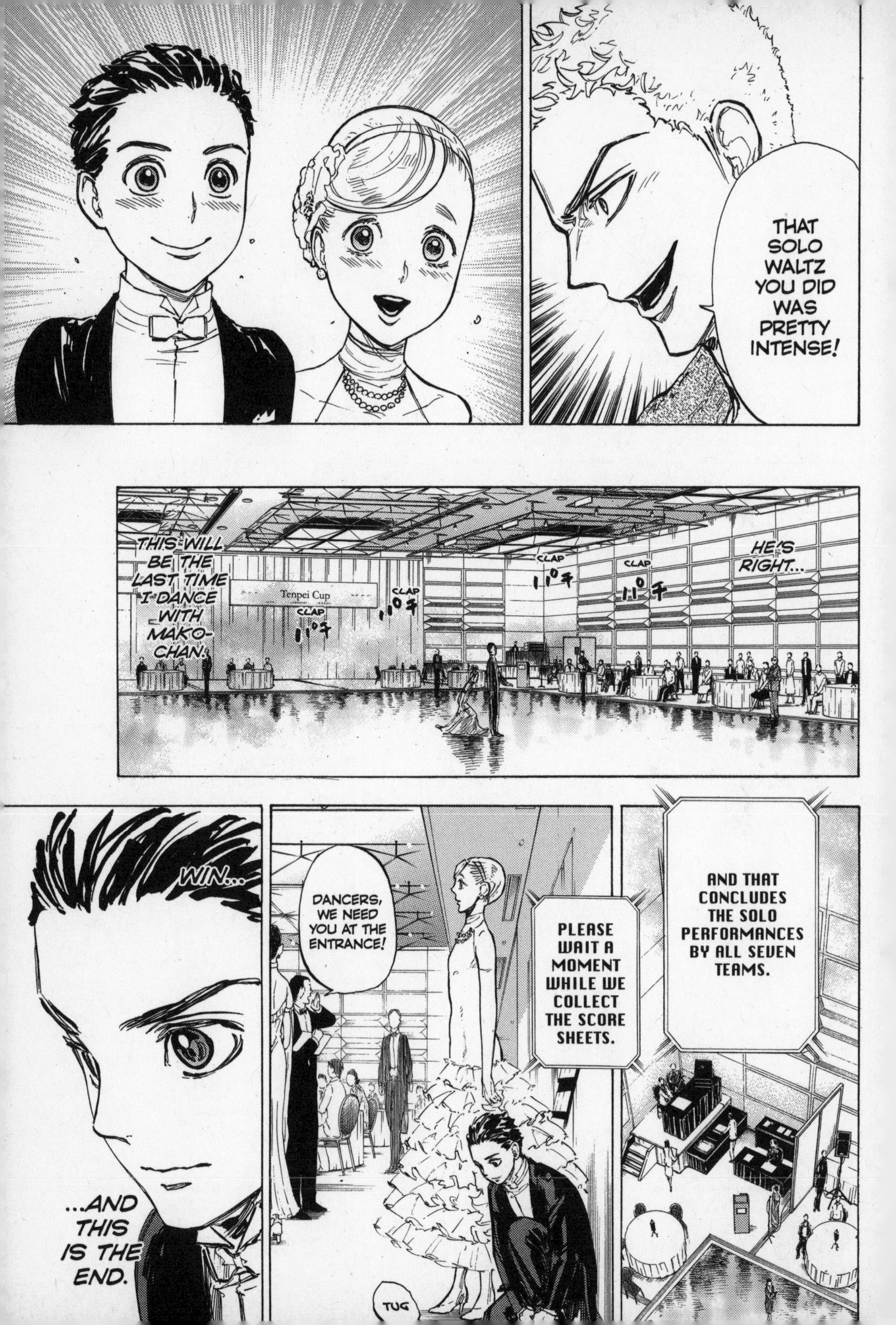
THAT SOLO WALTZ YOU DID WAS PRETTY INTENSE!
HE'S RIGHT...
CLAP パチ
CLAP パチ
CLAP パチ
CLAP パチ
Tenpei Cup
THIS WILL BE THE LAST TIME I DANCE WITH MAKO-CHAN.
AND THAT CONCLUDES THE SOLO PERFORMANCES BY ALL SEVEN TEAMS.
PLEASE WAIT A MOMENT WHILE WE COLLECT THE SCORE SHEETS.
DANCERS, WE NEED YOU AT THE ENTRANCE!
TUG
WIN...
...AND THIS IS THE END.

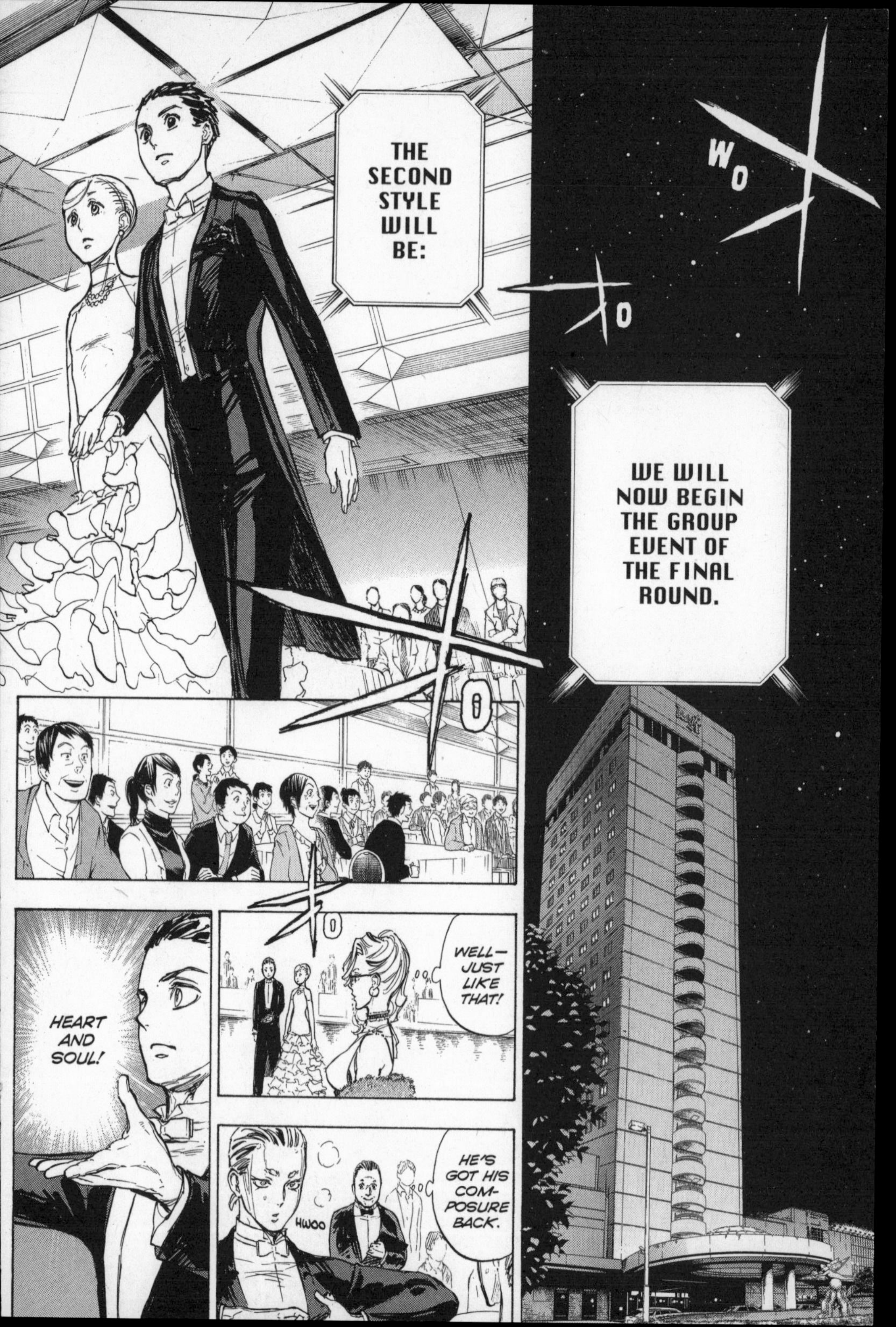
WO
O
WE WILL NOW BEGIN THE GROUP EVENT OF THE FINAL ROUND.
THE SECOND STYLE WILL BE:
O
O
WELL— JUST LIKE THAT!
HEART AND SOUL!
HE'S GOT HIS COM-POSURE BACK.
HWOO

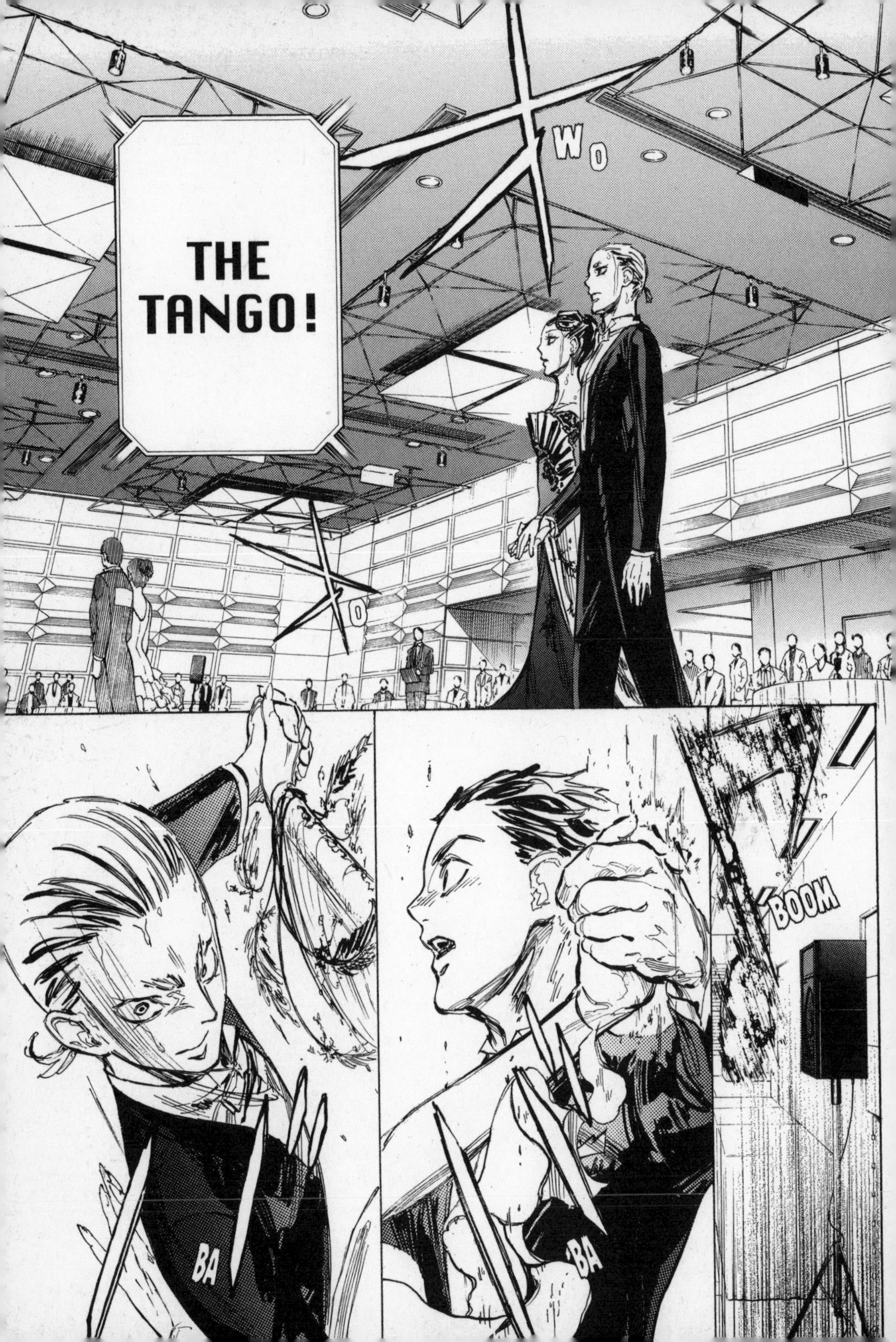

WO
THE TANGO!
O
BOOM
BA
BA

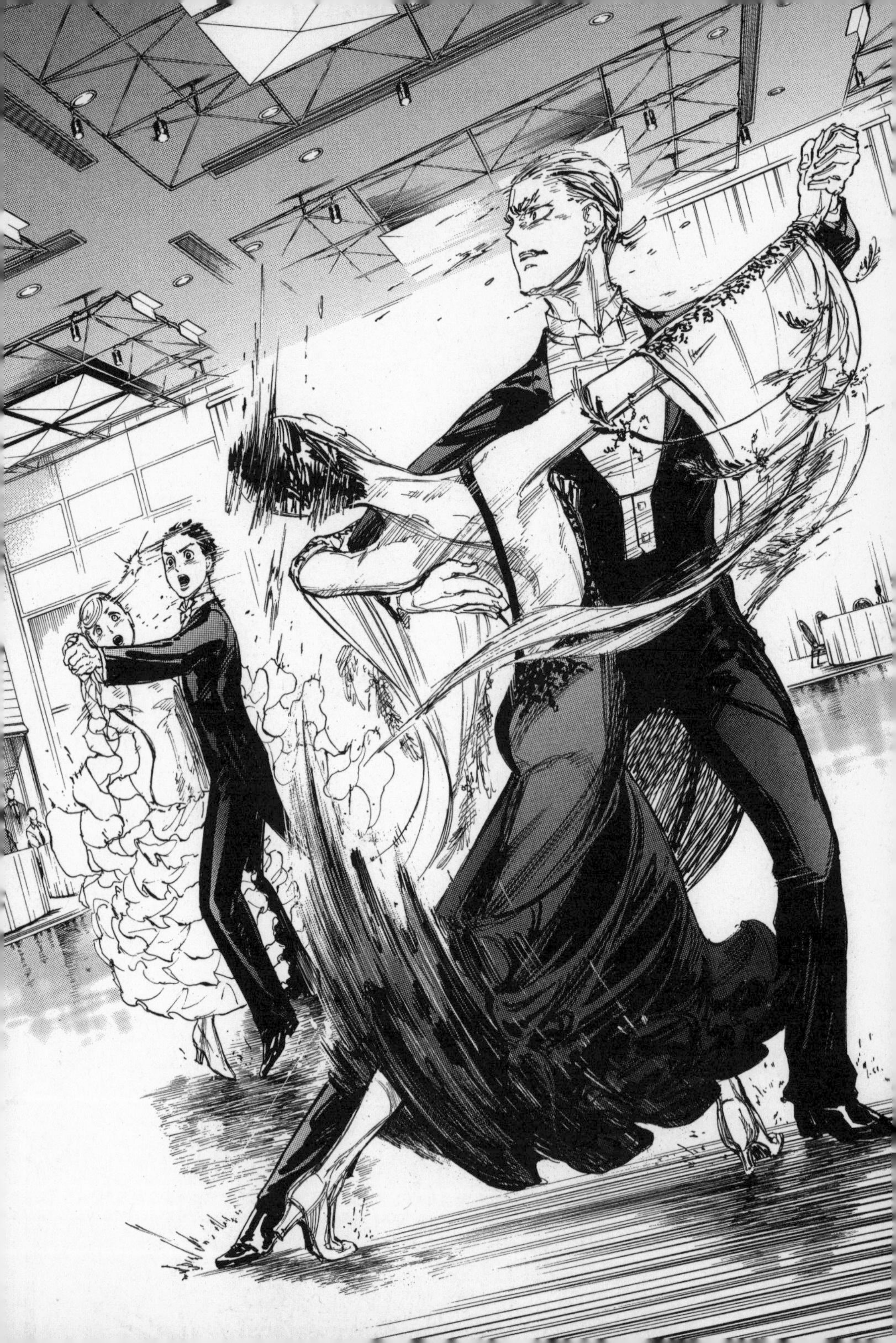

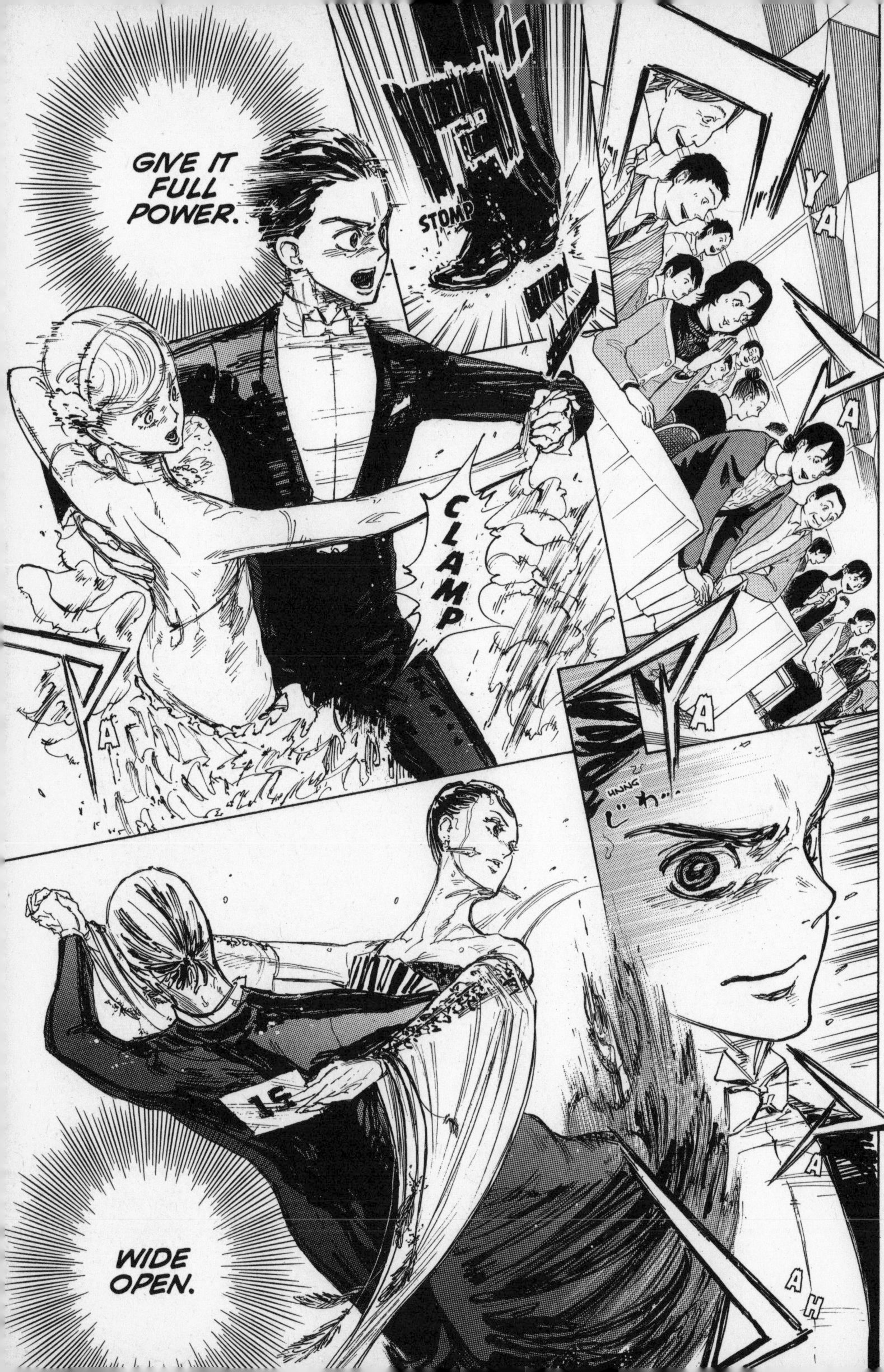

YA
YA
STOMP
GIVE IT FULL POWER.
CLAMP
YA
YA
HNNG
YA
AH
WIDE OPEN.

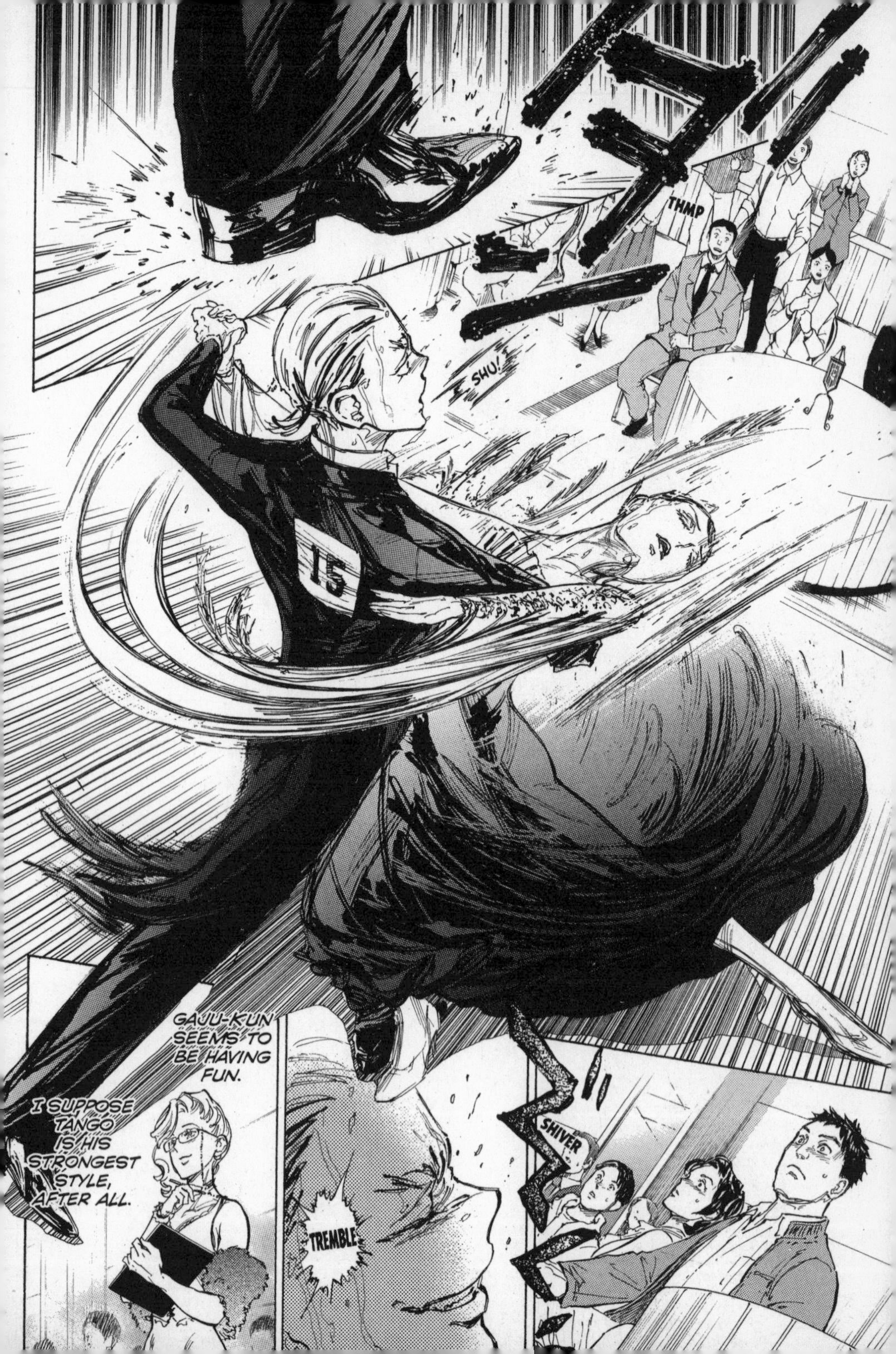
THMP
SHU!
SHIVER
TREMBLE
GAJU-KUN SEEMS TO BE HAVING FUN.
I SUPPOSE TANGO IS HIS STRONGEST STYLE, AFTER ALL.

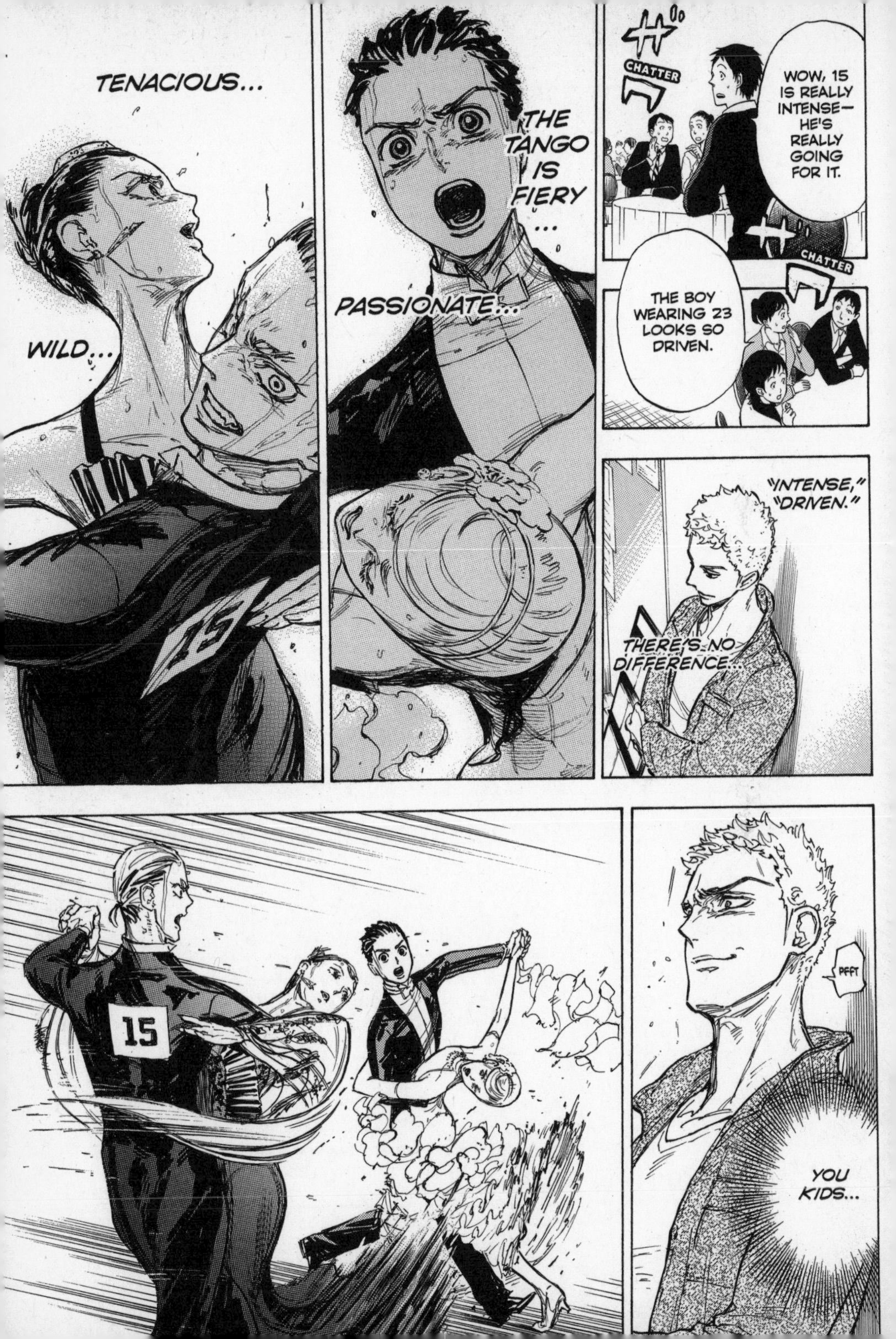
CHATTER
WOW, 15 IS REALLY INTENSE— HE'S REALLY GOING FOR IT.
CHATTER
THE BOY WEARING 23 LOOKS SO DRIVEN.
"INTENSE," "DRIVEN."
THERE'S NO DIFFERENCE...
THE TANGO IS FIERY...
PASSIONATE...
TENACIOUS...
WILD...
15
PFFT
YOU KIDS...
15

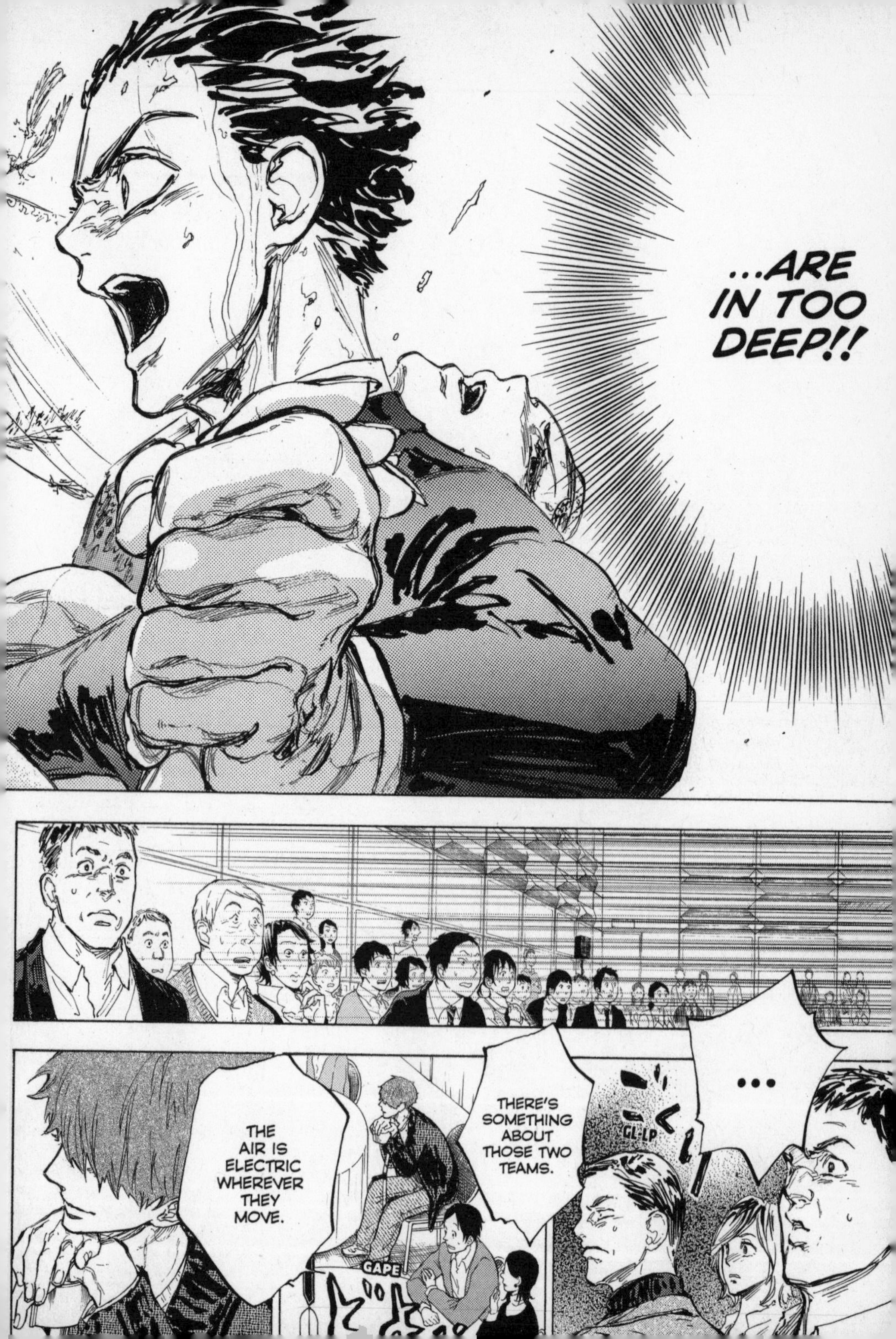
...ARE IN TOO DEEP!!
...
GL-LP
THERE'S SOMETHING ABOUT THOSE TWO TEAMS.
GAPE
THE AIR IS ELECTRIC WHEREVER THEY MOVE.

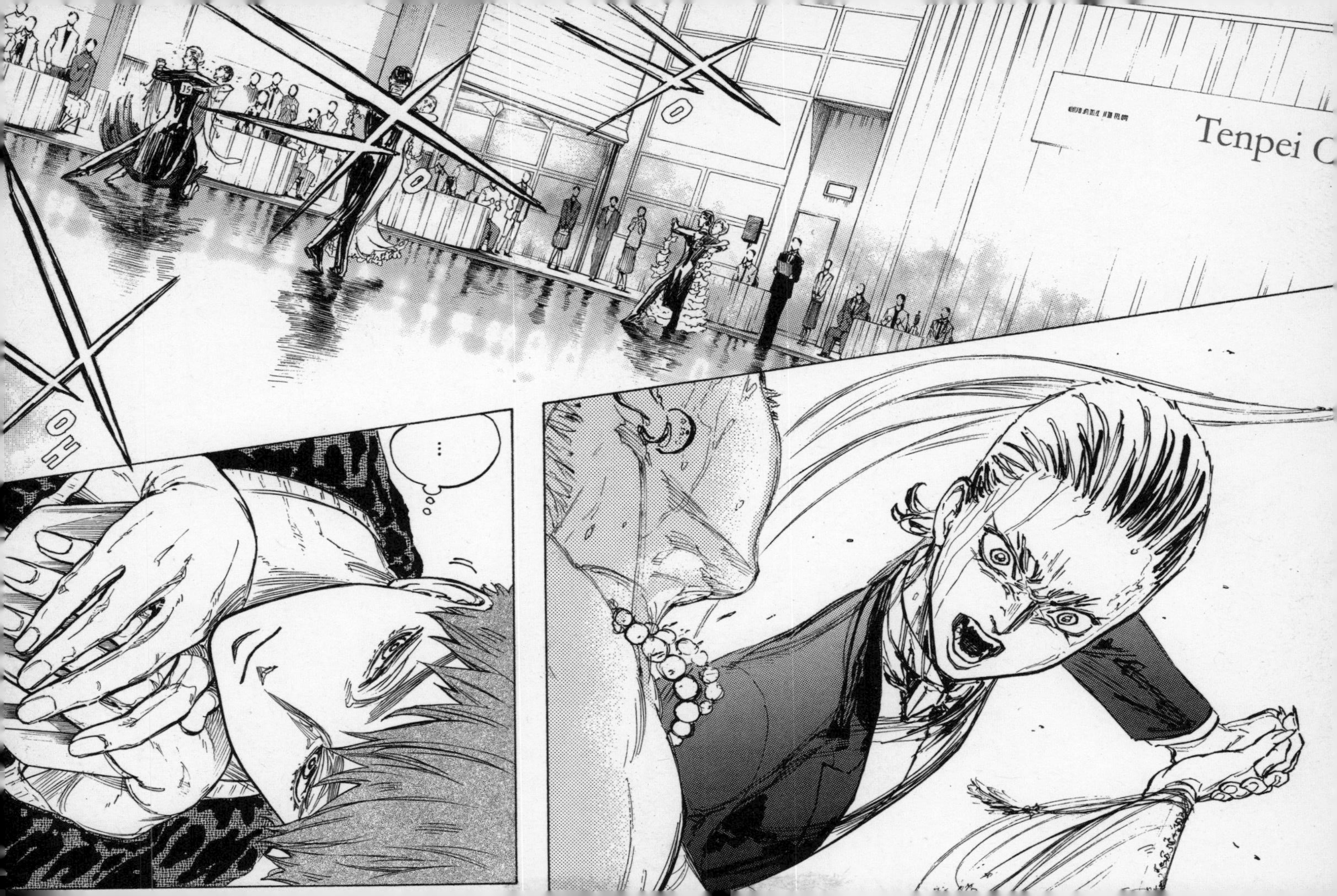
Tenpei C
O
O
OH
...

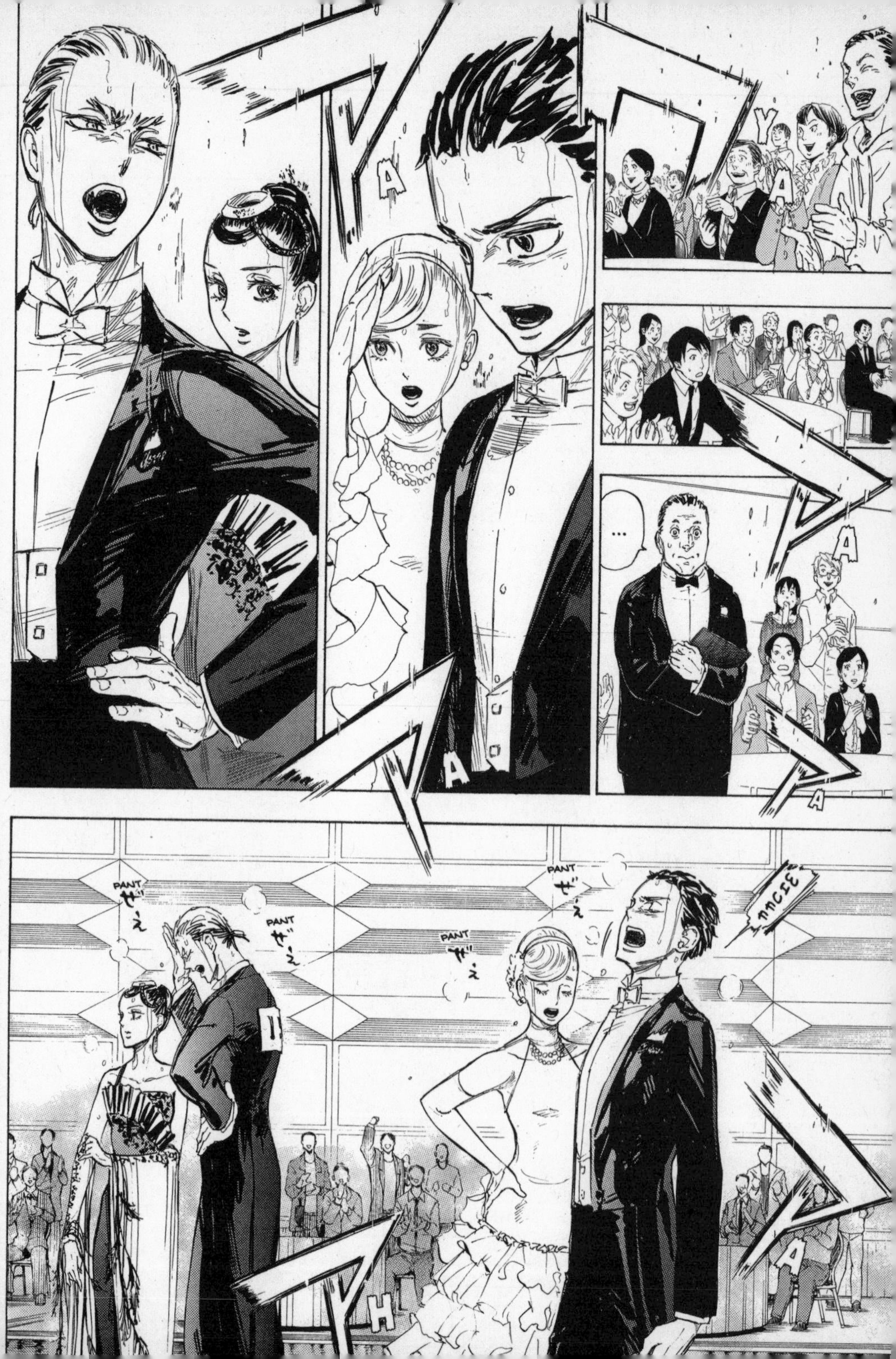

Y
A
A
A
...
A
A
A
PANT
ぜえ
PANT
ぜえ
PANT
ぜえ
PANT
ぜえ
A
H

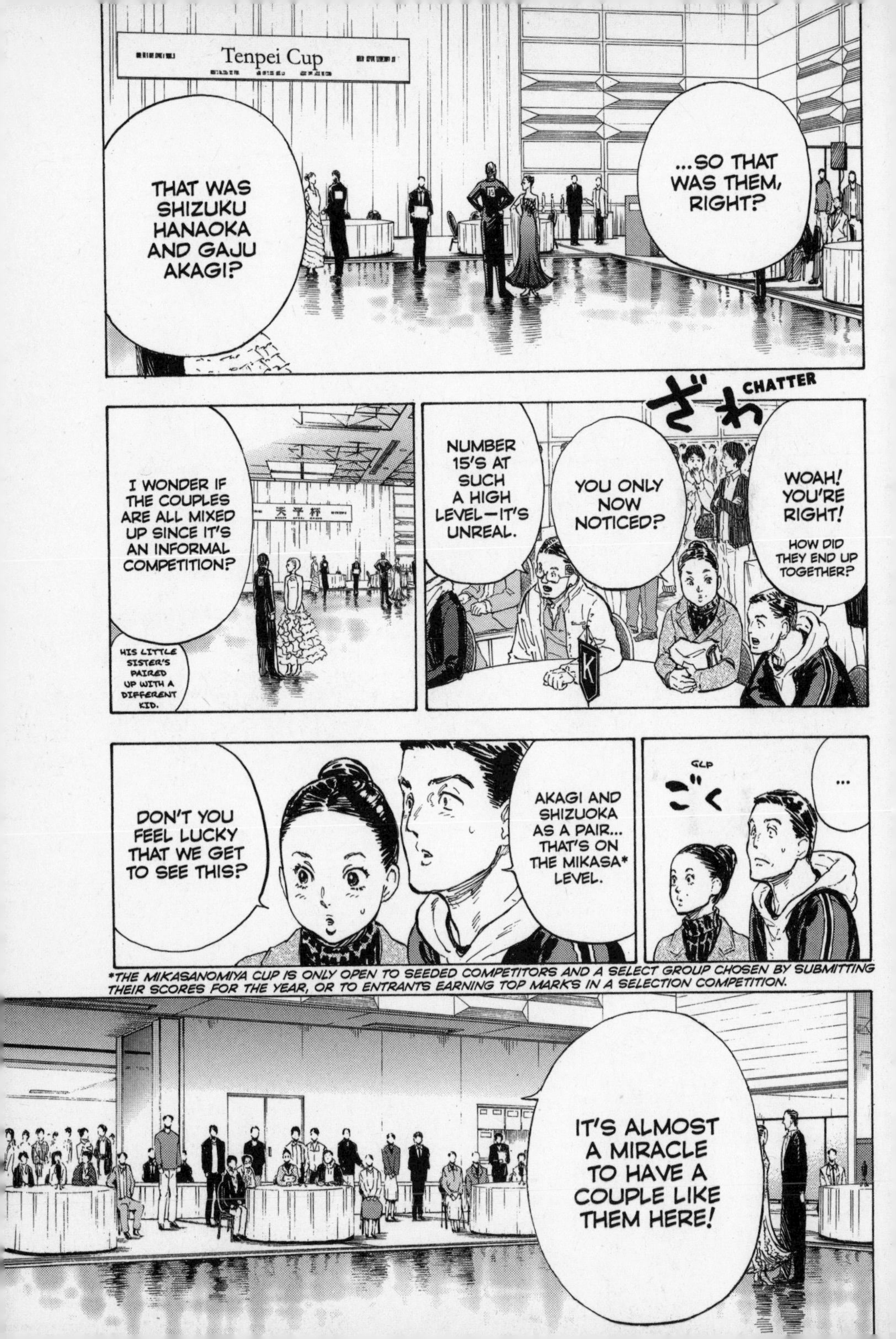
Tenpei Cup
...SO THAT WAS THEM, RIGHT?
THAT WAS SHIZUKU HANAOKA AND GAJU AKAGI?
ざわ CHATTER
WOAH! YOU'RE RIGHT!
HOW DID THEY END UP TOGETHER?
YOU ONLY NOW NOTICED?
NUMBER 15'S AT SUCH A HIGH LEVEL—IT'S UNREAL.
K
天平杯
I WONDER IF THE COUPLES ARE ALL MIXED UP SINCE IT'S AN INFORMAL COMPETITION?
HIS LITTLE SISTER'S PAIRED UP WITH A DIFFERENT KID.
...
ごく GLP
AKAGI AND SHIZUOKA AS A PAIR... THAT'S ON THE MIKASA* LEVEL.
DON'T YOU FEEL LUCKY THAT WE GET TO SEE THIS?
*THE MIKASANOMIYA CUP IS ONLY OPEN TO SEEDED COMPETITORS AND A SELECT GROUP CHOSEN BY SUBMITTING THEIR SCORES FOR THE YEAR, OR TO ENTRANTS EARNING TOP MARKS IN A SELECTION COMPETITION.
IT'S ALMOST A MIRACLE TO HAVE A COUPLE LIKE THEM HERE!

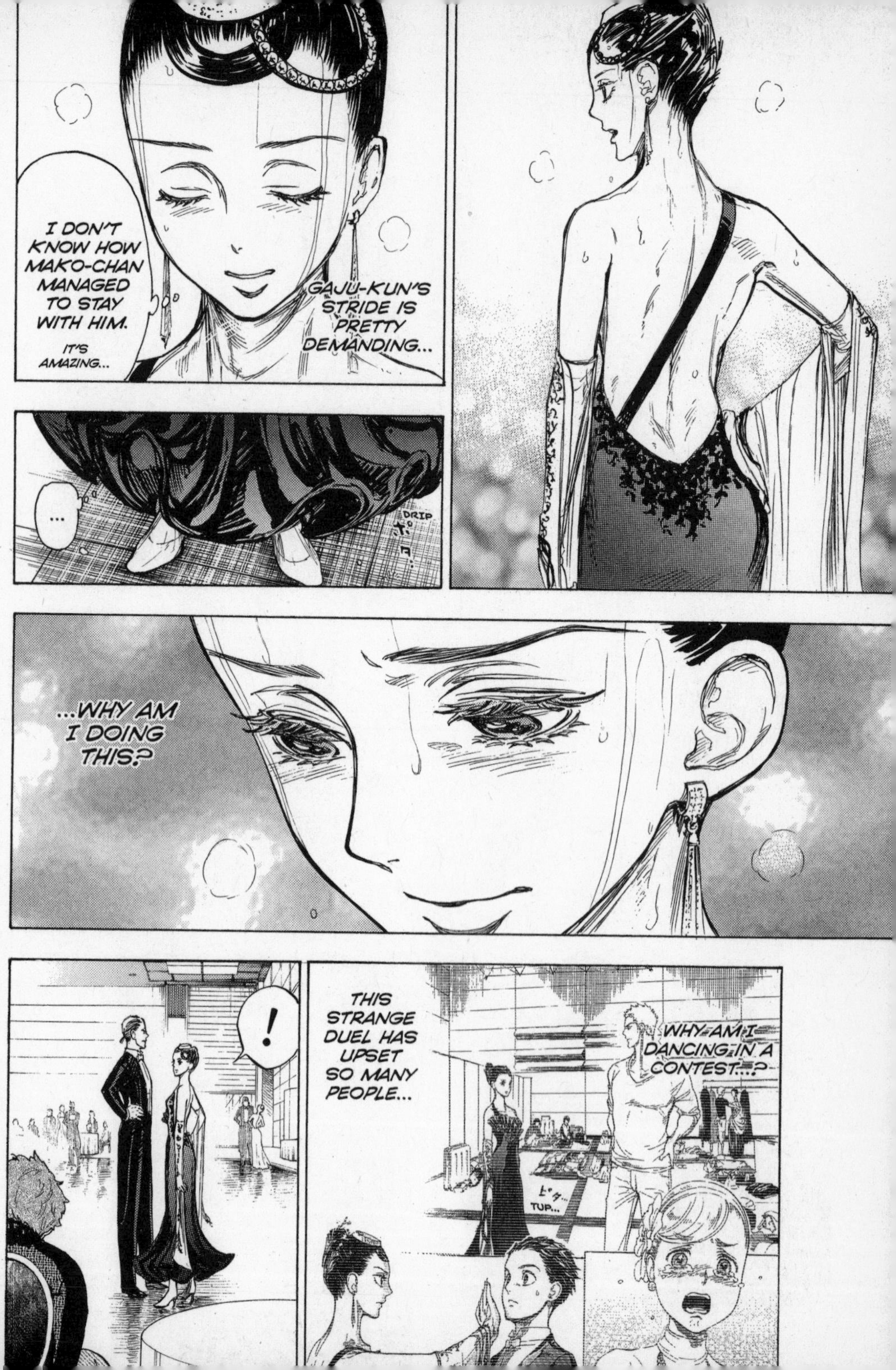
GAJU-KUN'S STRIDE IS PRETTY DEMANDING...
I DON'T KNOW HOW MAKO-CHAN MANAGED TO STAY WITH HIM.
IT'S AMAZING...
DRIP
...
...WHY AM I DOING THIS?
WHY AM I DANCING IN A CONTEST...?
THIS STRANGE DUEL HAS UPSET SO MANY PEOPLE...
TUP...
!

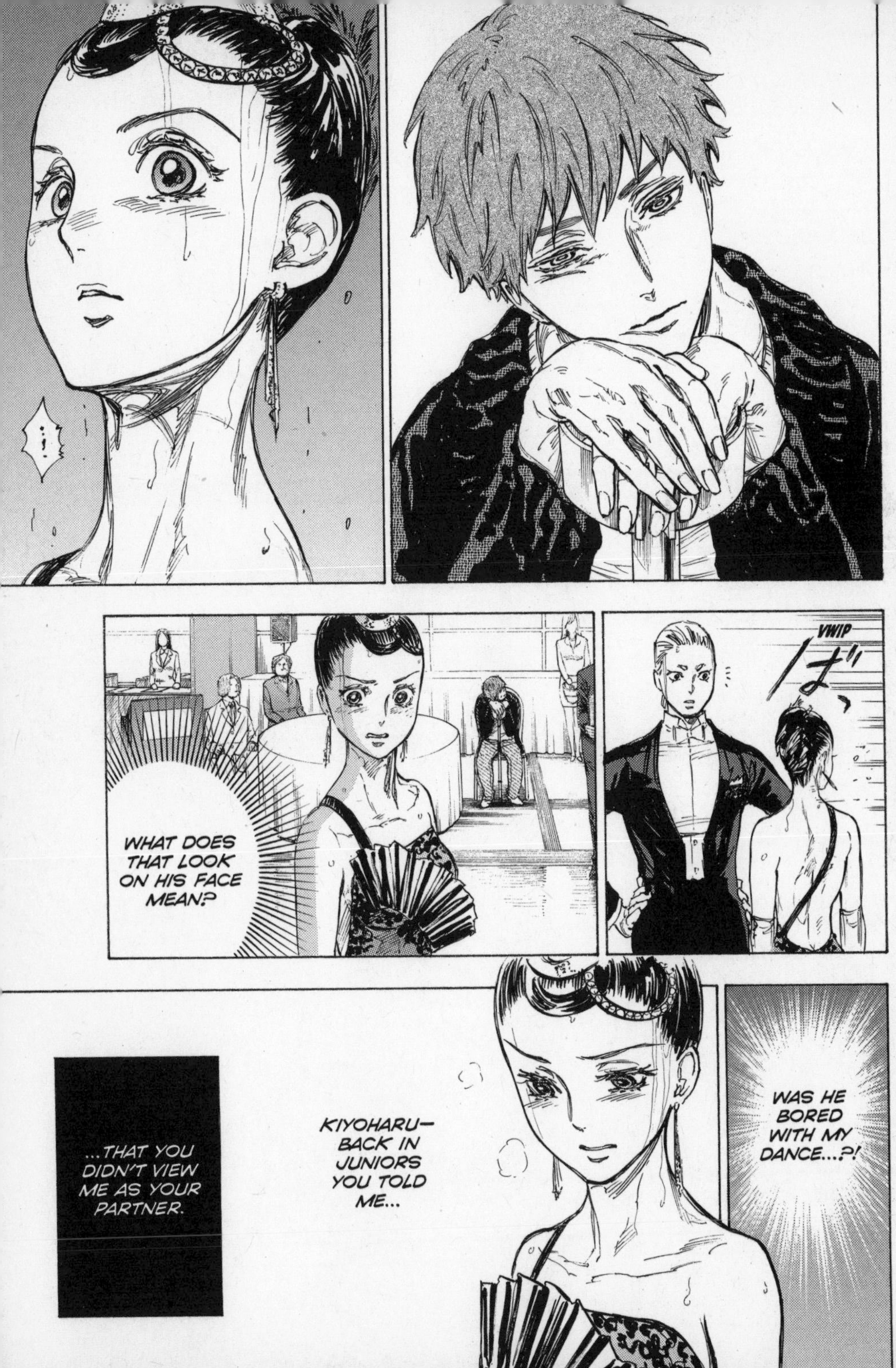
...!
VWIP
WHAT DOES THAT LOOK ON HIS FACE MEAN?
WAS HE BORED WITH MY DANCE...?!
KIYOHARU— BACK IN JUNIORS YOU TOLD ME...
...THAT YOU DIDN'T VIEW ME AS YOUR PARTNER.

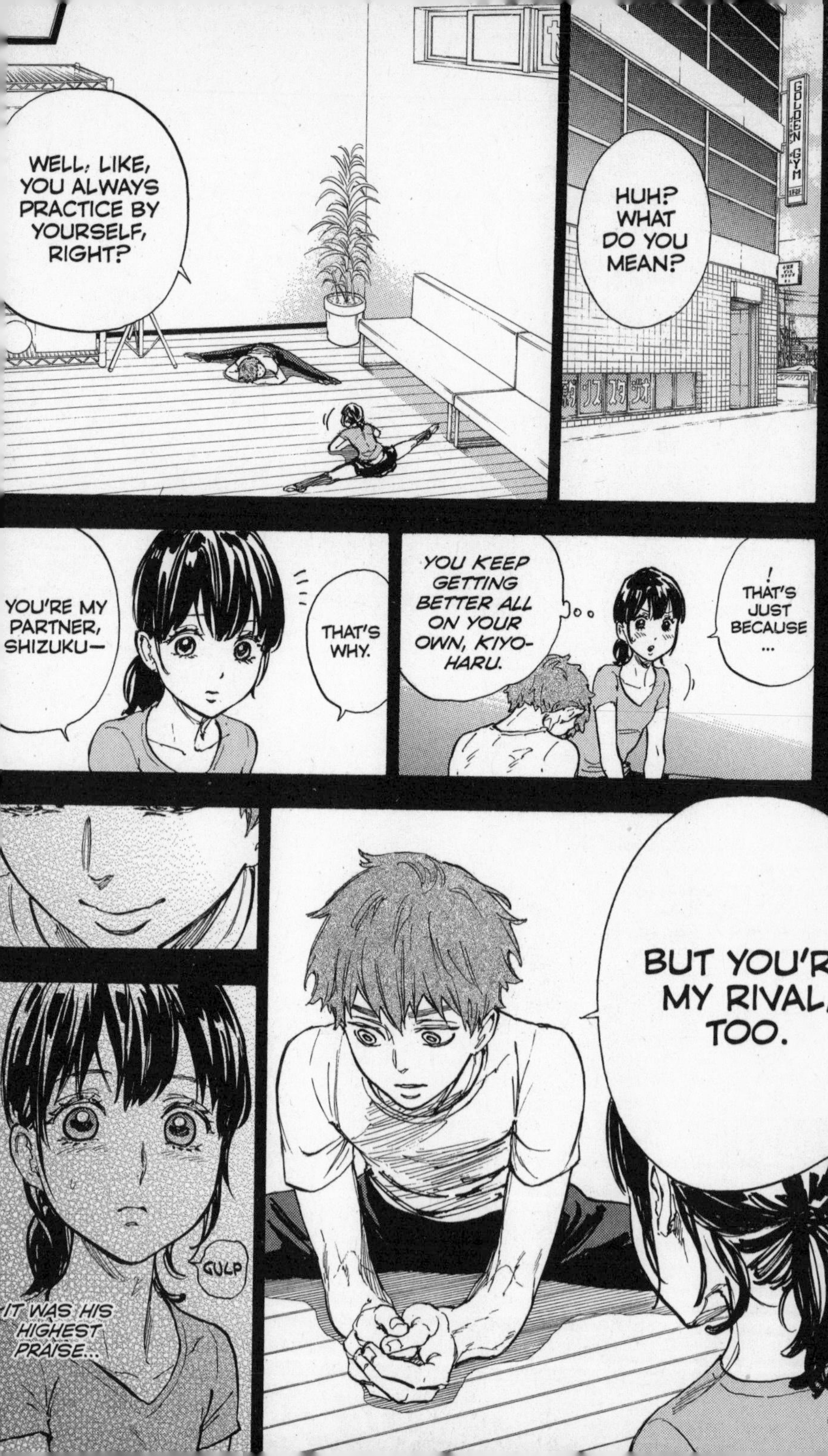
GOLDEN GYM
HUH? WHAT DO YOU MEAN?
WELL, LIKE, YOU ALWAYS PRACTICE BY YOURSELF, RIGHT?
! THAT'S JUST BECAUSE ...
YOU KEEP GETTING BETTER ALL ON YOUR OWN, KIYO-HARU.
THAT'S WHY.
YOU'RE MY PARTNER, SHIZUKU—
BUT YOU'RE MY RIVAL, TOO.
GULP
IT WAS HIS HIGHEST PRAISE...

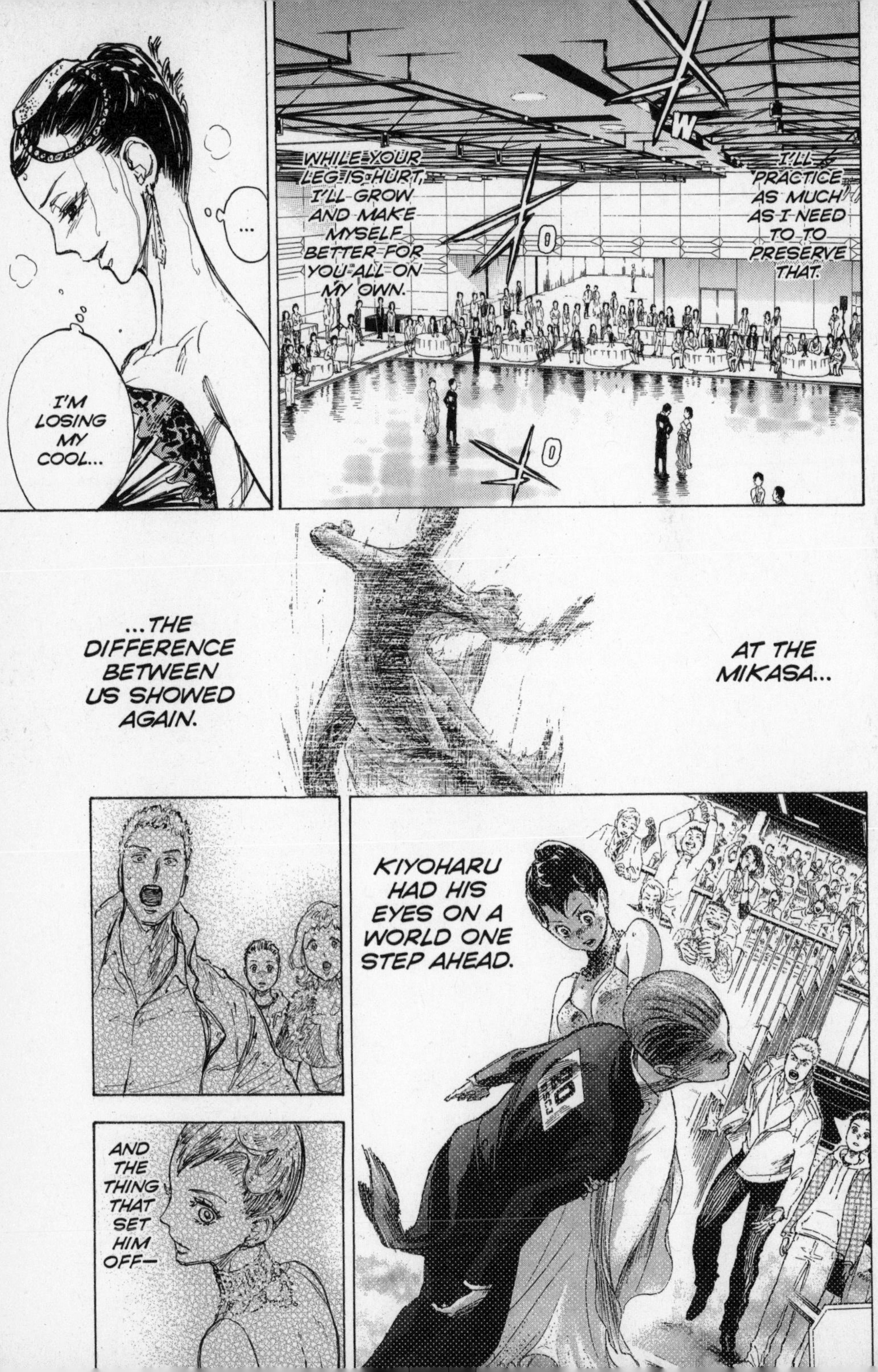
WHILE YOUR LEG IS HURT, I'LL GROW AND MAKE MYSELF BETTER FOR YOU ALL ON MY OWN.
I'LL PRACTICE AS MUCH AS I NEED TO TO PRESERVE THAT.
W
O
O
...
I'M LOSING MY COOL...
AT THE MIKASA...
...THE DIFFERENCE BETWEEN US SHOWED AGAIN.
KIYOHARU HAD HIS EYES ON A WORLD ONE STEP AHEAD.
AND THE THING THAT SET HIM OFF—

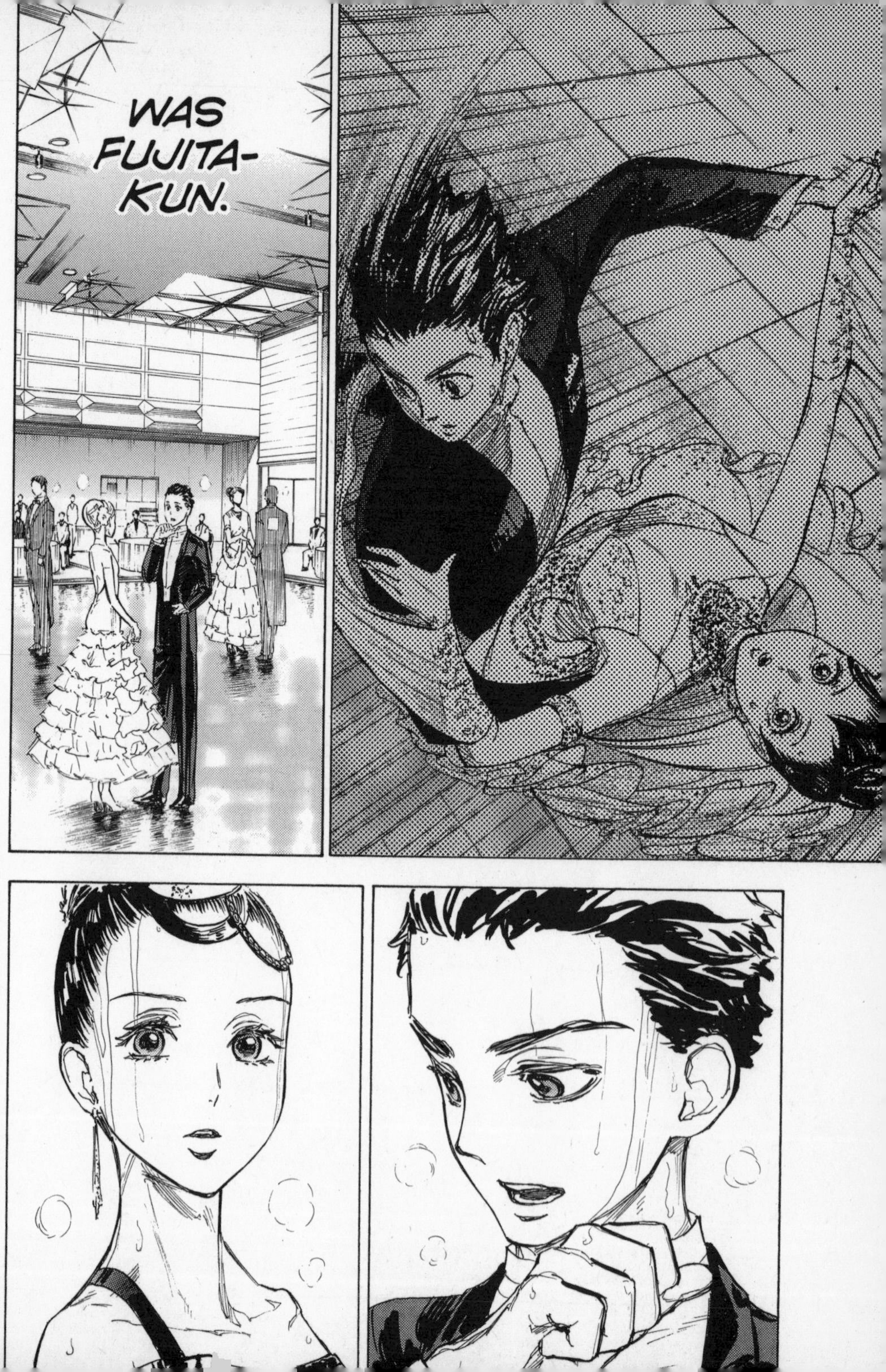
WAS FUJITA-KUN.

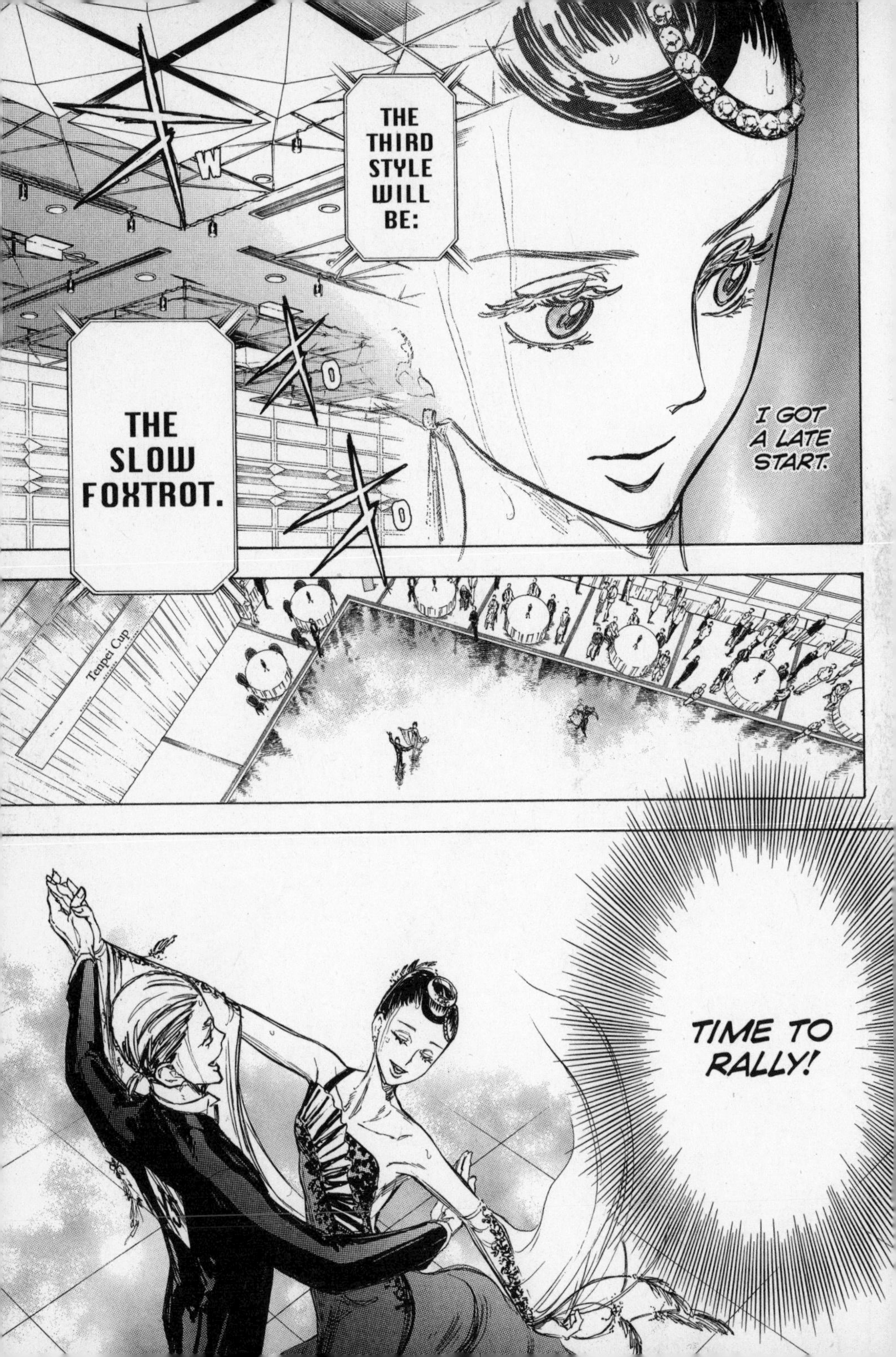
THE THIRD STYLE WILL BE:
WOO
THE SLOW FOXTROT.
I GOT A LATE START.
Tenpei Cup
TIME TO RALLY!

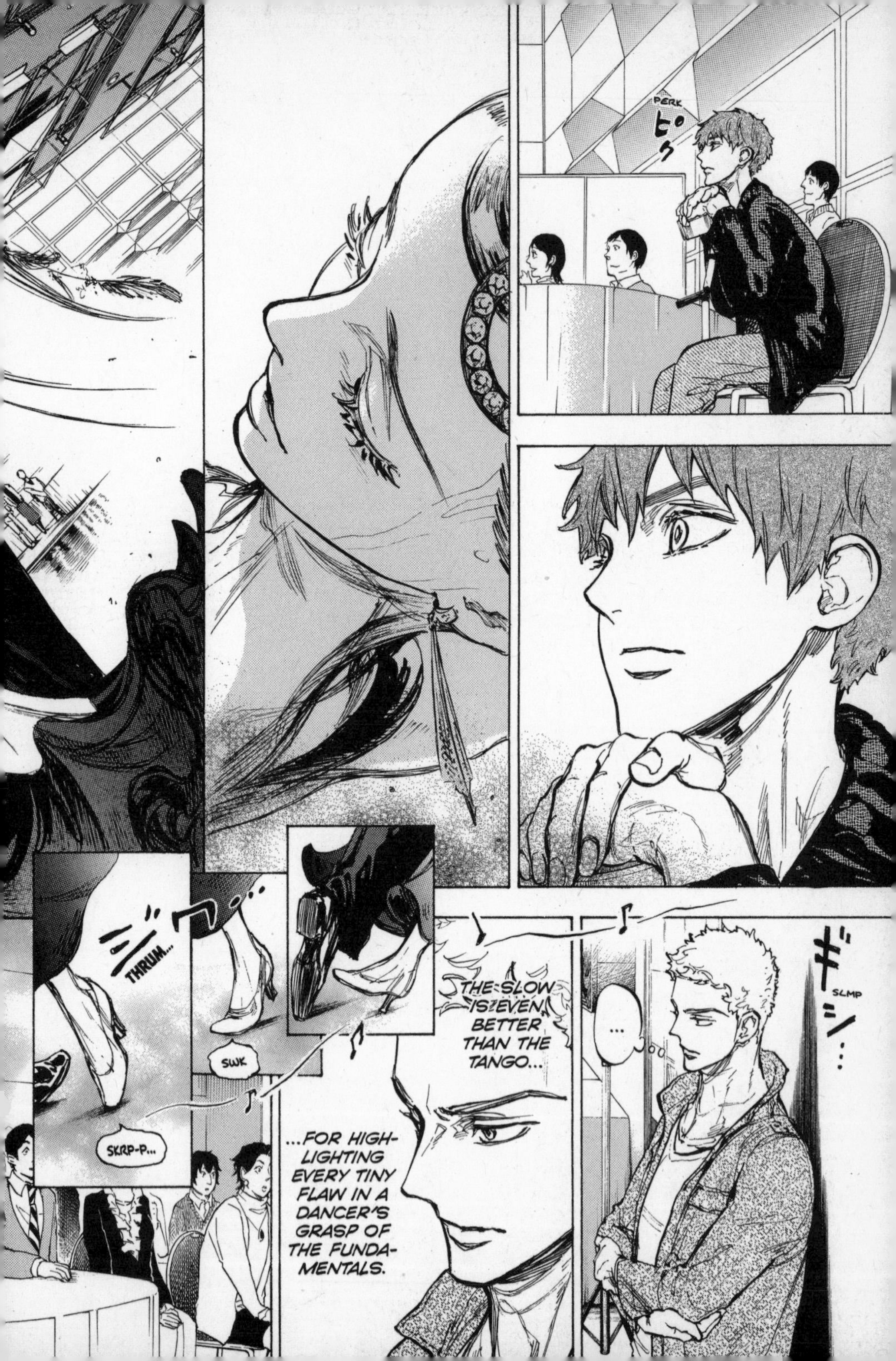

PERK
ピク
ギシ…
SLMP
…
THE SLOW IS EVEN BETTER THAN THE TANGO…
…FOR HIGH-LIGHTING EVERY TINY FLAW IN A DANCER'S GRASP OF THE FUNDAMENTALS.
SWK
…
THRUM…
SKRP-P…

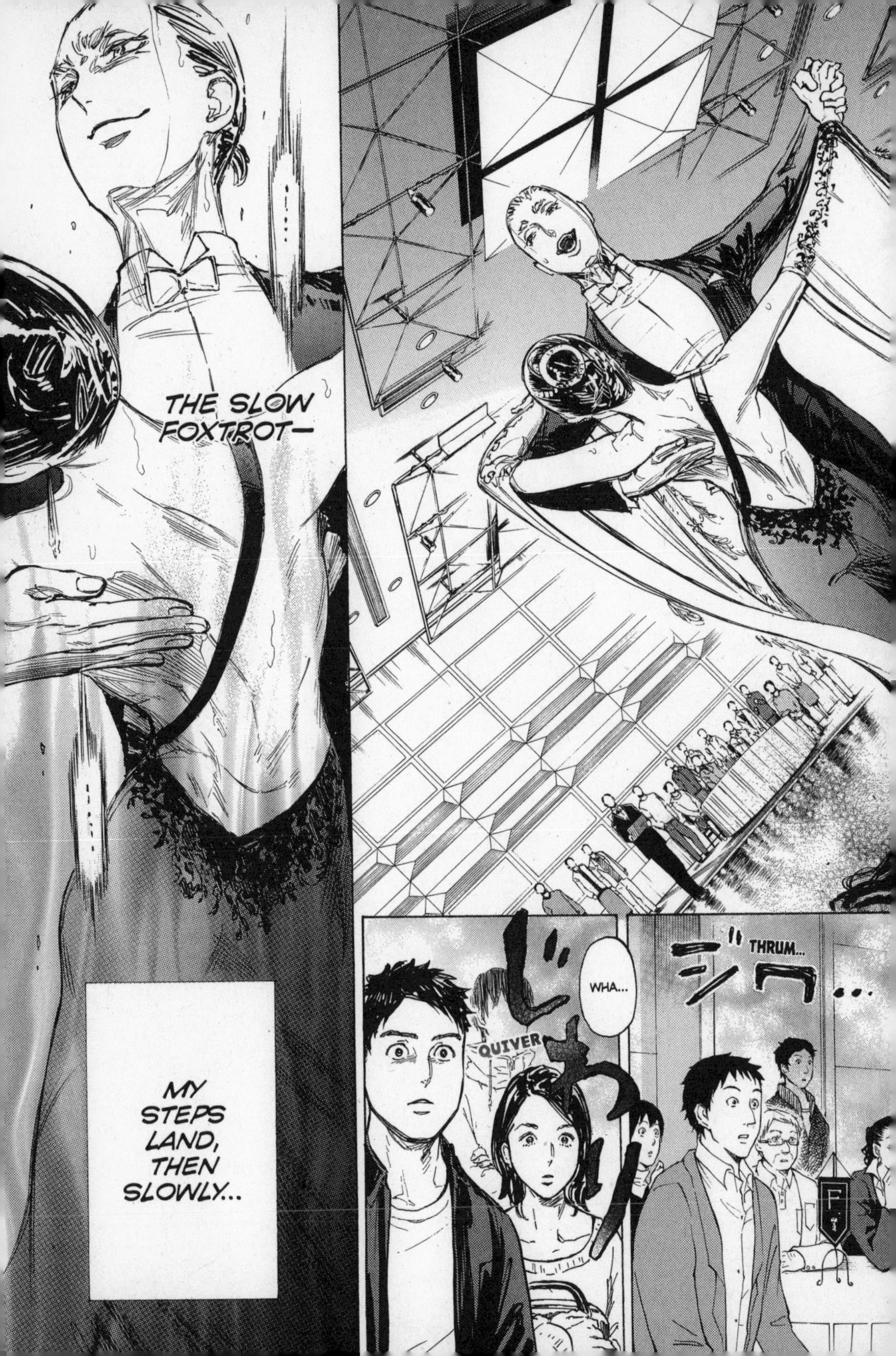
THRUM...
WHA...
QUIVER
THE SLOW FOXTROT—
MY STEPS LAND, THEN SLOWLY...

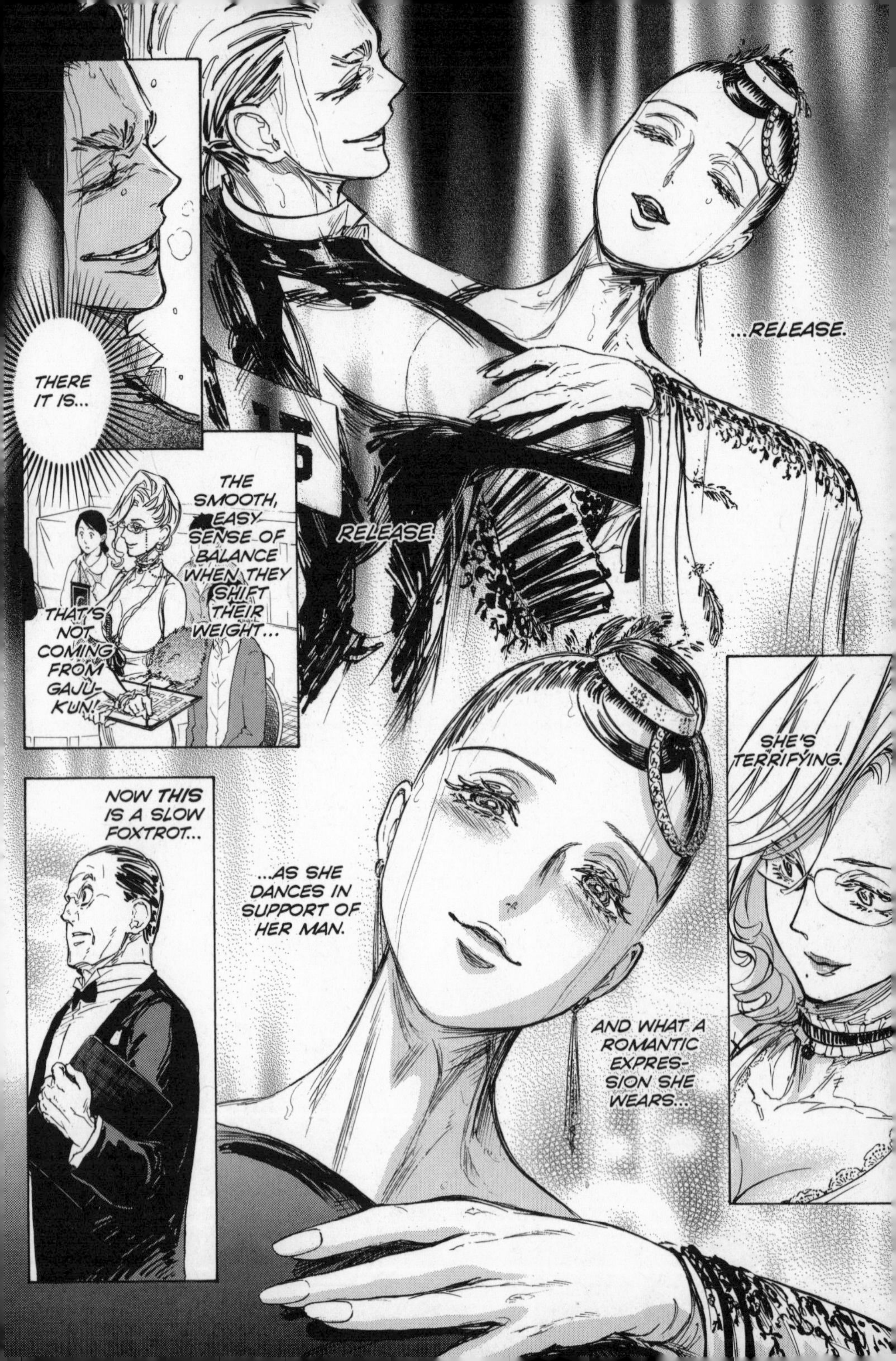
...RELEASE.
RELEASE.
THERE IT IS...
THE SMOOTH, EASY SENSE OF BALANCE WHEN THEY SHIFT THEIR WEIGHT...
THAT'S NOT COMING FROM GAJU-KUN!
SHE'S TERRIFYING.
...AS SHE DANCES IN SUPPORT OF HER MAN.
AND WHAT A ROMANTIC EXPRES-SION SHE WEARS...
NOW THIS IS A SLOW FOXTROT...

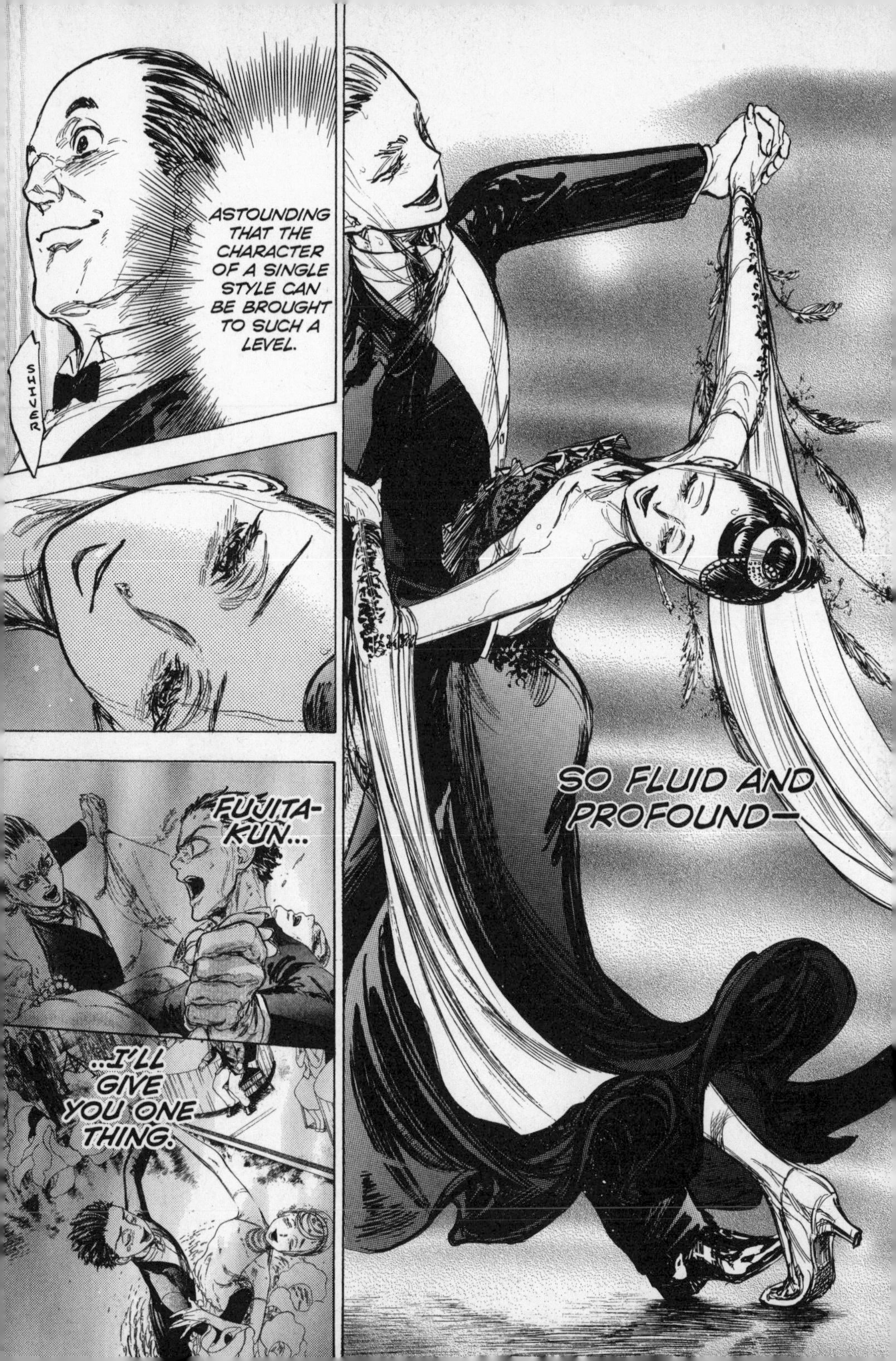
SO FLUID AND PROFOUND—
SHIVER
ASTOUNDING THAT THE CHARACTER OF A SINGLE STYLE CAN BE BROUGHT TO SUCH A LEVEL.
FUJITA-KUN...
...I'LL GIVE YOU ONE THING.

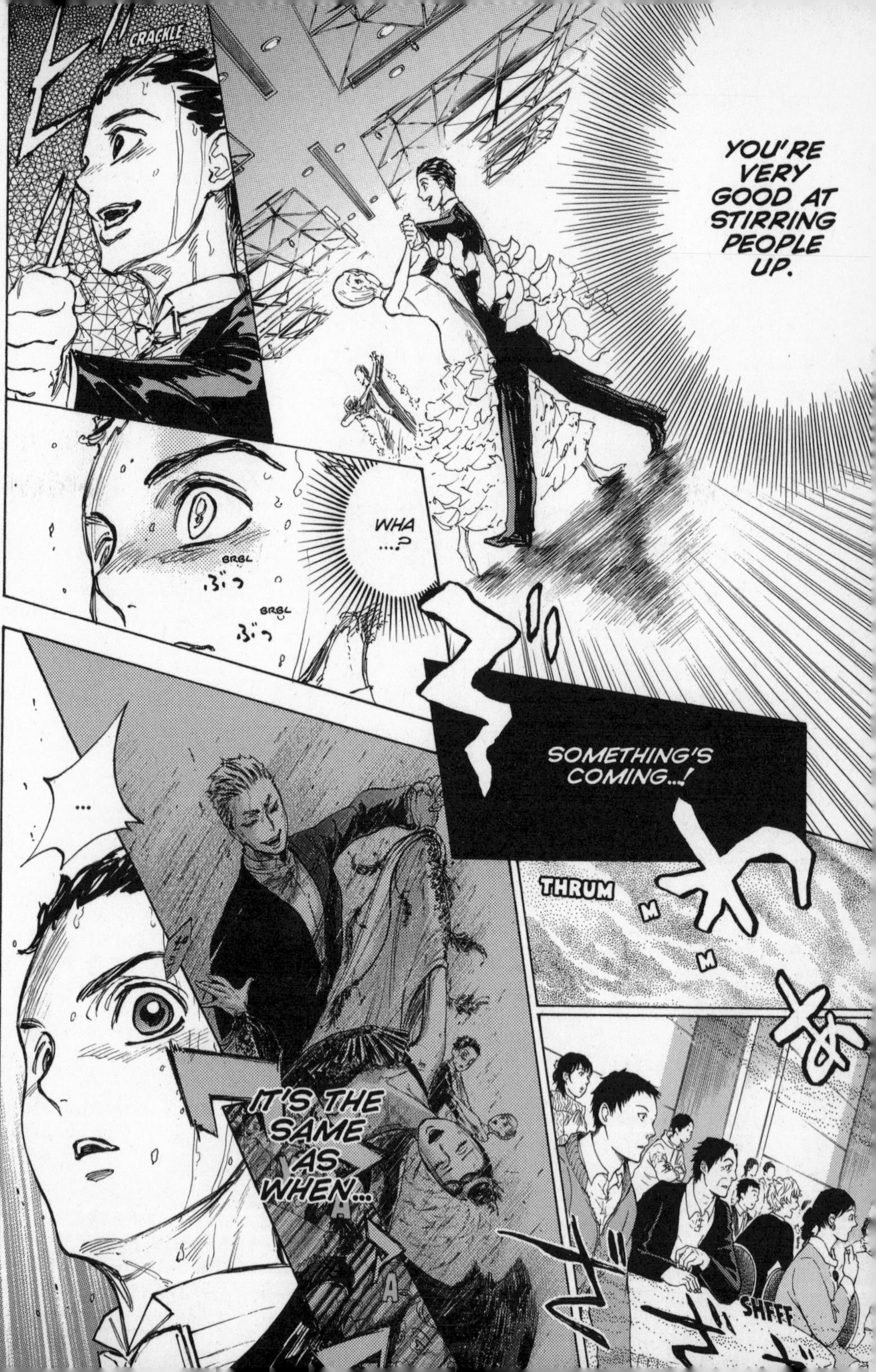
YOU'RE VERY GOOD AT STIRRING PEOPLE UP.
CRACKLE
WHA ...?
BRBL
ぶっ
BRBL
ぶっ
SOMETHING'S COMING...!
THRUM
M
M
SHFFF
...
IT'S THE SAME AS WHEN...

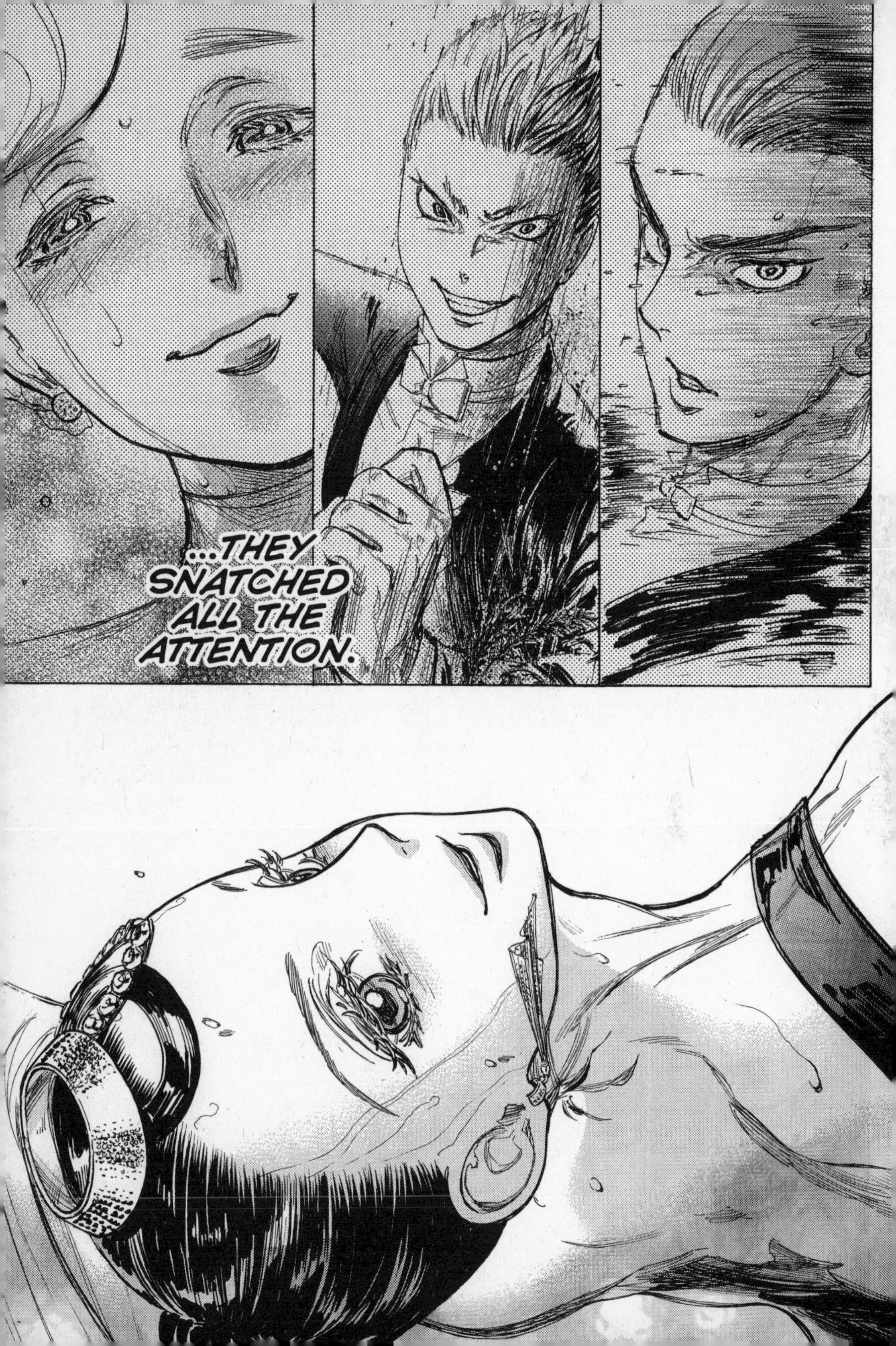
...THEY SNATCHED ALL THE ATTENTION.

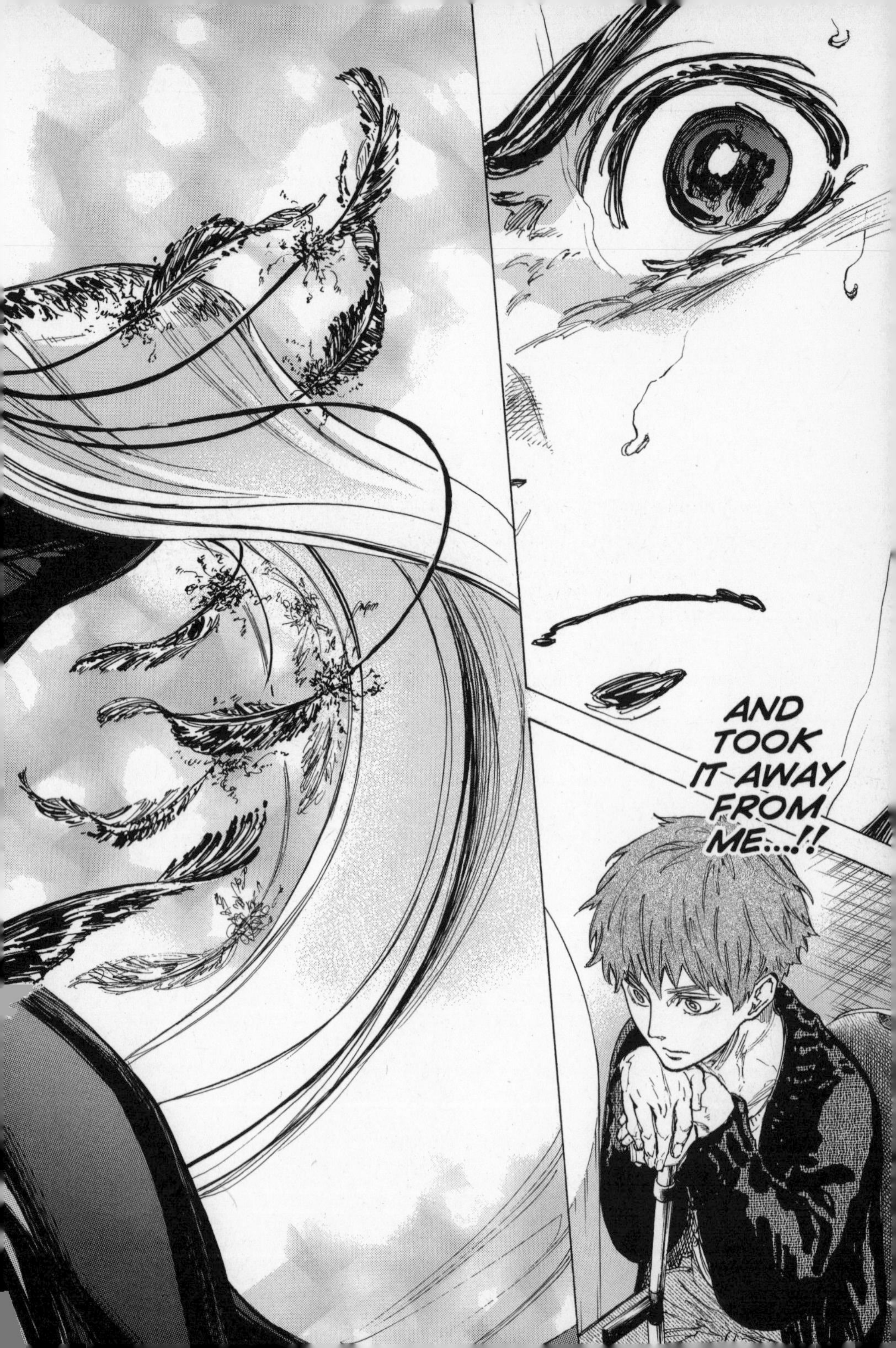
AND TOOK IT AWAY FROM ME...!!

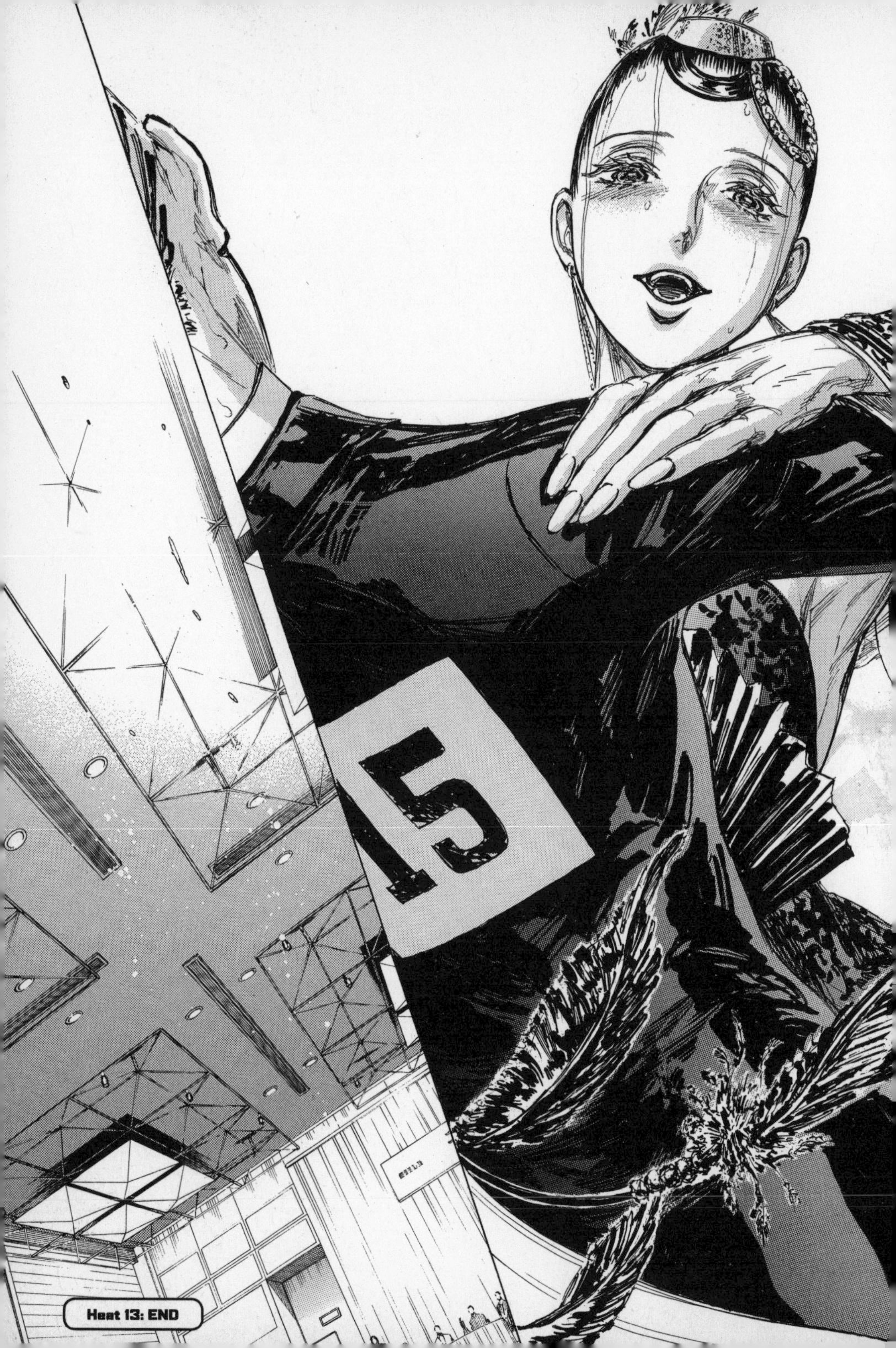
15
Heat 13: END

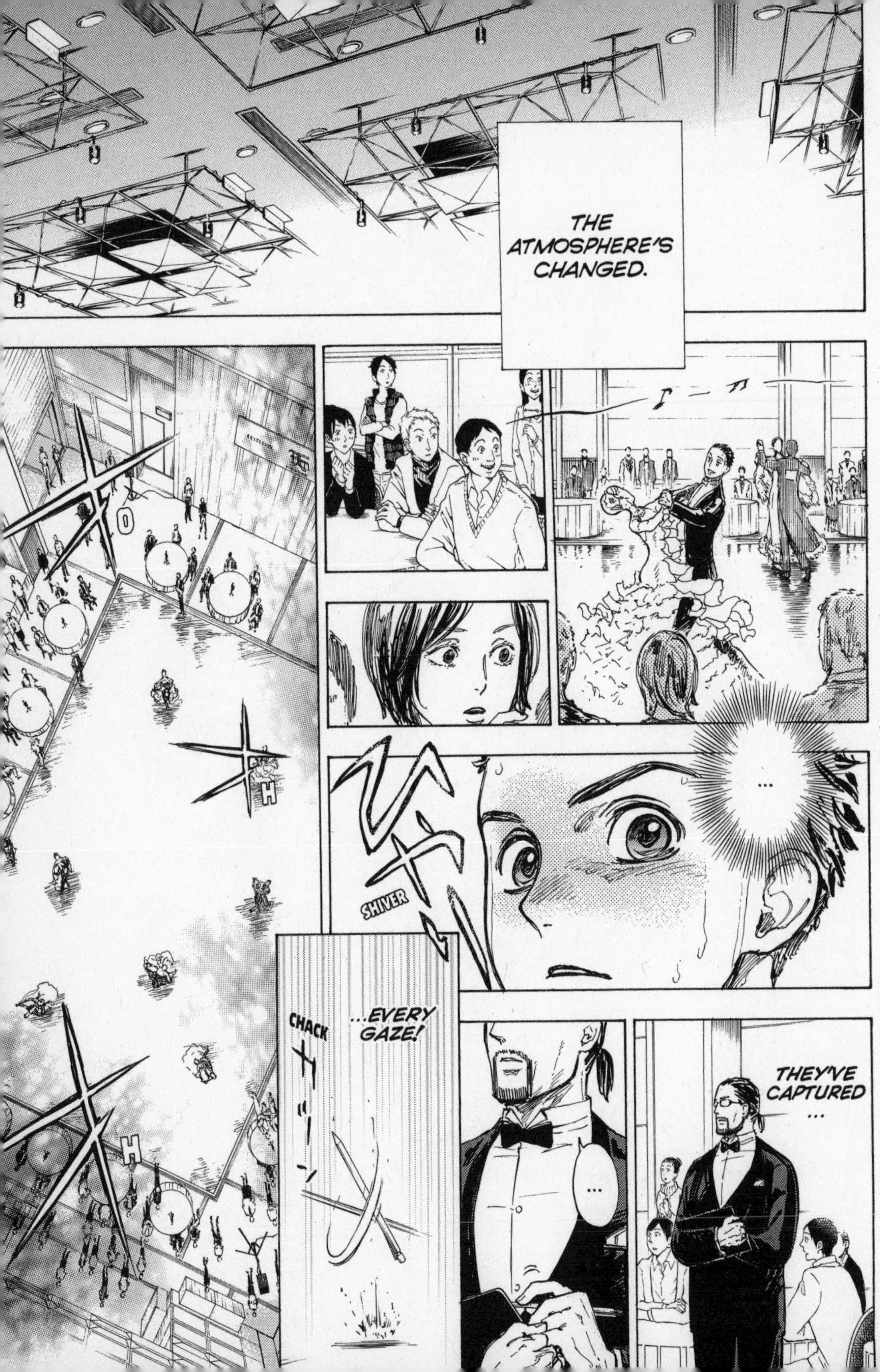
THE ATMOSPHERE'S CHANGED.
...
SHIVER
THEY'VE CAPTURED ...
...
...EVERY GAZE!
CHACK
O
H
H

# Heat 14
# Radiation

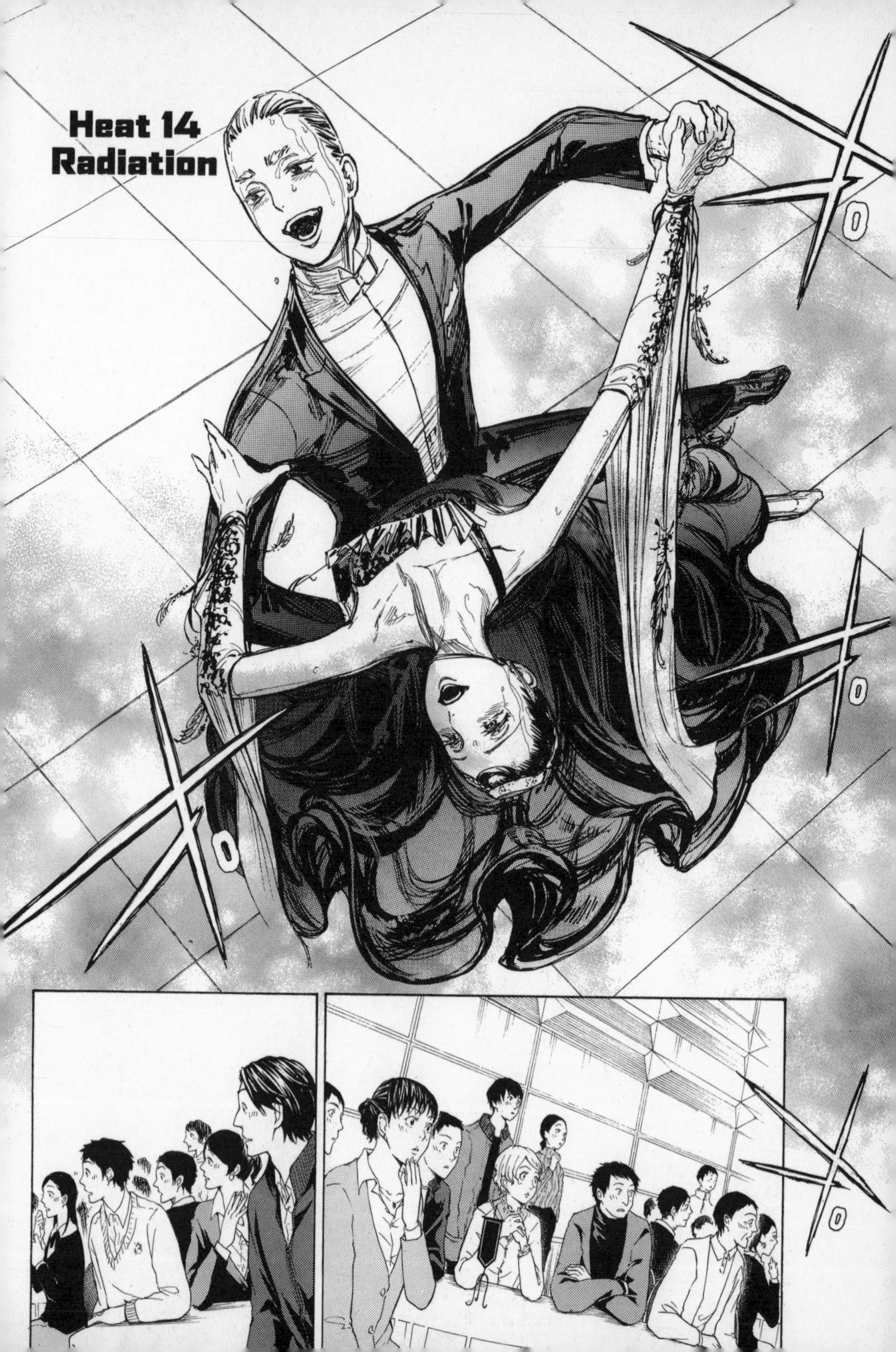
O
O
O
O

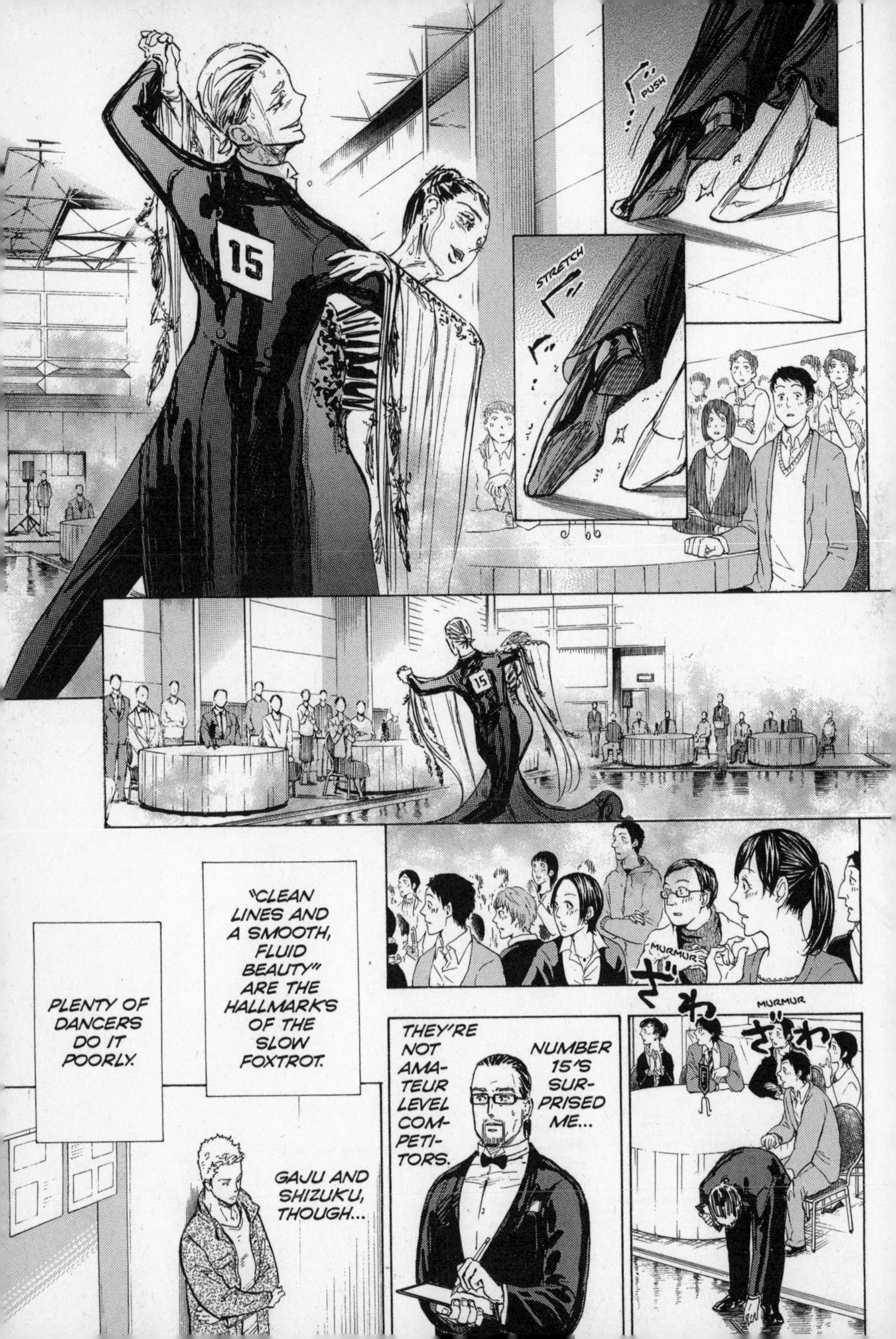
PUSH
STRETCH
MURMUR
ざわ
"CLEAN LINES AND A SMOOTH, FLUID BEAUTY" ARE THE HALLMARKS OF THE SLOW FOXTROT.
PLENTY OF DANCERS DO IT POORLY.
MURMUR
ざわ
NUMBER 15'S SURPRISED ME...
THEY'RE NOT AMATEUR LEVEL COMPETITORS.
GAJU AND SHIZUKU, THOUGH...

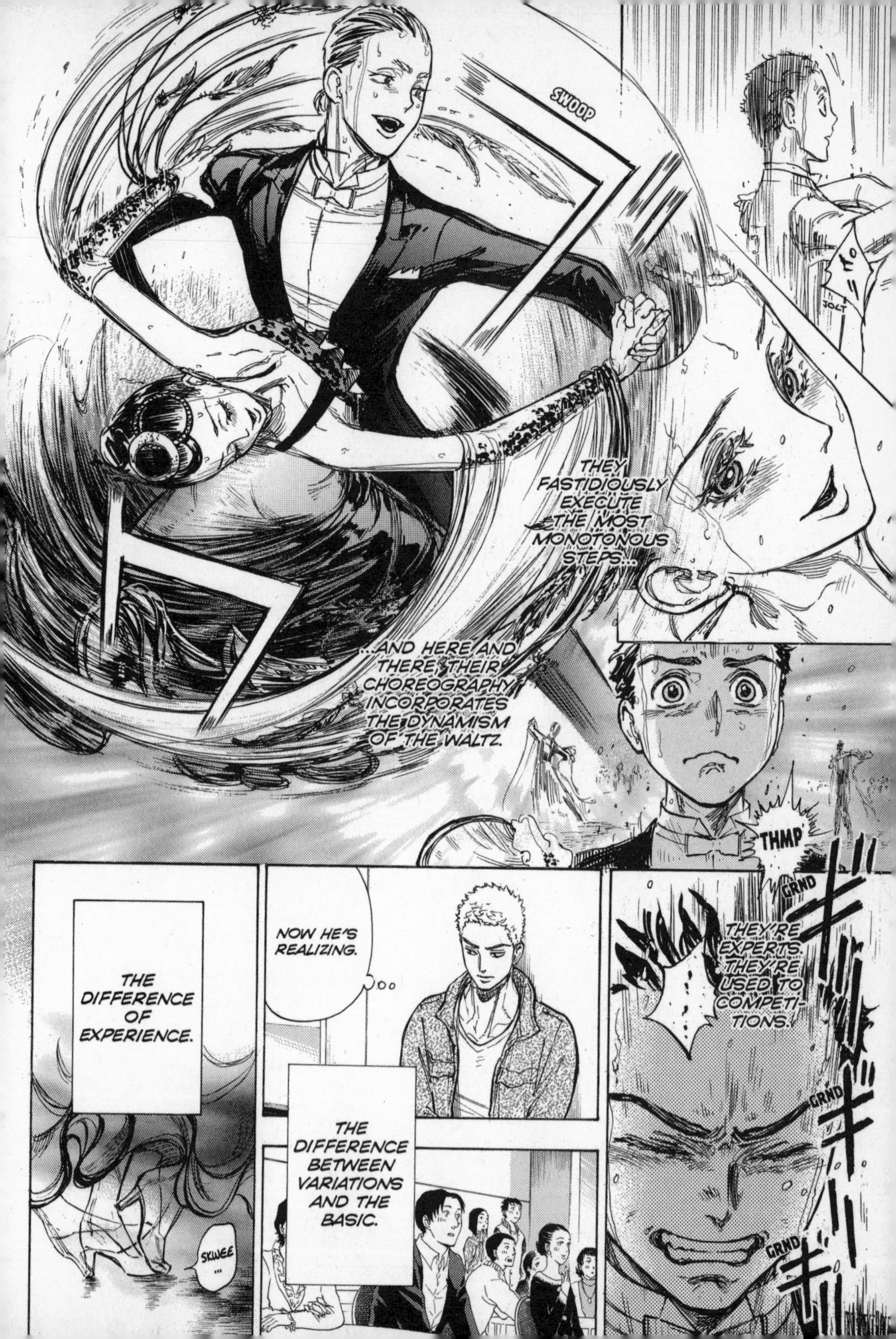
JOLT
SWOOP
THEY FASTIDIOUSLY EXECUTE THE MOST MONOTONOUS STEPS...
...AND HERE AND THERE THEIR CHOREOGRAPHY INCORPORATES THE DYNAMISM OF THE WALTZ.
THMP
GRND
THEY'RE EXPERTS. THEY'RE USED TO COMPETITIONS.
GRND
GRND
NOW HE'S REALIZING.
THE DIFFERENCE BETWEEN VARIATIONS AND THE BASIC.
THE DIFFERENCE OF EXPERIENCE.
SKWEE ...

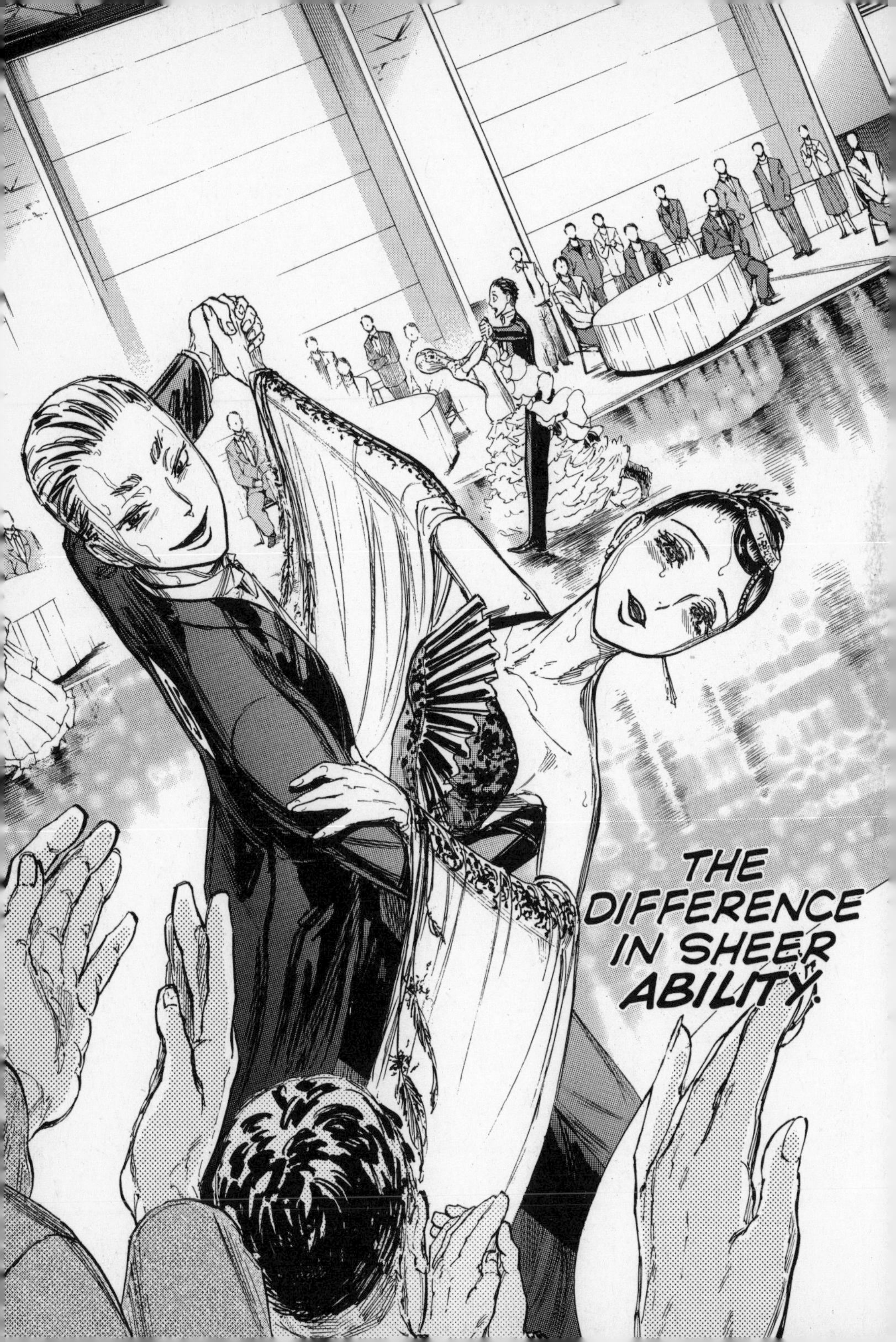
THE DIFFERENCE IN SHEER ABILITY.

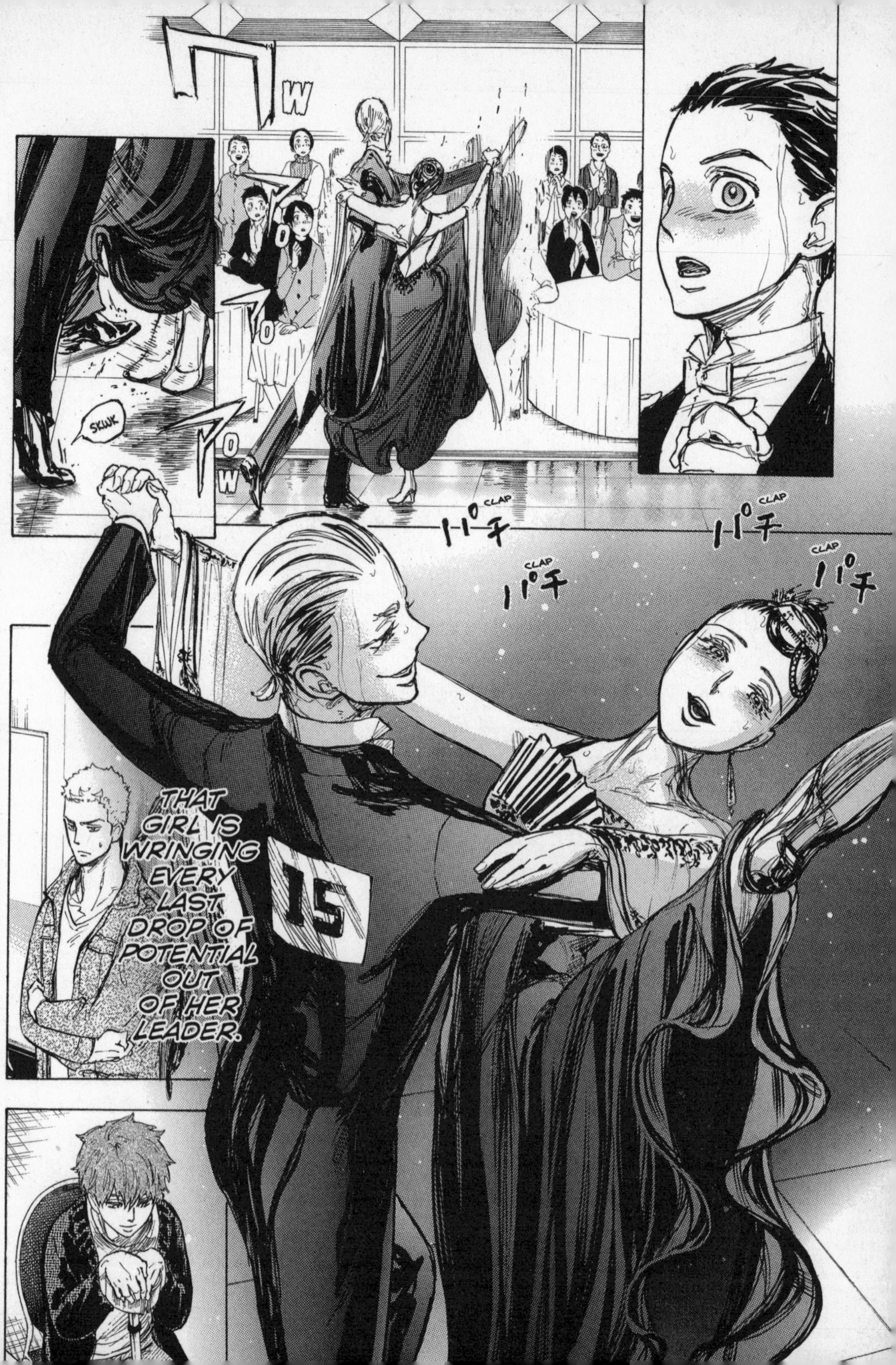
WOOOW
SKWK
パチ CLAP
パチ CLAP
パチ CLAP
パチ CLAP
THAT GIRL IS WRINGING EVERY LAST DROP OF POTENTIAL OUT OF HER LEADER.

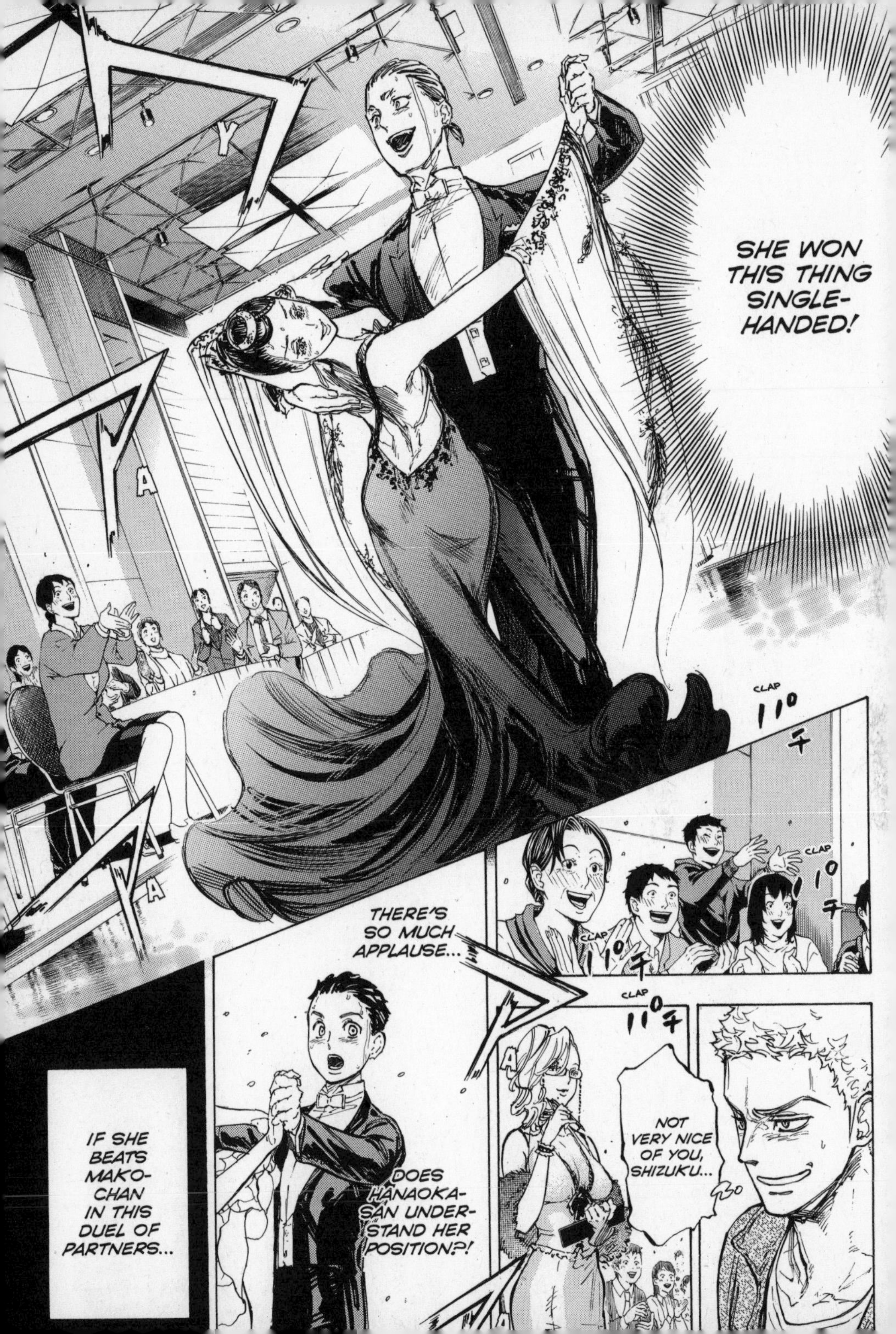SHE WON THIS THING SINGLE-HANDED!
Y
A
A
CLAP
CLAP
THERE'S SO MUCH APPLAUSE...
CLAP
CLAP
NOT VERY NICE OF YOU, SHIZUKU...
A
DOES HANAOKA-SAN UNDERSTAND HER POSITION?!
IF SHE BEATS MAKO-CHAN IN THIS DUEL OF PARTNERS...

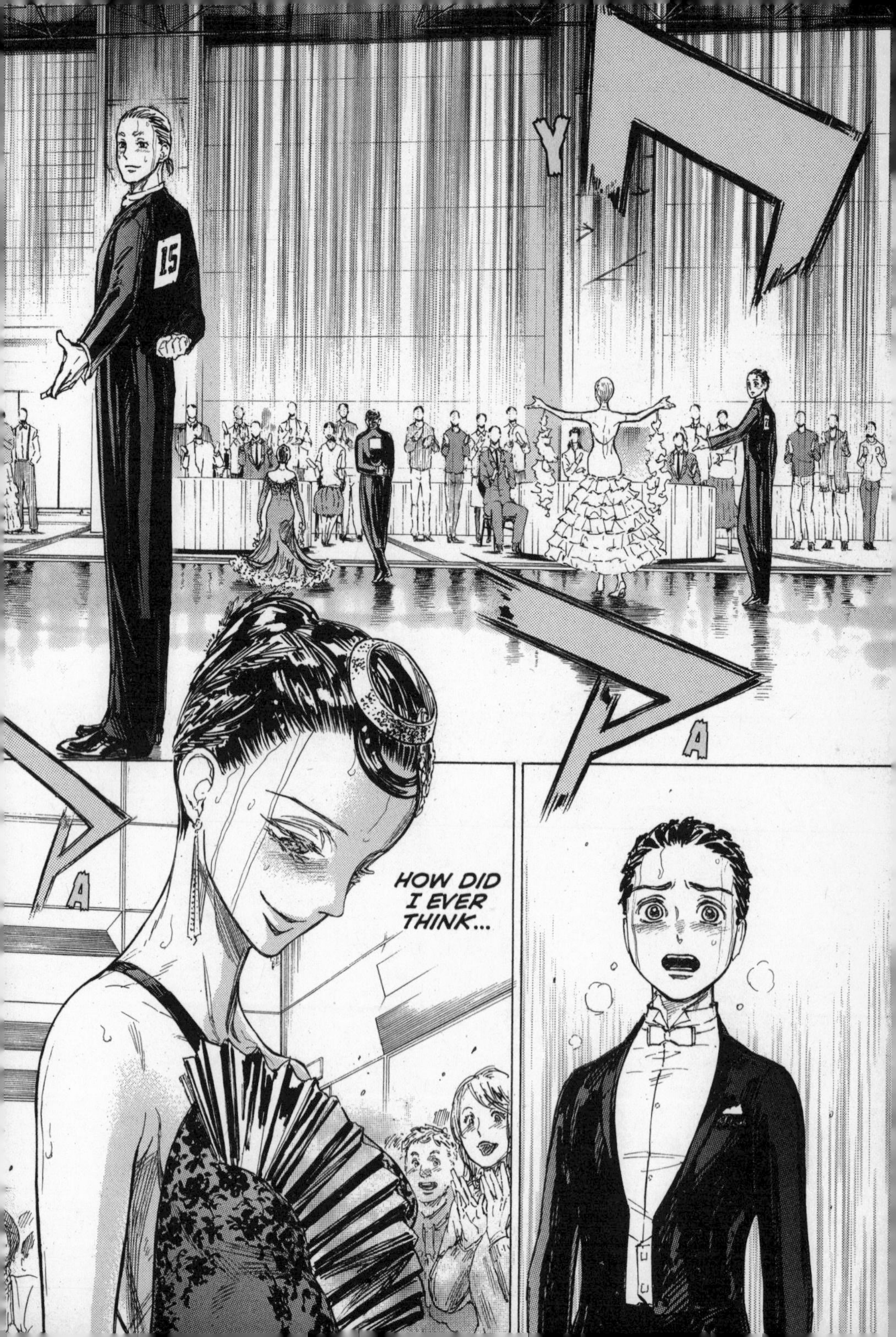
Y
A
A
HOW DID I EVER THINK...

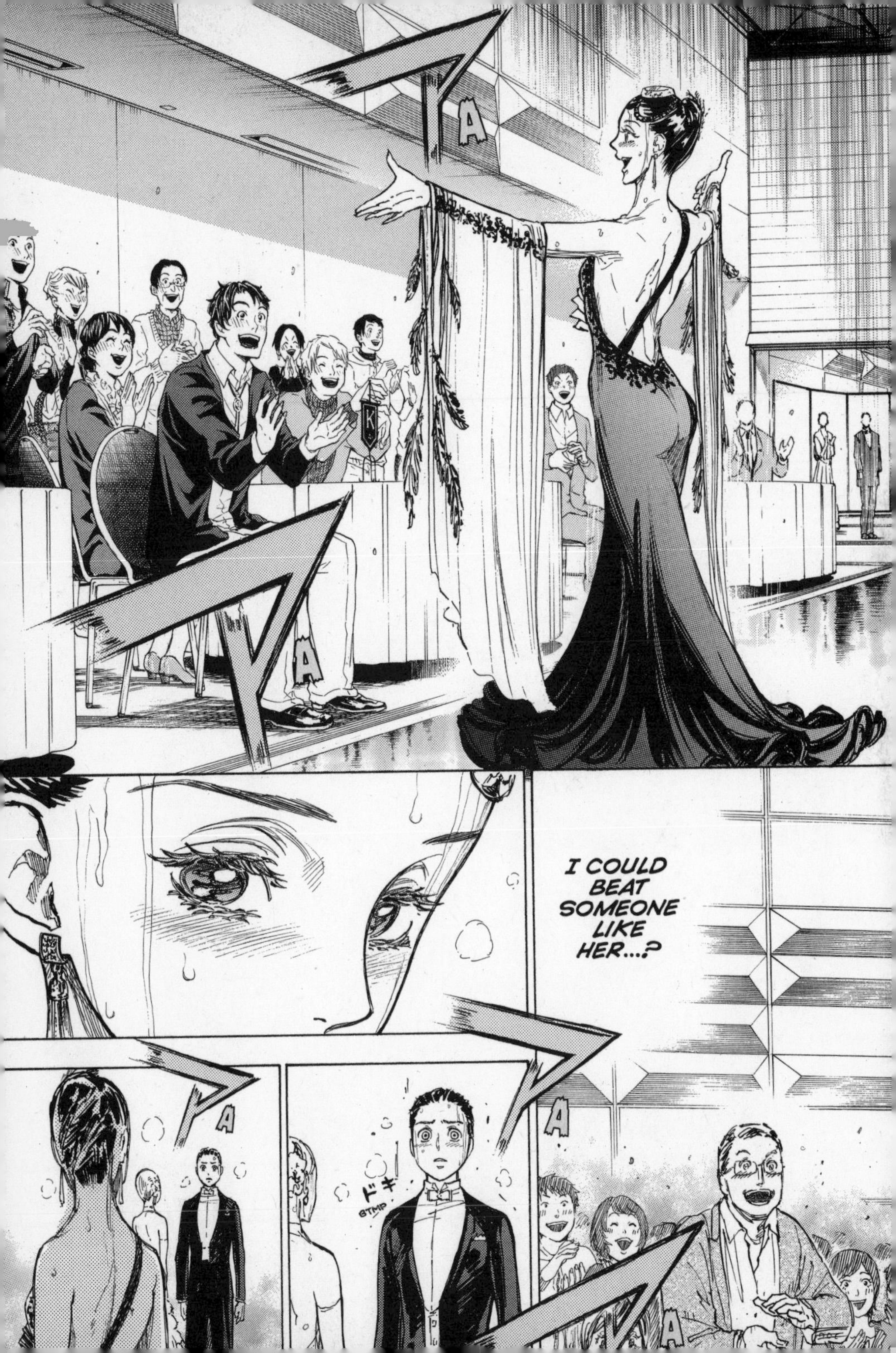
A
A
I COULD BEAT SOMEONE LIKE HER...?
A
A
ドキ
BTMP
A

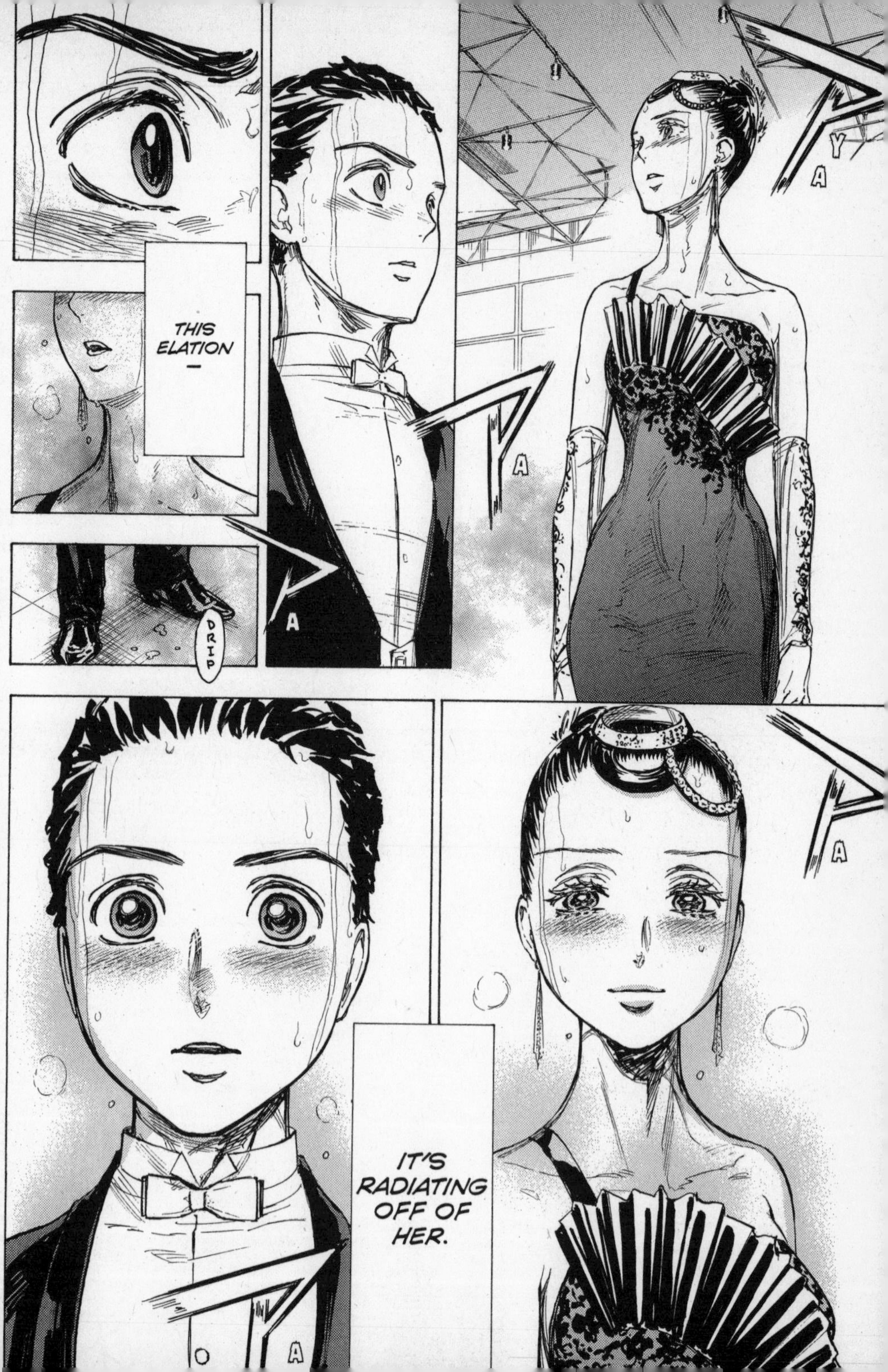

PYA
PA
PA
THIS ELATION —
DRIP
PA
IT'S RADIATING OFF OF HER.
PA

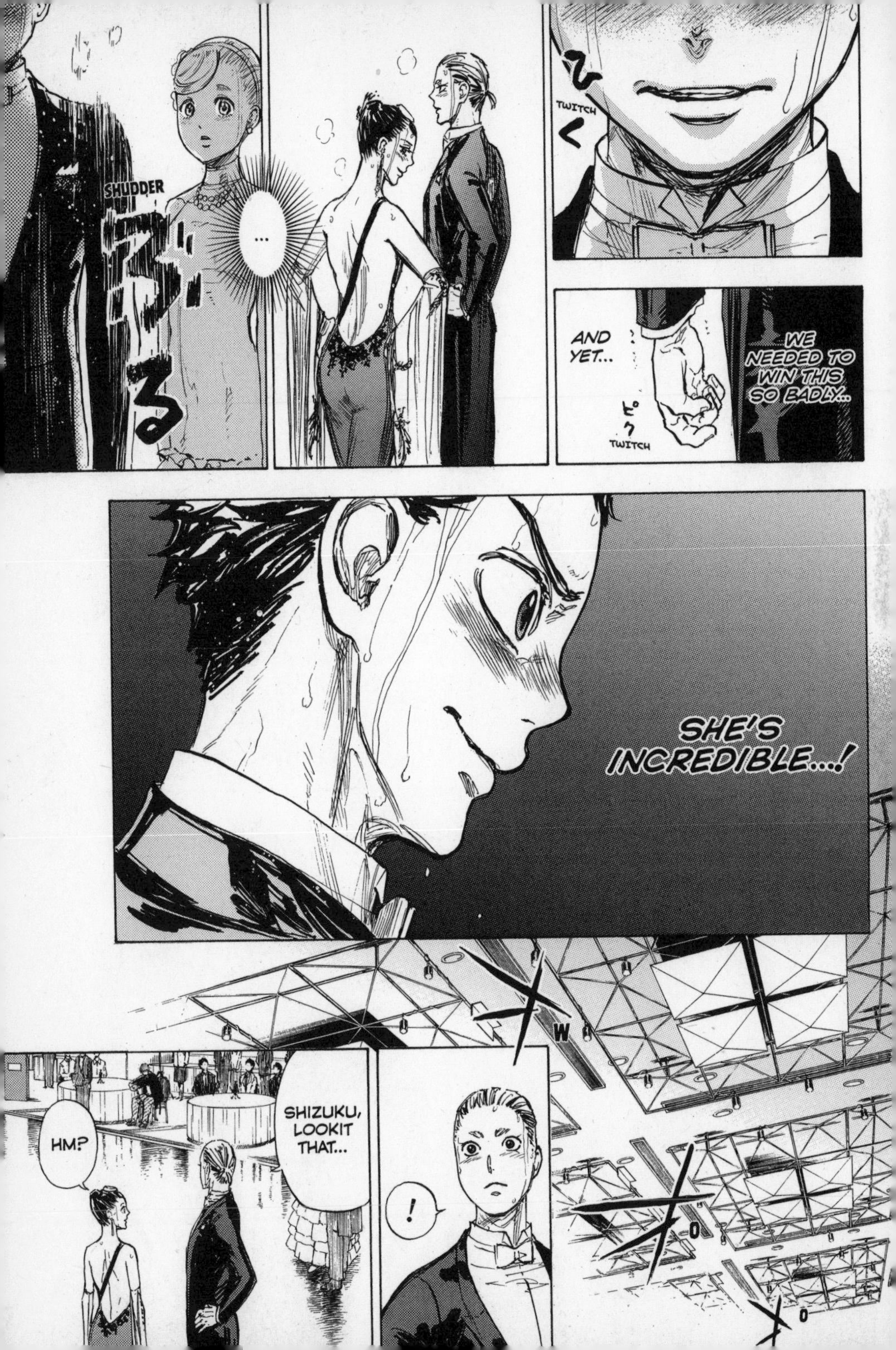
TWITCH
WE NEEDED TO WIN THIS SO BADLY...
AND YET...
ピク
TWITCH
SHUDDER
...
SHE'S INCREDIBLE...!
W
O
O
!
SHIZUKU, LOOKIT THAT...
HM?

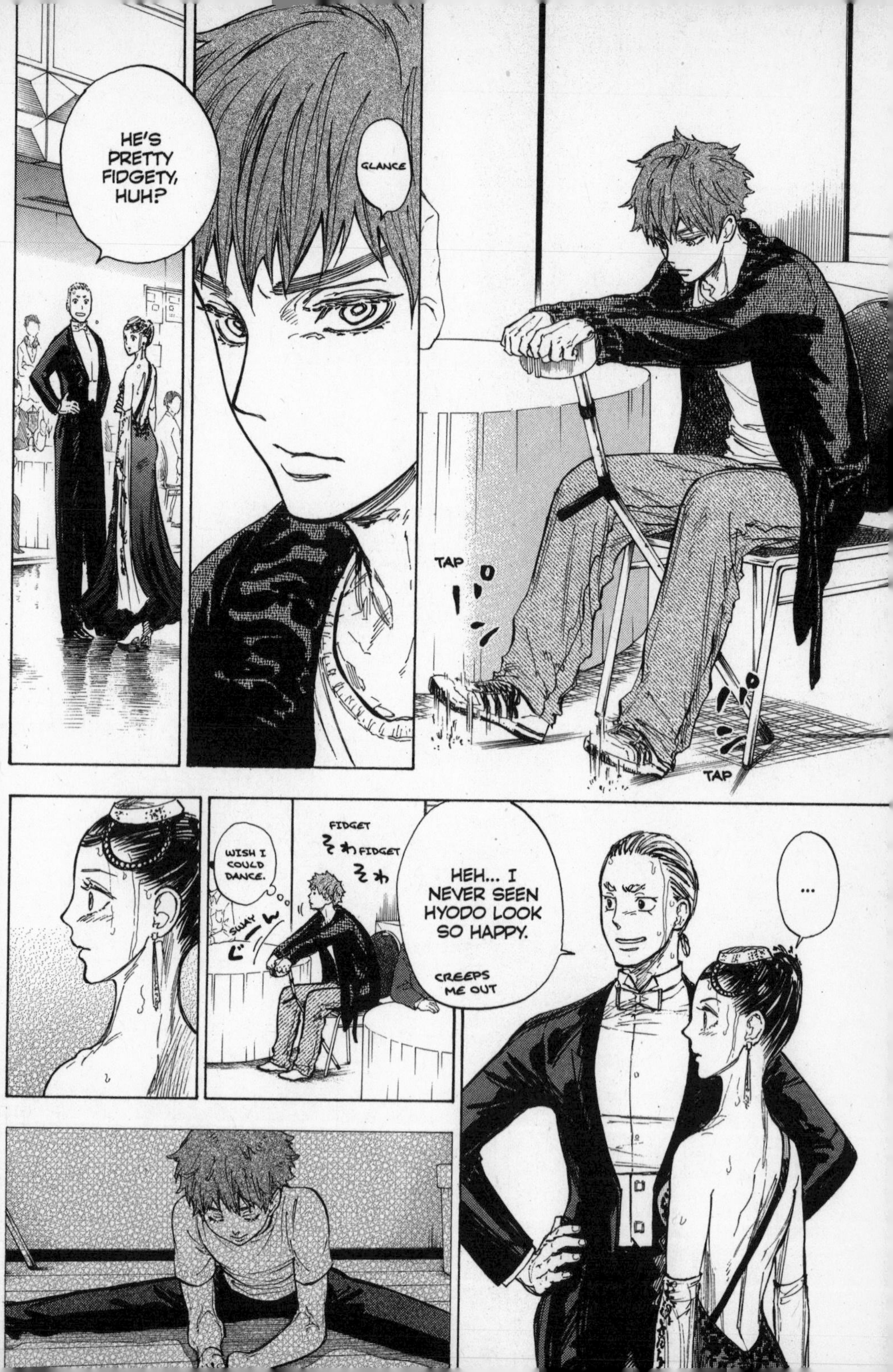
TAP
TAP
GLANCE
HE'S PRETTY FIDGETY, HUH?
HEH... I NEVER SEEN HYODO LOOK SO HAPPY.
CREEPS ME OUT
...
FIDGET
FIDGET
WISH I COULD DANCE.
SWAY

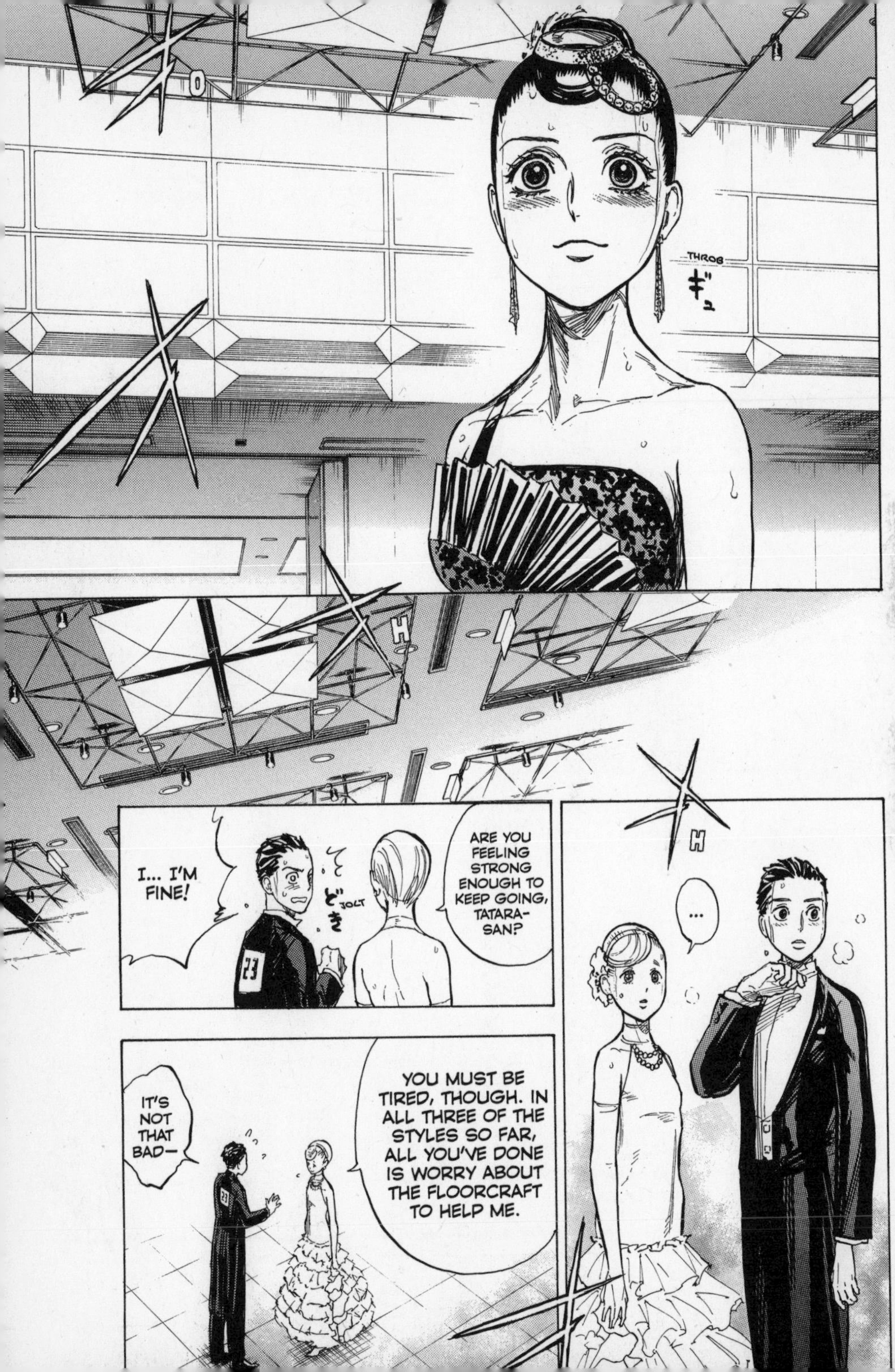
THROB
ギュ
...
ARE YOU FEELING STRONG ENOUGH TO KEEP GOING, TATARA-SAN?
JOLT
どき
I... I'M FINE!
YOU MUST BE TIRED, THOUGH. IN ALL THREE OF THE STYLES SO FAR, ALL YOU'VE DONE IS WORRY ABOUT THE FLOORCRAFT TO HELP ME.
IT'S NOT THAT BAD—

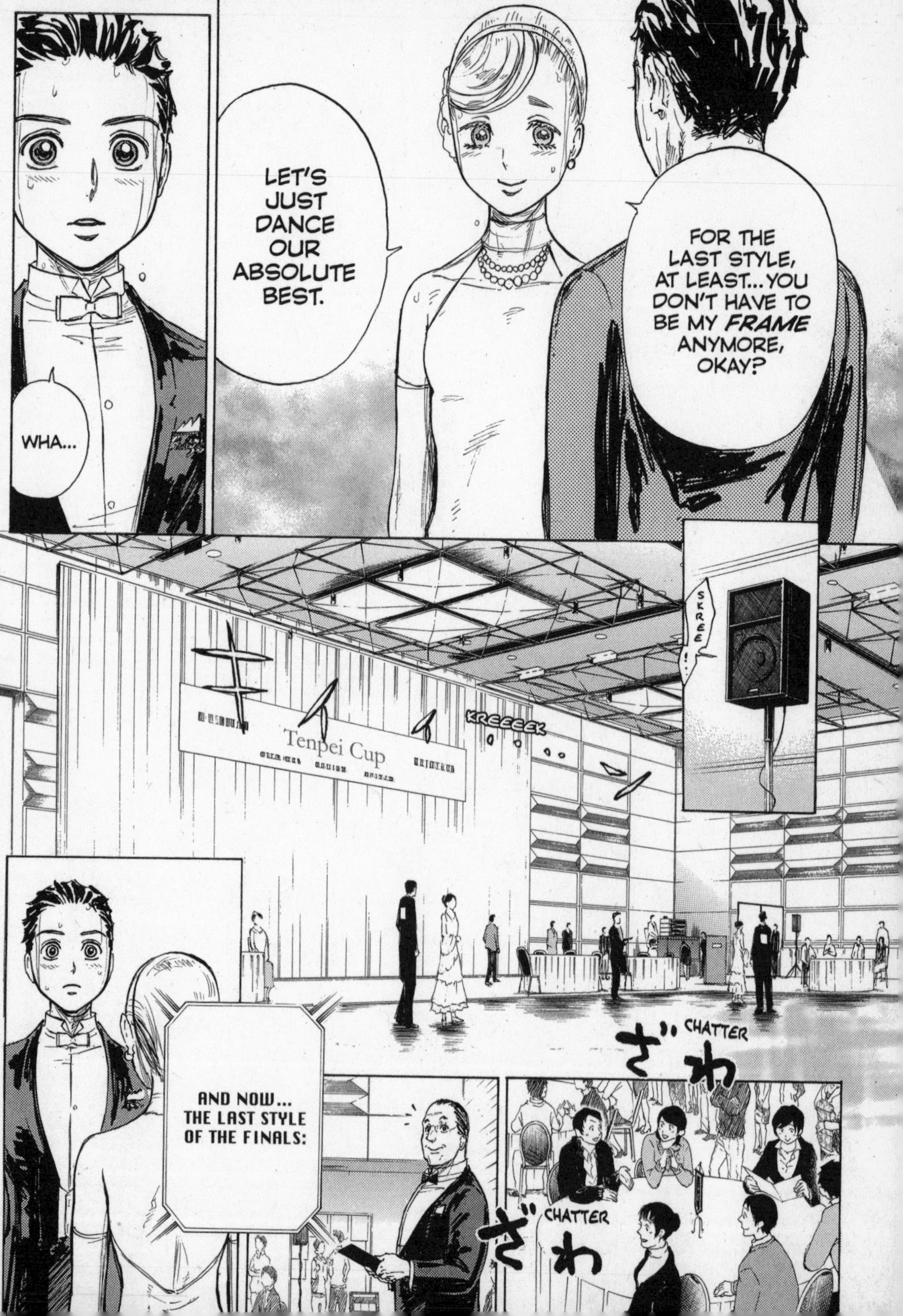
FOR THE LAST STYLE, AT LEAST...YOU DON'T HAVE TO BE MY *FRAME* ANYMORE, OKAY?
LET'S JUST DANCE OUR ABSOLUTE BEST.
WHA...
SKREE!
KREEEEK
Tenpei Cup
ざわ CHATTER
ざわ CHATTER
AND NOW... THE LAST STYLE OF THE FINALS:

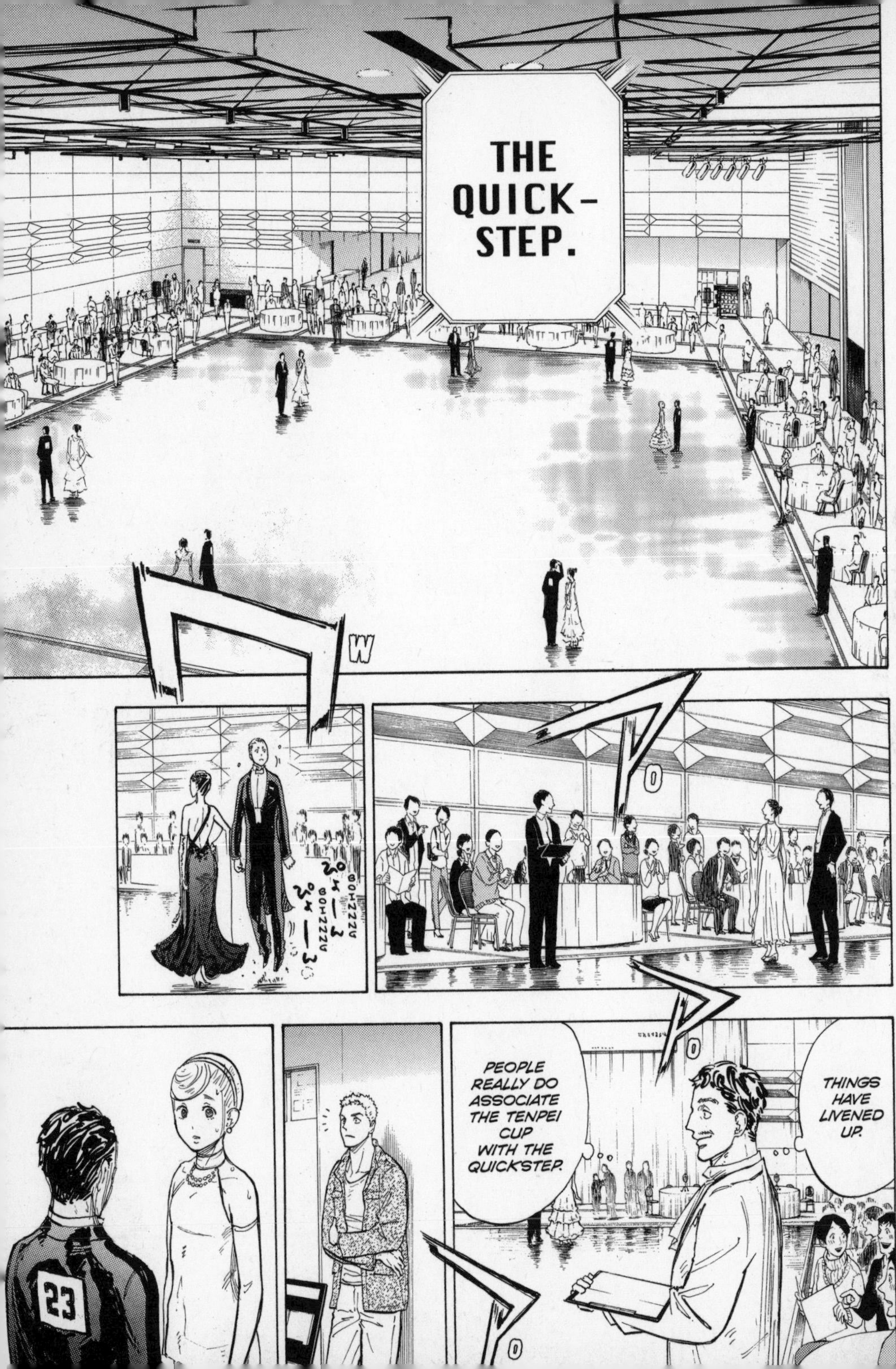
THE QUICK-STEP.
W
O
BOHZZZV
BOHZZZV
O
THINGS HAVE LIVENED UP.
PEOPLE REALLY DO ASSOCIATE THE TENPEI CUP WITH THE QUICKSTEP.
O

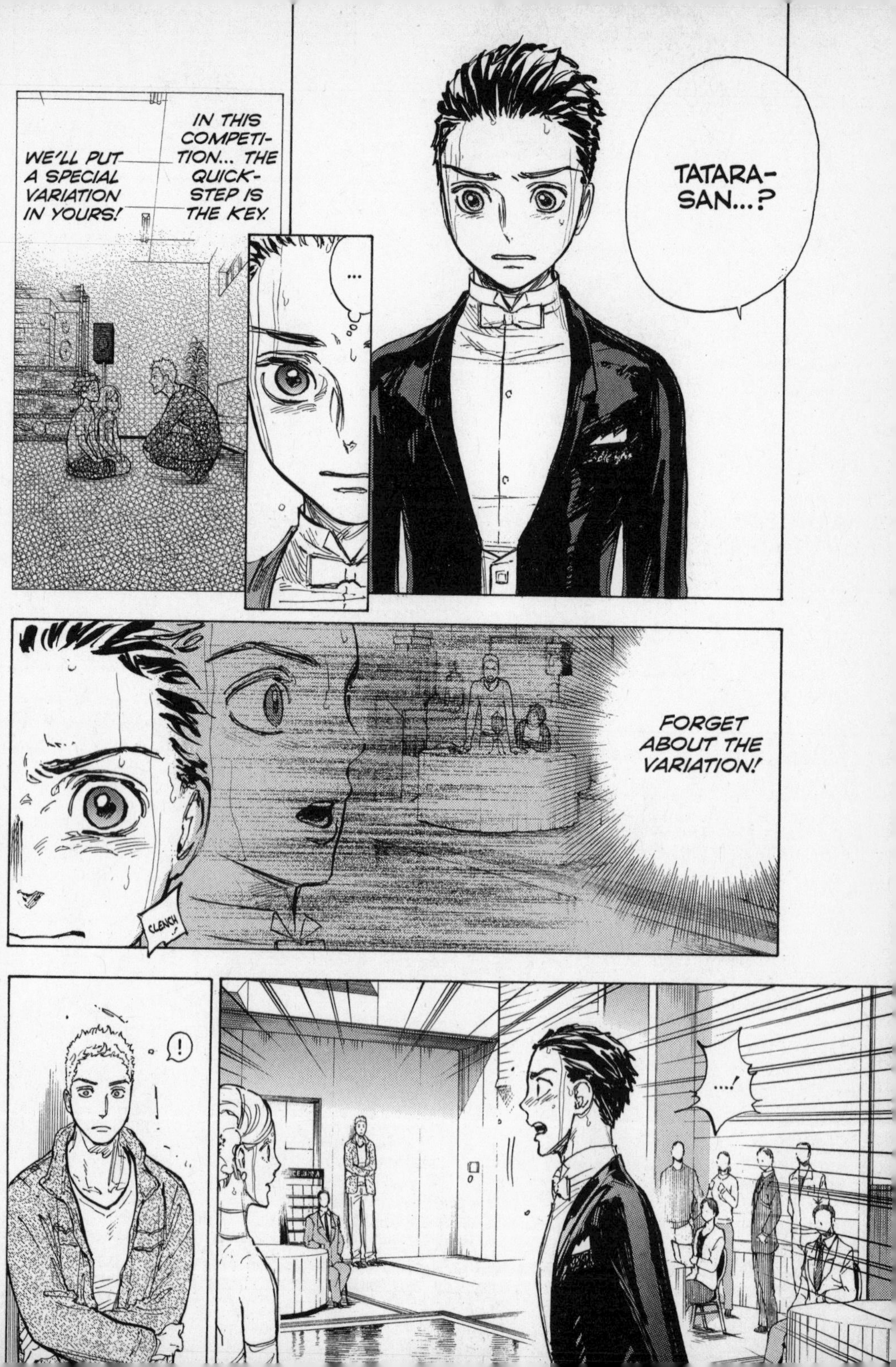
TATARA-SAN...?
...
IN THIS COMPETITION... THE QUICKSTEP IS THE KEY.
WE'LL PUT A SPECIAL VARIATION IN YOURS!
FORGET ABOUT THE VARIATION!
CLENCH
...!
!

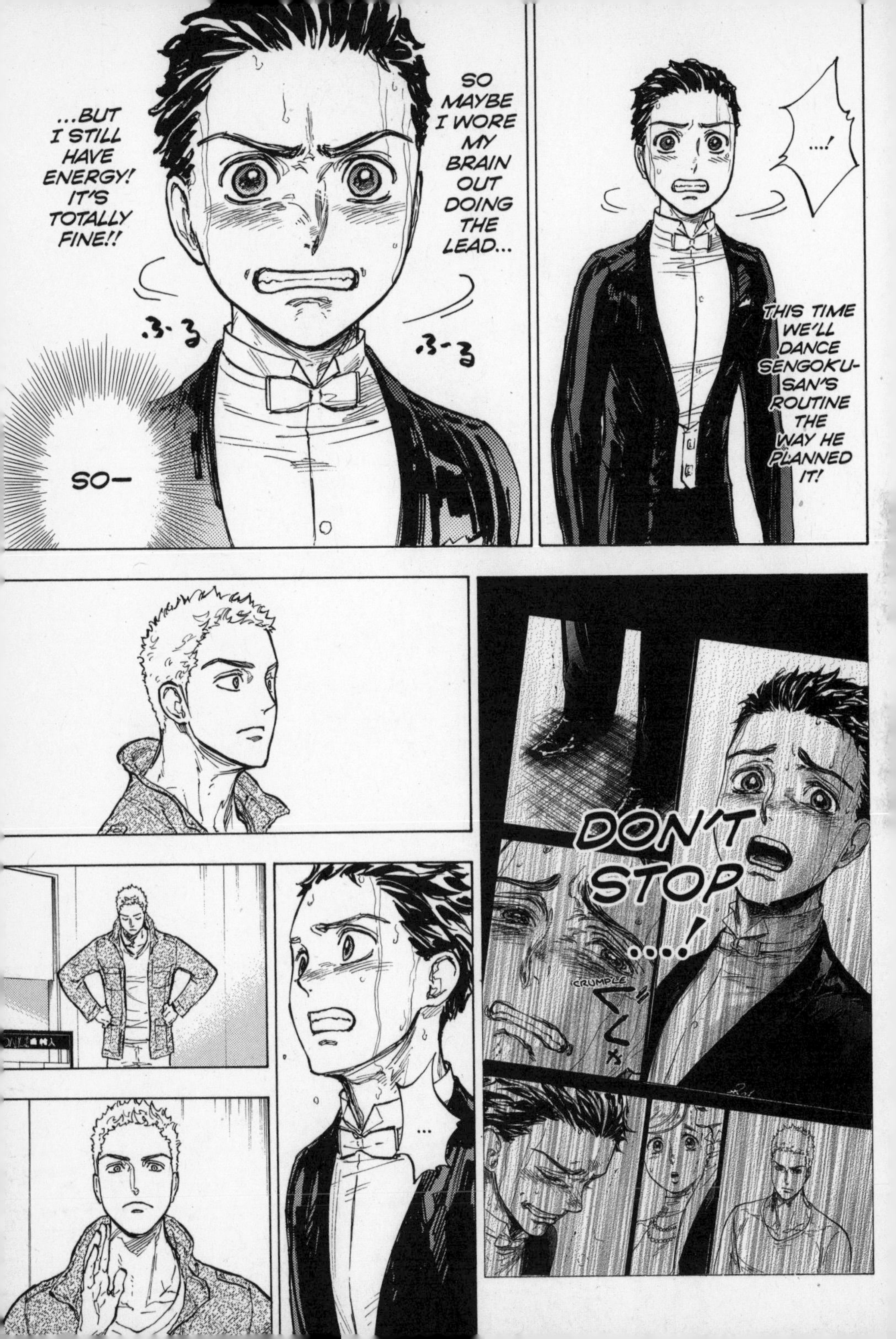

...!
THIS TIME WE'LL DANCE SENGOKU-SAN'S ROUTINE THE WAY HE PLANNED IT!
SO MAYBE I WORE MY BRAIN OUT DOING THE LEAD...
...BUT I STILL HAVE ENERGY! IT'S TOTALLY FINE!!
ふ・る
ふ・る
SO—
DON'T STOP....!
CRUMPLE
...

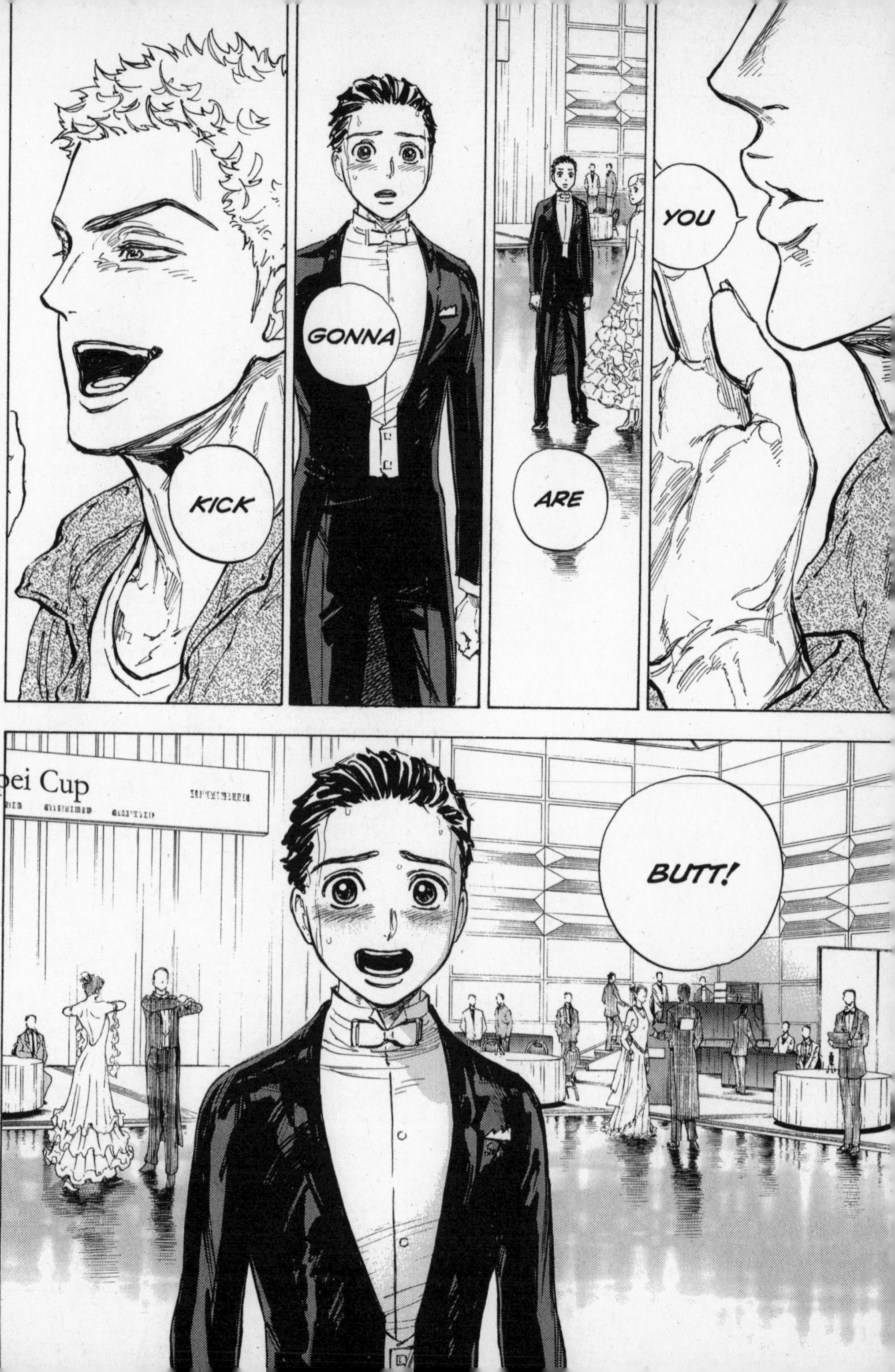
YOU
ARE
GONNA
KICK
BUTT!
npei Cup

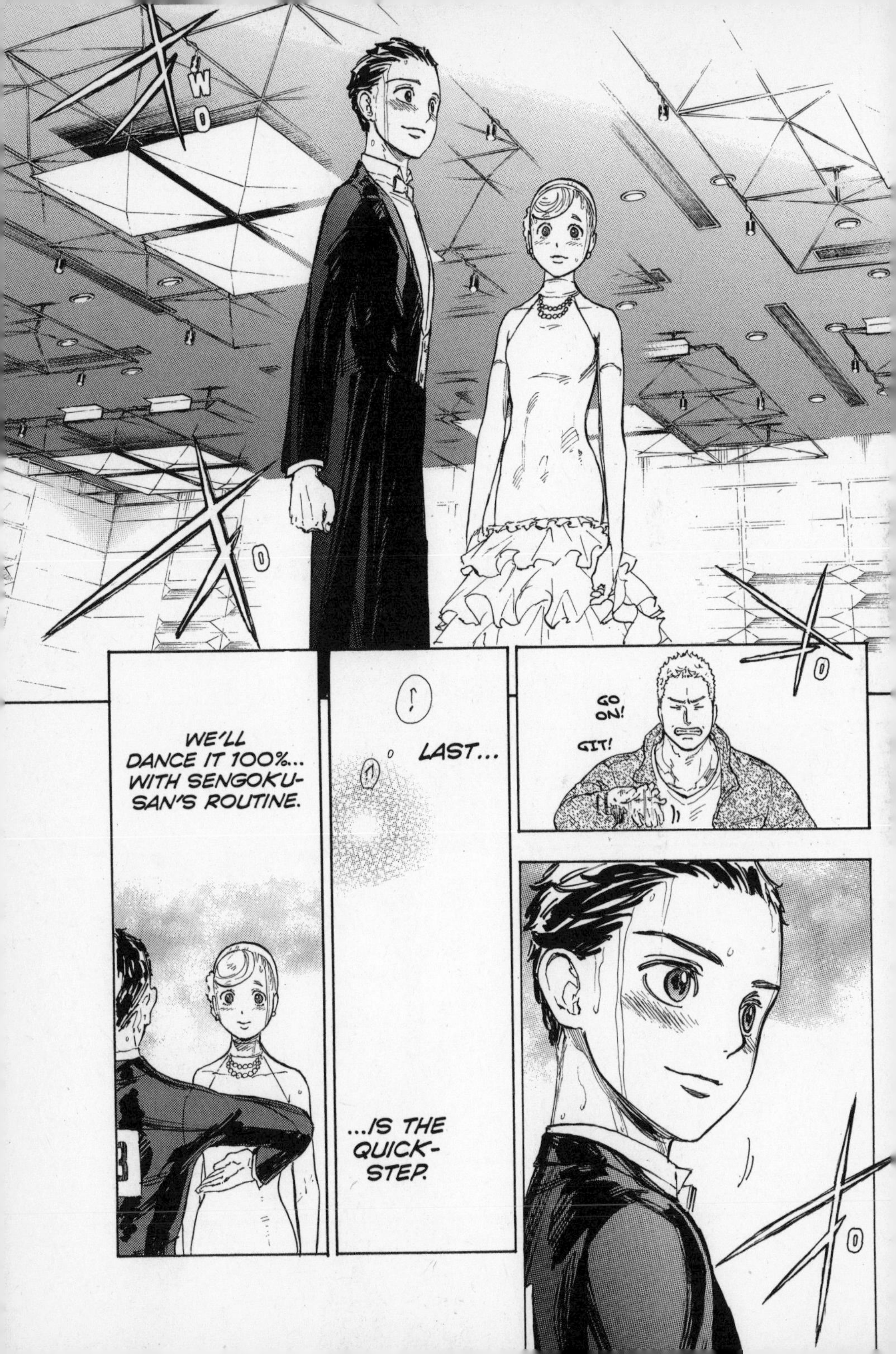
WO
O
O
O
GO ON!
GIT!
O
LAST...
...IS THE QUICK-STEP.
WE'LL DANCE IT 100%... WITH SENGOKU-SAN'S ROUTINE.

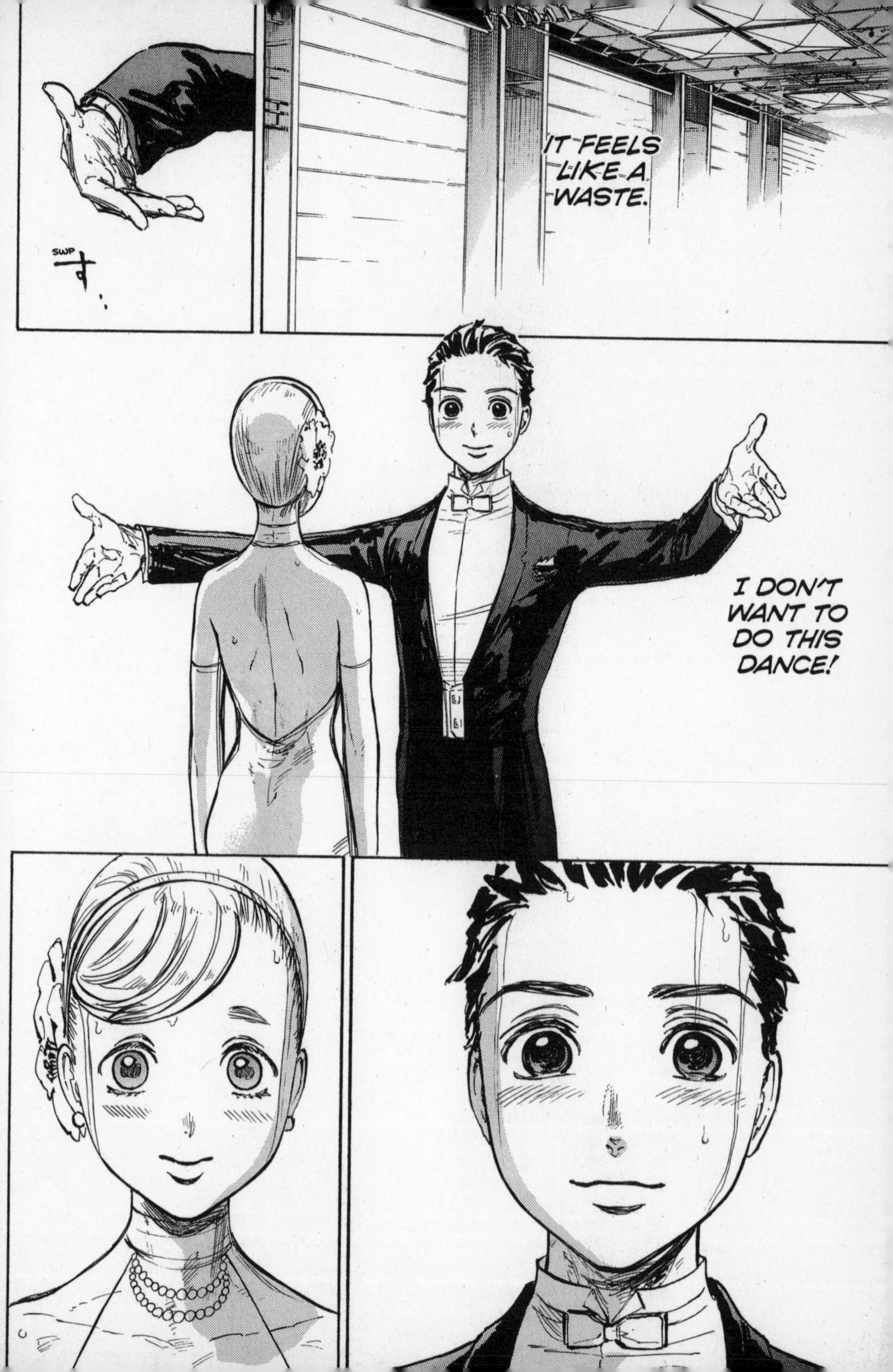
IT FEELS LIKE A WASTE.
SWP
す
I DON'T WANT TO DO THIS DANCE!

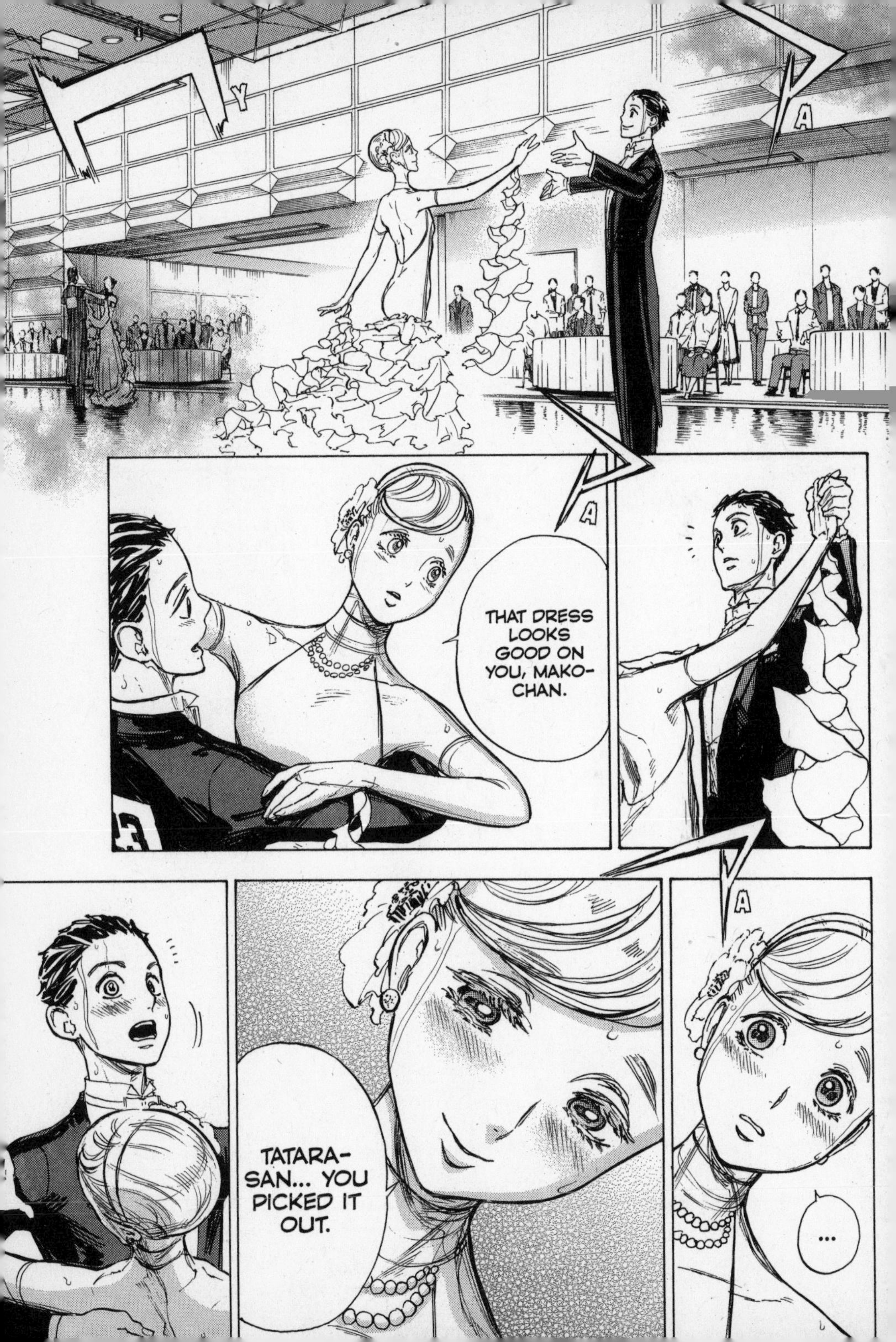
A
Y
A
THAT DRESS LOOKS GOOD ON YOU, MAKO-CHAN.
A
...
TATARA-SAN... YOU PICKED IT OUT.

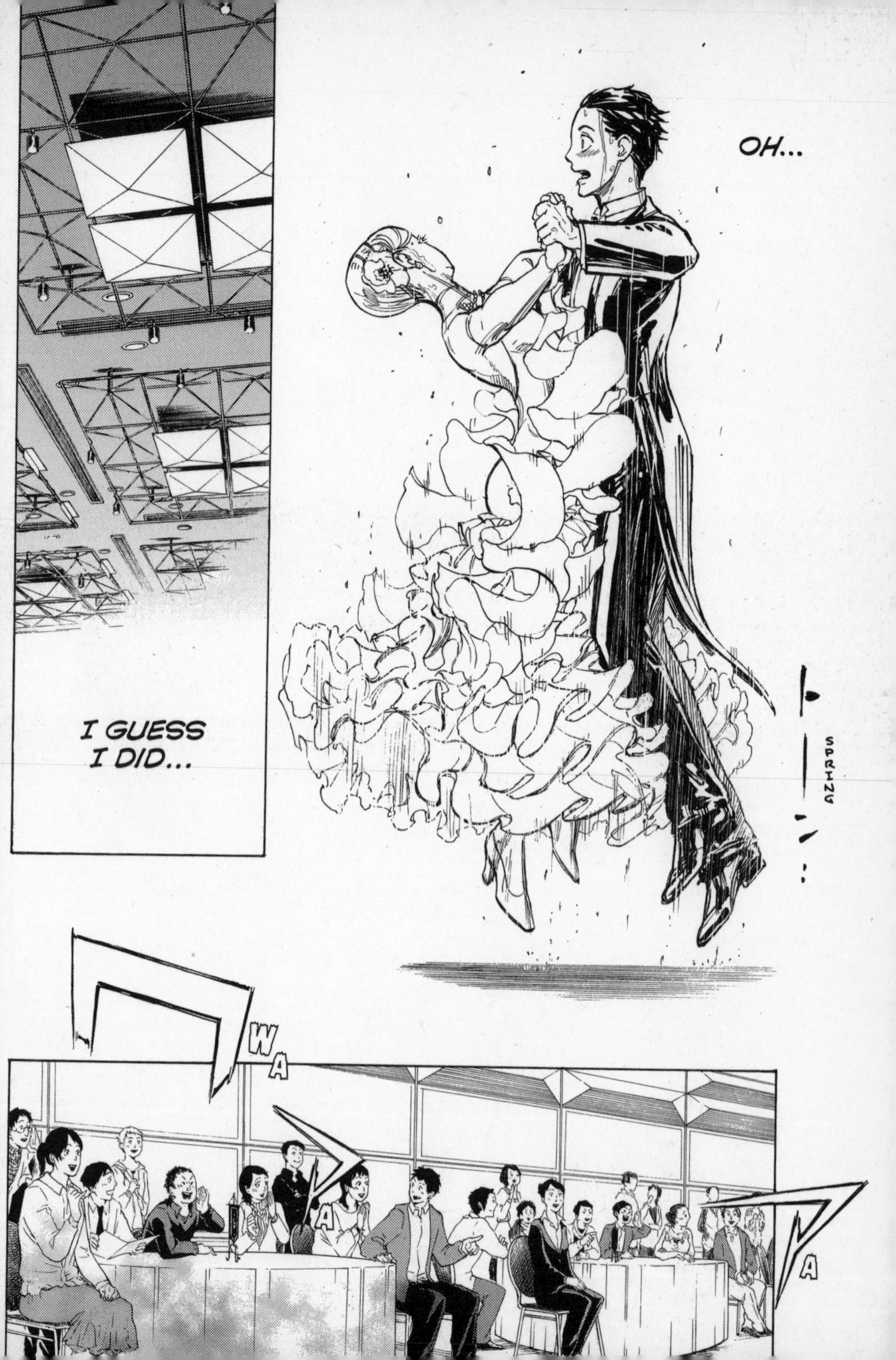
OH...
SPRING
I GUESS I DID...
WA
A
A
A

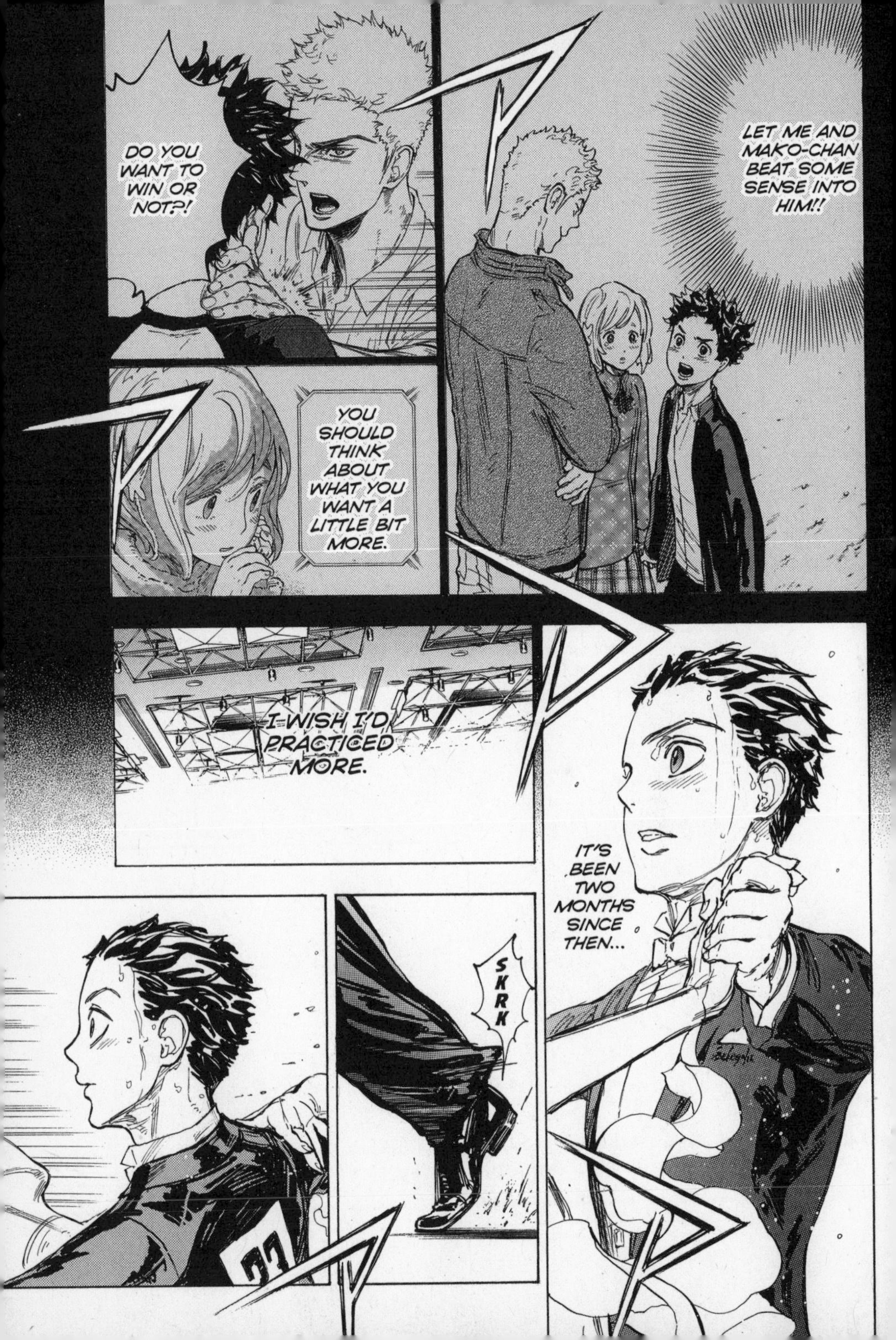
LET ME AND MAKO-CHAN BEAT SOME SENSE INTO HIM!!
DO YOU WANT TO WIN OR NOT?!
YOU SHOULD THINK ABOUT WHAT YOU WANT A LITTLE BIT MORE.
IT'S BEEN TWO MONTHS SINCE THEN...
I WISH I'D PRACTICED MORE.
SKRK

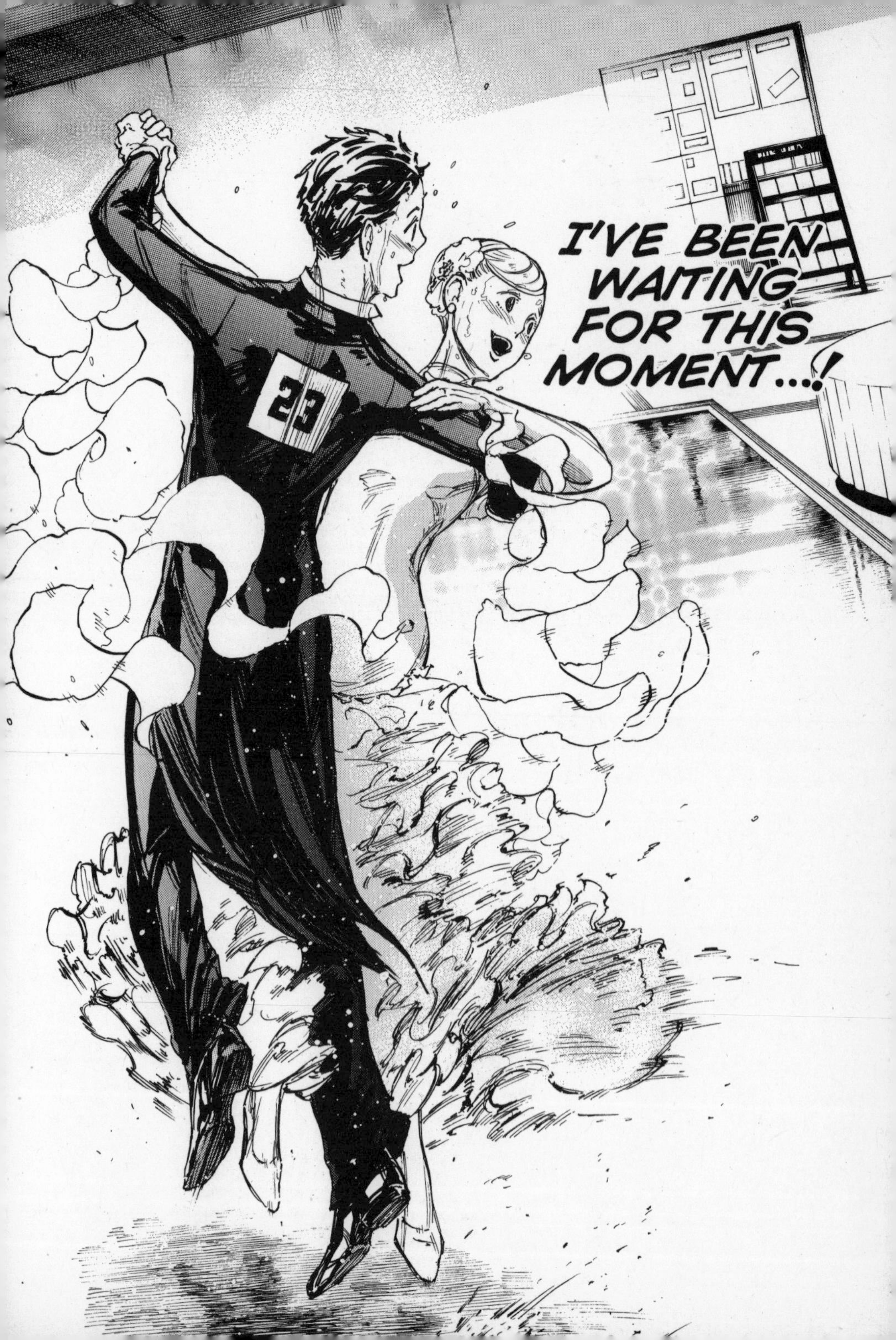
I'VE BEEN WAITING FOR THIS MOMENT...!
23

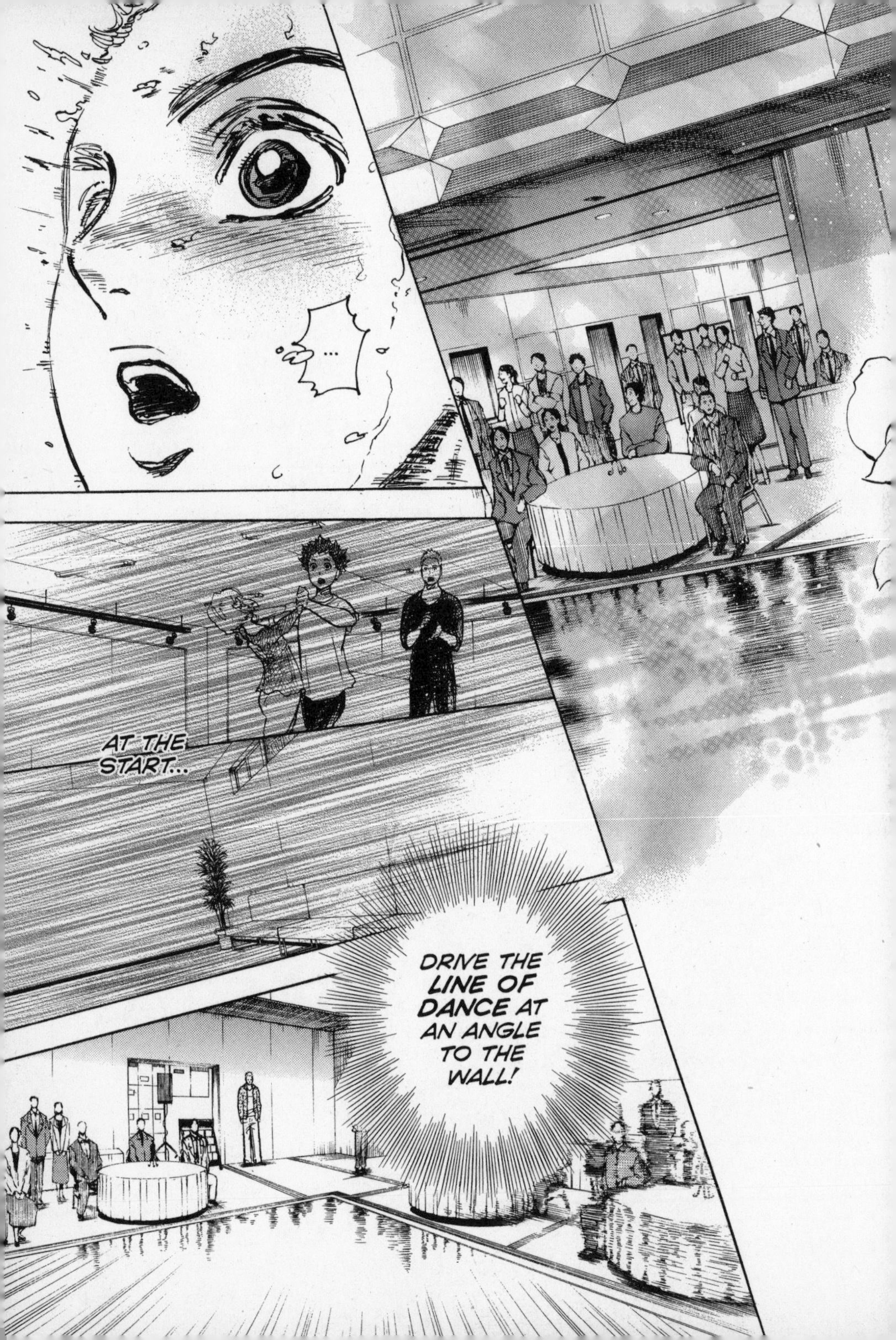
...
AT THE START...
DRIVE THE LINE OF DANCE AT AN ANGLE TO THE WALL!

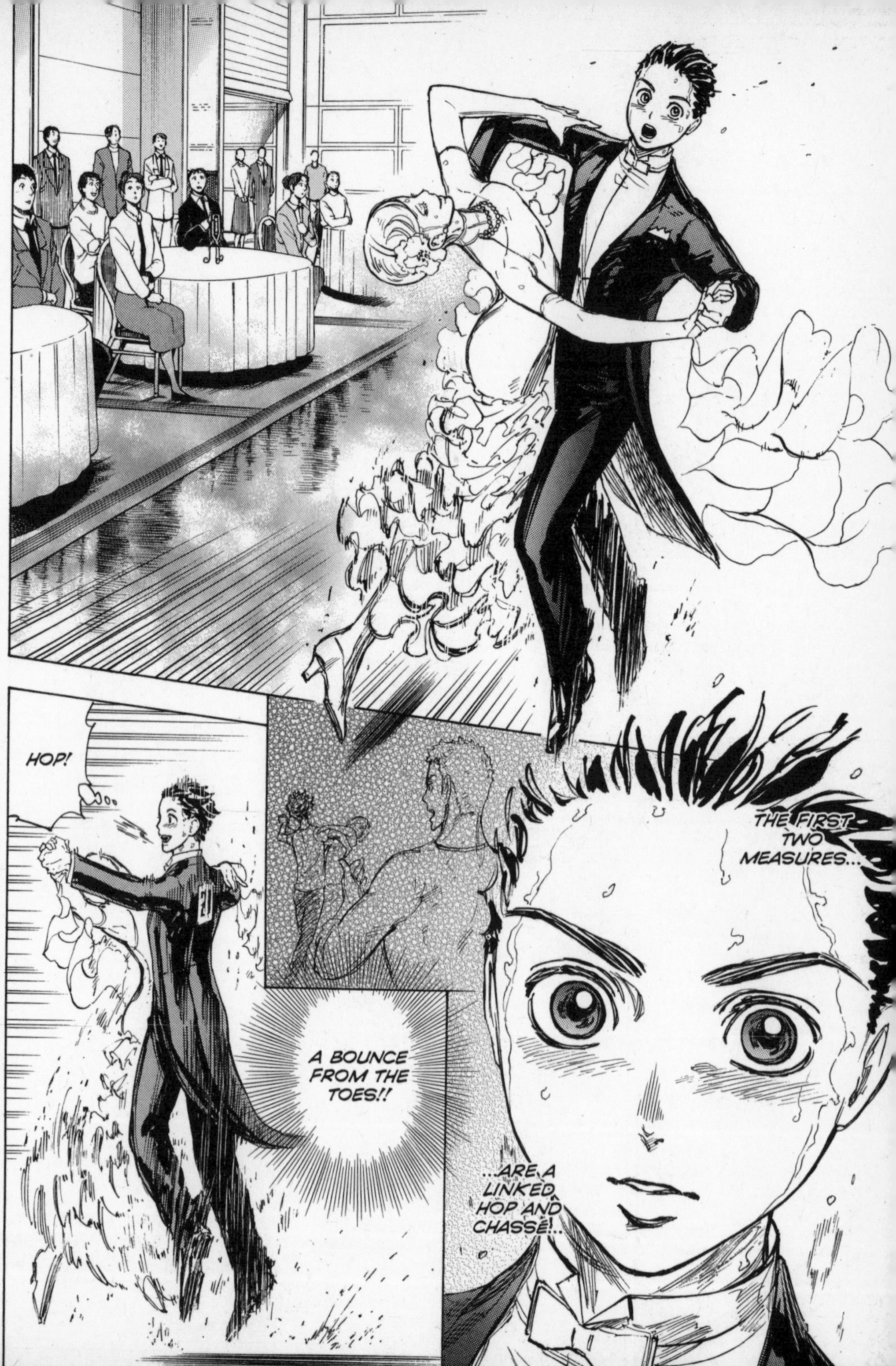
THE FIRST TWO MEASURES...
...ARE A LINKED HOP AND CHASSÉ!...
A BOUNCE FROM THE TOES!!
HOP!

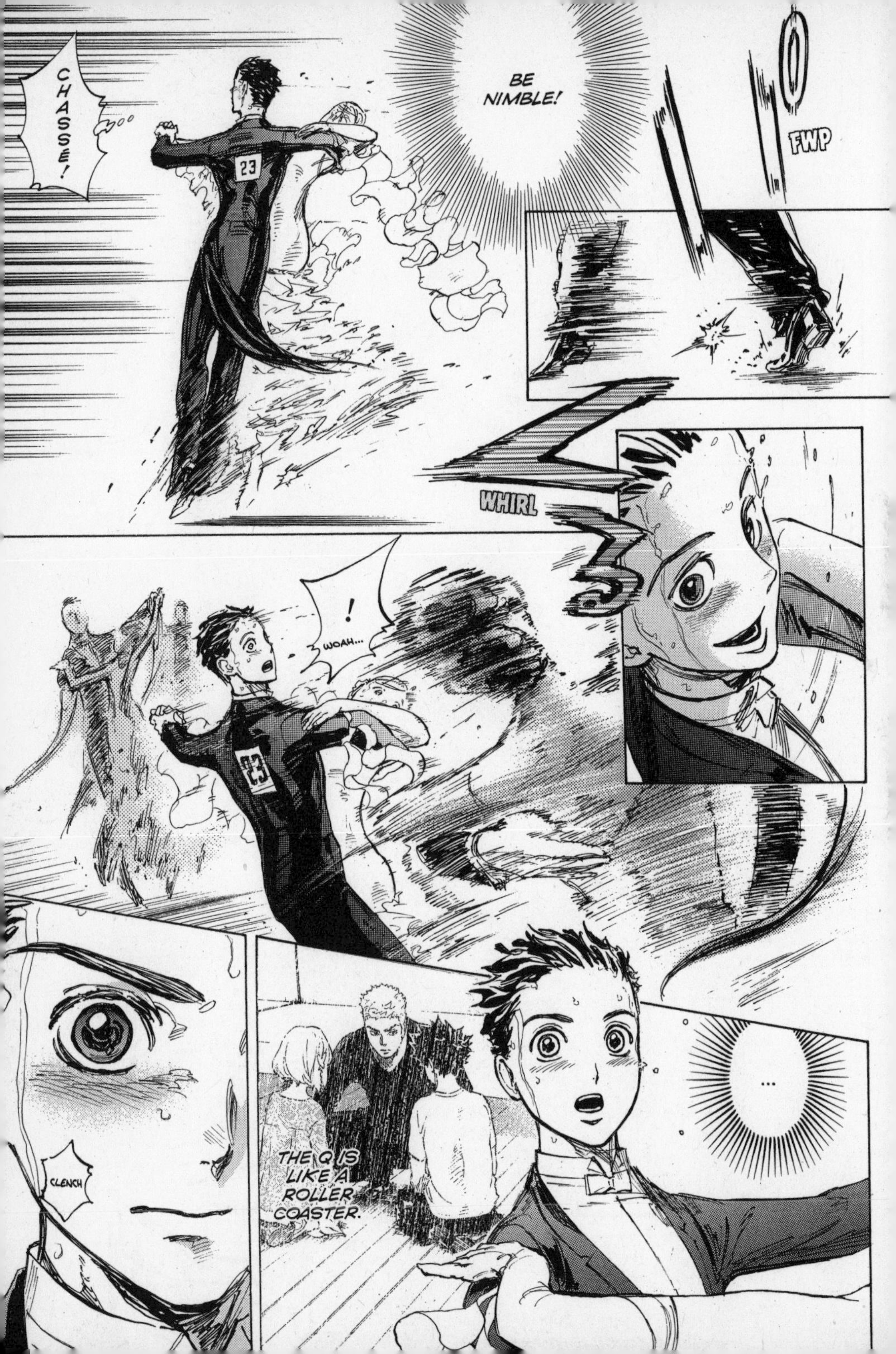
FWP
BE NIMBLE!
CHASSÉ!
WHIRL
!
WOAH...
...
THE Q IS LIKE A ROLLER COASTER.
CLENCH

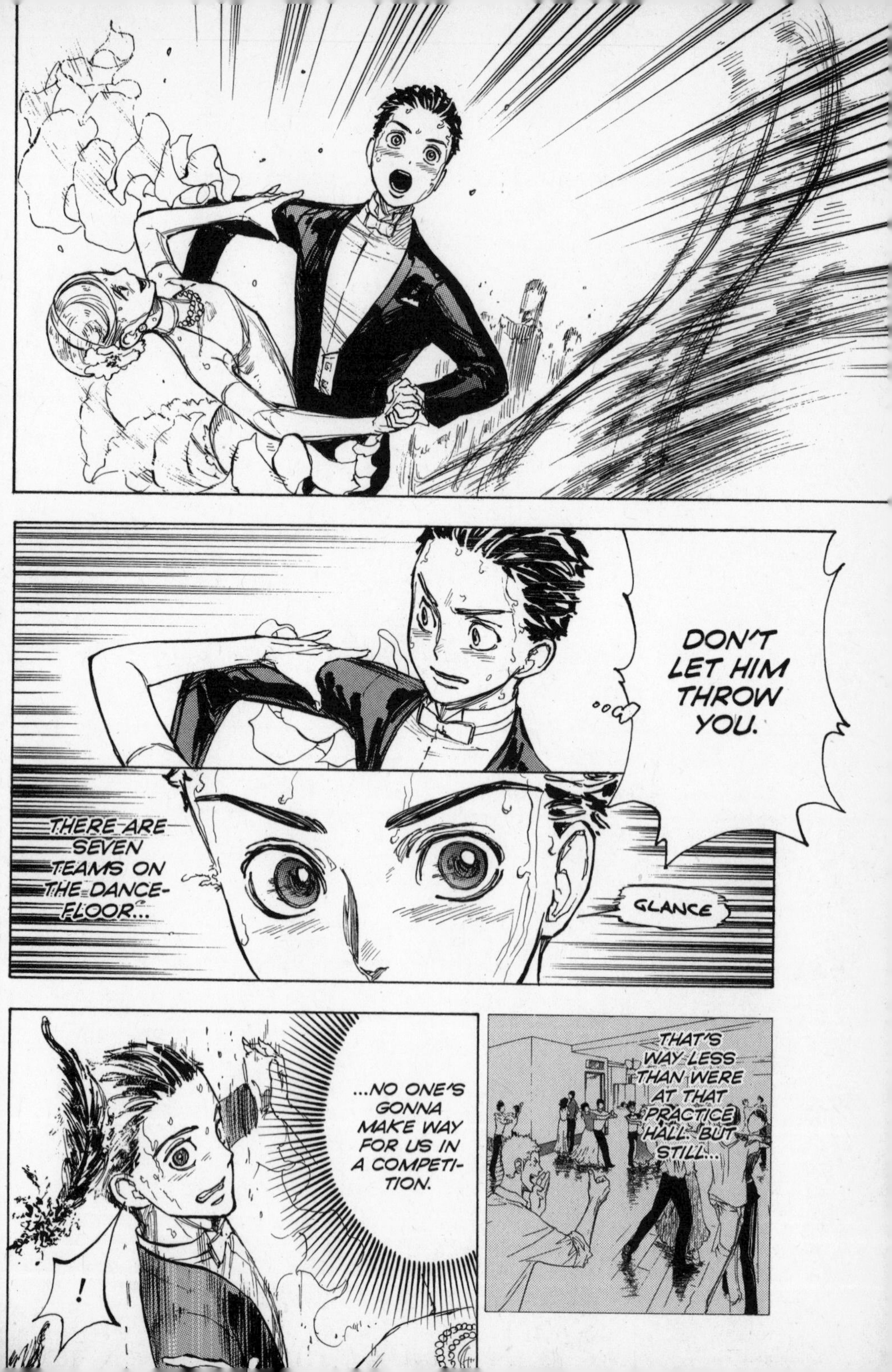
DON'T LET HIM THROW YOU.
GLANCE
THERE ARE SEVEN TEAMS ON THE DANCE-FLOOR...
THAT'S WAY LESS THAN WERE AT THAT PRACTICE HALL. BUT STILL...
...NO ONE'S GONNA MAKE WAY FOR US IN A COMPETITION.
!

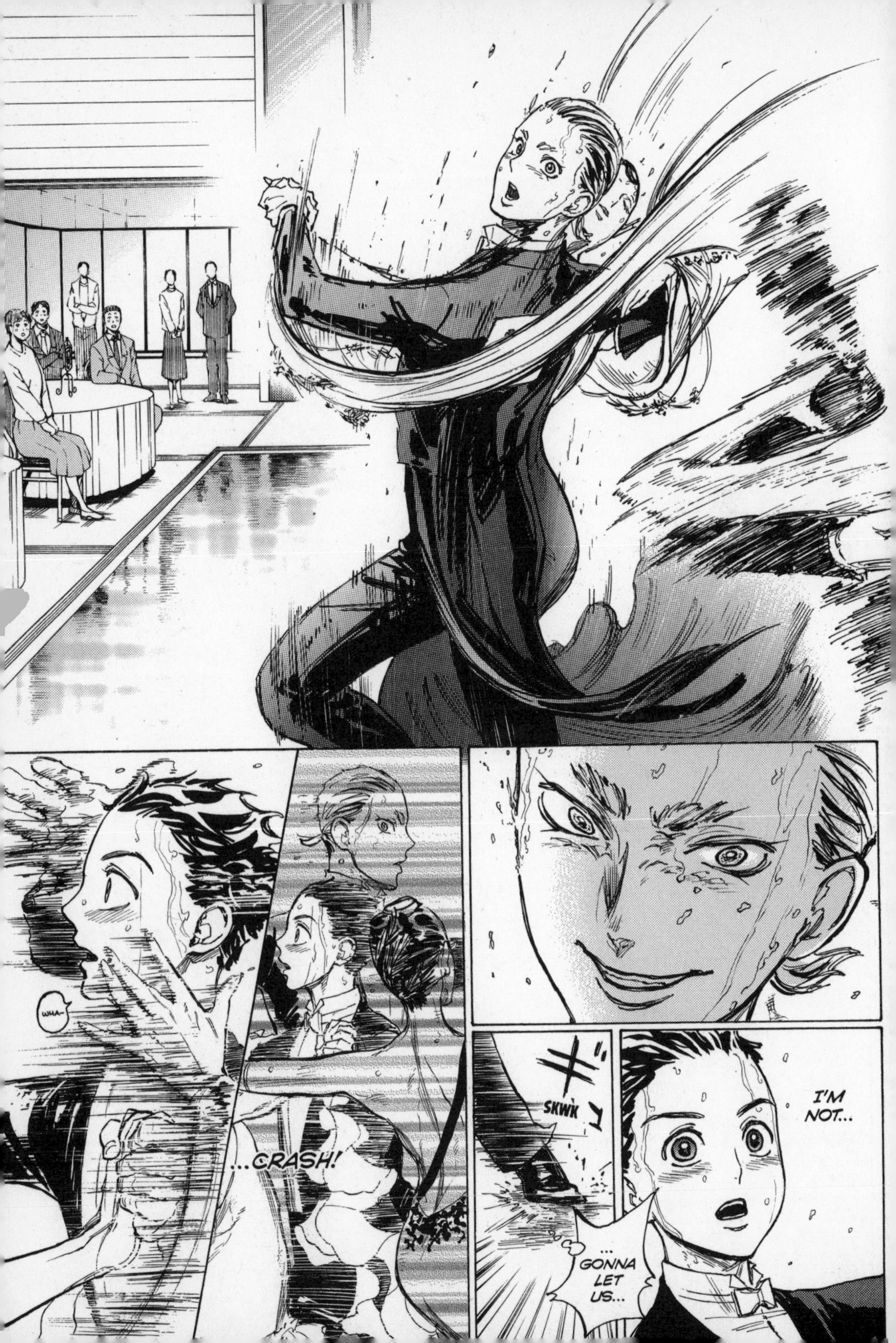
I'M NOT...
... GONNA LET US...
SKWK
...CRASH!
WHA-

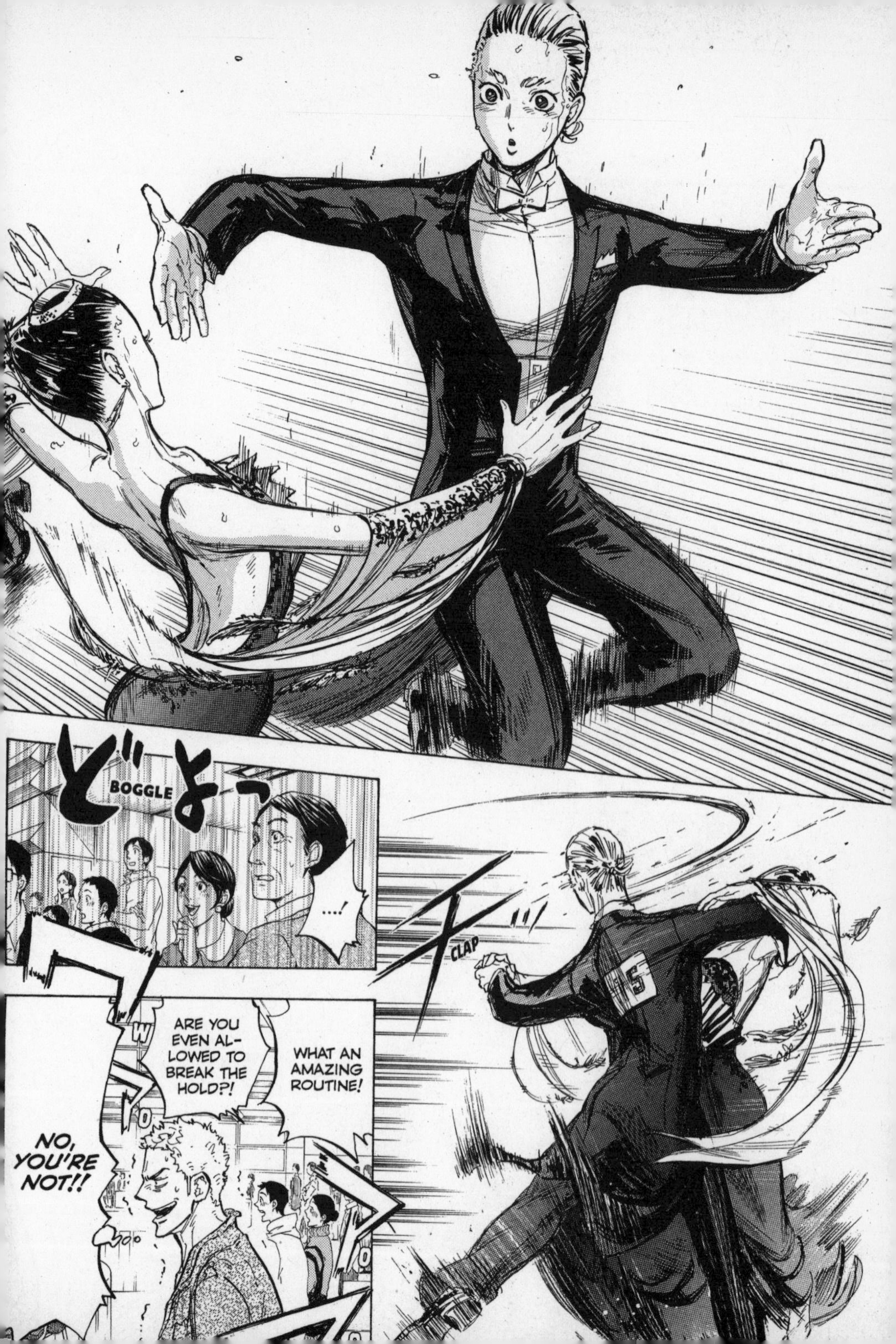

CLAP
BOGGLE
...!
WHAT AN AMAZING ROUTINE!
ARE YOU EVEN AL-LOWED TO BREAK THE HOLD?!
NO, YOU'RE NOT!!

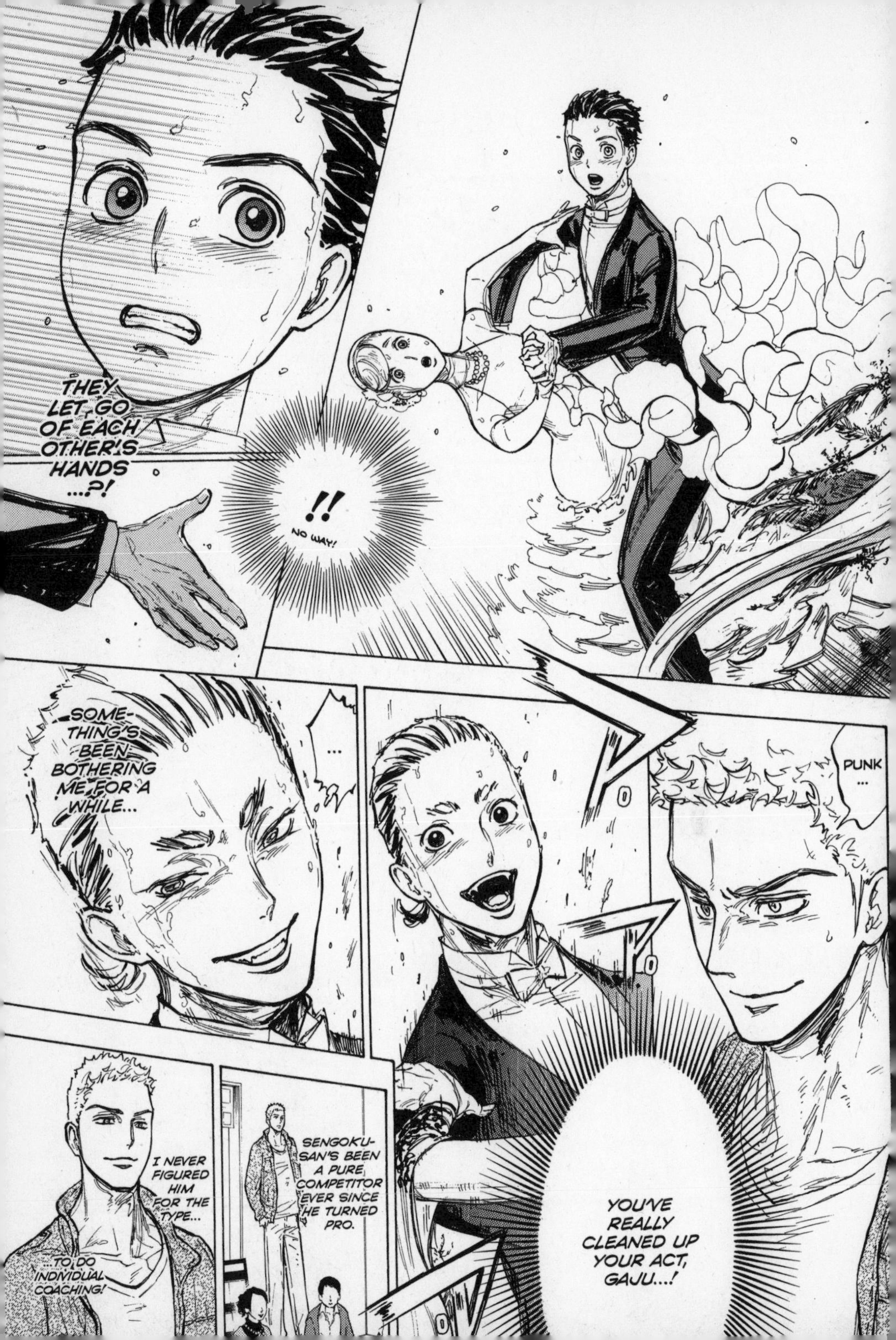
THEY LET GO OF EACH OTHER'S HANDS ...?!
!!
NO WAY!
PUNK ...
...
YOU'VE REALLY CLEANED UP YOUR ACT, GAJU...!
SOME-THING'S BEEN BOTHERING ME FOR A WHILE...
SENGOKU-SAN'S BEEN A PURE COMPETITOR EVER SINCE HE TURNED PRO.
I NEVER FIGURED HIM FOR THE TYPE...
...TO DO INDIVIDUAL COACHING!

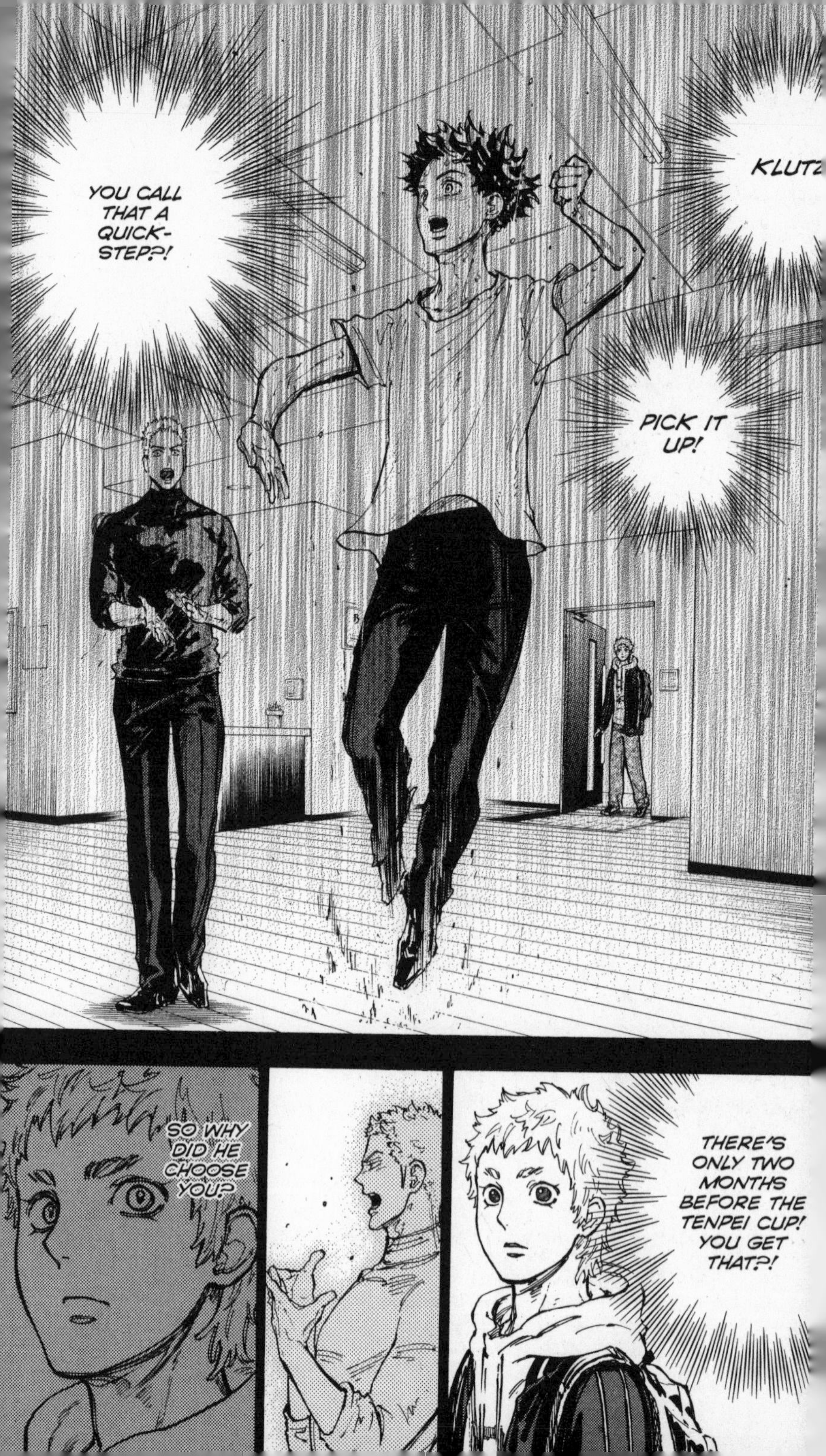
KLUTZ
YOU CALL THAT A QUICK-STEP?!
PICK IT UP!
THERE'S ONLY TWO MONTHS BEFORE THE TENPEI CUP! YOU GET THAT?!
SO WHY DID HE CHOOSE YOU?

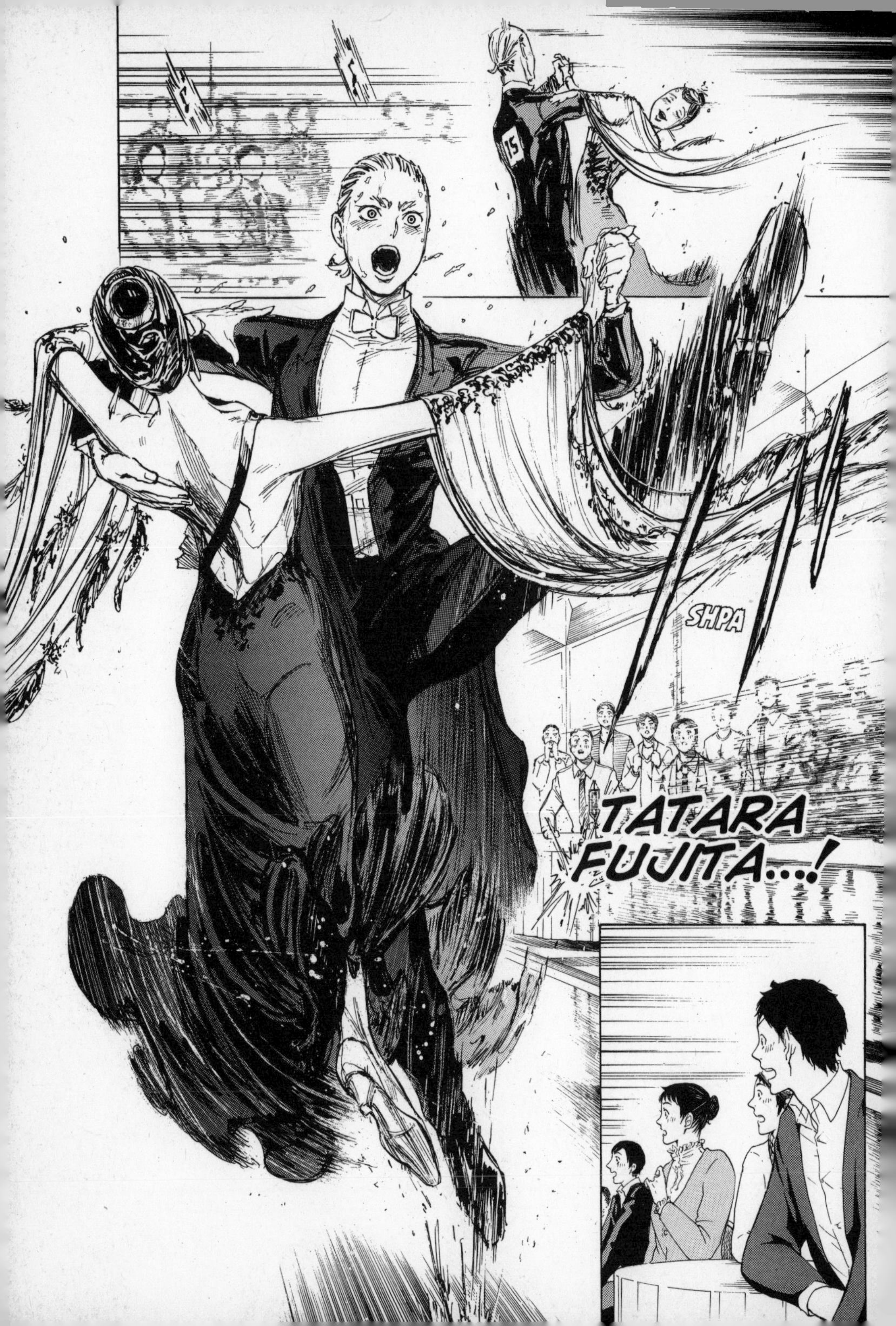
SHPA
TATARA FUJITA...!

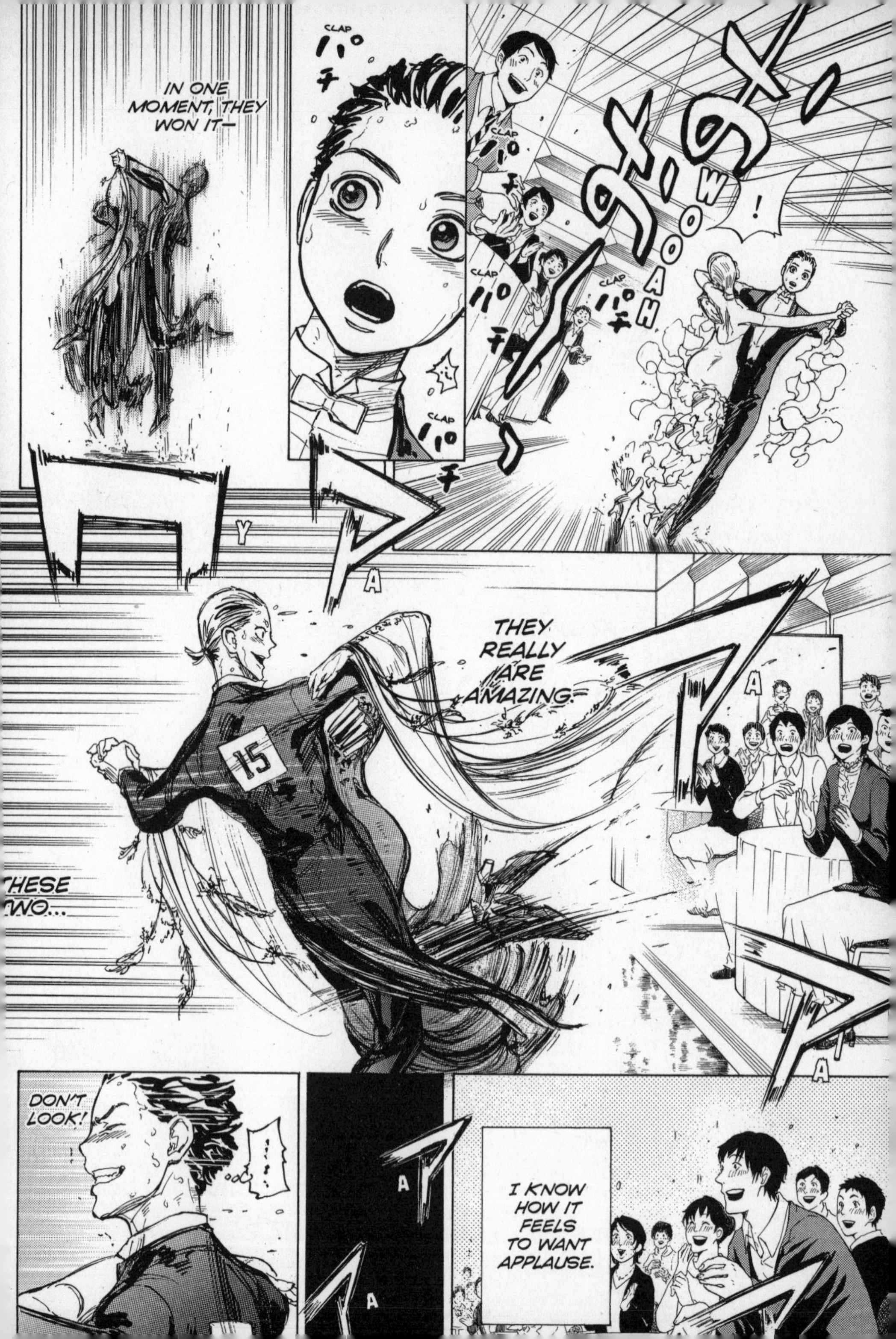
WOOOAH!
CLAP
CLAP
CLAP
CLAP
CLAP
IN ONE MOMENT, THEY WON IT—
Y
A
THEY REALLY ARE AMAZING.
A
A
THESE TWO...
I KNOW HOW IT FEELS TO WANT APPLAUSE.
A
A
DON'T LOOK!

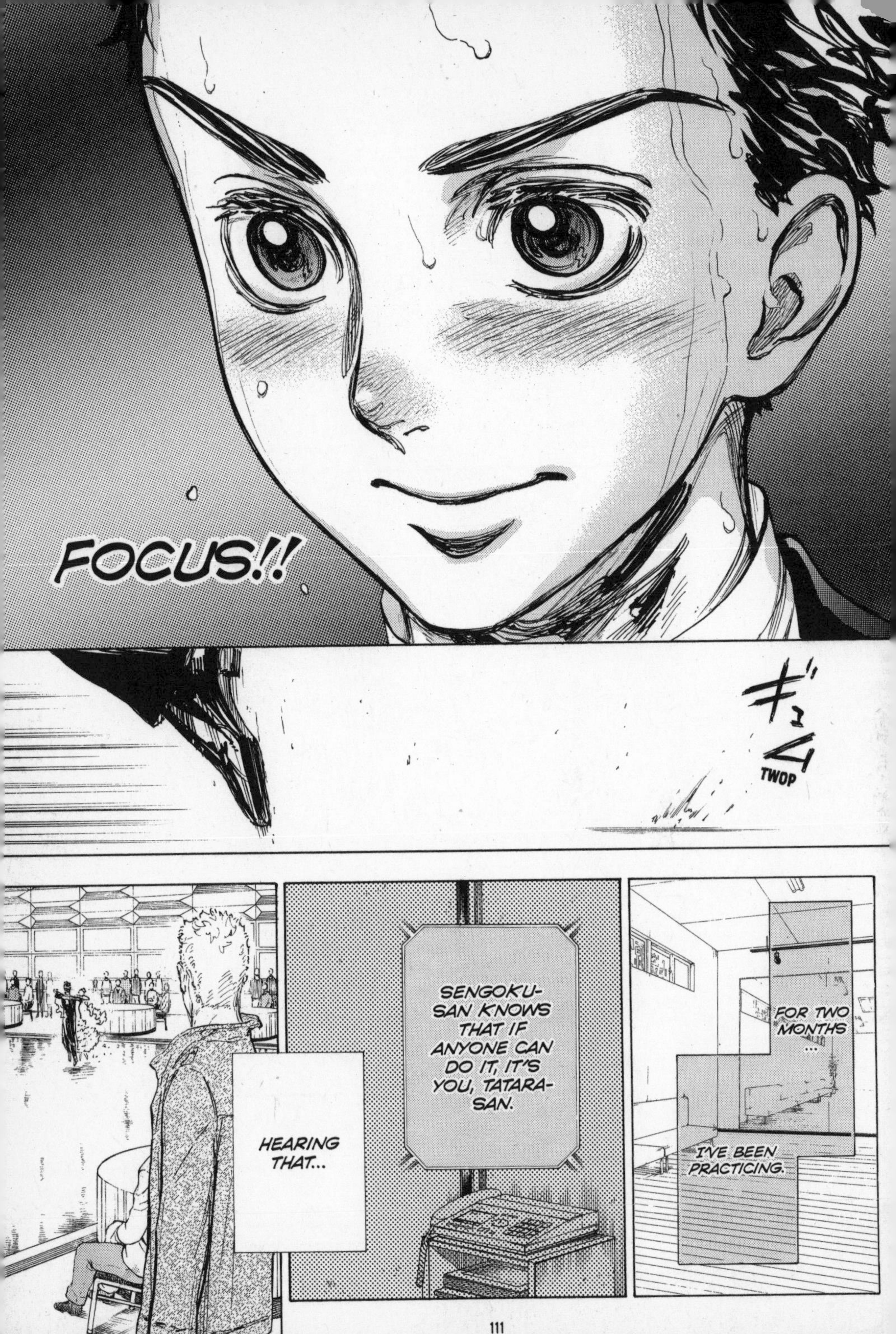
FOCUS!!
ギュム
TWOP
FOR TWO MONTHS ...
I'VE BEEN PRACTICING.
SENGOKU-SAN KNOWS THAT IF ANYONE CAN DO IT, IT'S YOU, TATARA-SAN.
HEARING THAT...

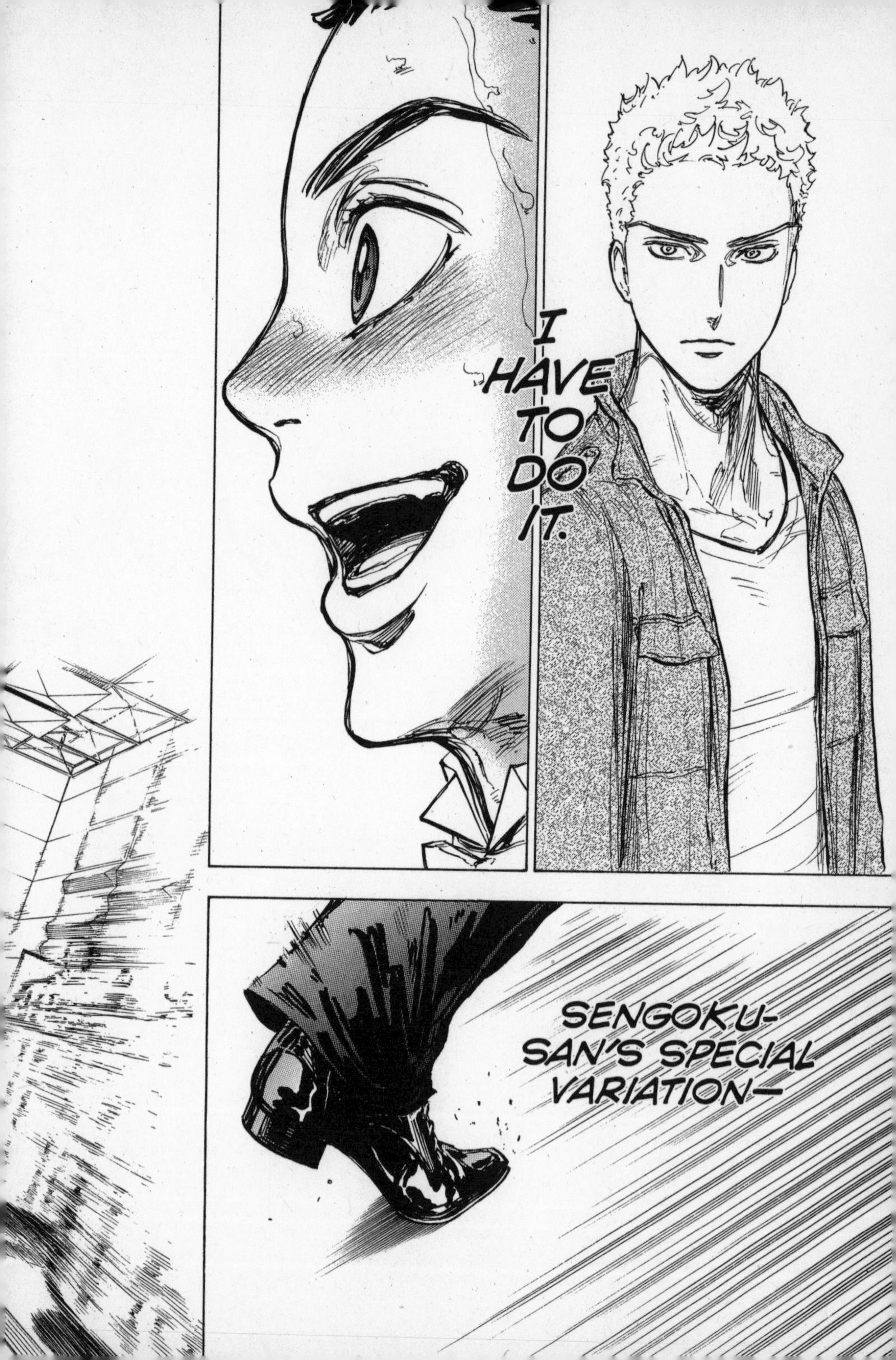
I HAVE TO DO IT.
SENGOKU-SAN'S SPECIAL VARIATION—

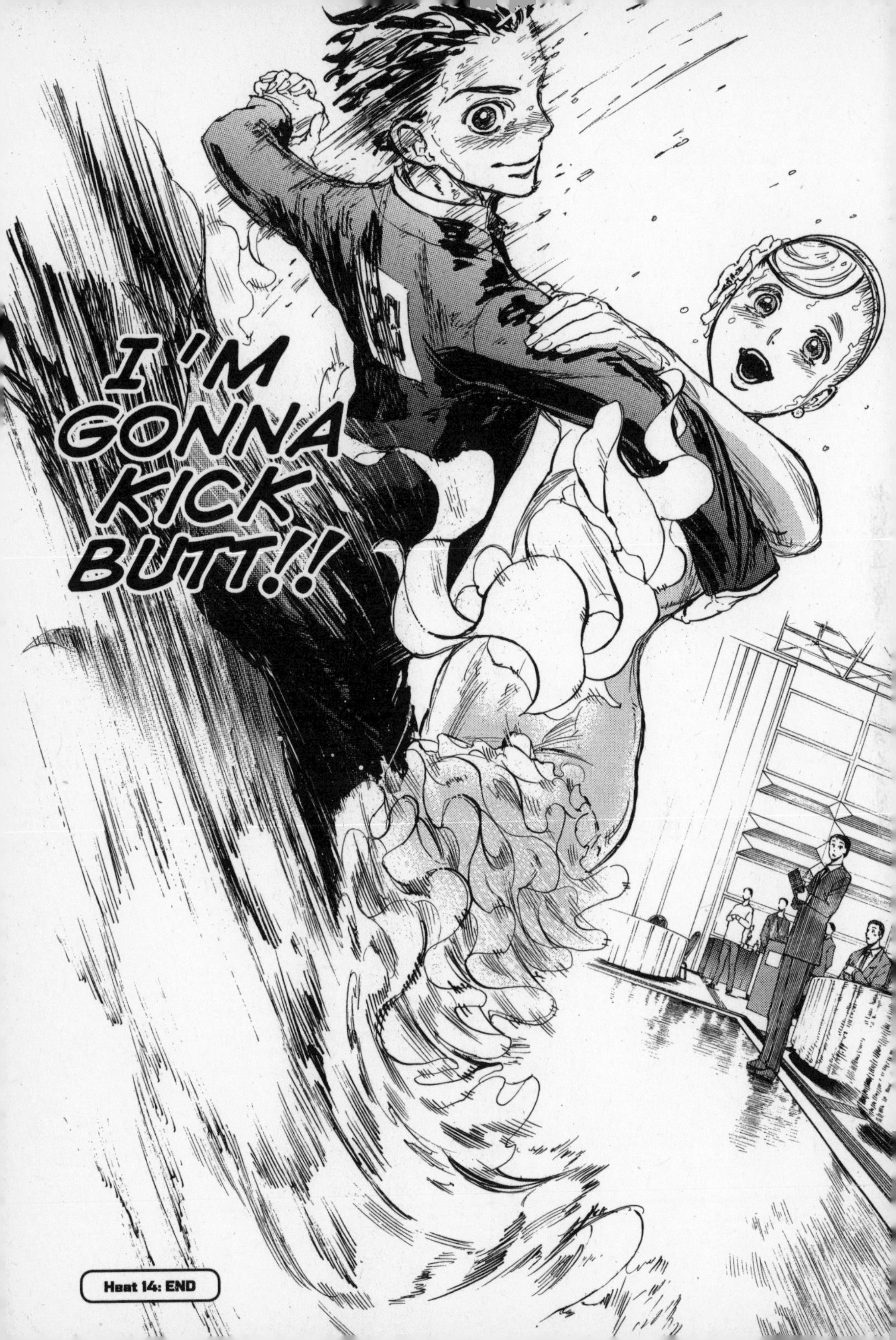
I'M GONNA KICK BUTT!!
Heat 14: END

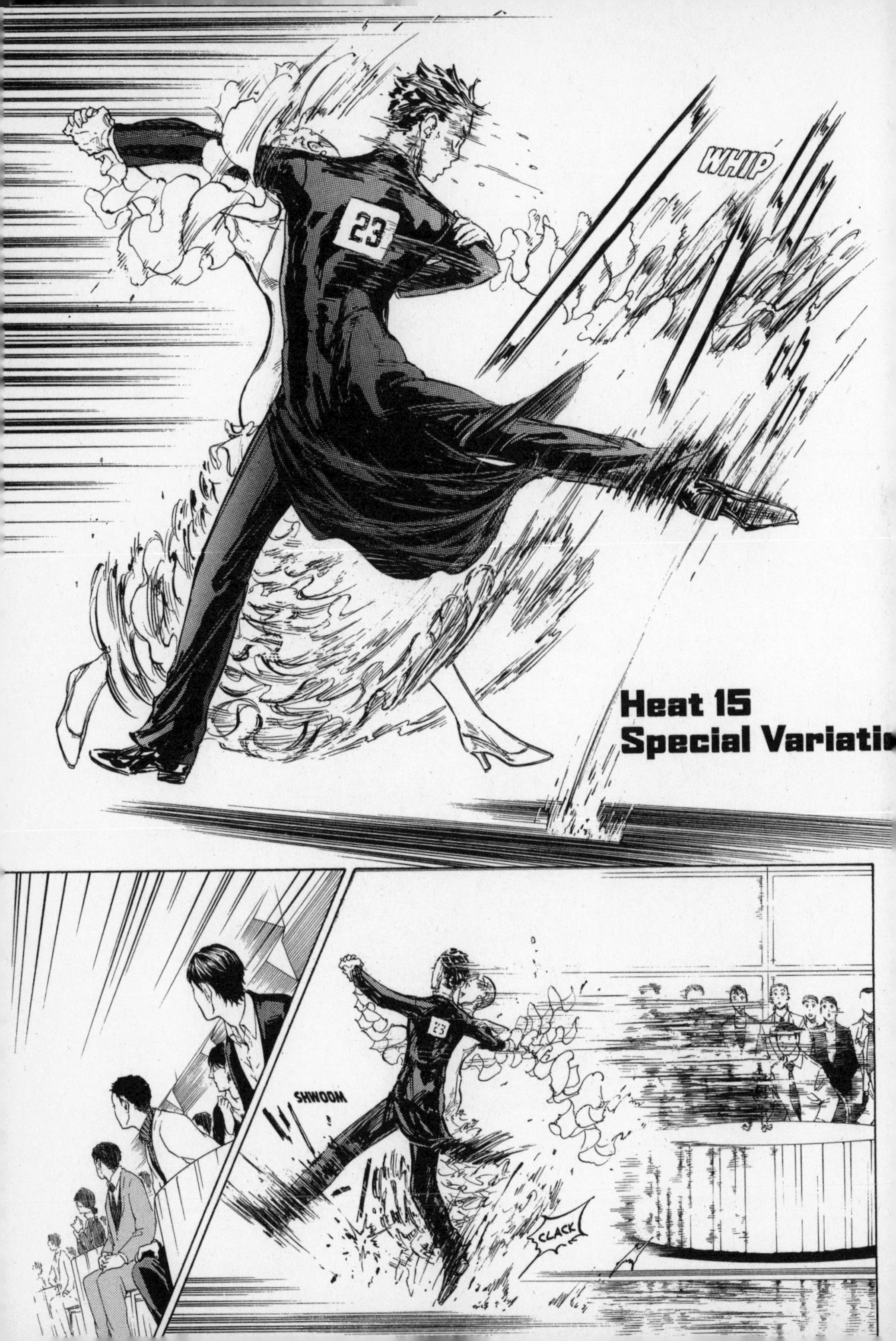
WHIP
Heat 15
Special Variati
SHWOOM
CLACK

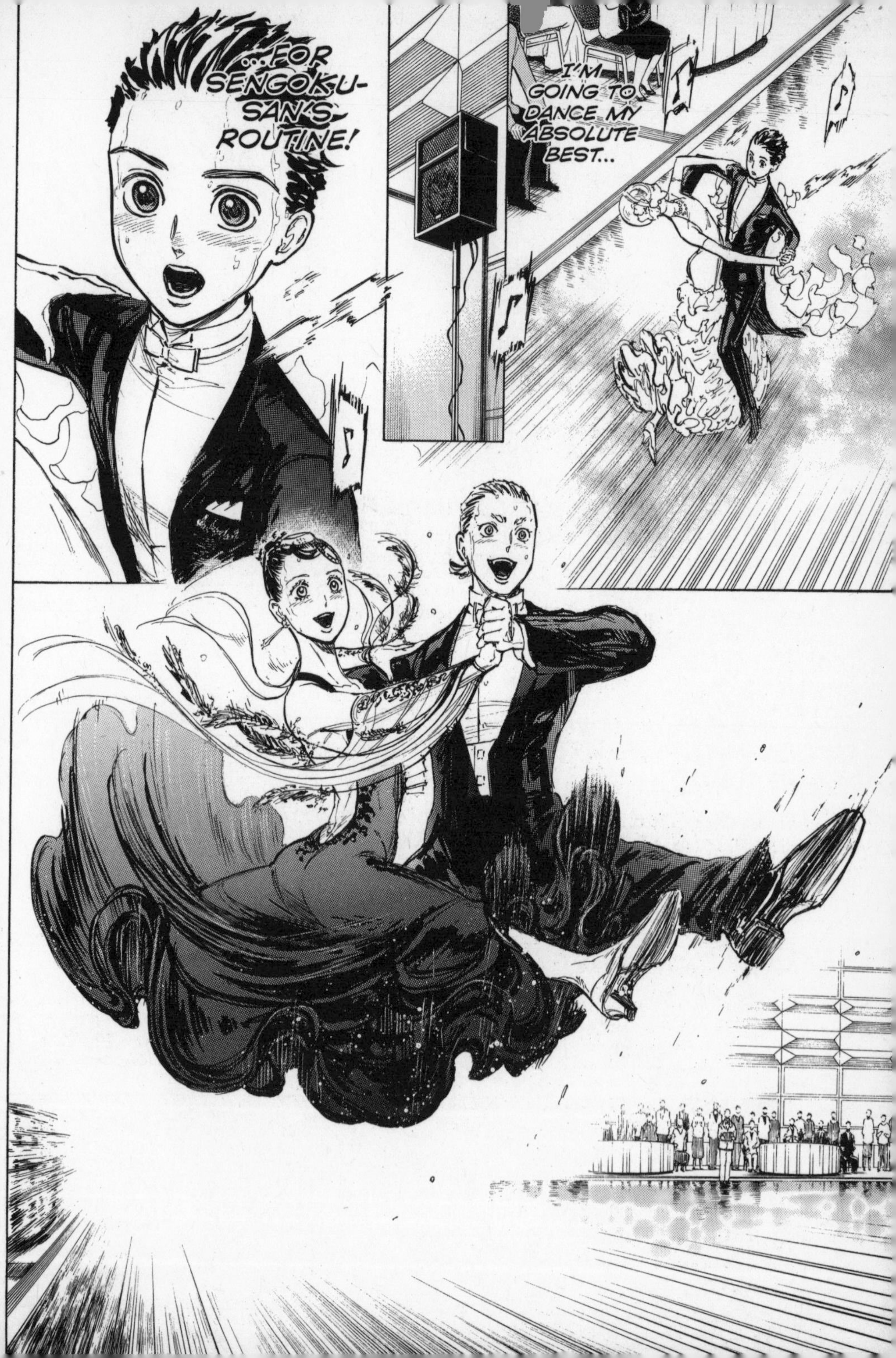
I'M GOING TO DANCE MY ABSOLUTE BEST...
...FOR SENGOKU-SAN'S ROUTINE!

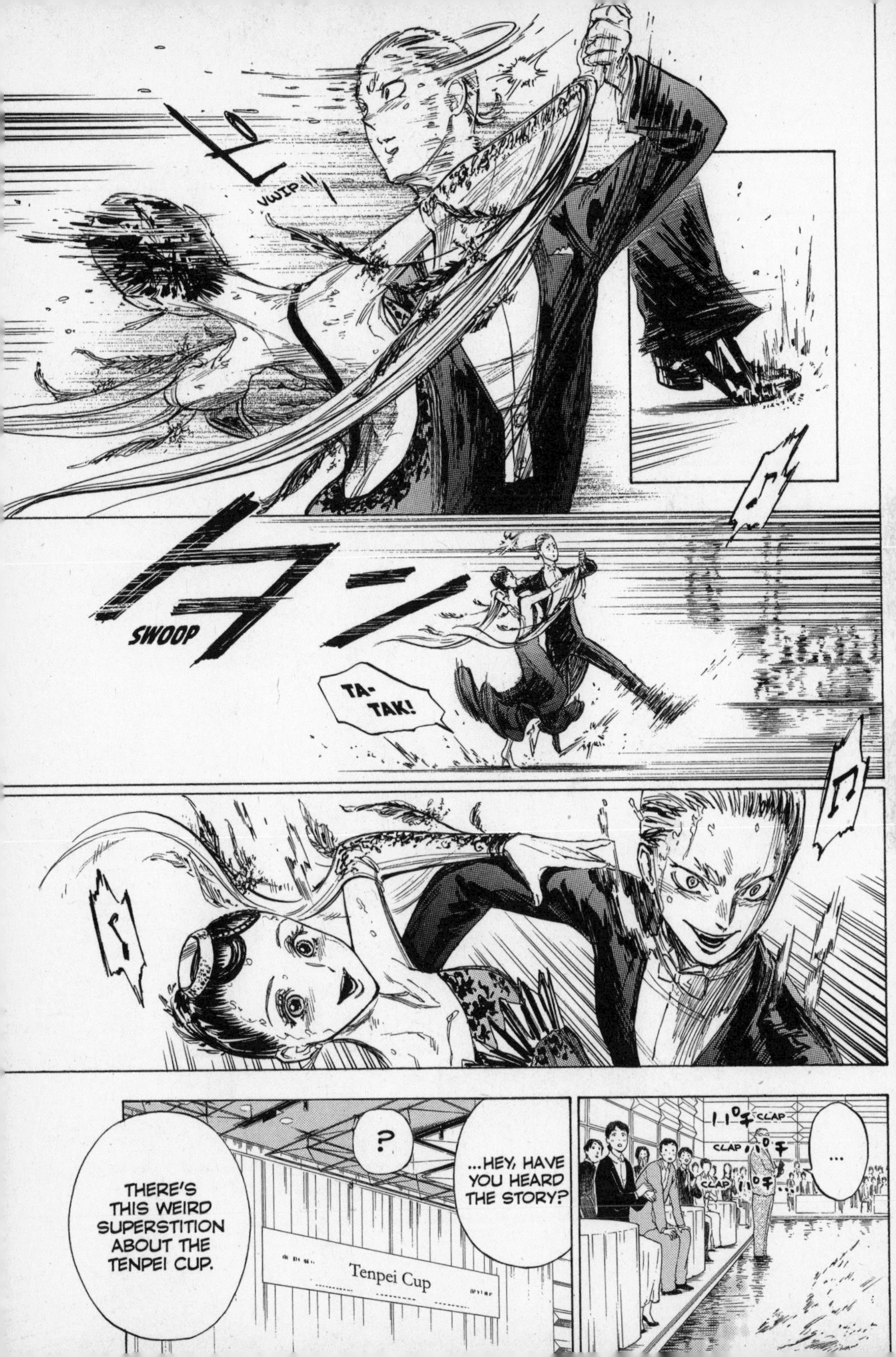
VWIP
SWOOP
TA-TAK!
CLAP
CLAP
CLAP
...
?
...HEY, HAVE YOU HEARD THE STORY?
THERE'S THIS WEIRD SUPERSTITION ABOUT THE TENPEI CUP.
Tenpei Cup

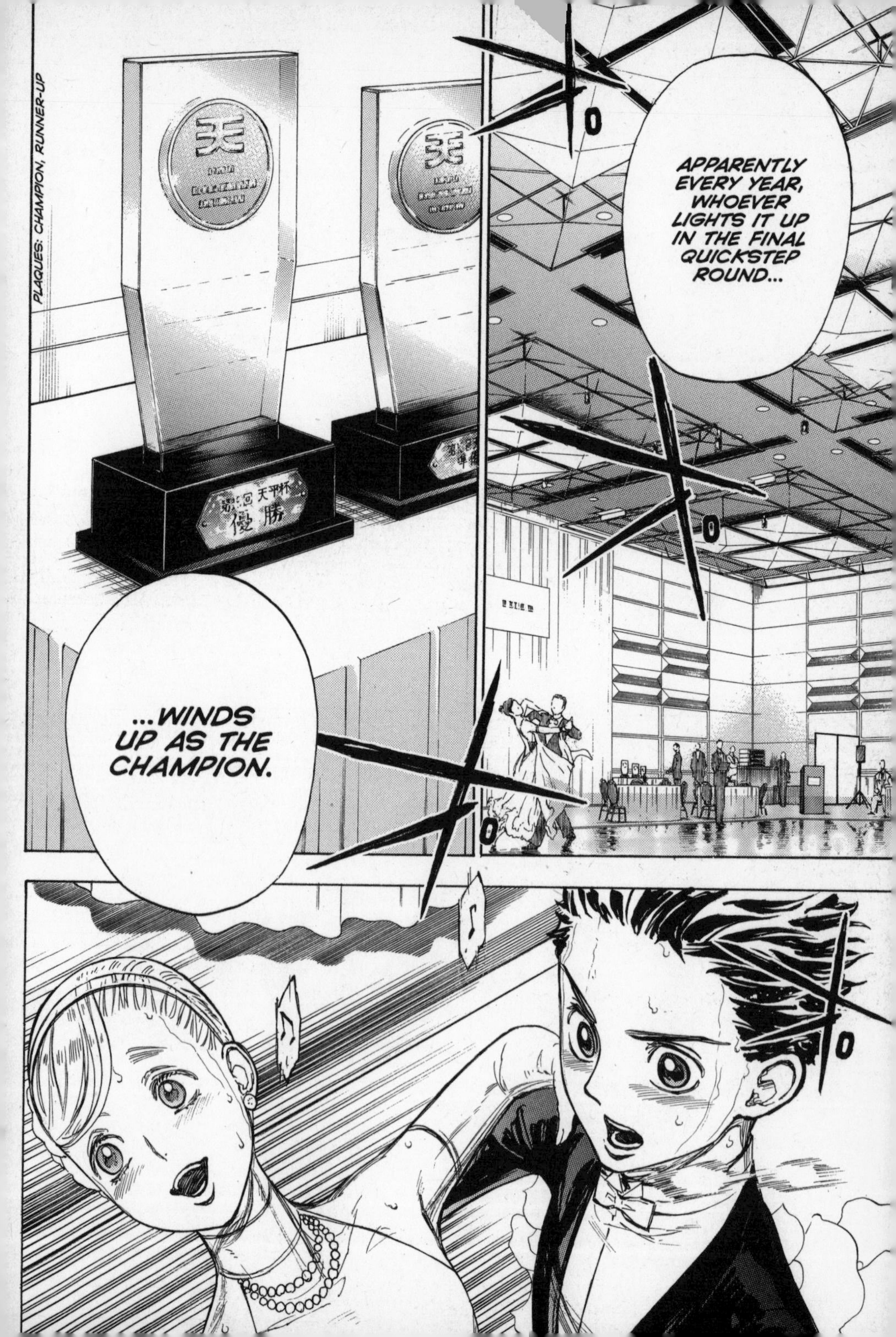
APPARENTLY EVERY YEAR, WHOEVER LIGHTS IT UP IN THE FINAL QUICKSTEP ROUND...
...WINDS UP AS THE CHAMPION.
PLAQUES: CHAMPION, RUNNER-UP

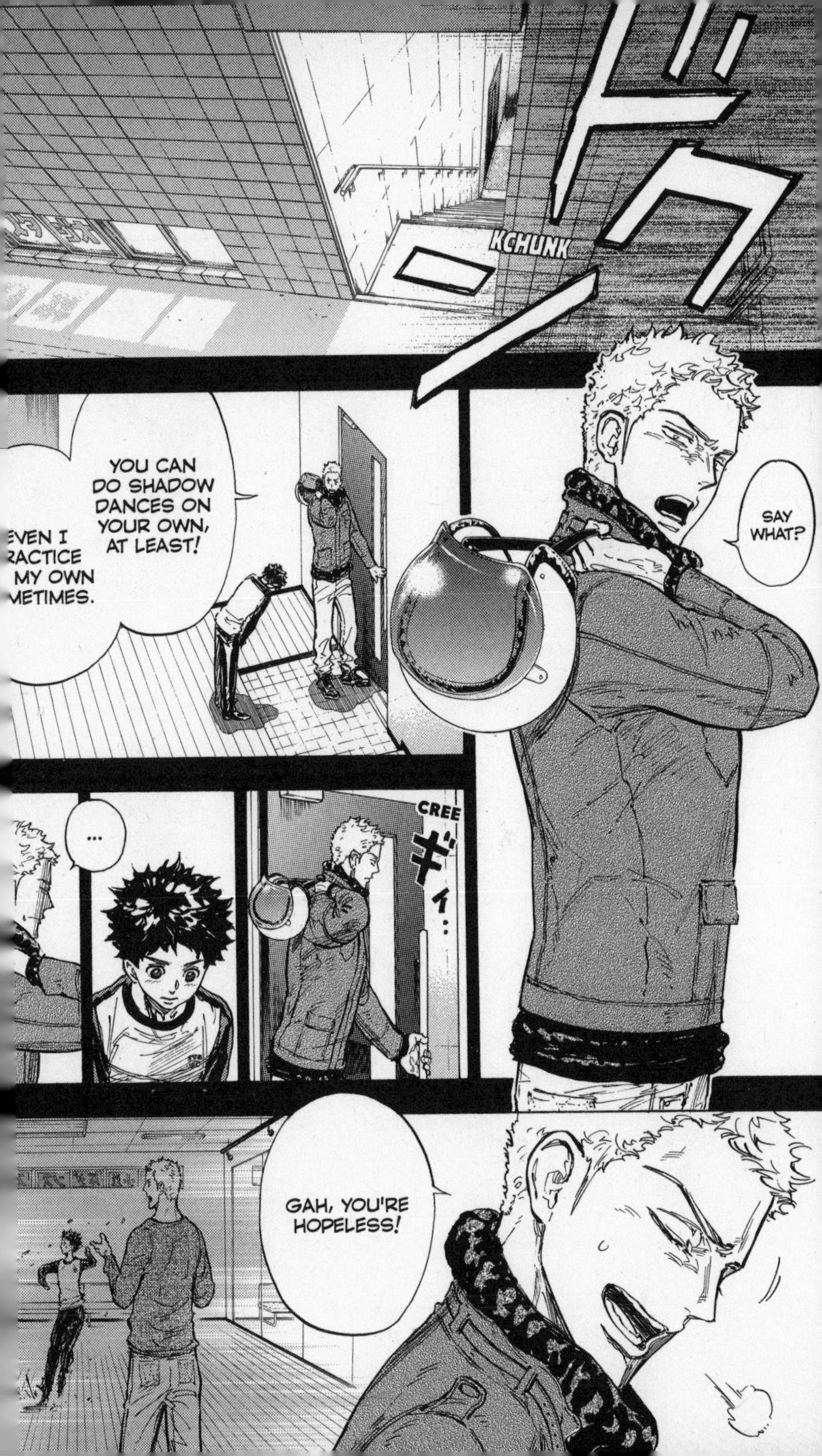
KCHUNK
SAY WHAT?
YOU CAN DO SHADOW DANCES ON YOUR OWN, AT LEAST!
EVEN I RACTICE MY OWN METIMES.
CREE
ギィ…
...
GAH, YOU'RE HOPELESS!

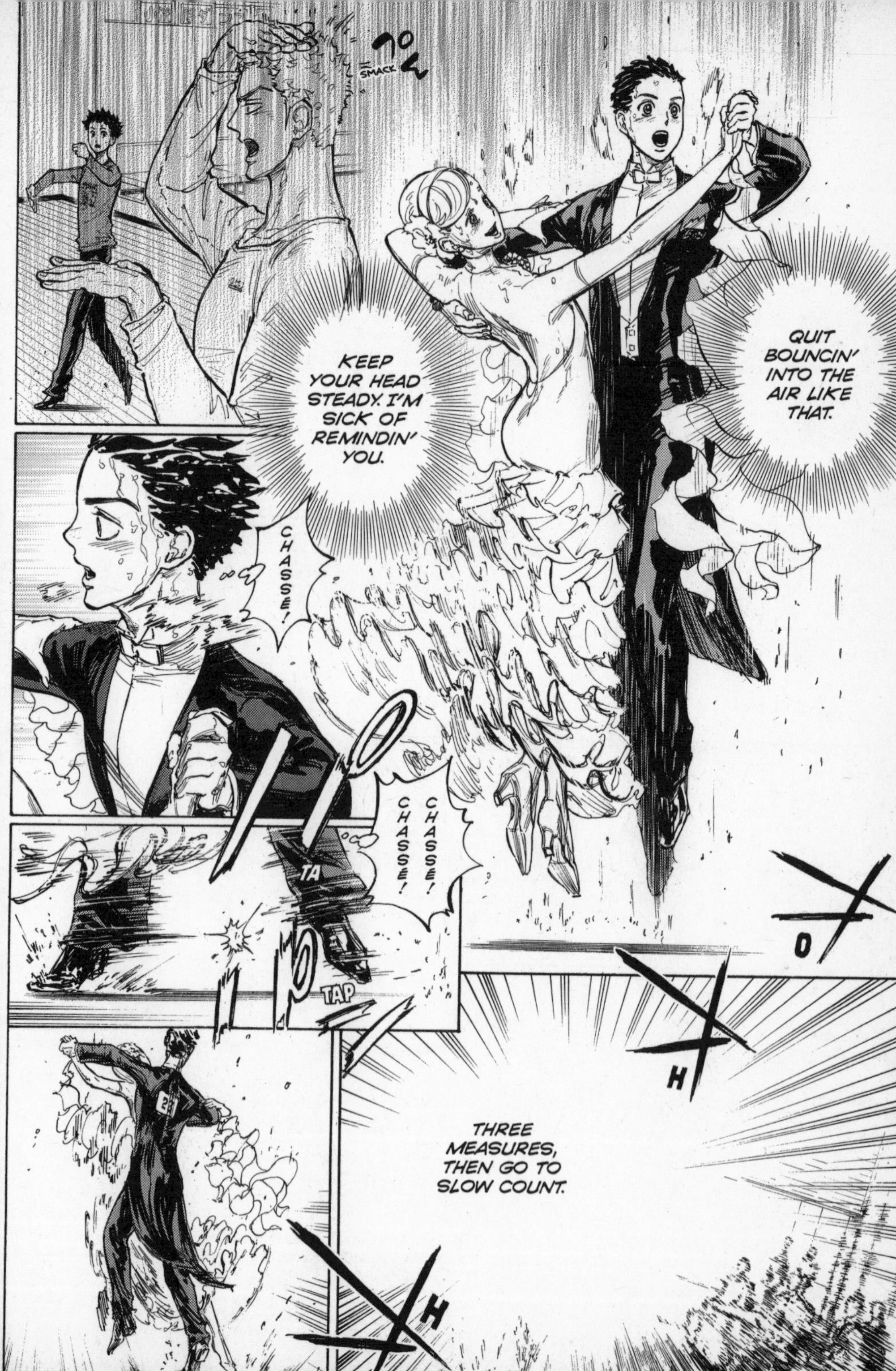
QUIT BOUNCIN' INTO THE AIR LIKE THAT.
KEEP YOUR HEAD STEADY. I'M SICK OF REMINDIN' YOU.
SMACK
CHASSÉ!
CHASSÉ!
CHASSÉ!
TA
TAP
O
H
THREE MEASURES, THEN GO TO SLOW COUNT.
H

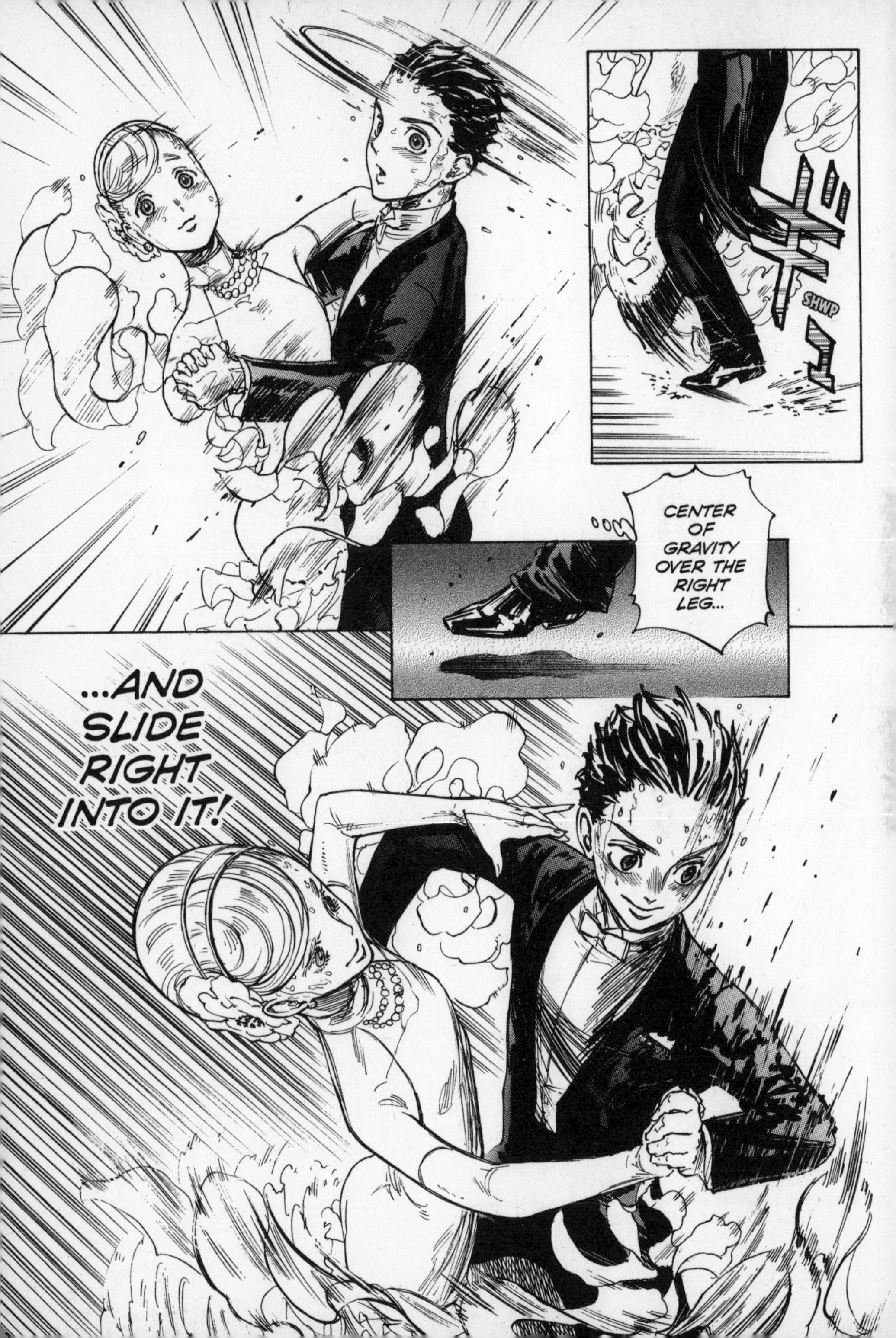
SHWP
CENTER OF GRAVITY OVER THE RIGHT LEG...
...AND SLIDE RIGHT INTO IT!

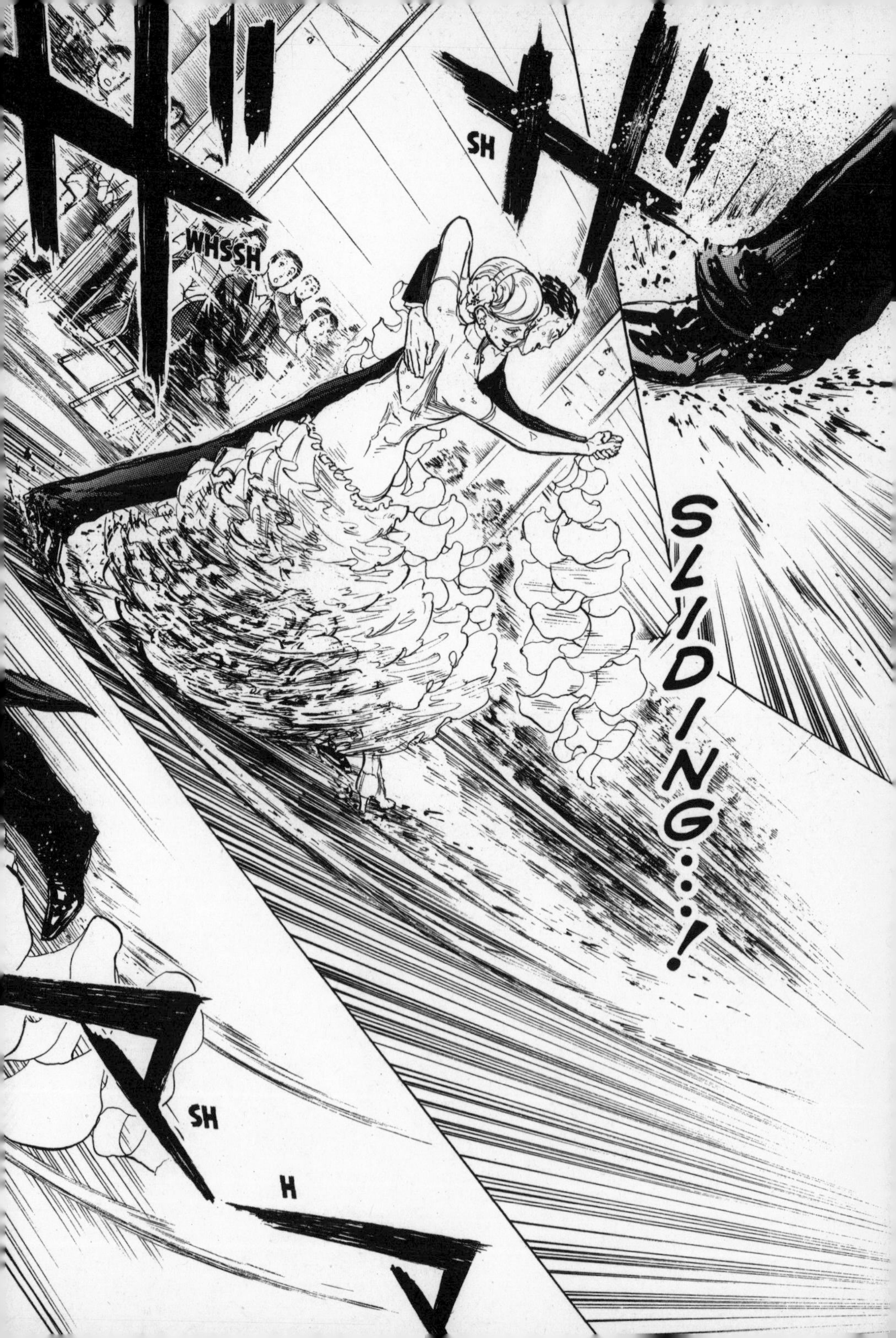
SH
WHSSH
SLIDING...!
SH
H

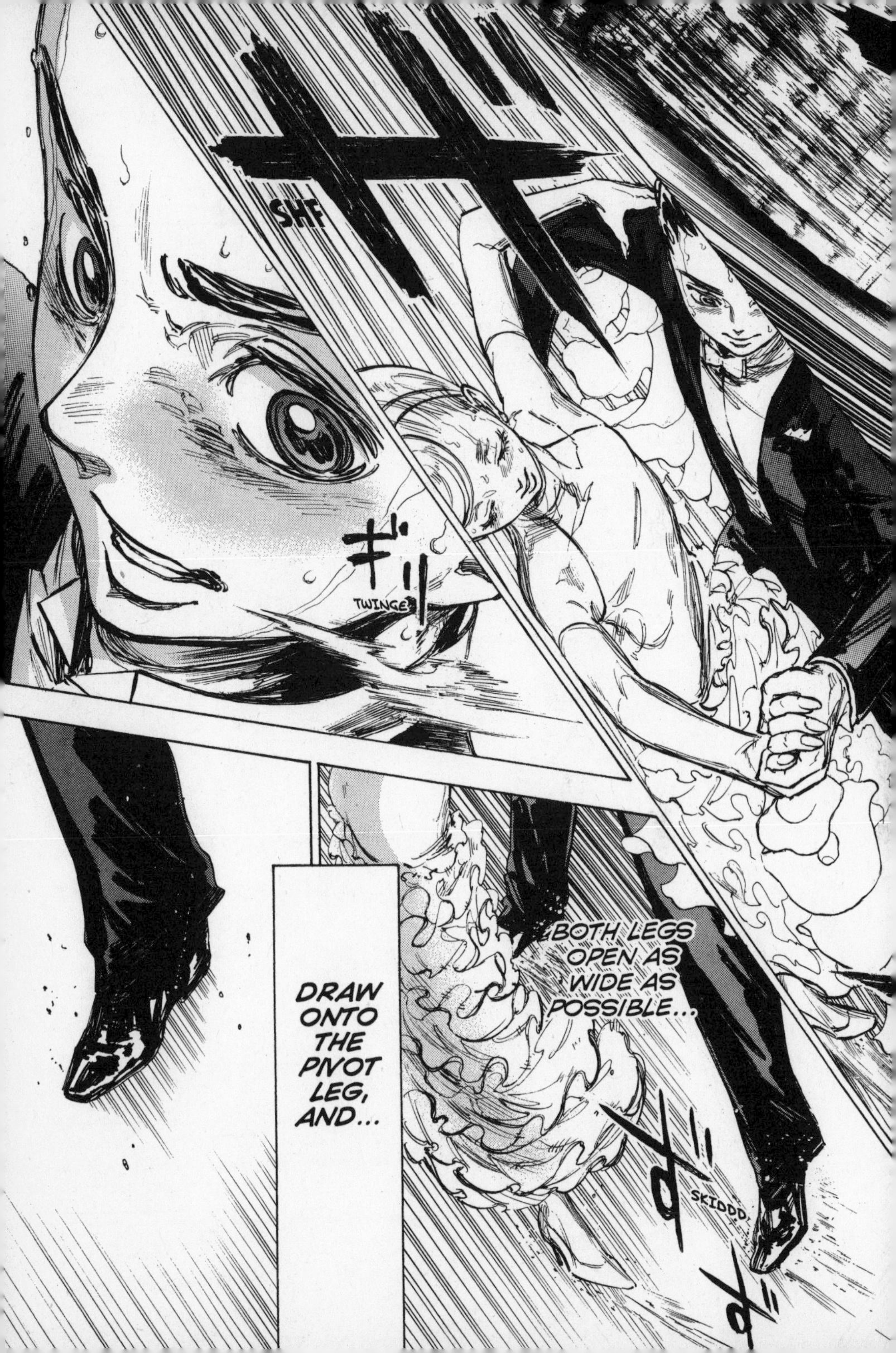
SHF
ギリ
TWINGE
BOTH LEGS OPEN AS WIDE AS POSSIBLE...
SKIDDD
DRAW ONTO THE PIVOT LEG, AND...

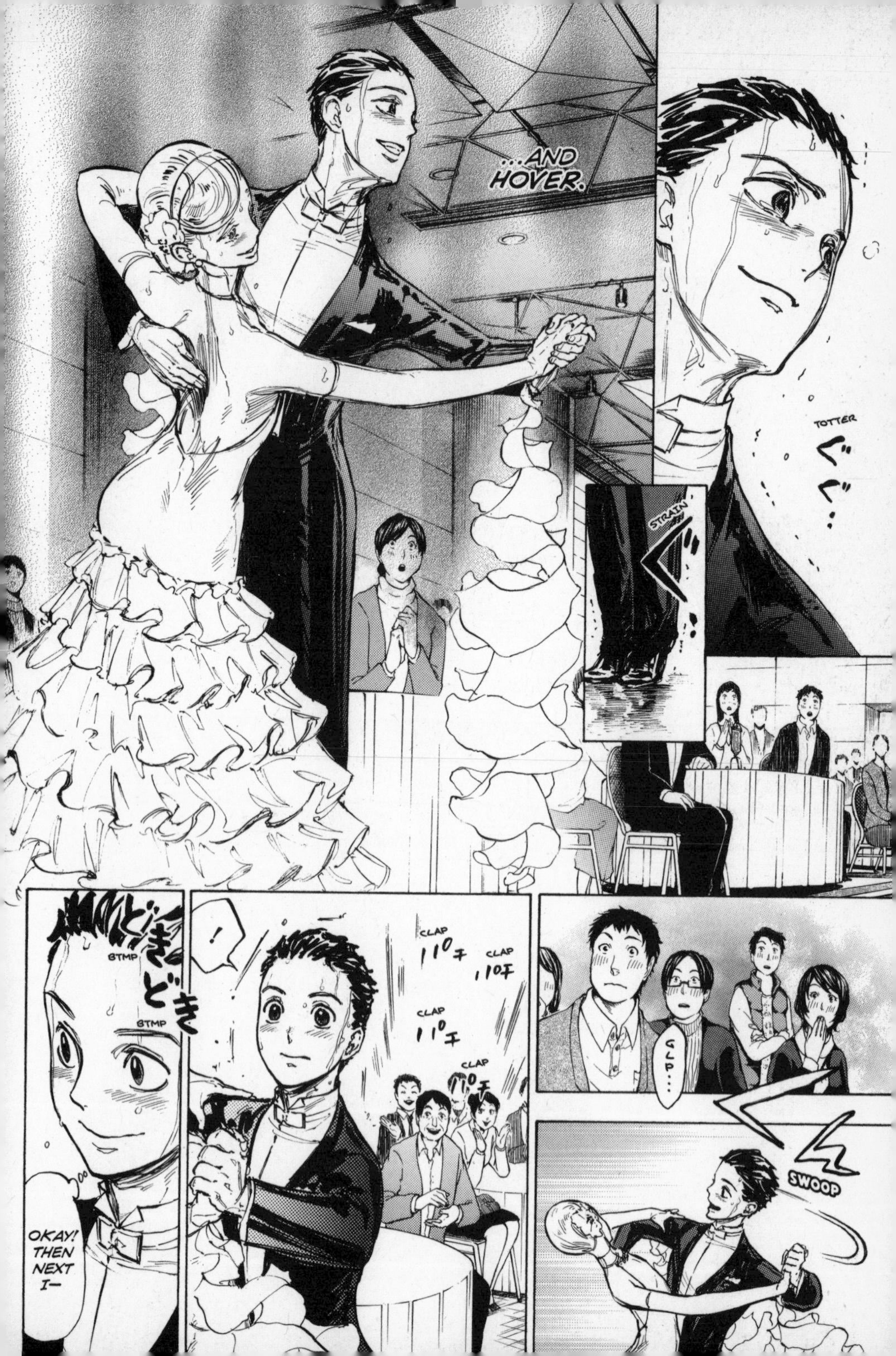
TOTTER
ぐぐ…
STRAIN
...AND HOVER.
GLP...
SWOOP
!
CLAP
CLAP
CLAP
CLAP
BTMP
BTMP
どき
どき
OKAY! THEN NEXT I—

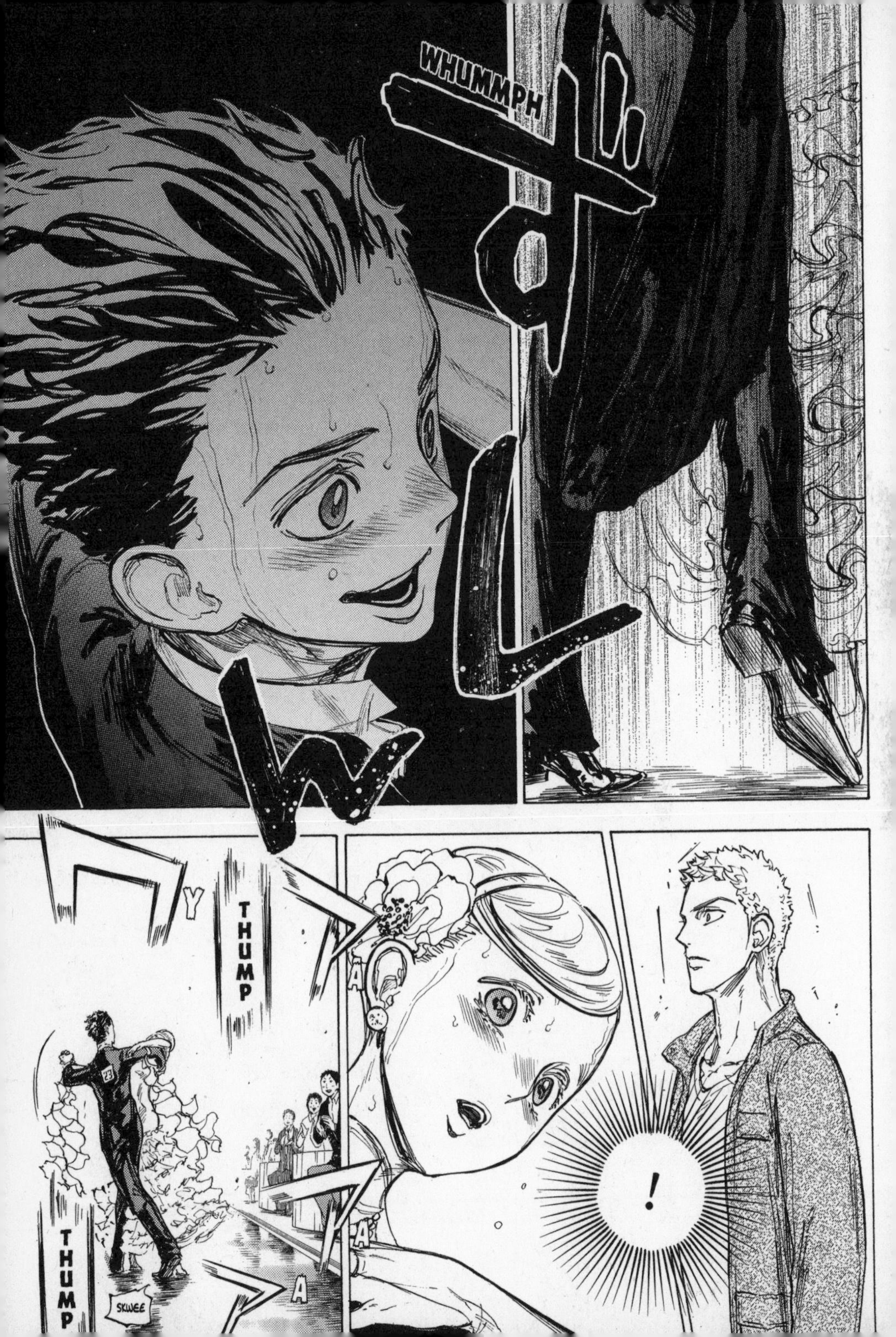
WHUMMPH
!
A
A
A
Y
THUMP
THUMP
SKWEE

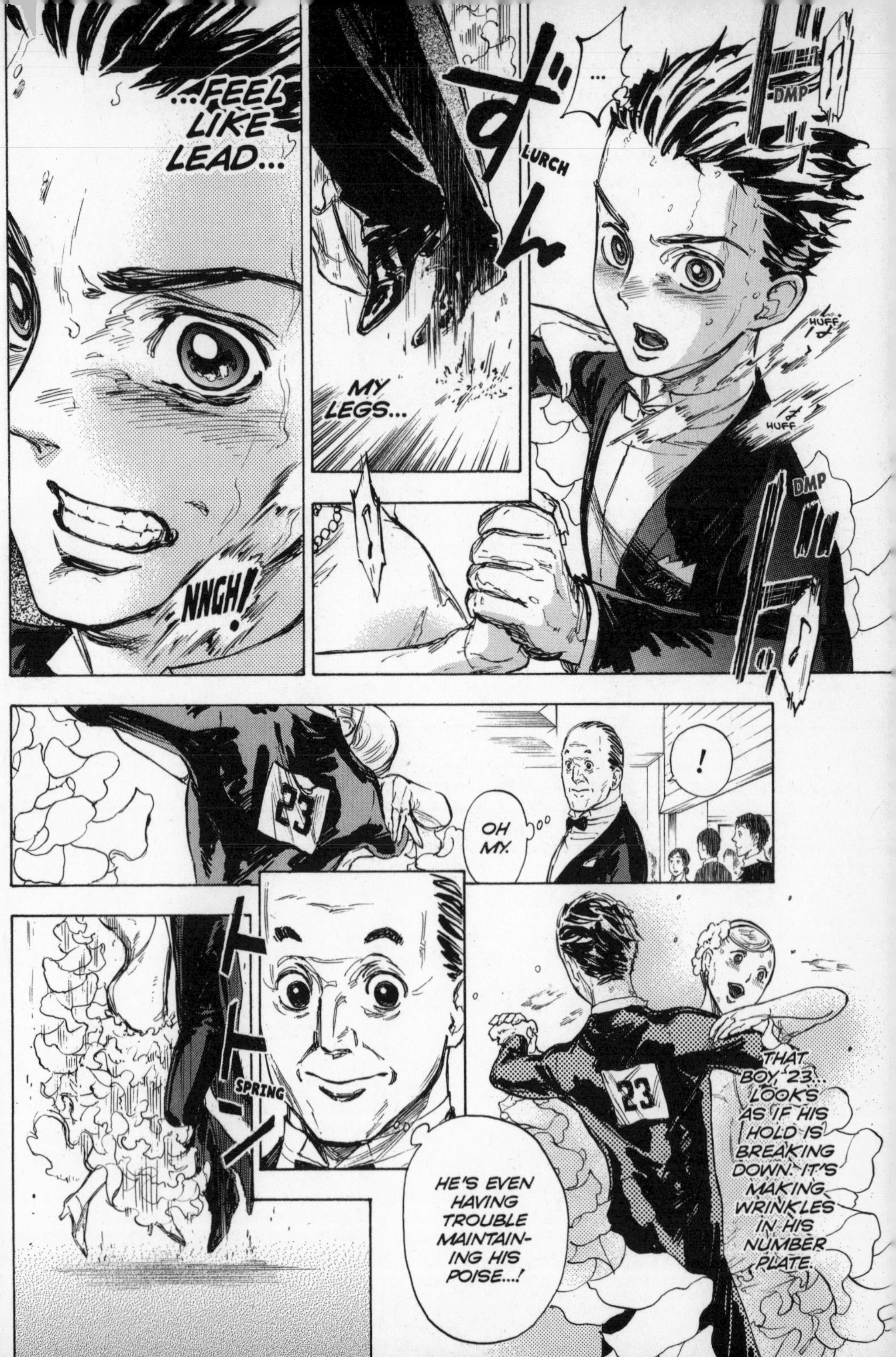
...
DMP
HUFF
HUFF
DMP
LURCH
MY LEGS...
...FEEL LIKE LEAD...
NNGH!
!
OH MY.
THAT BOY, 23... LOOKS AS IF HIS HOLD IS BREAKING DOWN. IT'S MAKING WRINKLES IN HIS NUMBER PLATE.
HE'S EVEN HAVING TROUBLE MAINTAIN-ING HIS POISE...!
SPRING

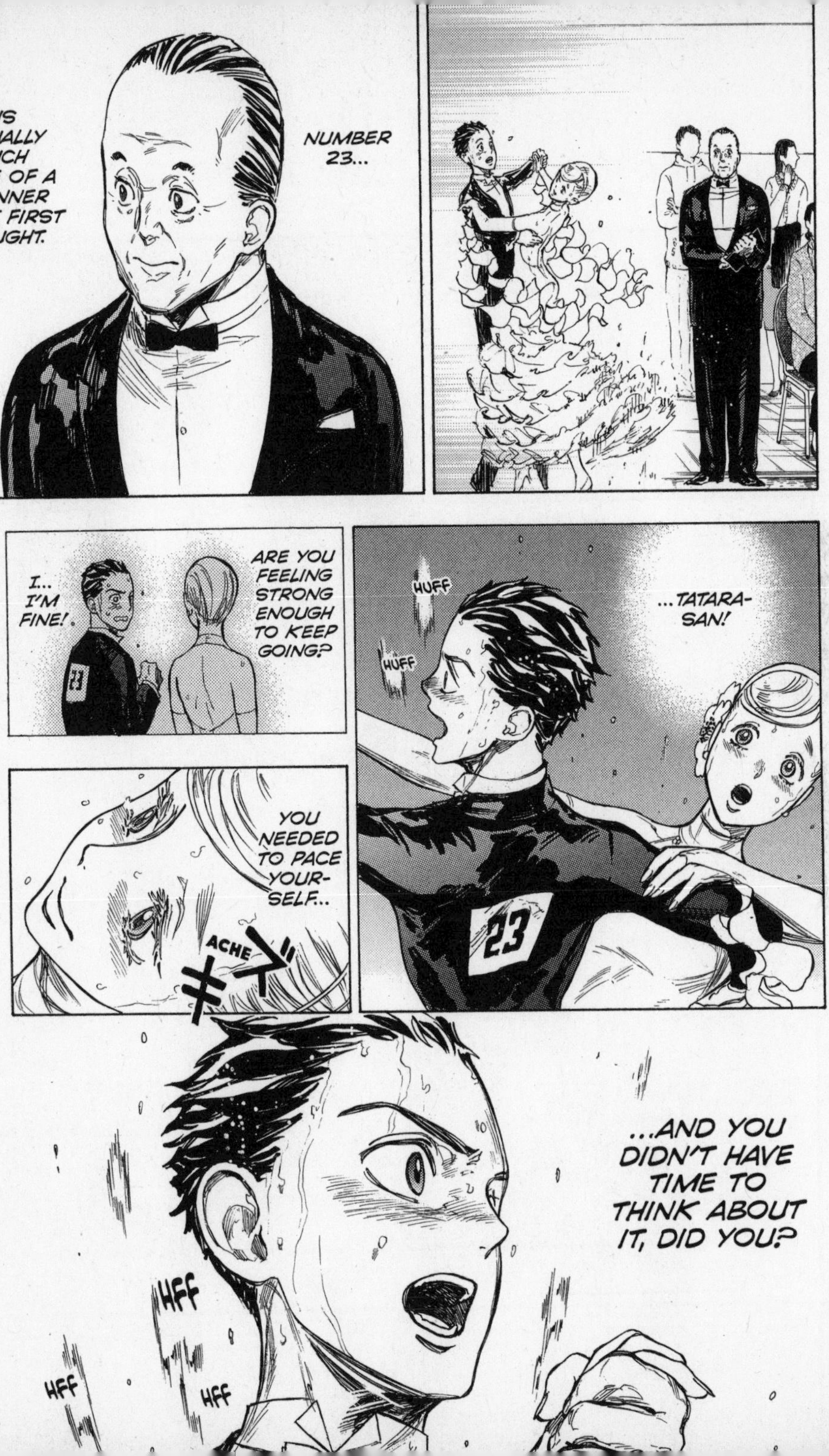
NUMBER 23...
...IS ACTUALLY MUCH MORE OF A BEGINNER THAN I FIRST THOUGHT.
HUFF
HUFF
...TATARA-SAN!
ARE YOU FEELING STRONG ENOUGH TO KEEP GOING?
I... I'M FINE!
YOU NEEDED TO PACE YOURSELF...
ACHE
...AND YOU DIDN'T HAVE TIME TO THINK ABOUT IT, DID YOU?
HFF
HFF
HFF

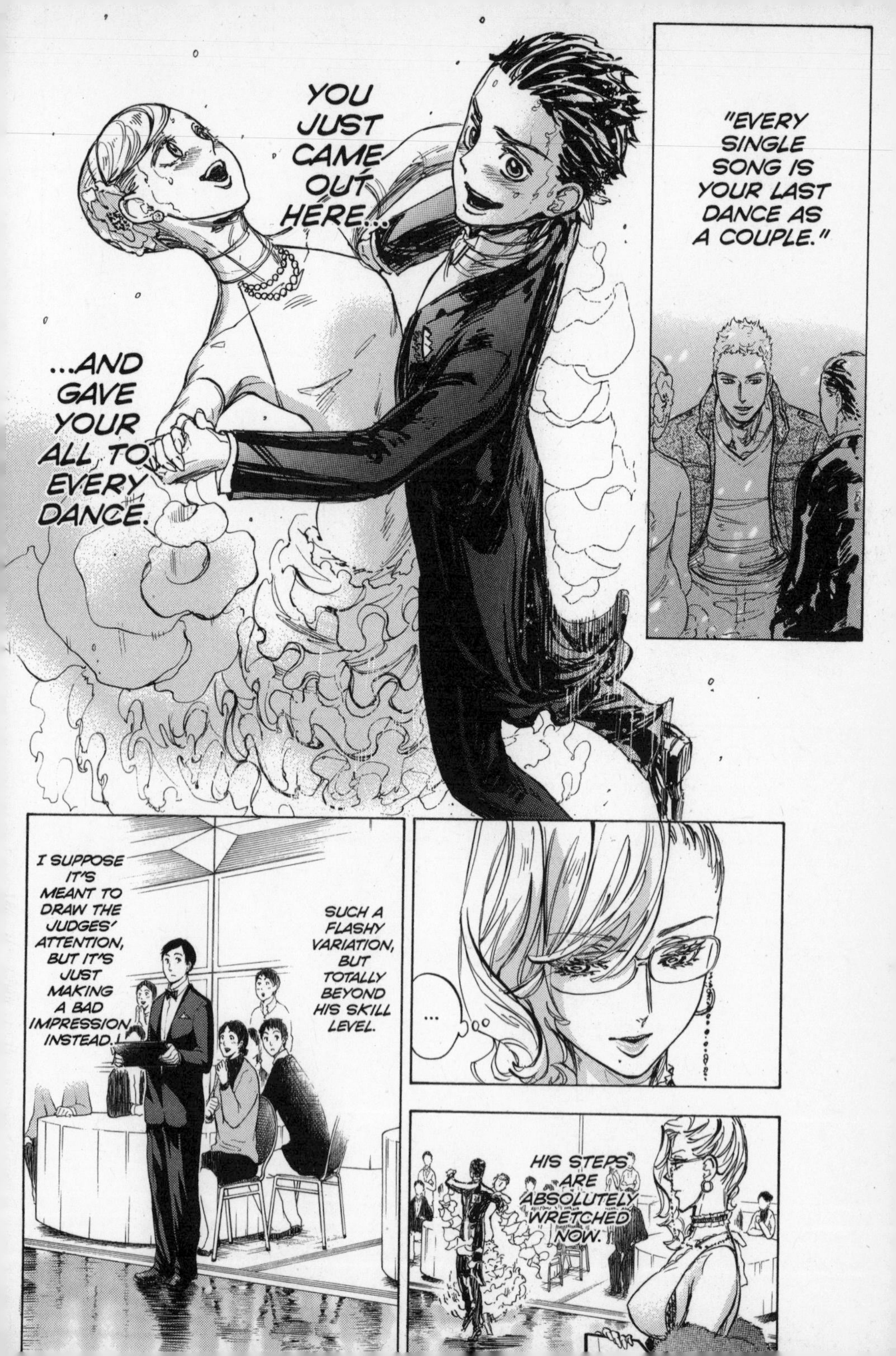
"EVERY SINGLE SONG IS YOUR LAST DANCE AS A COUPLE."
YOU JUST CAME OUT HERE...
...AND GAVE YOUR ALL TO EVERY DANCE.
...
HIS STEPS ARE ABSOLUTELY WRETCHED NOW.
SUCH A FLASHY VARIATION, BUT TOTALLY BEYOND HIS SKILL LEVEL.
I SUPPOSE IT'S MEANT TO DRAW THE JUDGES' ATTENTION, BUT IT'S JUST MAKING A BAD IMPRESSION INSTEAD...!

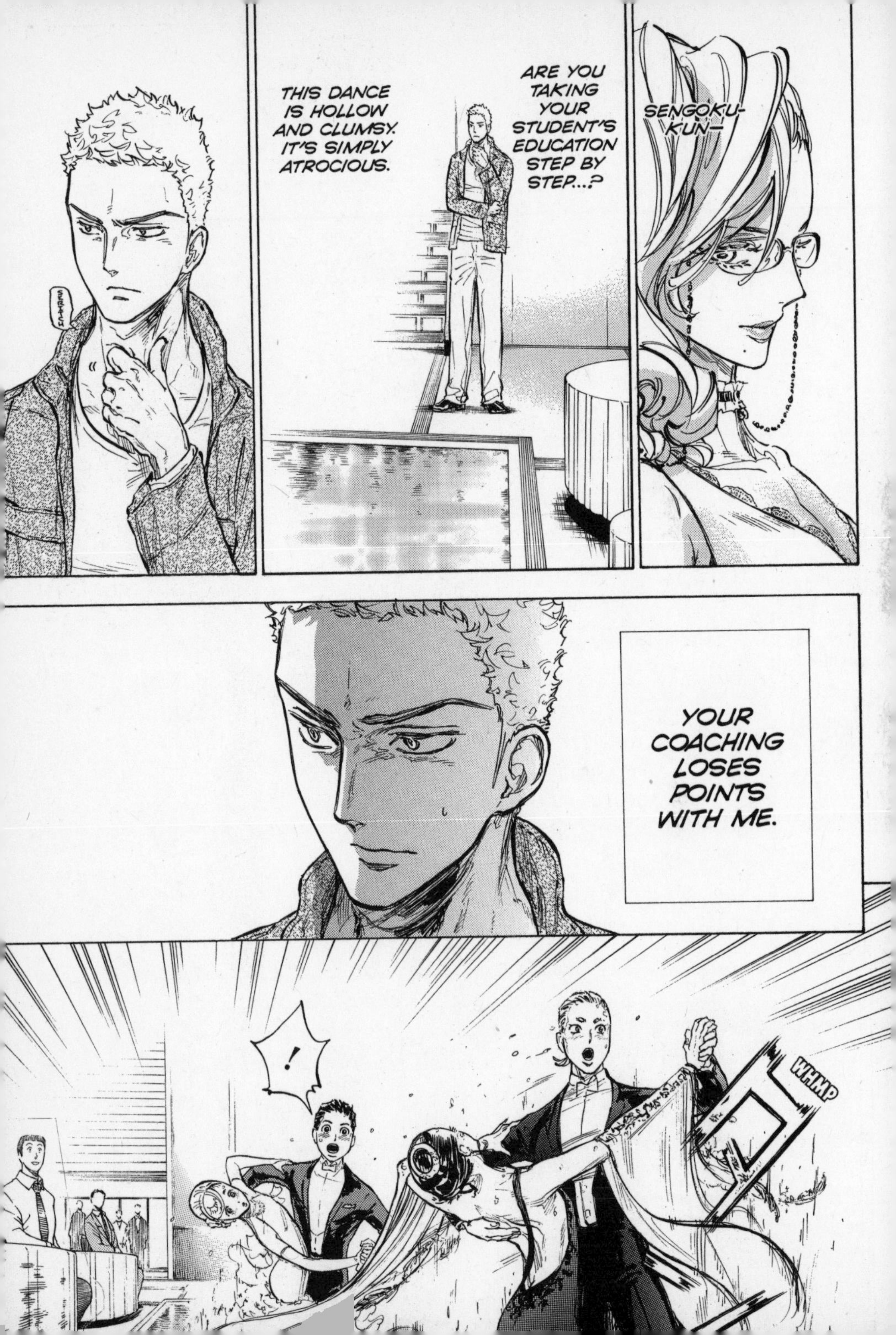
SENGOKU-KUN—
ARE YOU TAKING YOUR STUDENT'S EDUCATION STEP BY STEP...?
THIS DANCE IS HOLLOW AND CLUMSY. IT'S SIMPLY ATROCIOUS.
YOUR COACHING LOSES POINTS WITH ME.
WHMP
!

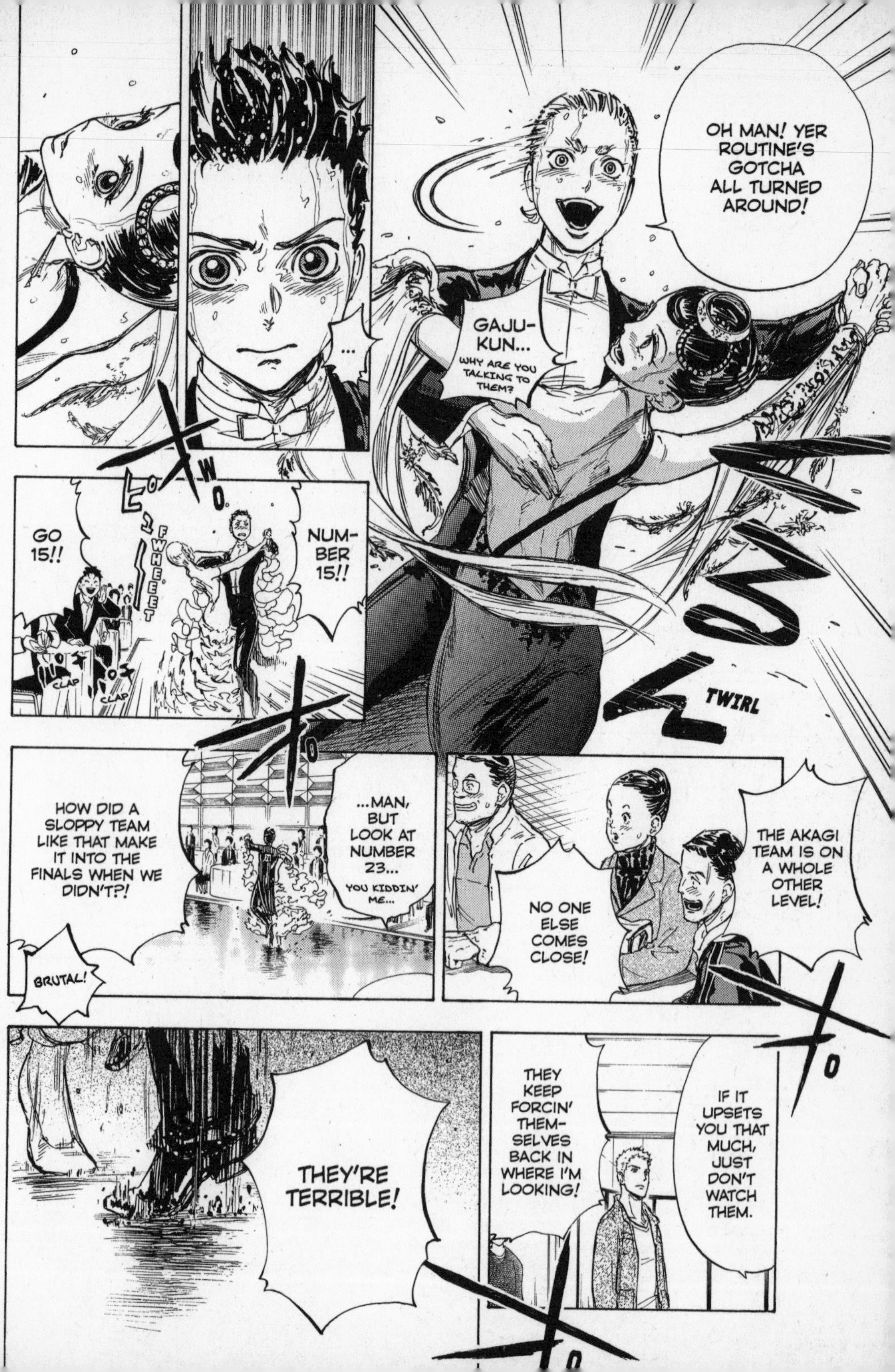
OH MAN! YER ROUTINE'S GOTCHA ALL TURNED AROUND!
GAJU-KUN... WHY ARE YOU TALKING TO THEM?
TWIRL
...
WO
O
NUMBER 15!!
FWHEEET
GO 15!!
CLAP
CLAP
O
THE AKAGI TEAM IS ON A WHOLE OTHER LEVEL!
NO ONE ELSE COMES CLOSE!
...MAN, BUT LOOK AT NUMBER 23...
YOU KIDDIN' ME...
HOW DID A SLOPPY TEAM LIKE THAT MAKE IT INTO THE FINALS WHEN WE DIDN'T?!
BRUTAL!
O
IF IT UPSETS YOU THAT MUCH, JUST DON'T WATCH THEM.
THEY KEEP FORCIN' THEMSELVES BACK IN WHERE I'M LOOKING!
THEY'RE TERRIBLE!
O

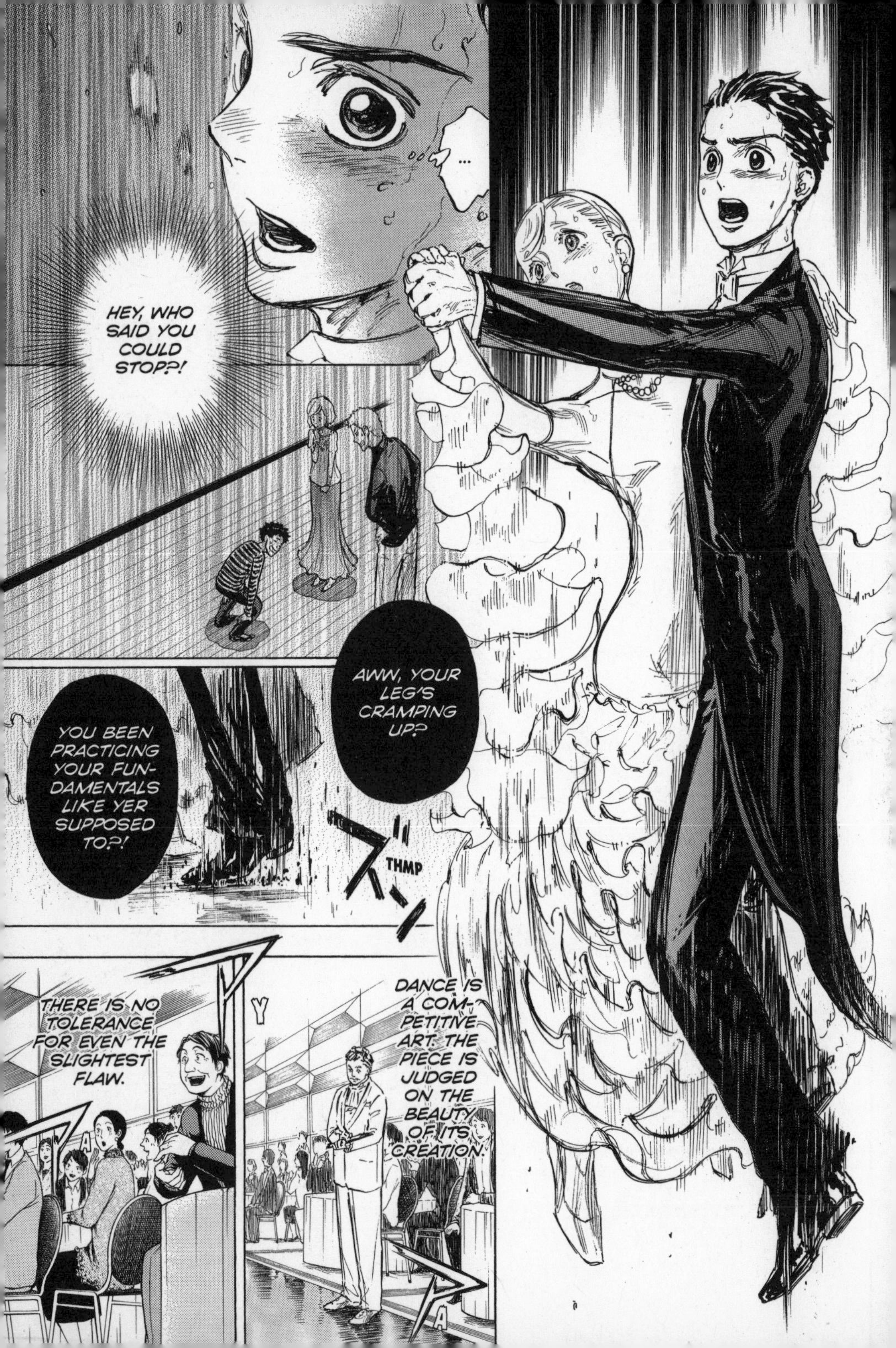
...
HEY, WHO SAID YOU COULD STOP?!
AWW, YOUR LEG'S CRAMPING UP?
YOU BEEN PRACTICING YOUR FUN-DAMENTALS LIKE YER SUPPOSED TO?!
THMP
DANCE IS A COM-PETITIVE ART. THE PIECE IS JUDGED ON THE BEAUTY OF ITS CREATION.
THERE IS NO TOLERANCE FOR EVEN THE SLIGHTEST FLAW.

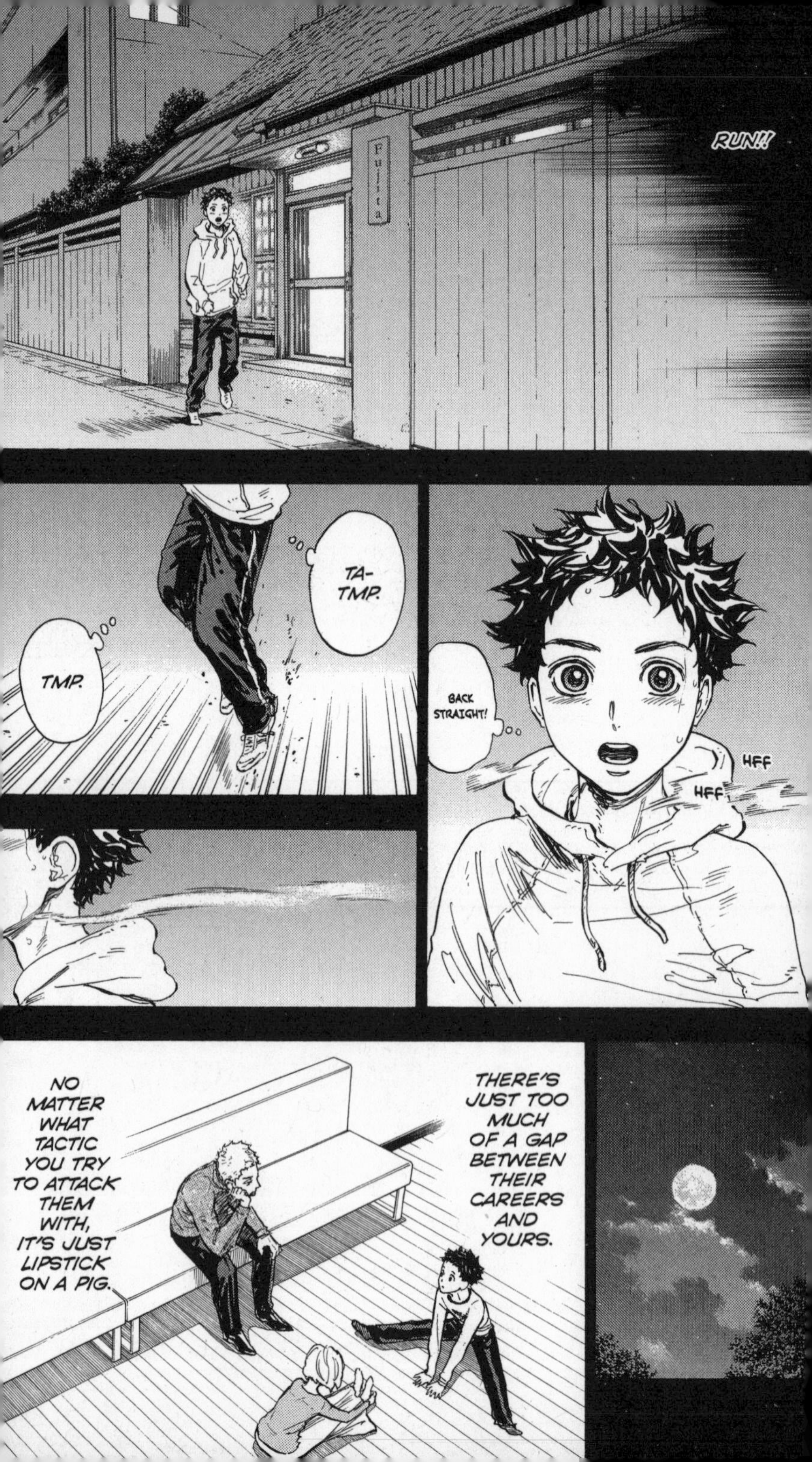
RUN!!
BACK STRAIGHT!
HFF
HFF
TA-TMP.
TMP.
THERE'S JUST TOO MUCH OF A GAP BETWEEN THEIR CAREERS AND YOURS.
NO MATTER WHAT TACTIC YOU TRY TO ATTACK THEM WITH, IT'S JUST LIPSTICK ON A PIG.

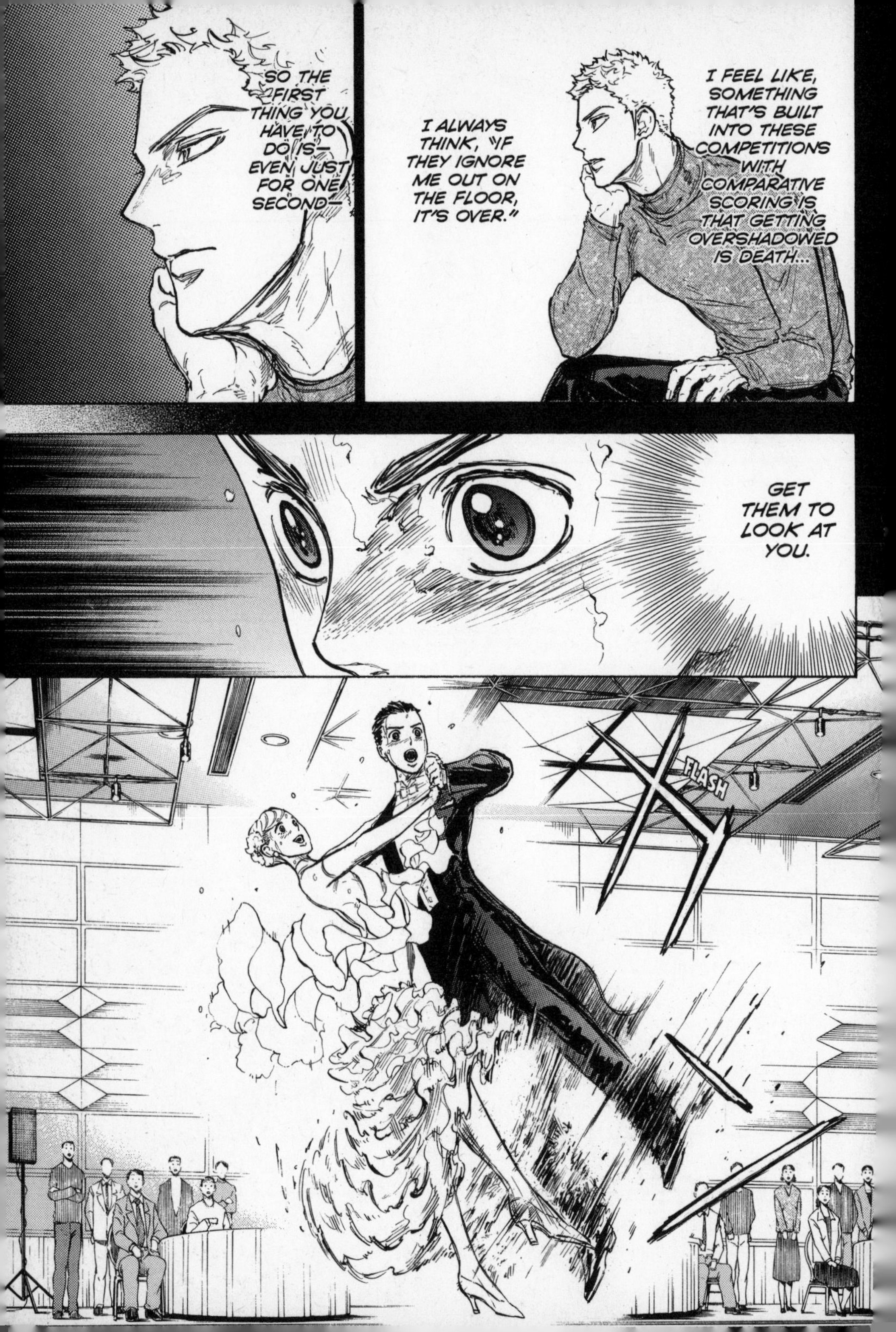
I FEEL LIKE, SOMETHING THAT'S BUILT INTO THESE COMPETITIONS WITH COMPARATIVE SCORING IS THAT GETTING OVERSHADOWED IS DEATH...
I ALWAYS THINK, "IF THEY IGNORE ME OUT ON THE FLOOR, IT'S OVER."
SO THE FIRST THING YOU HAVE TO DO IS— EVEN JUST FOR ONE SECOND—
GET THEM TO LOOK AT YOU.
FLASH

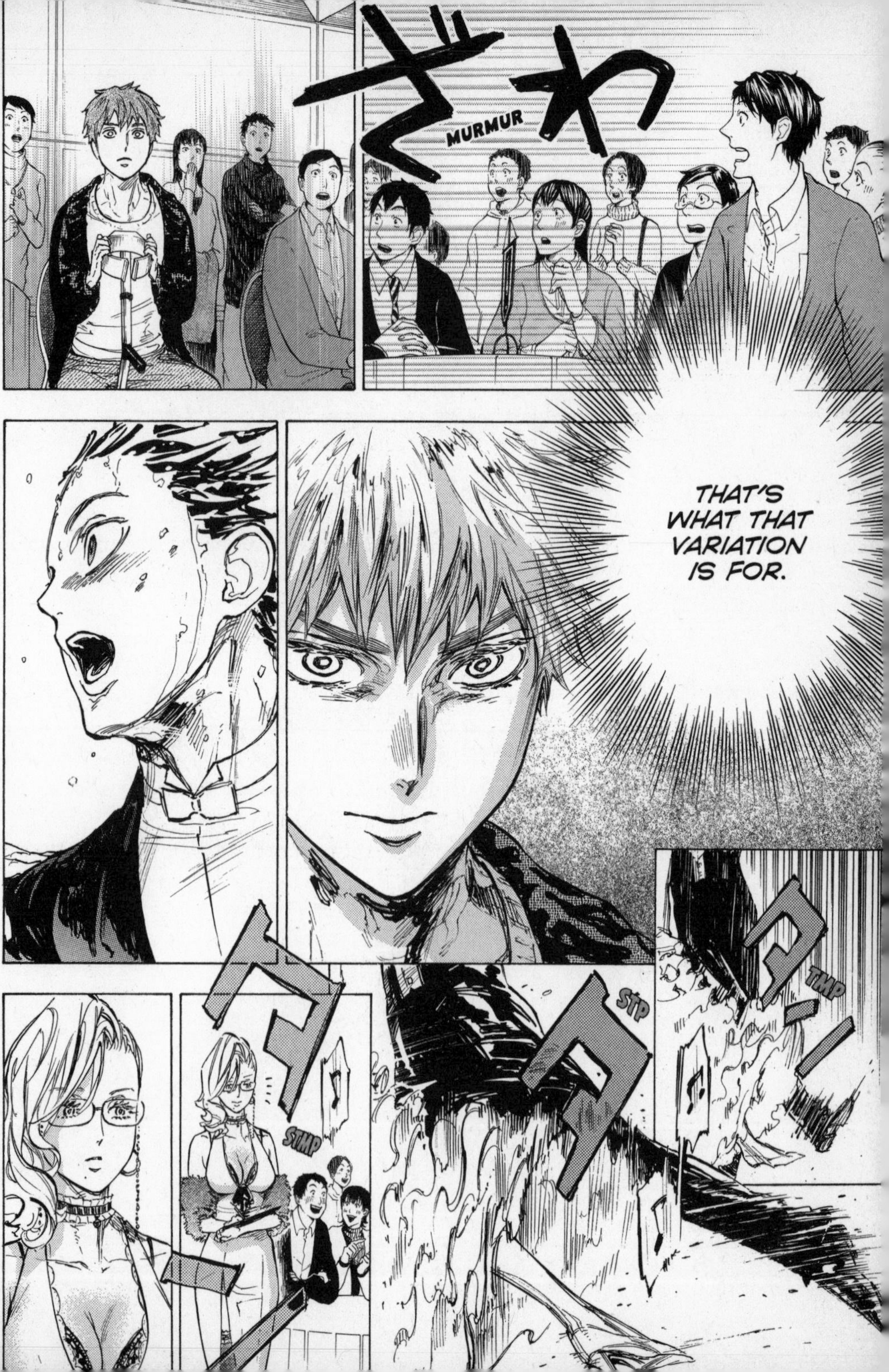
ざわ
MURMUR
THAT'S WHAT THAT VARIATION IS FOR.
TMP
STP
STMP

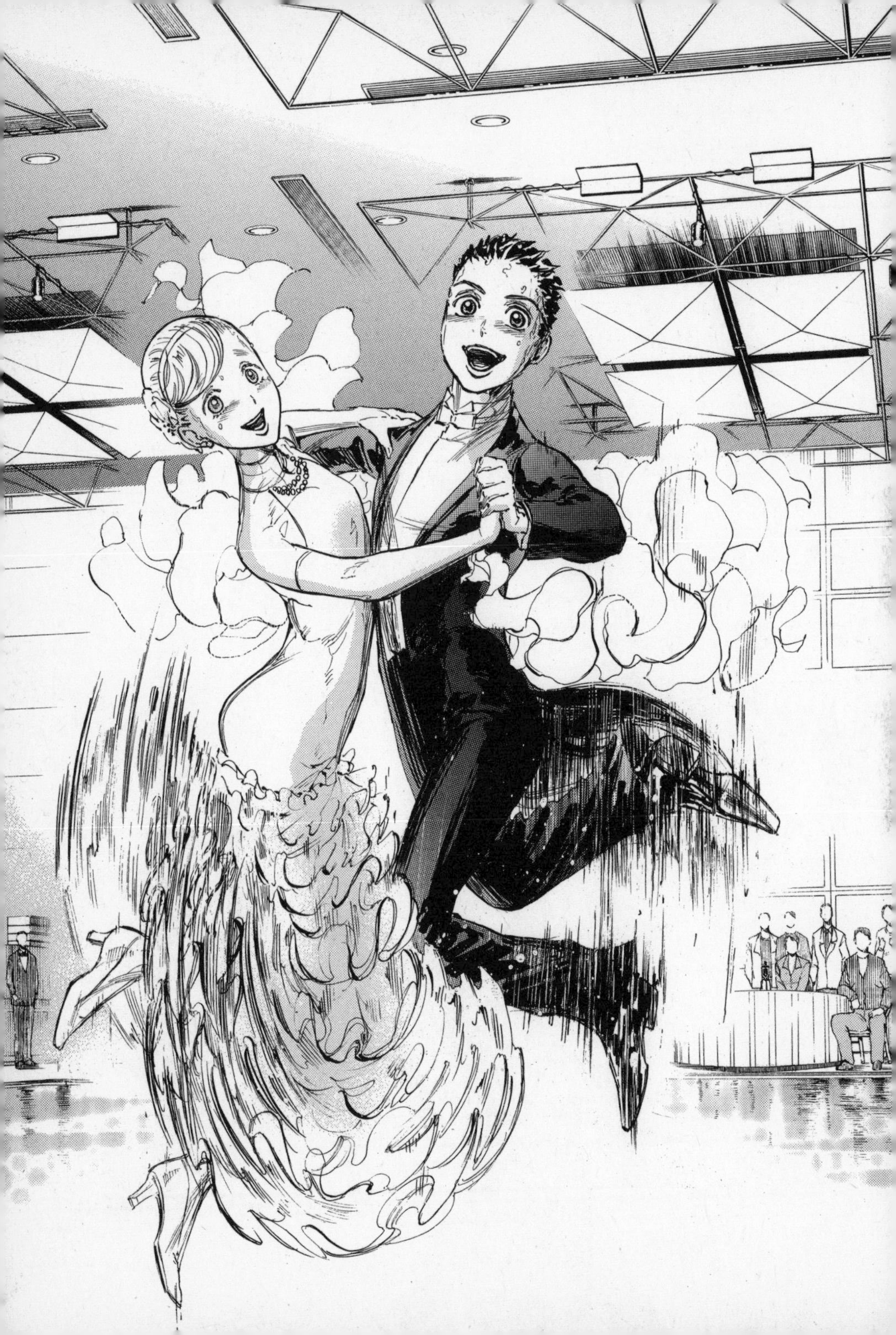

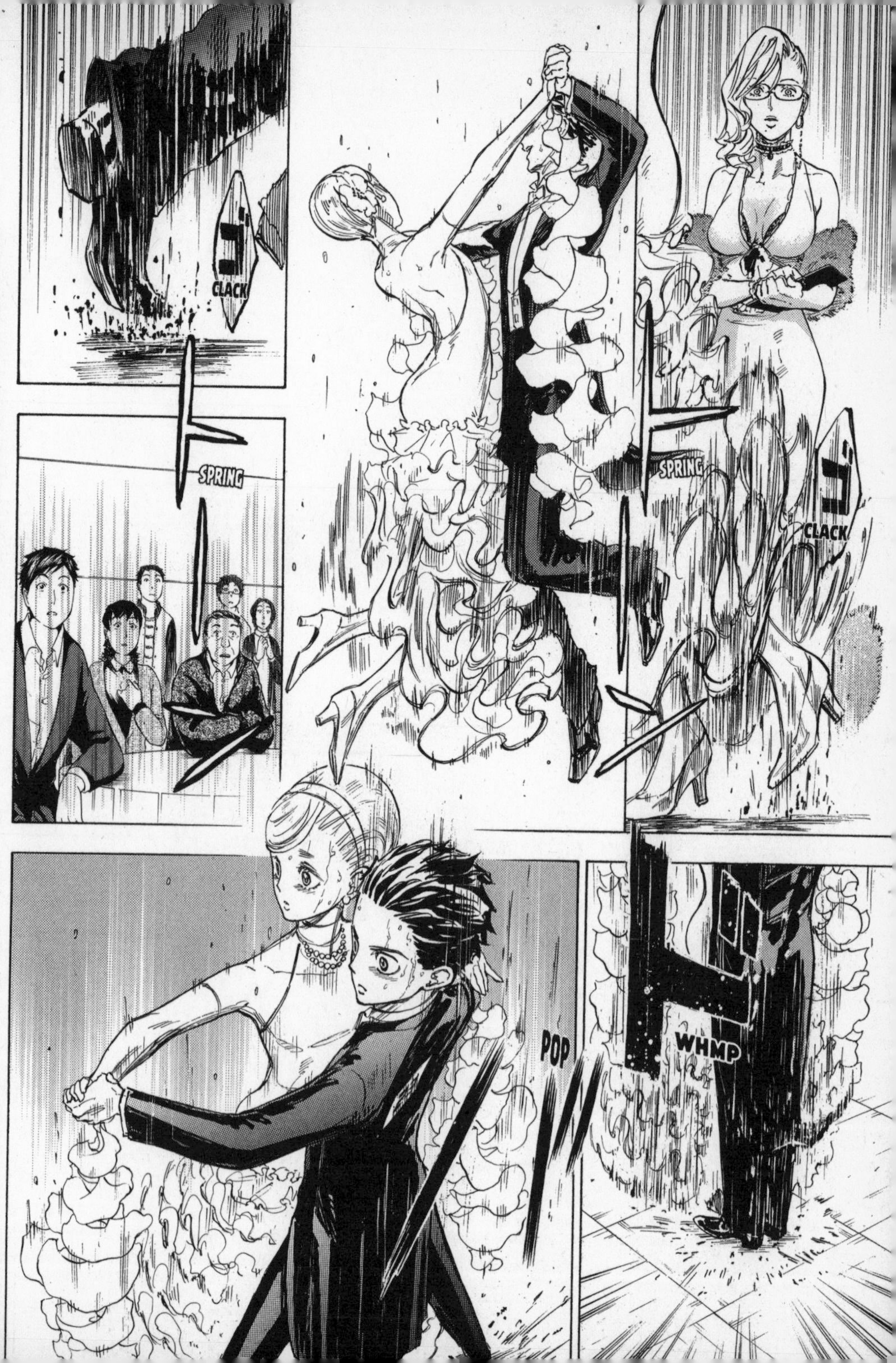
SPRING
ゴ
CLACK
ゴ
CLACK
SPRING
WHMP
POP

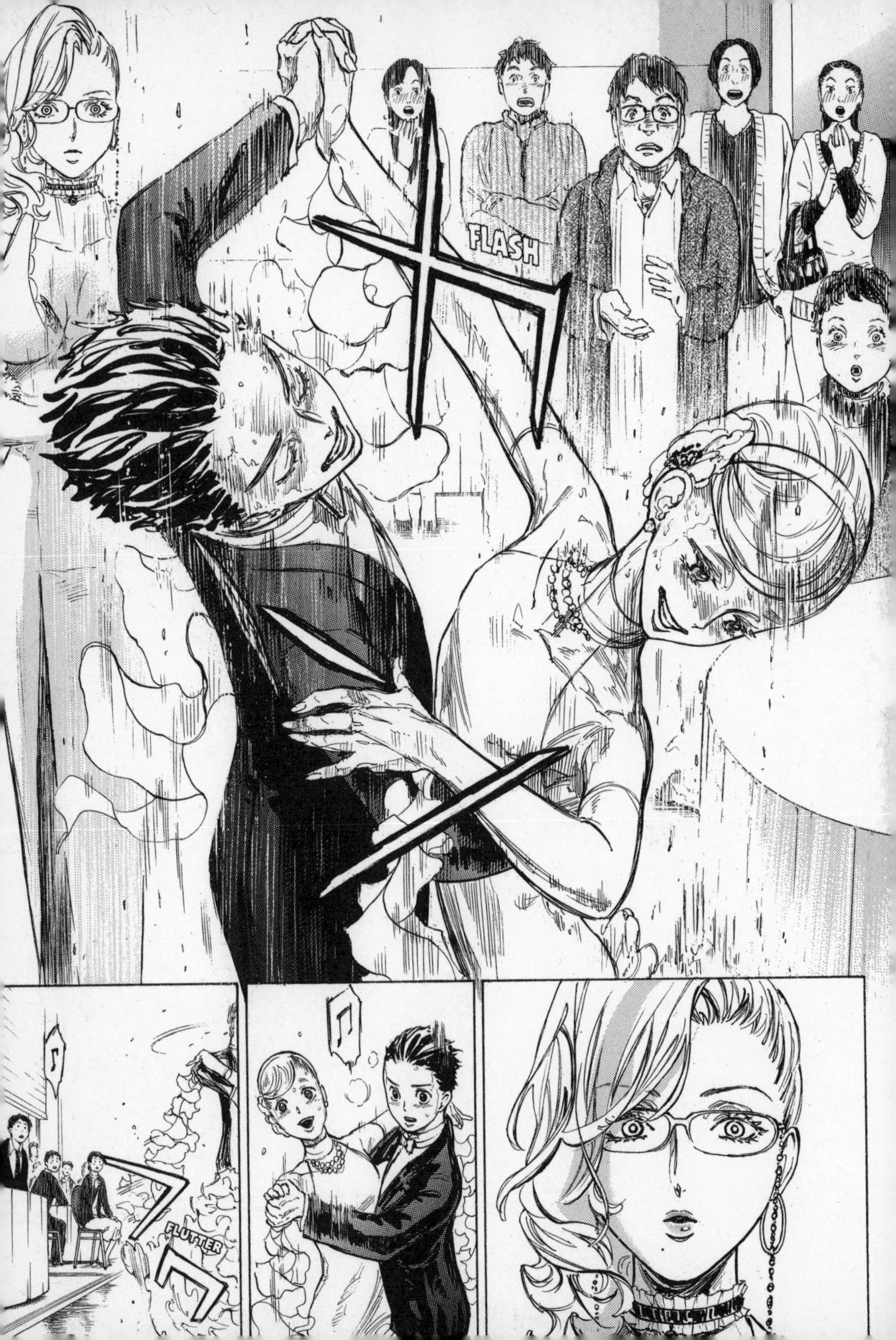
FLASH
FLUTTER

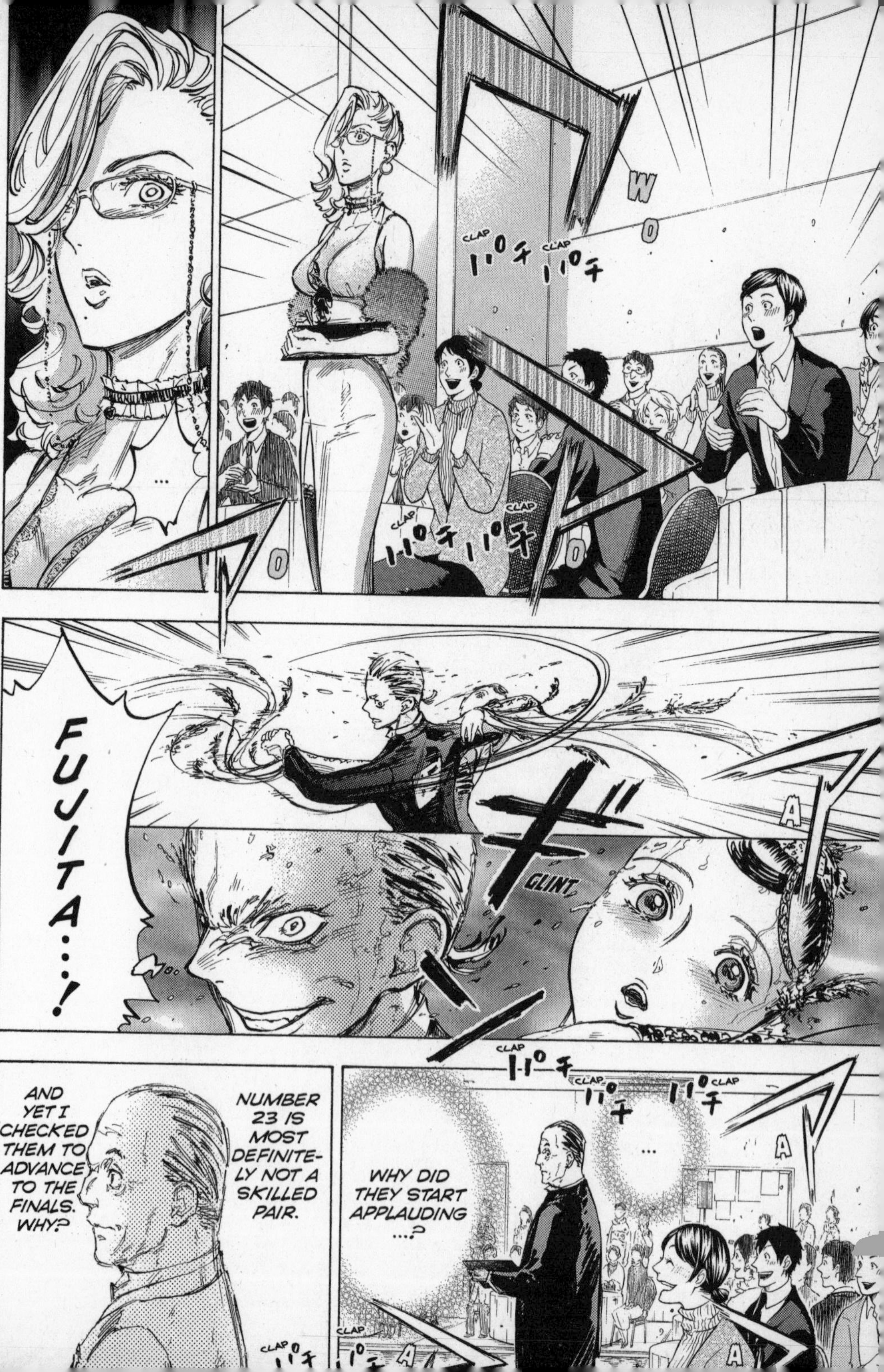
W
O
CLAP パチ CLAP パチ
CLAP パチ CLAP パチ
O
O
...
A
GLINT
FUJITA...!
CLAP パチ CLAP パチ CLAP パチ
A
...
WHY DID THEY START APPLAUDING ...?
A
A
CLAP パチ パチ
NUMBER 23 IS MOST DEFINITE-LY NOT A SKILLED PAIR.
AND YET I CHECKED THEM TO ADVANCE TO THE FINALS. WHY?

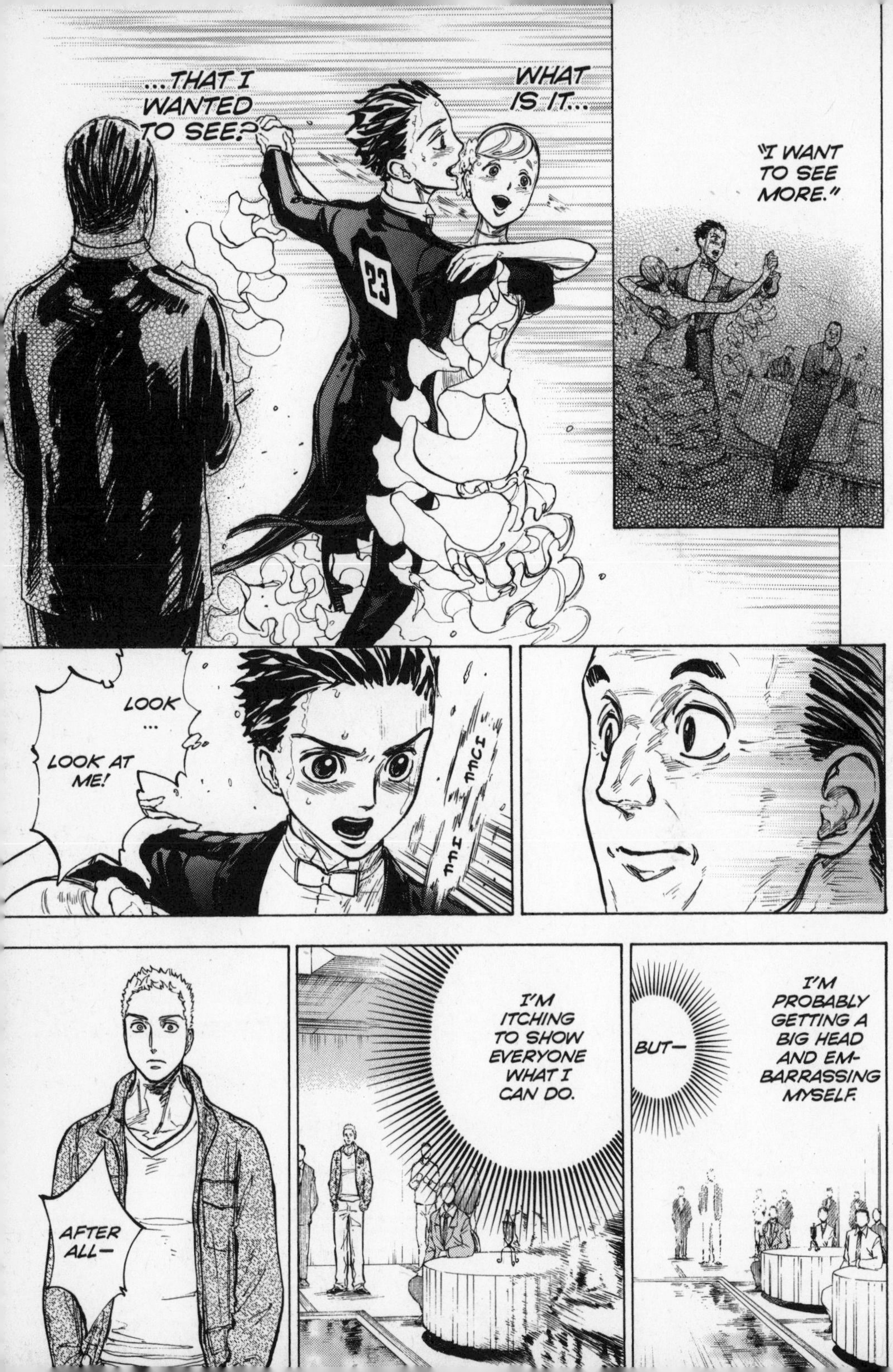
"I WANT TO SEE MORE."
WHAT IS IT...
...THAT I WANTED TO SEE?
LOOK ... LOOK AT ME!
HUFF HUFF
I'M PROBABLY GETTING A BIG HEAD AND EMBARRASSING MYSELF.
BUT—
I'M ITCHING TO SHOW EVERYONE WHAT I CAN DO.
AFTER ALL—

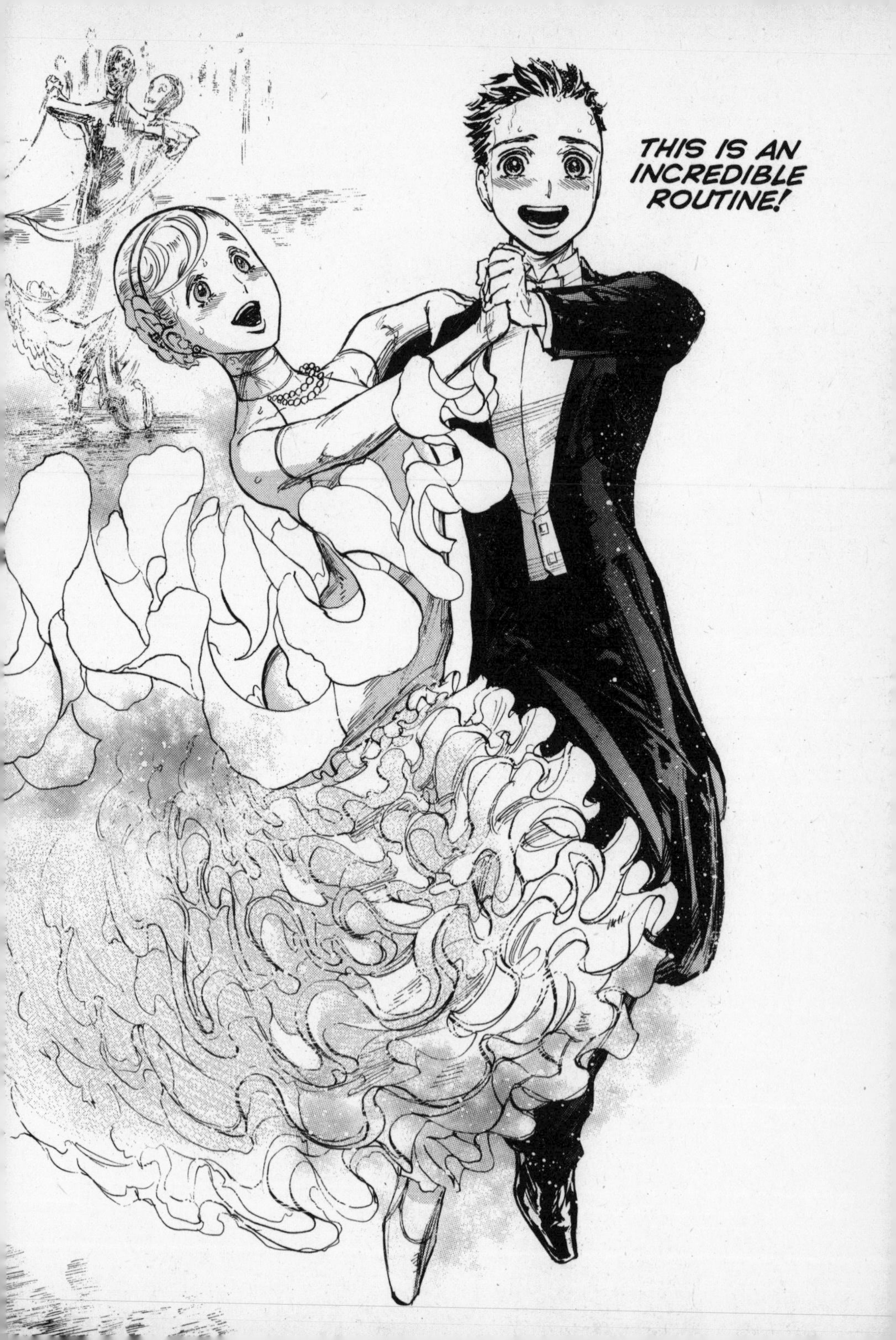
THIS IS AN INCREDIBLE ROUTINE!

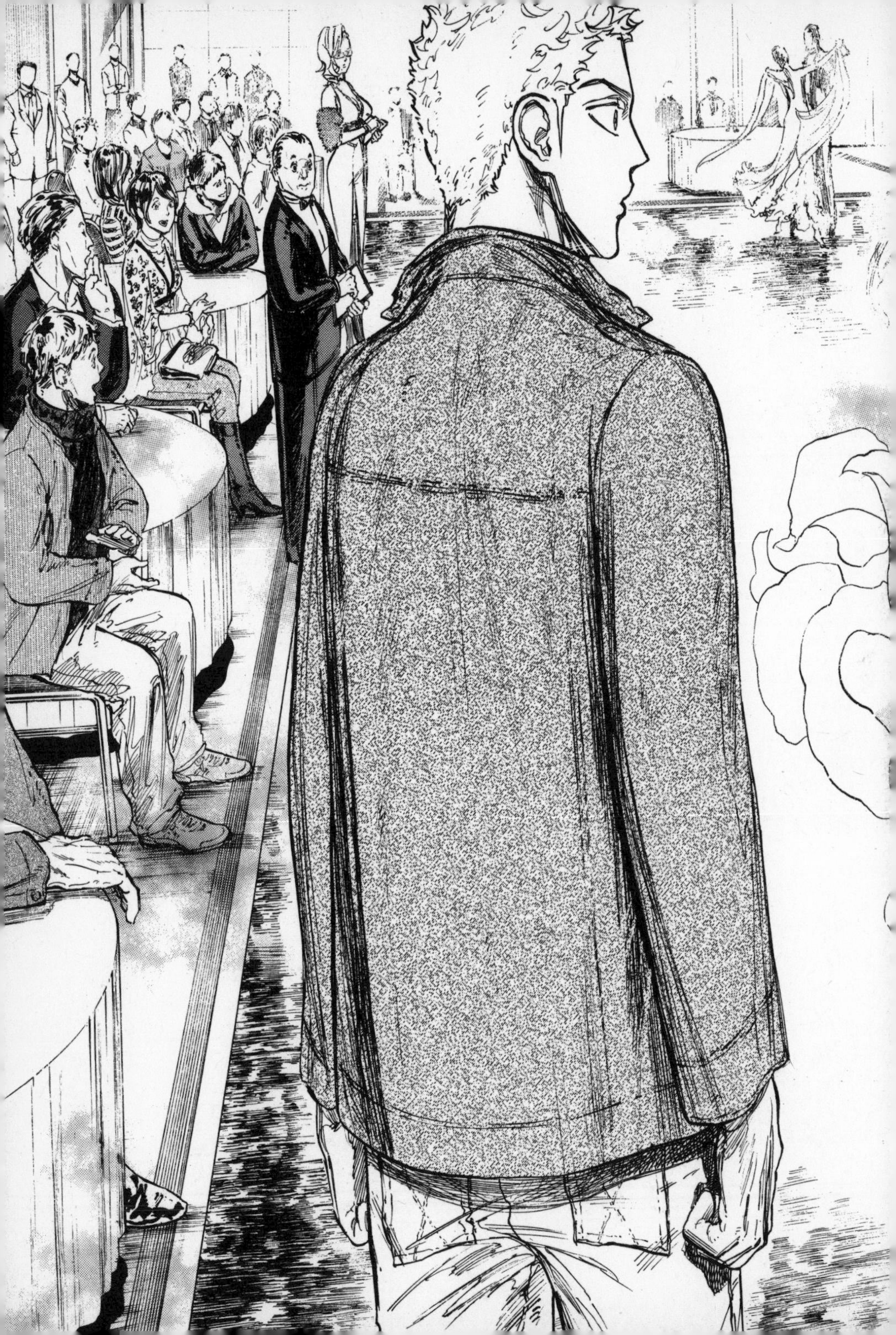

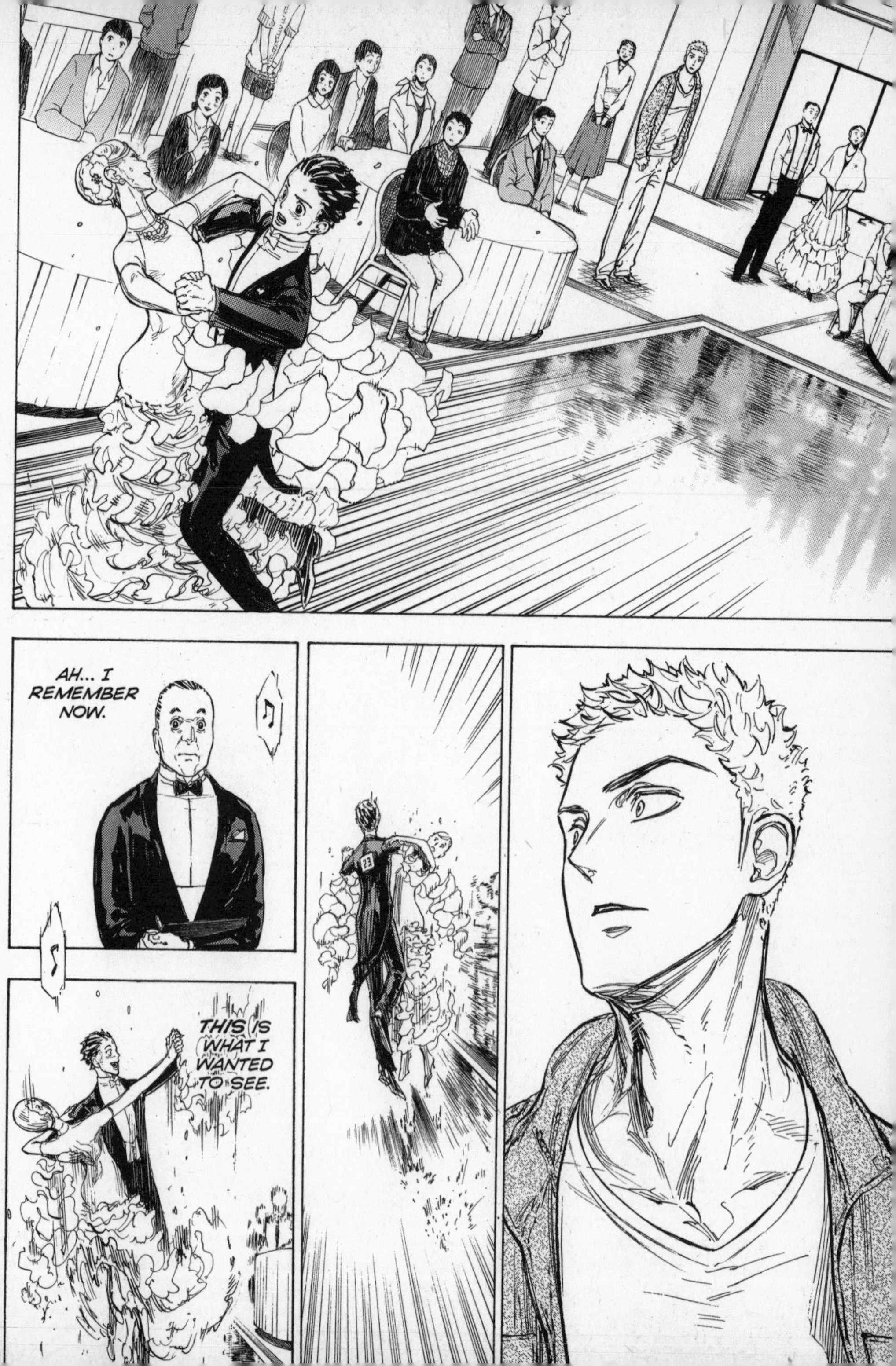
AH... I REMEMBER NOW.
THIS IS WHAT I WANTED TO SEE.

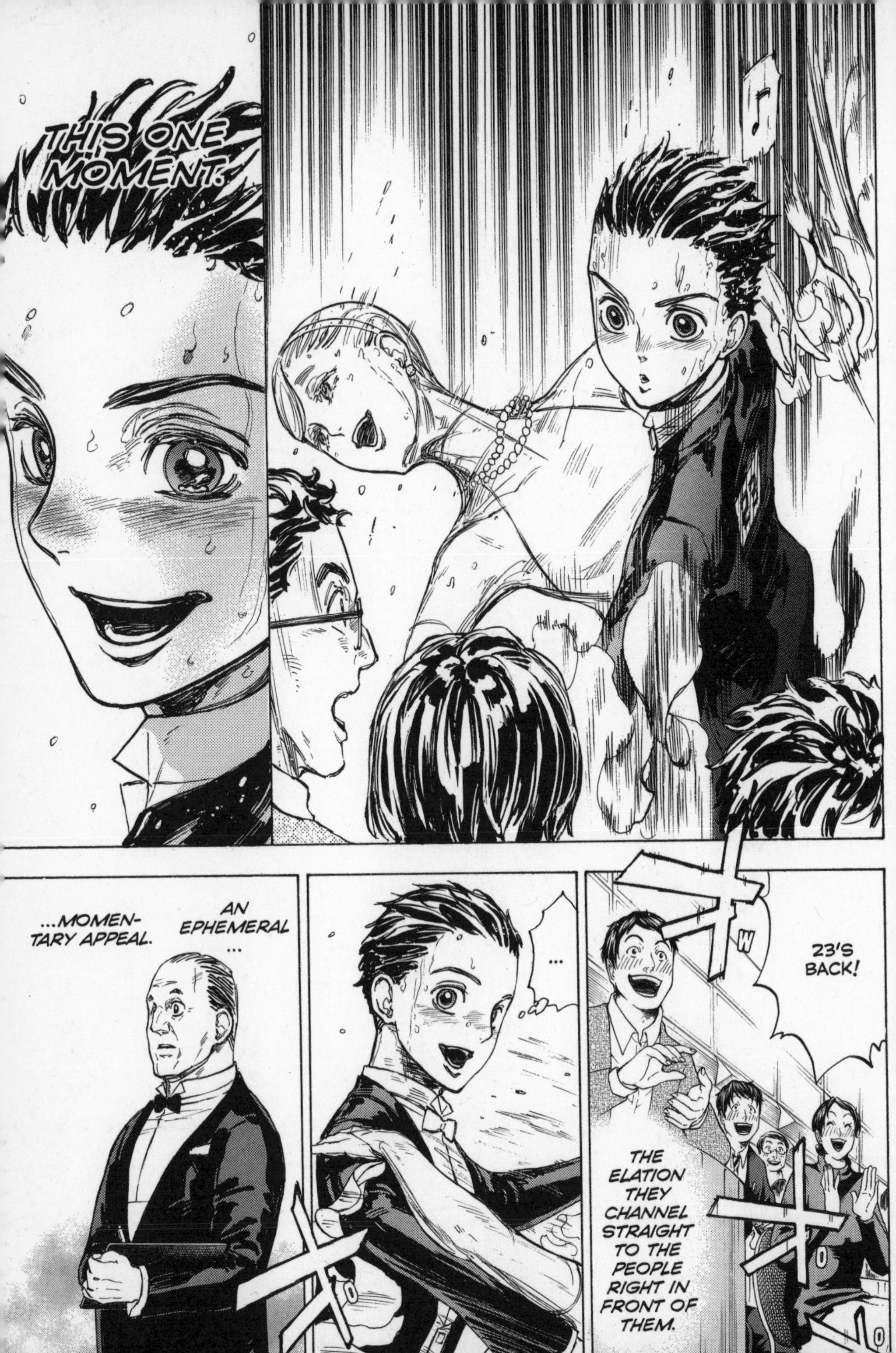
THIS ONE MOMENT.
23'S BACK!
THE ELATION THEY CHANNEL STRAIGHT TO THE PEOPLE RIGHT IN FRONT OF THEM.
...
AN EPHEMERAL ...
...MOMEN-TARY APPEAL.

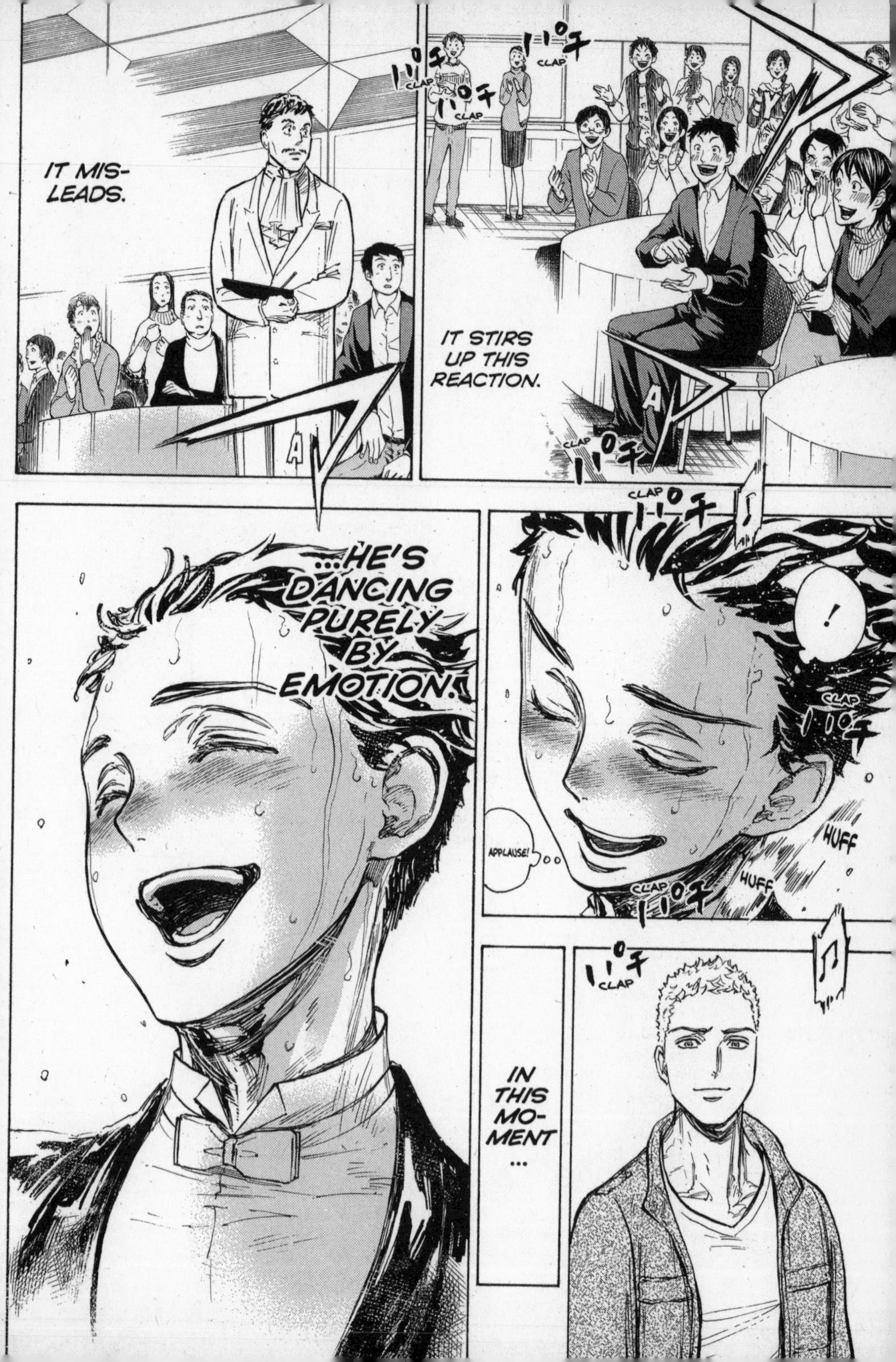

パチ CLAP
パチ CLAP
パチ CLAP
IT STIRS UP THIS REACTION.
A
パチ CLAP
IT MIS-LEADS.
A
パチ CLAP
!
パチ CLAP
APPLAUSE!
HUFF
HUFF
パチ CLAP
パチ CLAP
IN THIS MO-MENT...
...HE'S DANCING PURELY BY EMOTION.

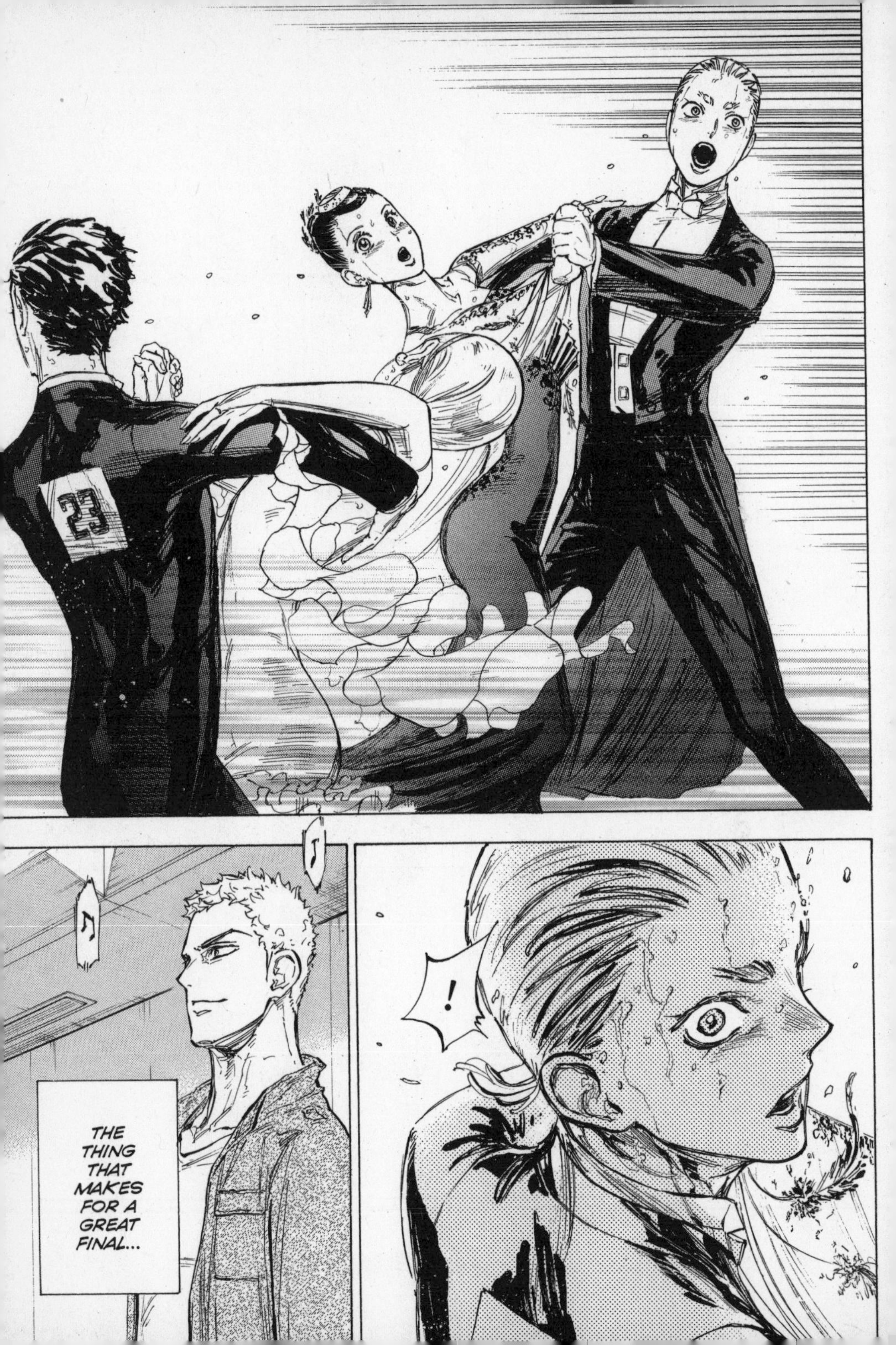
23
!
THE THING THAT MAKES FOR A GREAT FINAL...

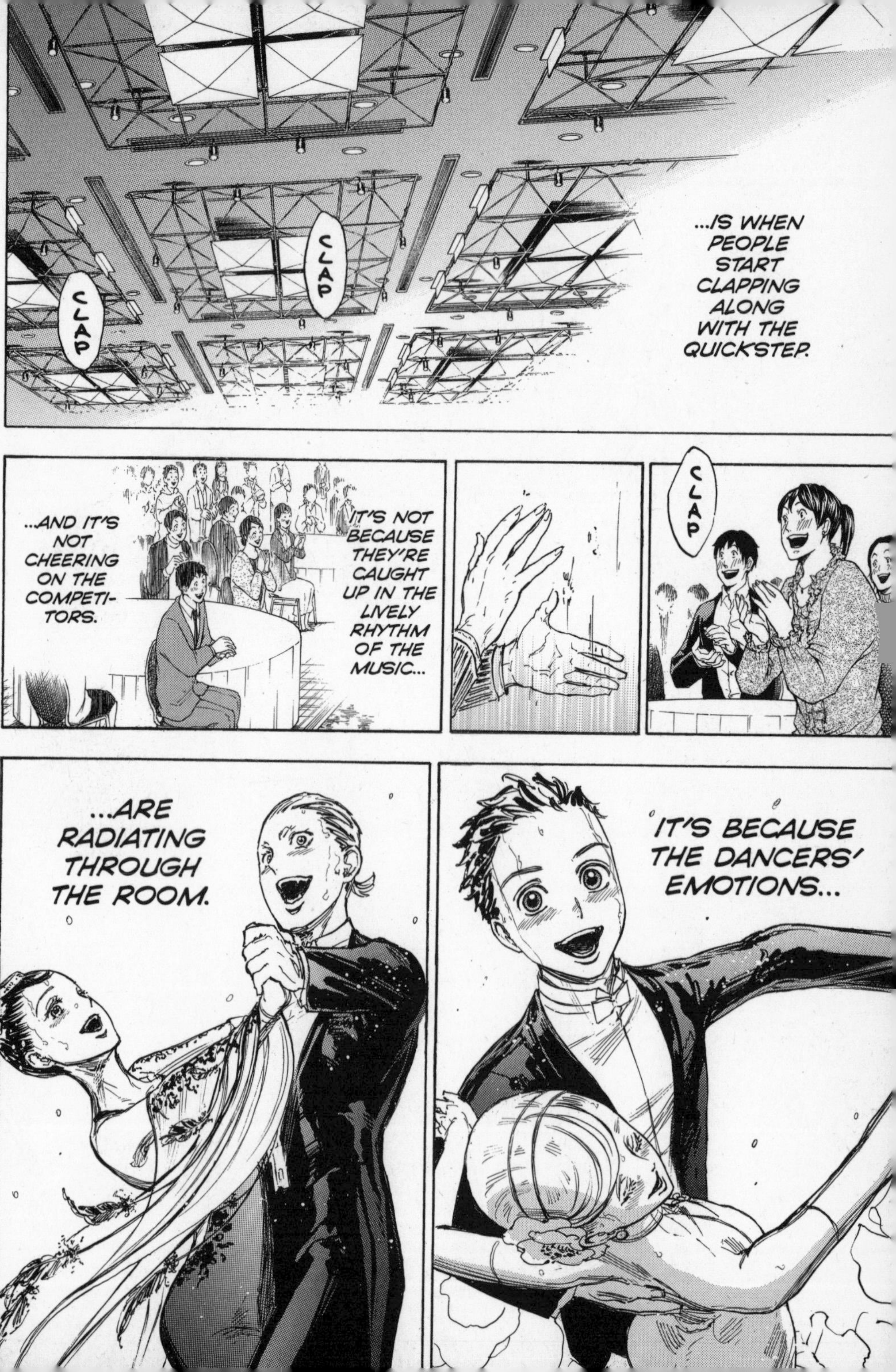
...IS WHEN PEOPLE START CLAPPING ALONG WITH THE QUICKSTEP.
CLAP
CLAP
CLAP
IT'S NOT BECAUSE THEY'RE CAUGHT UP IN THE LIVELY RHYTHM OF THE MUSIC...
...AND IT'S NOT CHEERING ON THE COMPETITORS.
IT'S BECAUSE THE DANCERS' EMOTIONS...
...ARE RADIATING THROUGH THE ROOM.

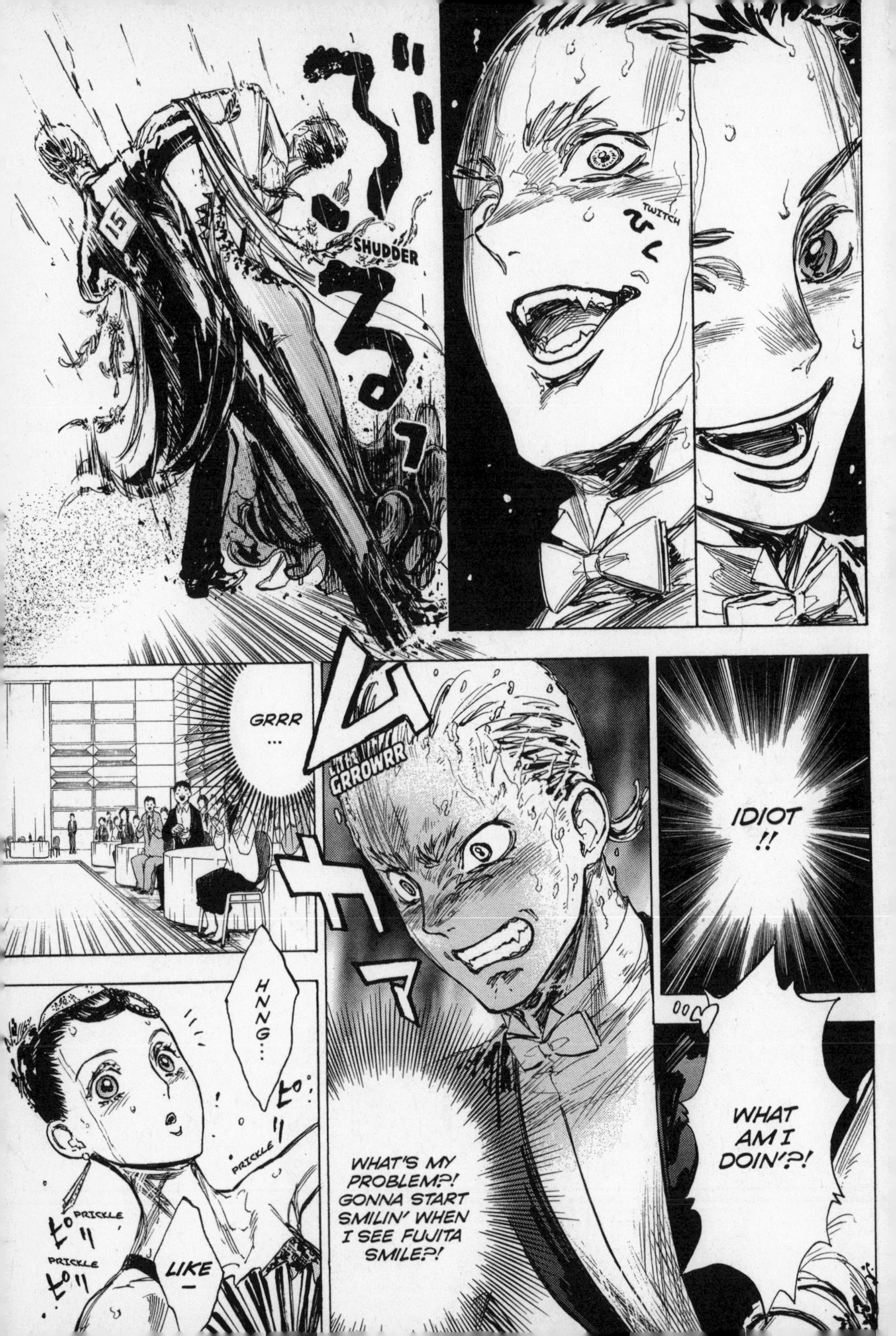
TWITCH
SHUDDER
IDIOT!!
WHAT AM I DOIN'?!
GRROWRR
WHAT'S MY PROBLEM?! GONNA START SMILIN' WHEN I SEE FUJITA SMILE?!
GRRR...
HNNG...
PRICKLE
PRICKLE
PRICKLE
LIKE—

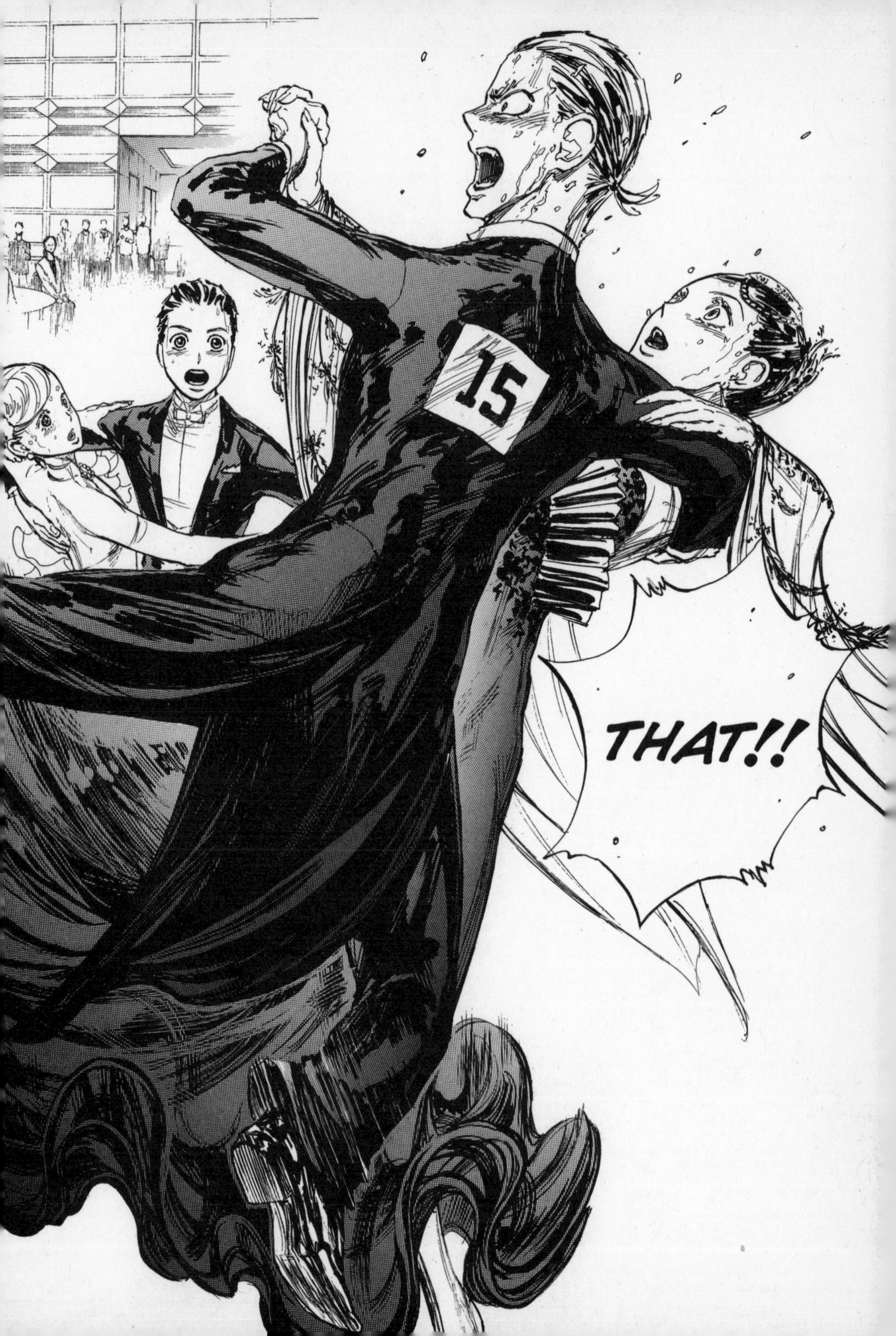
15
THAT!!

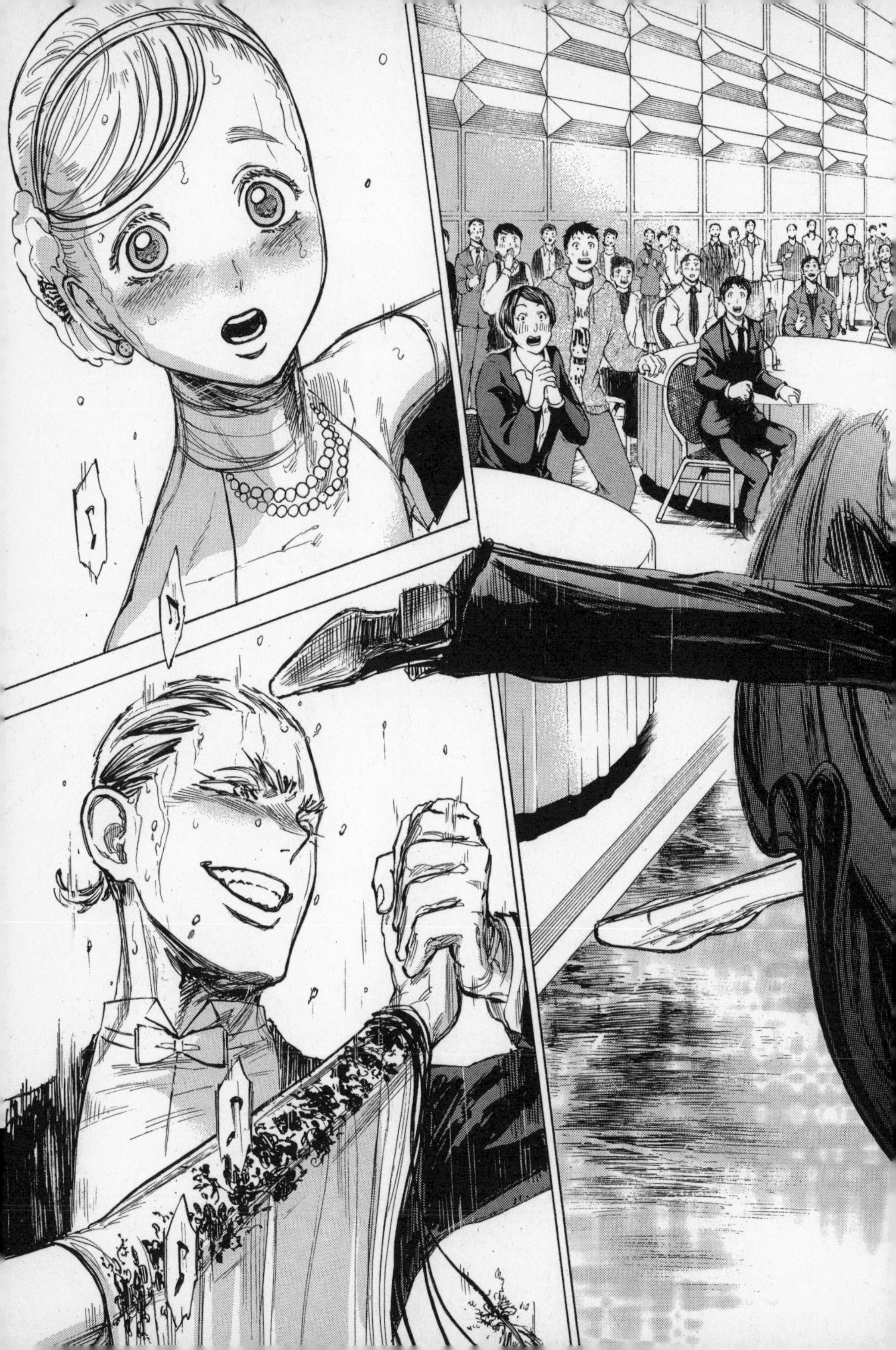

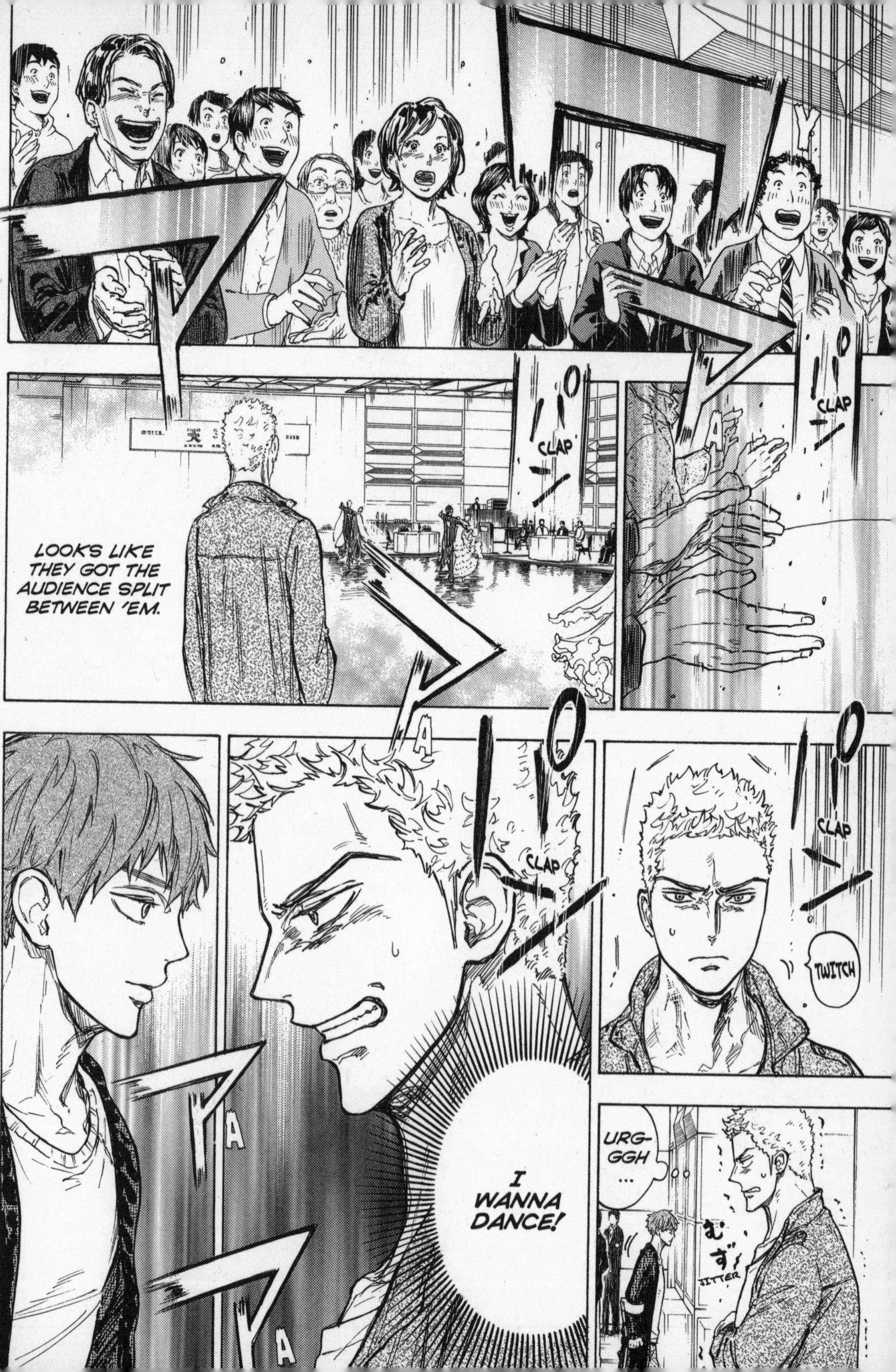

CLAP
CLAP
LOOKS LIKE THEY GOT THE AUDIENCE SPLIT BETWEEN 'EM.
CLAP
TWITCH
URG-GGH ...
むず
JITTER
CLAP
I WANNA DANCE!

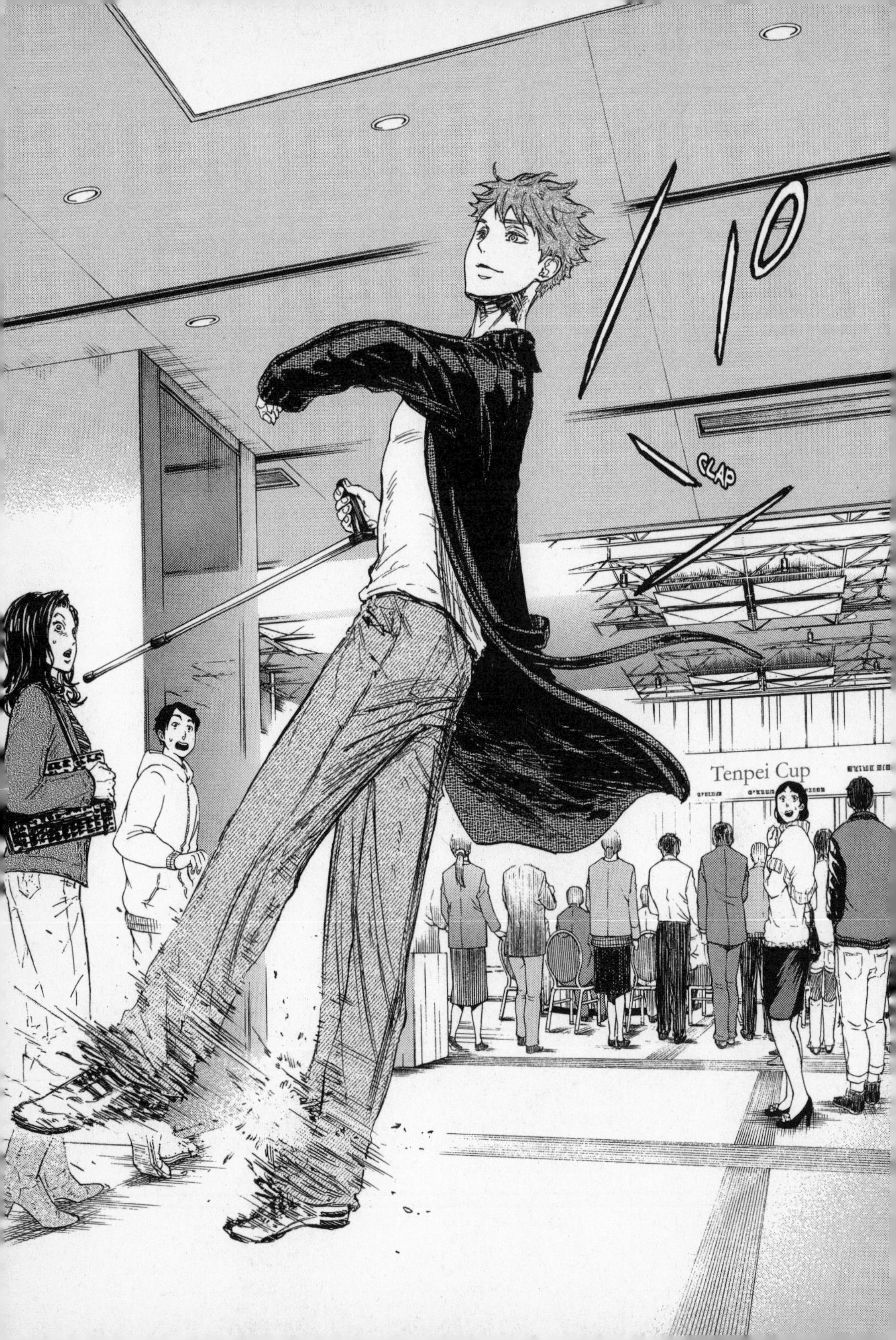
CLAP
Tenpei Cup

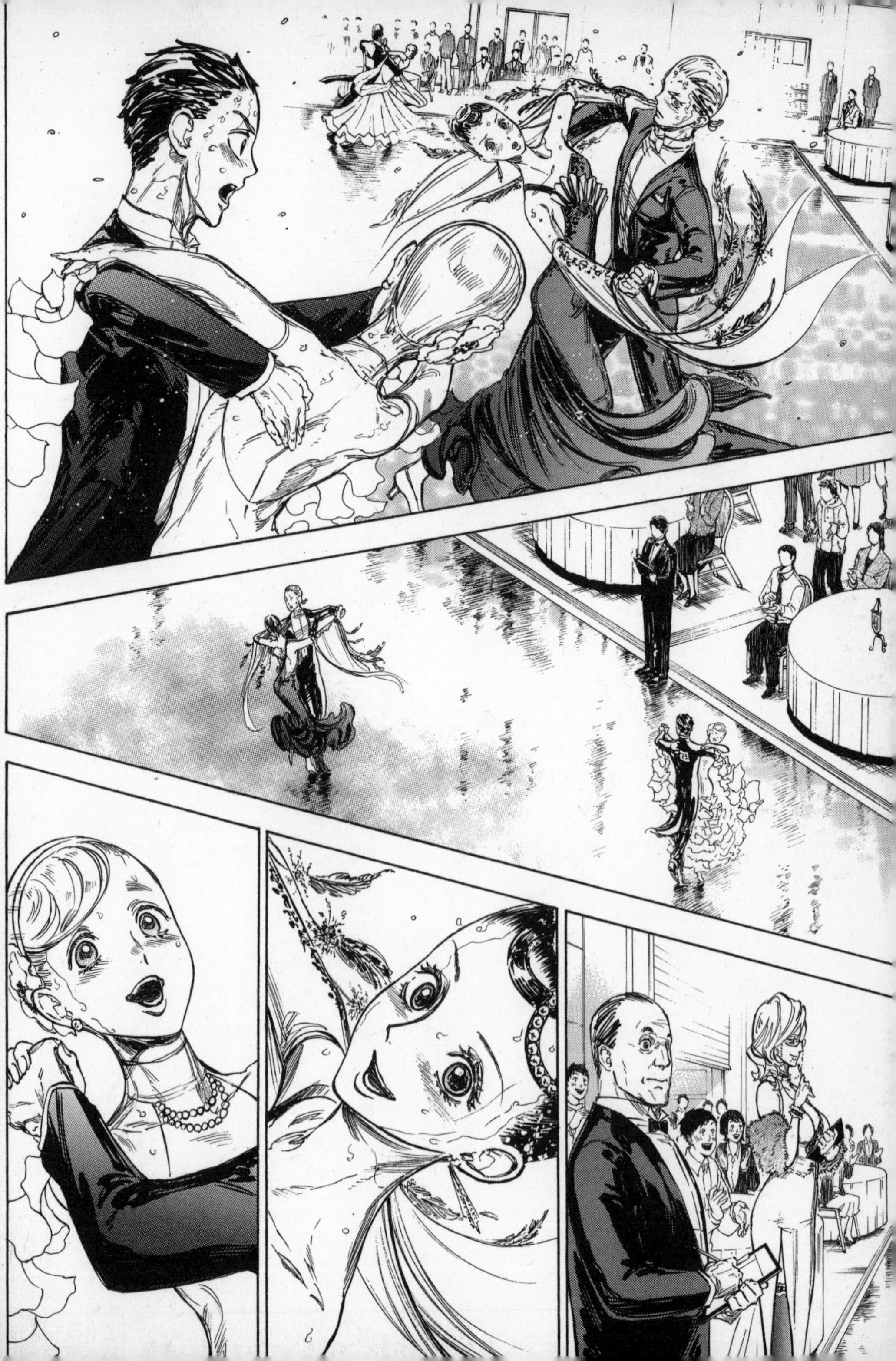

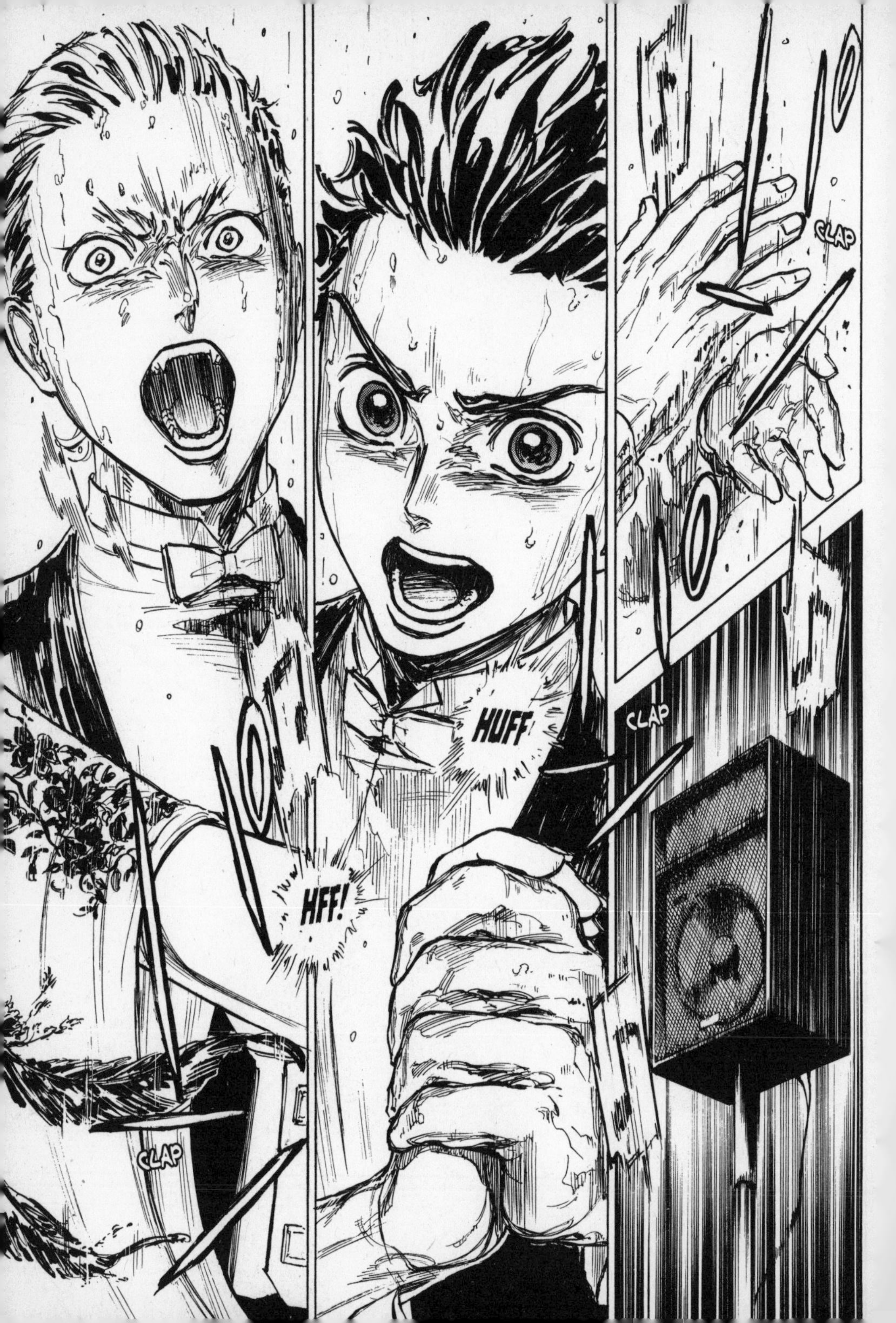
CLAP
CLAP
HUFF
HFF!
CLAP

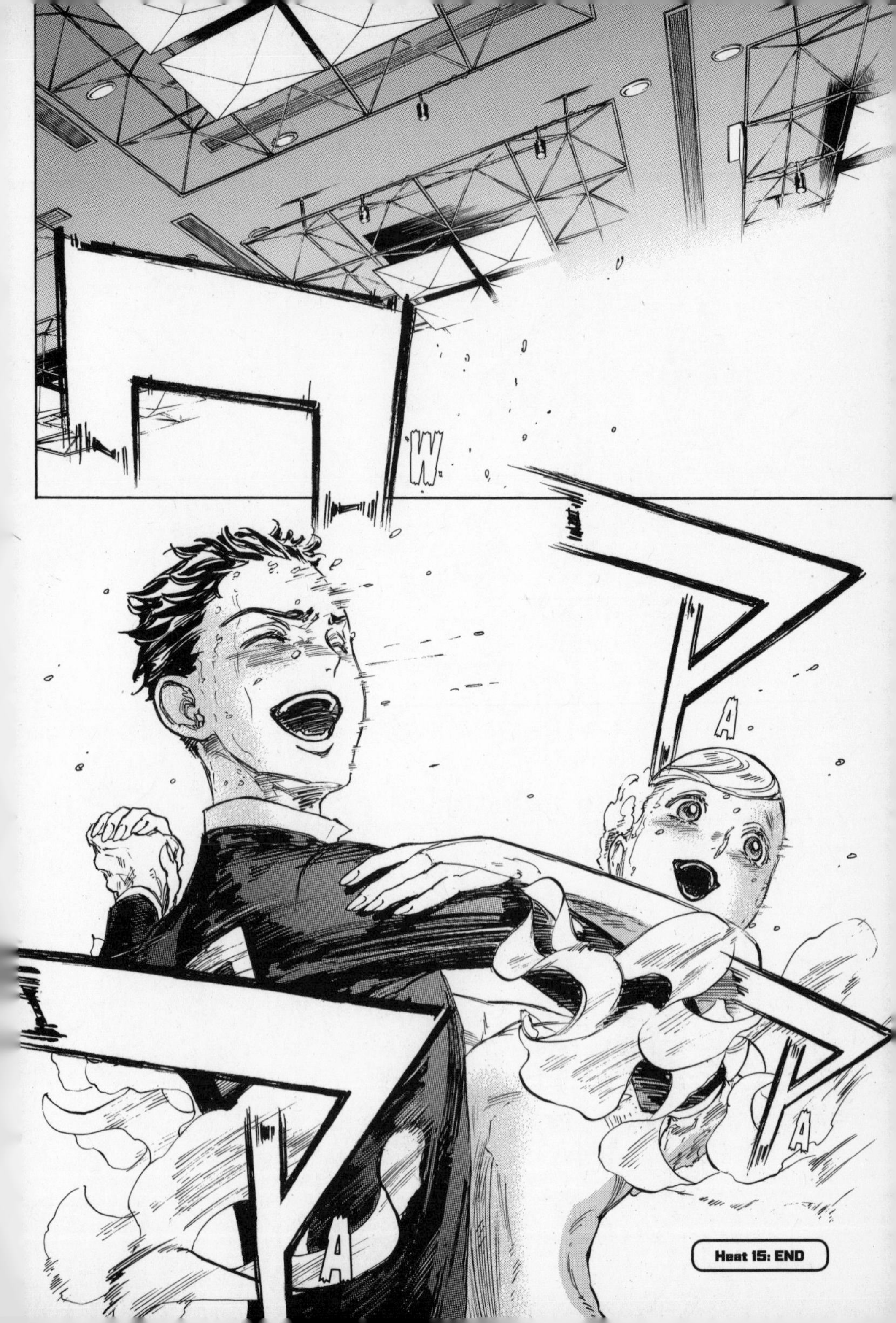
W
A
A
A

Heat 15: END

# WELCOME TO THE BALLROOM

*Special Thanks!*

**For help with waltz variations**
Mr. Masayuki Ishihara
Ms. Saori Ito

**For help with tango
& slow foxtrot variations**
Mr. Yoshihiro Miwa
Ms. Tomoko Miwa

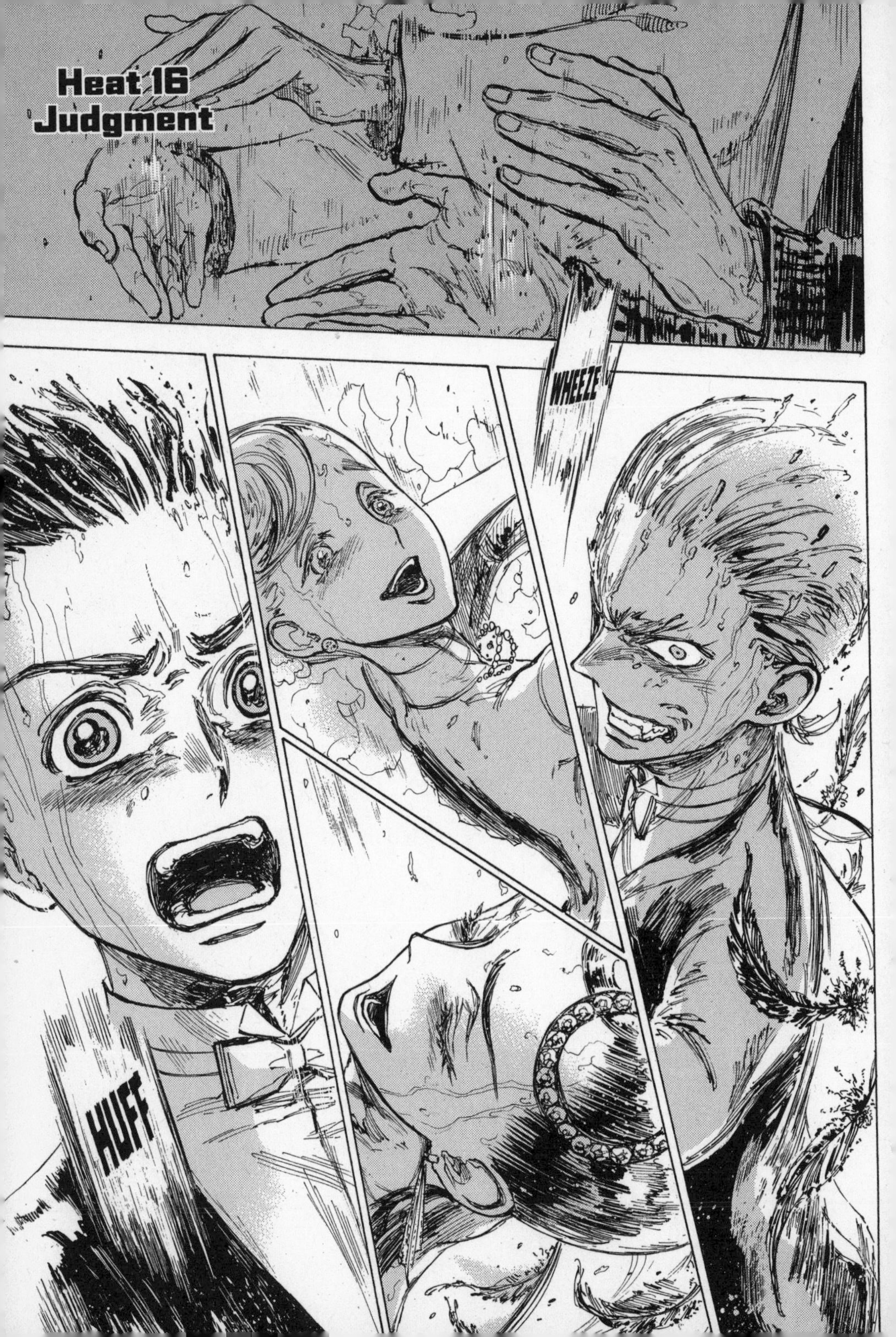
Heat 16
Judgment
WHEEZE
HUFF

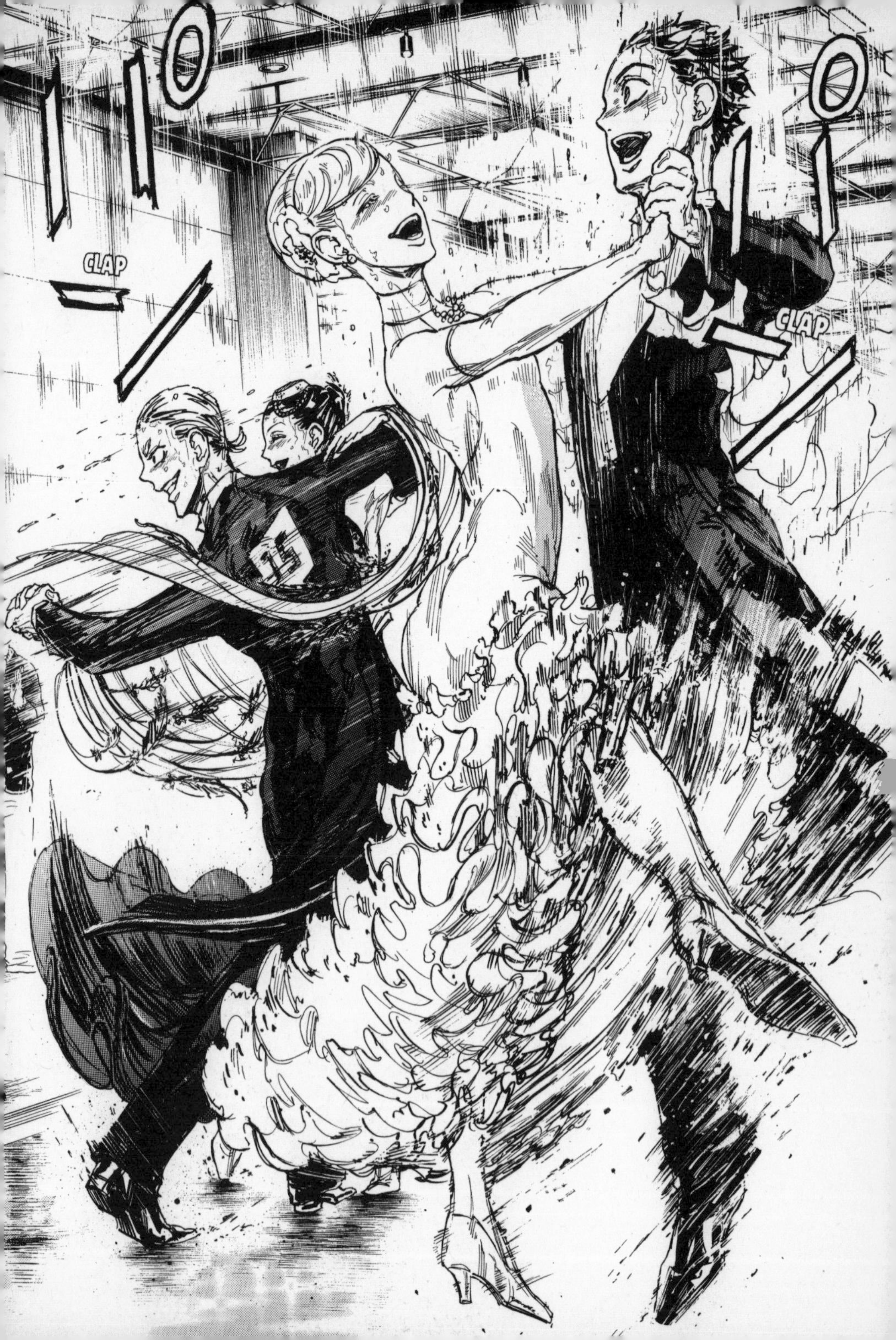
CLAP
CLAP

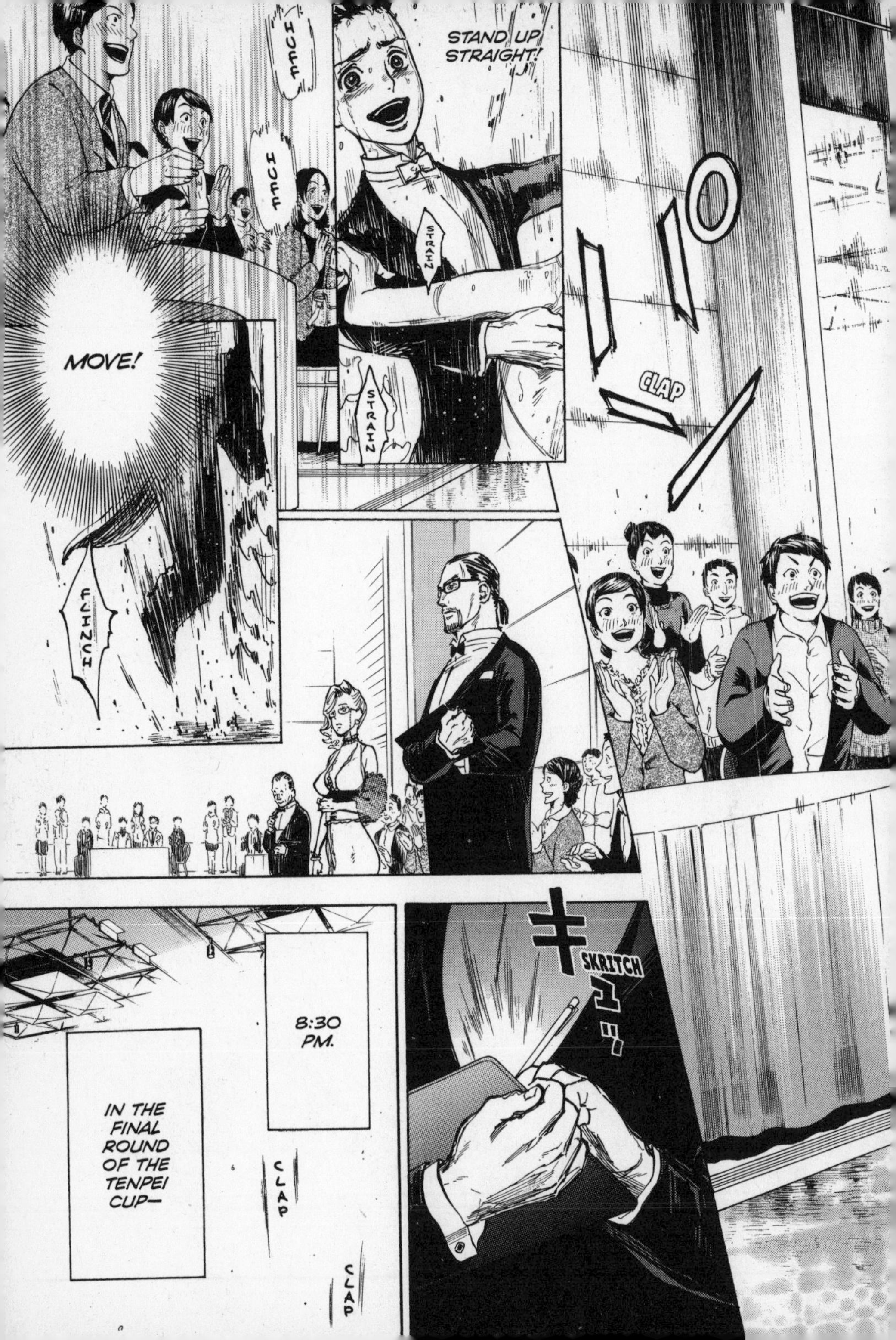
CLAP
STAND UP STRAIGHT!
STRAIN
STRAIN
HUFF
HUFF
MOVE!
FLINCH
キュッ
SKRITCH
8:30 PM.
IN THE FINAL ROUND OF THE TENPEI CUP—
CLAP
CLAP
CLAP
CLAP

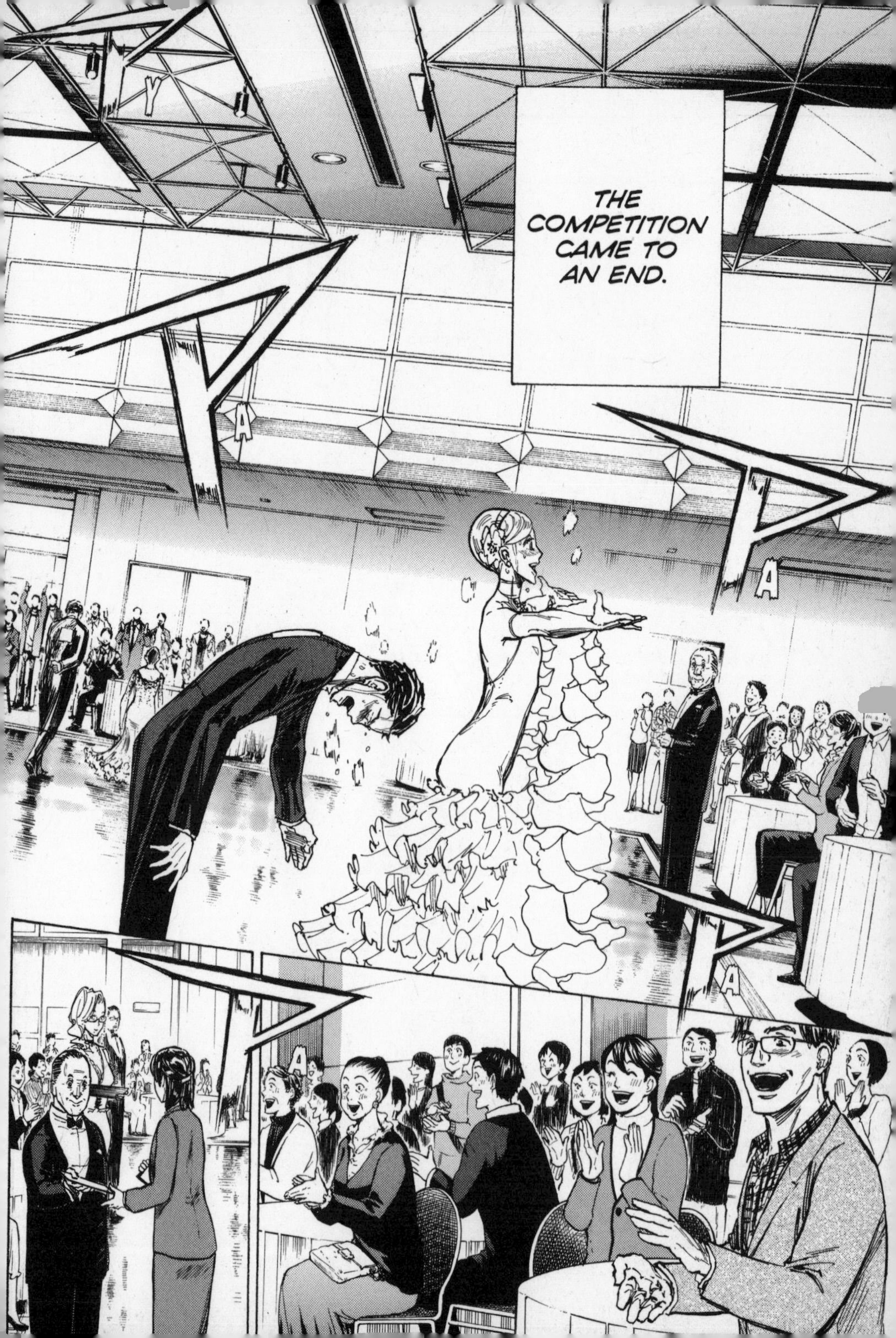
THE COMPETITION CAME TO AN END.
PA
PA
PA
PA

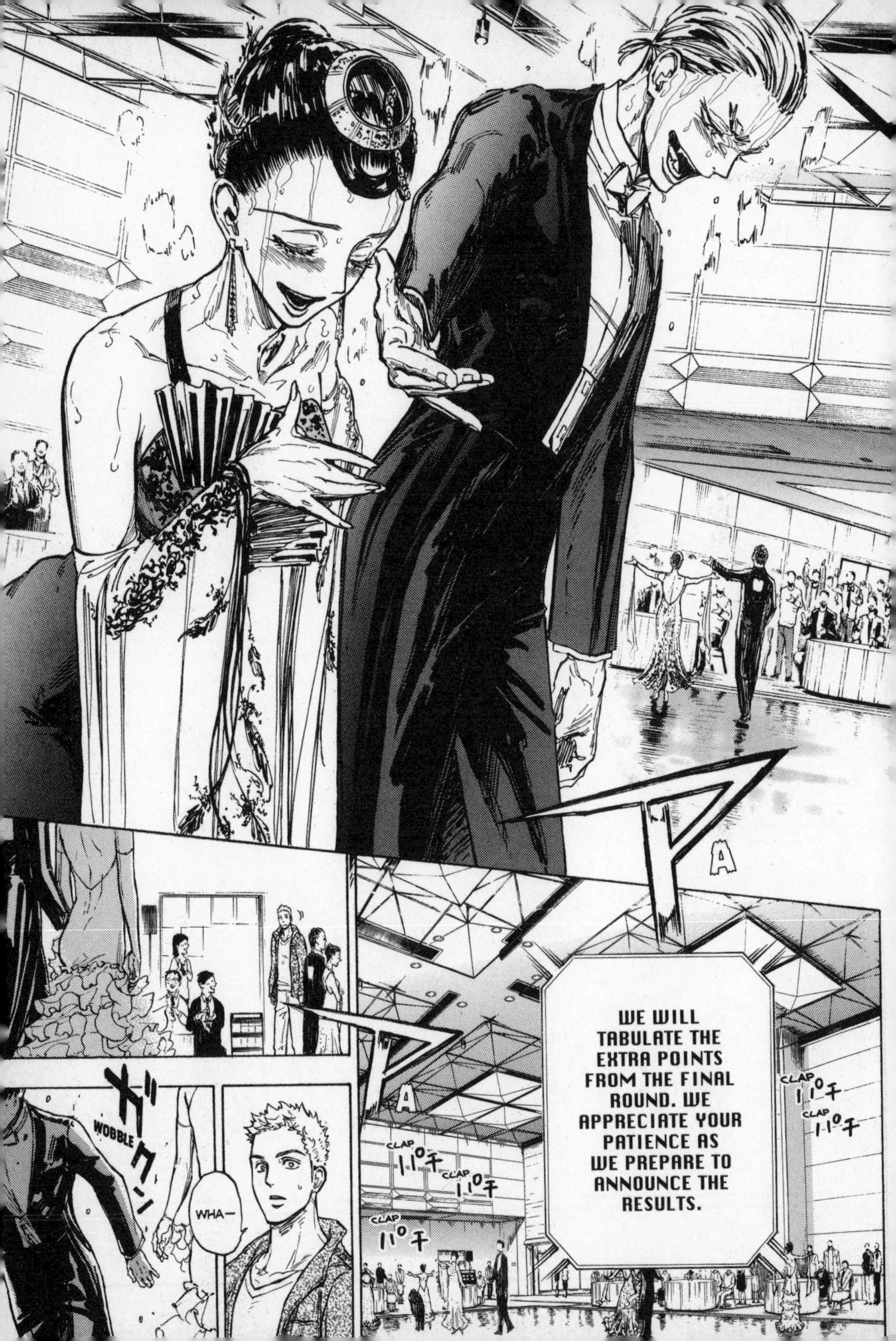
A
A
WE WILL TABULATE THE EXTRA POINTS FROM THE FINAL ROUND. WE APPRECIATE YOUR PATIENCE AS WE PREPARE TO ANNOUNCE THE RESULTS.
CLAP
CLAP
CLAP
CLAP
CLAP
WHA—
WOBBLE

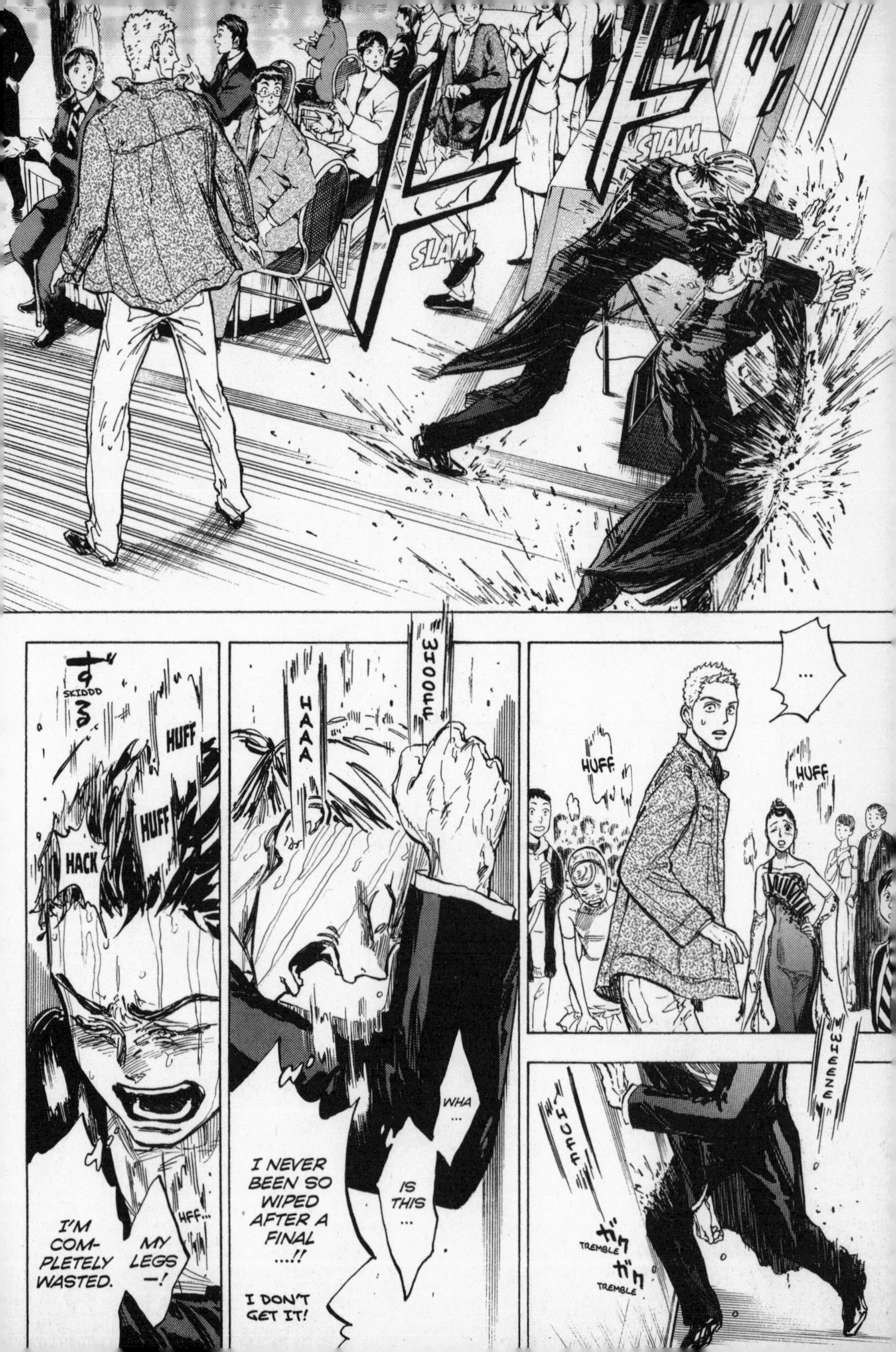
SLAM
SLAM
...
HUFF
HUFF
WHEEZE
HUFF
TREMBLE
TREMBLE
HAAA
WHA ...
IS THIS ...
I NEVER BEEN SO WIPED AFTER A FINAL ....!!
I DON'T GET IT!
SKIDDD
HUFF
HUFF
HACK
HFF...
MY LEGS —!
I'M COMPLETELY WASTED.

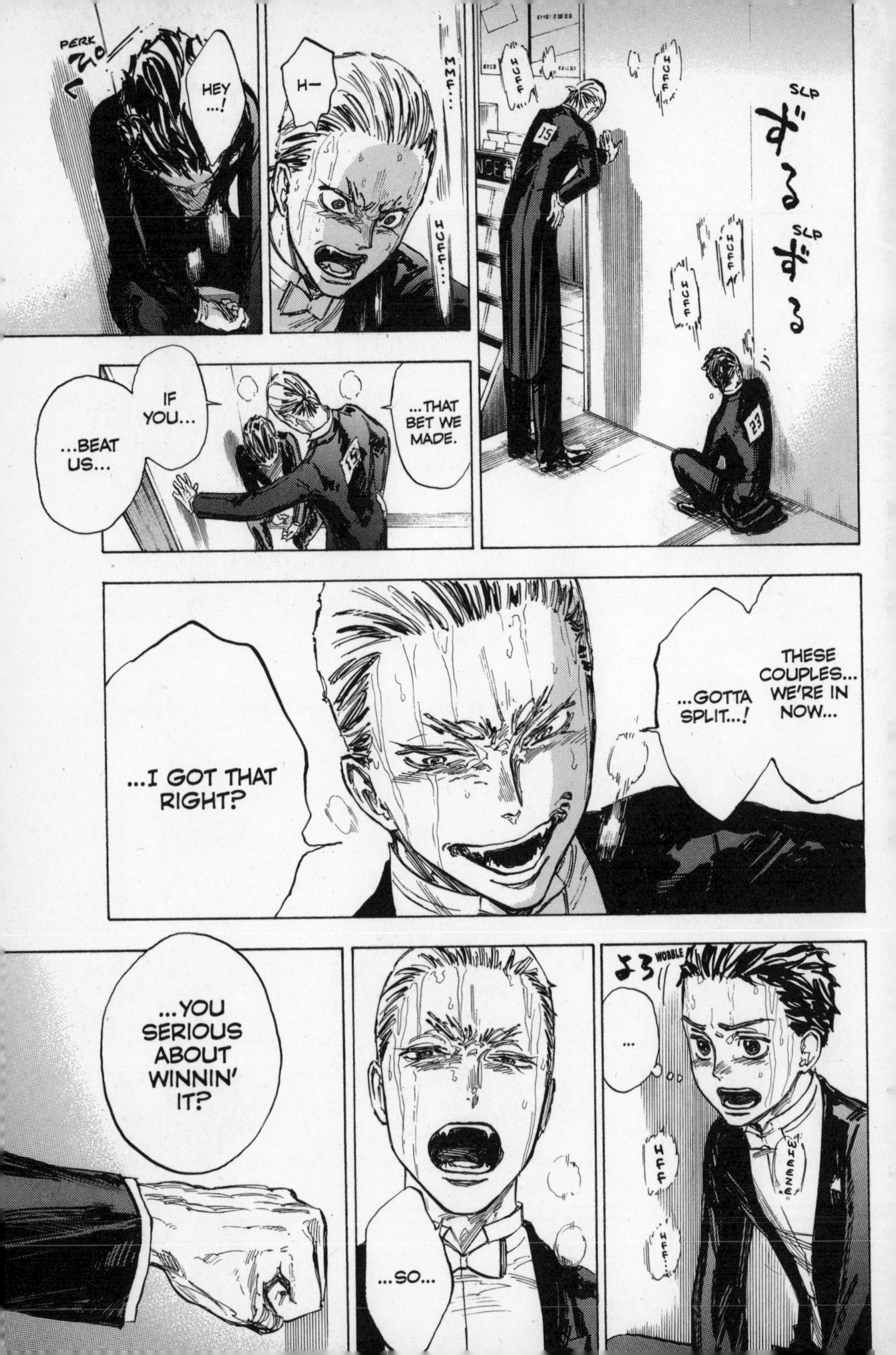
HUFF
HUFF
HUFF
SLP ずる
SLP ずる
HUFF
HUFF
H—
MMF...
HUFF...
PERK
HEY ...!
...THAT BET WE MADE.
IF YOU...
...BEAT US...
THESE COUPLES... WE'RE IN NOW...
...GOTTA SPLIT...!
...I GOT THAT RIGHT?
よろ WOBBLE
...
HFF
WHEEZE
HFF...
...SO...
...YOU SERIOUS ABOUT WINNIN' IT?

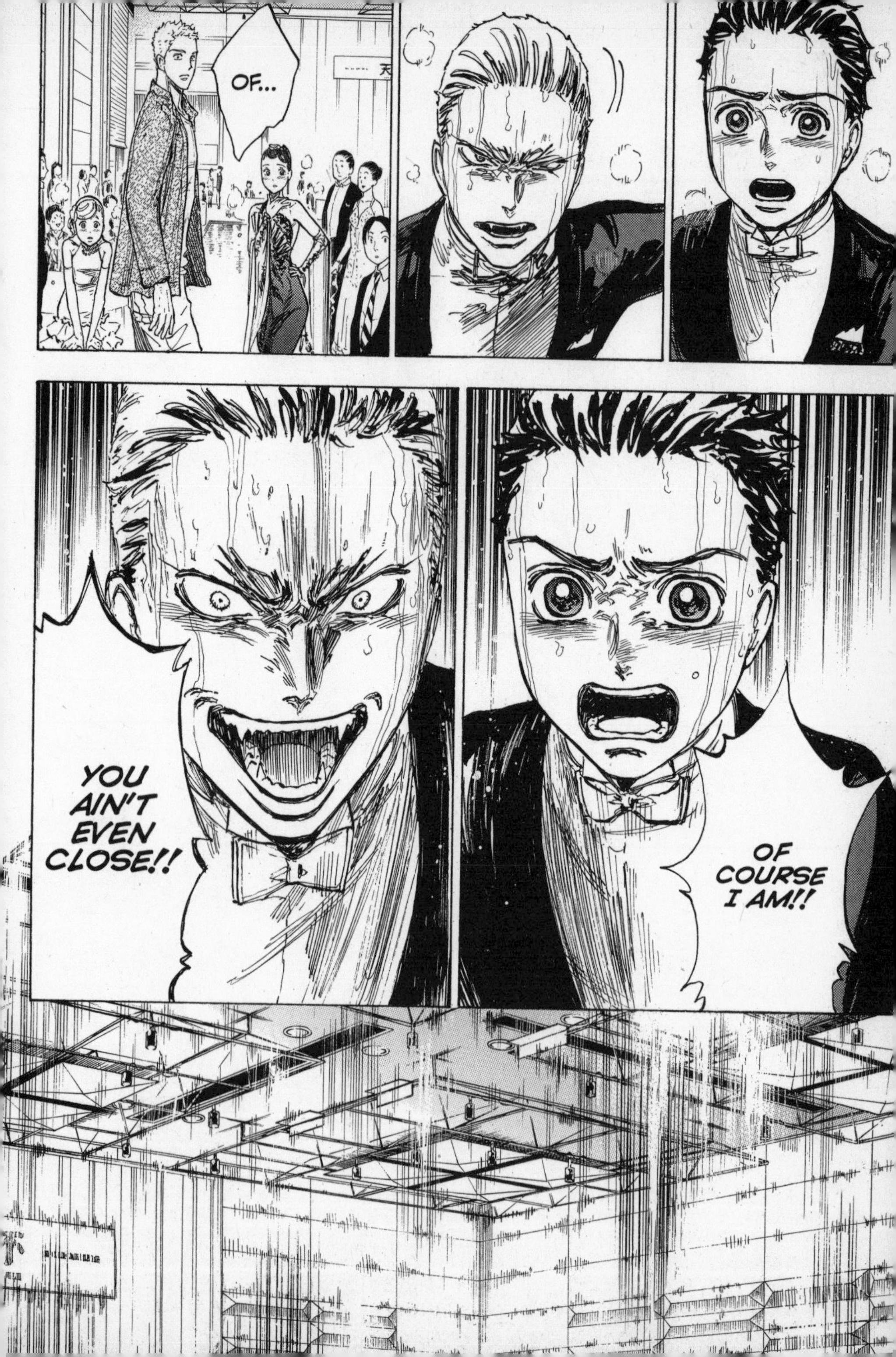
OF...
OF COURSE I AM!!
YOU AIN'T EVEN CLOSE!!

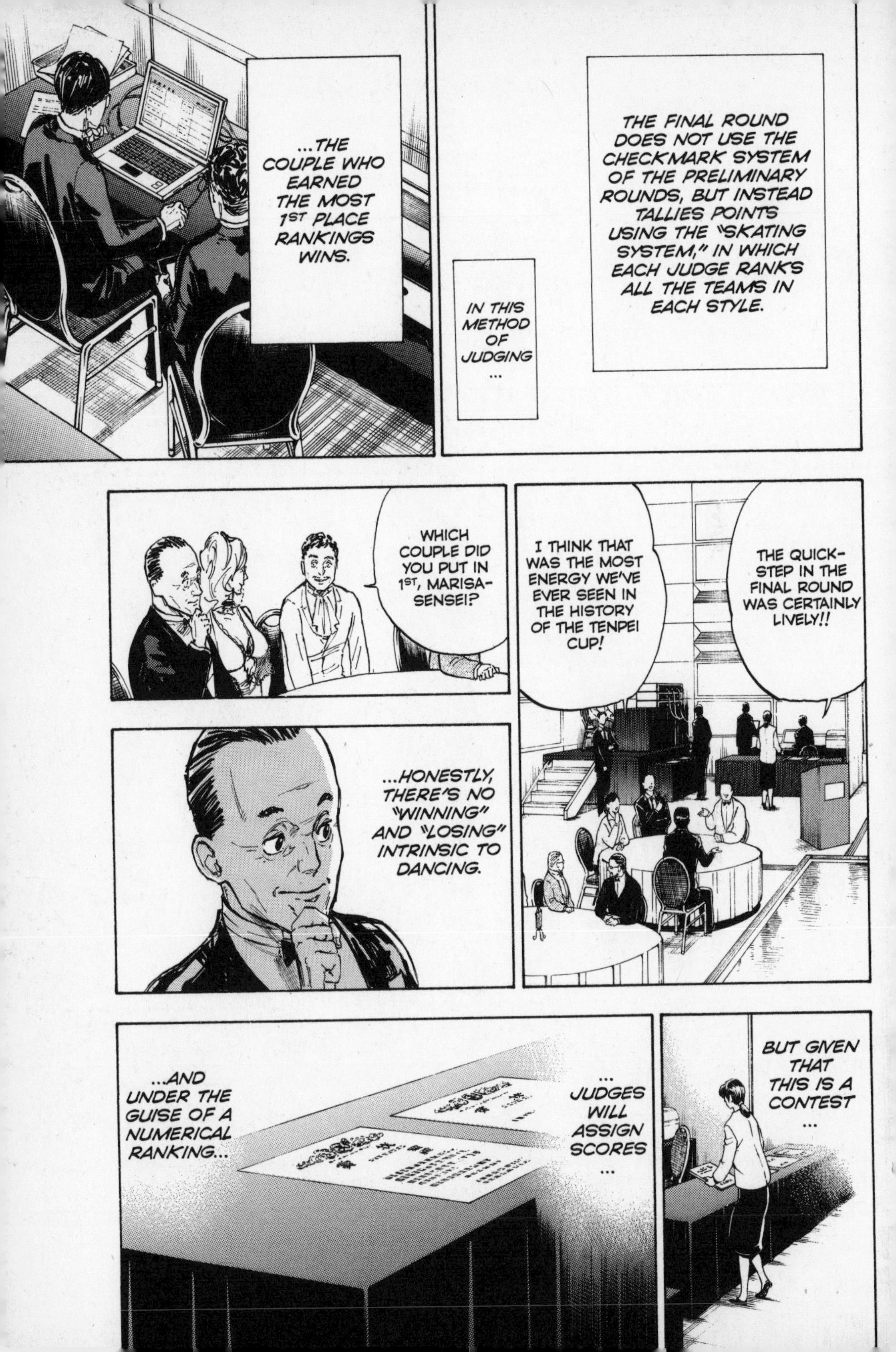
THE FINAL ROUND DOES NOT USE THE CHECKMARK SYSTEM OF THE PRELIMINARY ROUNDS, BUT INSTEAD TALLIES POINTS USING THE "SKATING SYSTEM," IN WHICH EACH JUDGE RANKS ALL THE TEAMS IN EACH STYLE.
IN THIS METHOD OF JUDGING ...
...THE COUPLE WHO EARNED THE MOST 1ST PLACE RANKINGS WINS.
THE QUICK-STEP IN THE FINAL ROUND WAS CERTAINLY LIVELY!!
I THINK THAT WAS THE MOST ENERGY WE'VE EVER SEEN IN THE HISTORY OF THE TENPEI CUP!
WHICH COUPLE DID YOU PUT IN 1ST, MARISA-SENSEI?
...HONESTLY, THERE'S NO "WINNING" AND "LOSING" INTRINSIC TO DANCING.
BUT GIVEN THAT THIS IS A CONTEST ...
... JUDGES WILL ASSIGN SCORES ...
...AND UNDER THE GUISE OF A NUMERICAL RANKING...

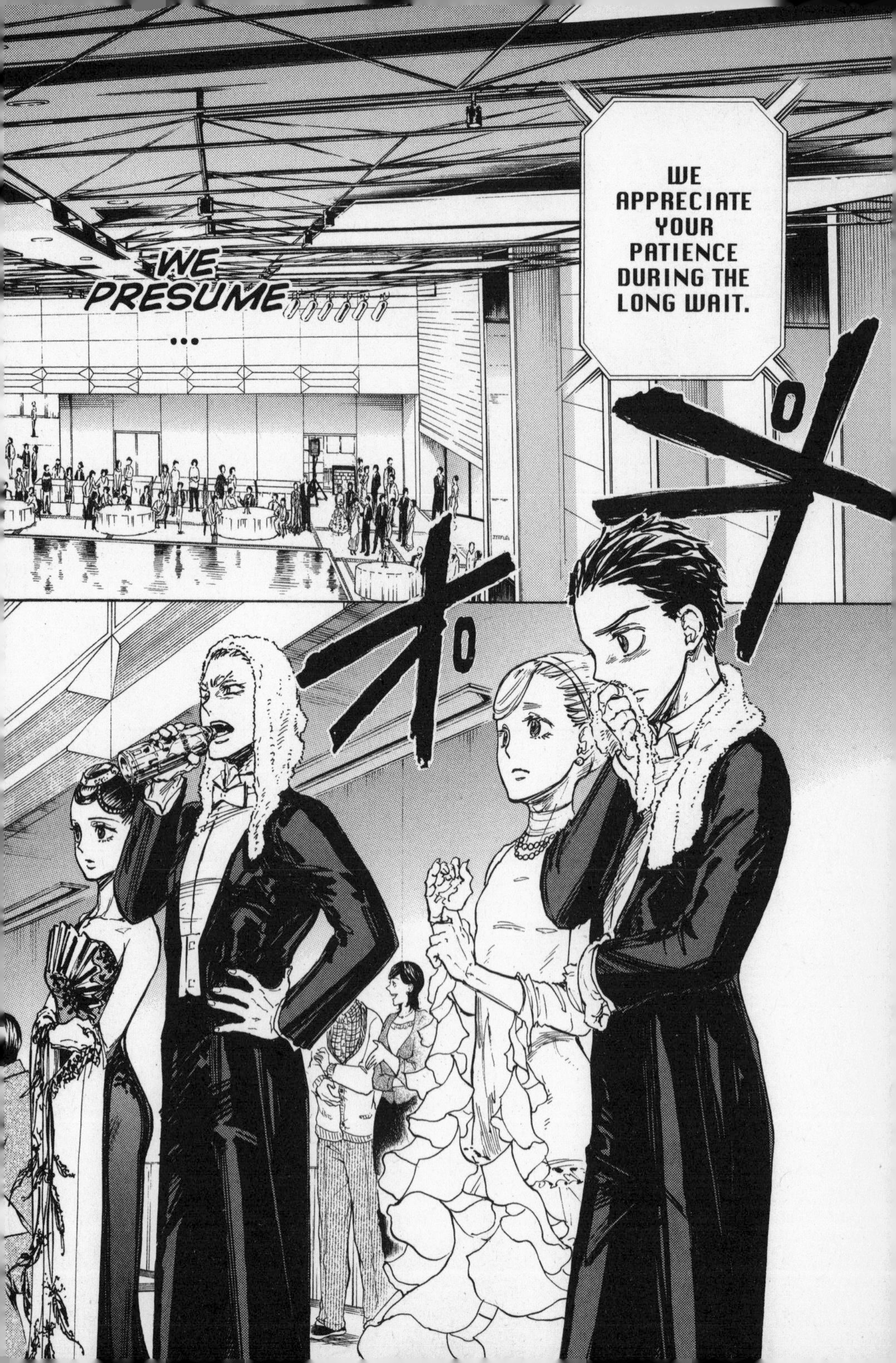
WE APPRECIATE YOUR PATIENCE DURING THE LONG WAIT.
WE PRESUME...

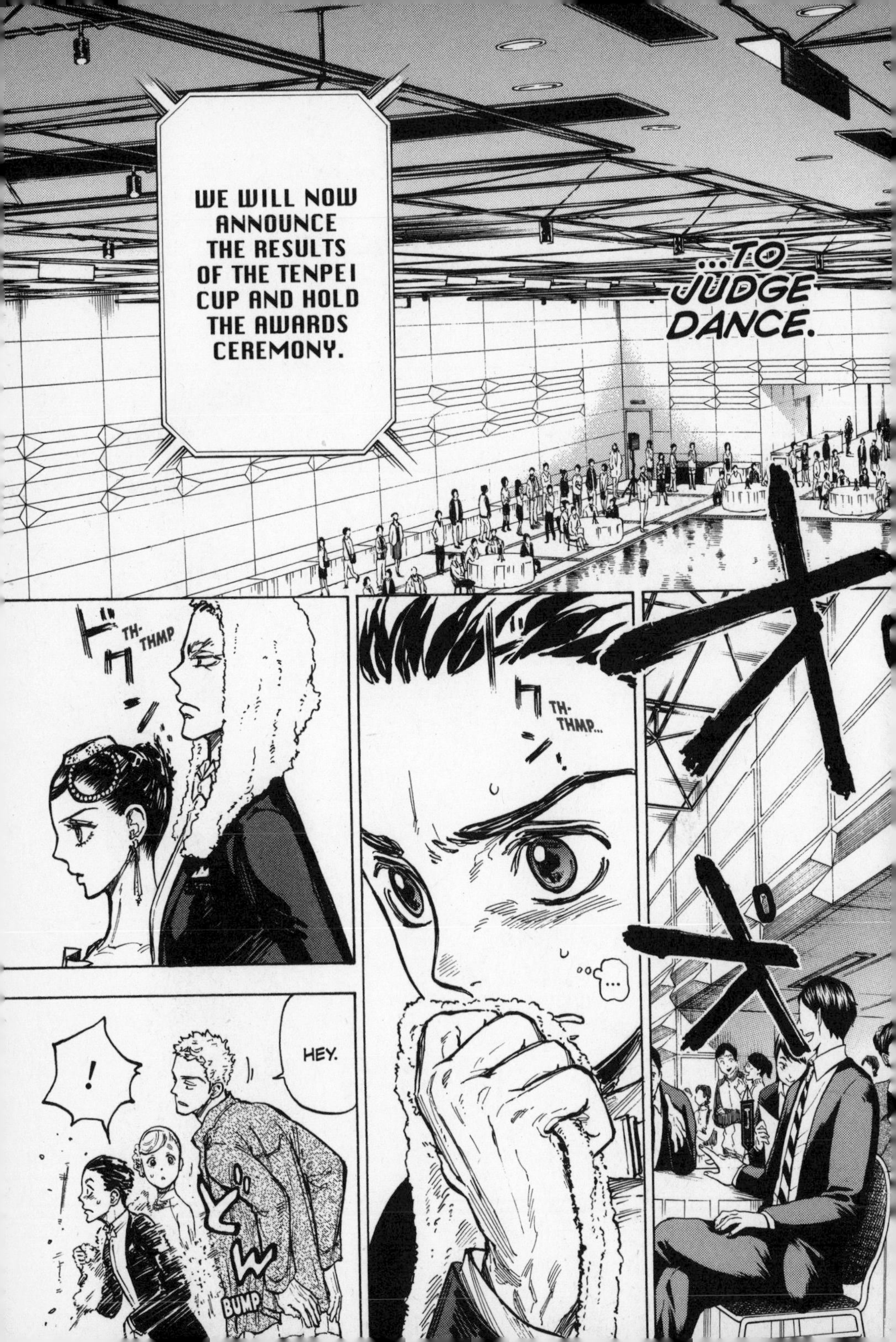

...TO JUDGE DANCE.
WE WILL NOW ANNOUNCE THE RESULTS OF THE TENPEI CUP AND HOLD THE AWARDS CEREMONY.
TH-THMP...
...
TH-THMP
HEY.
!
BUMP

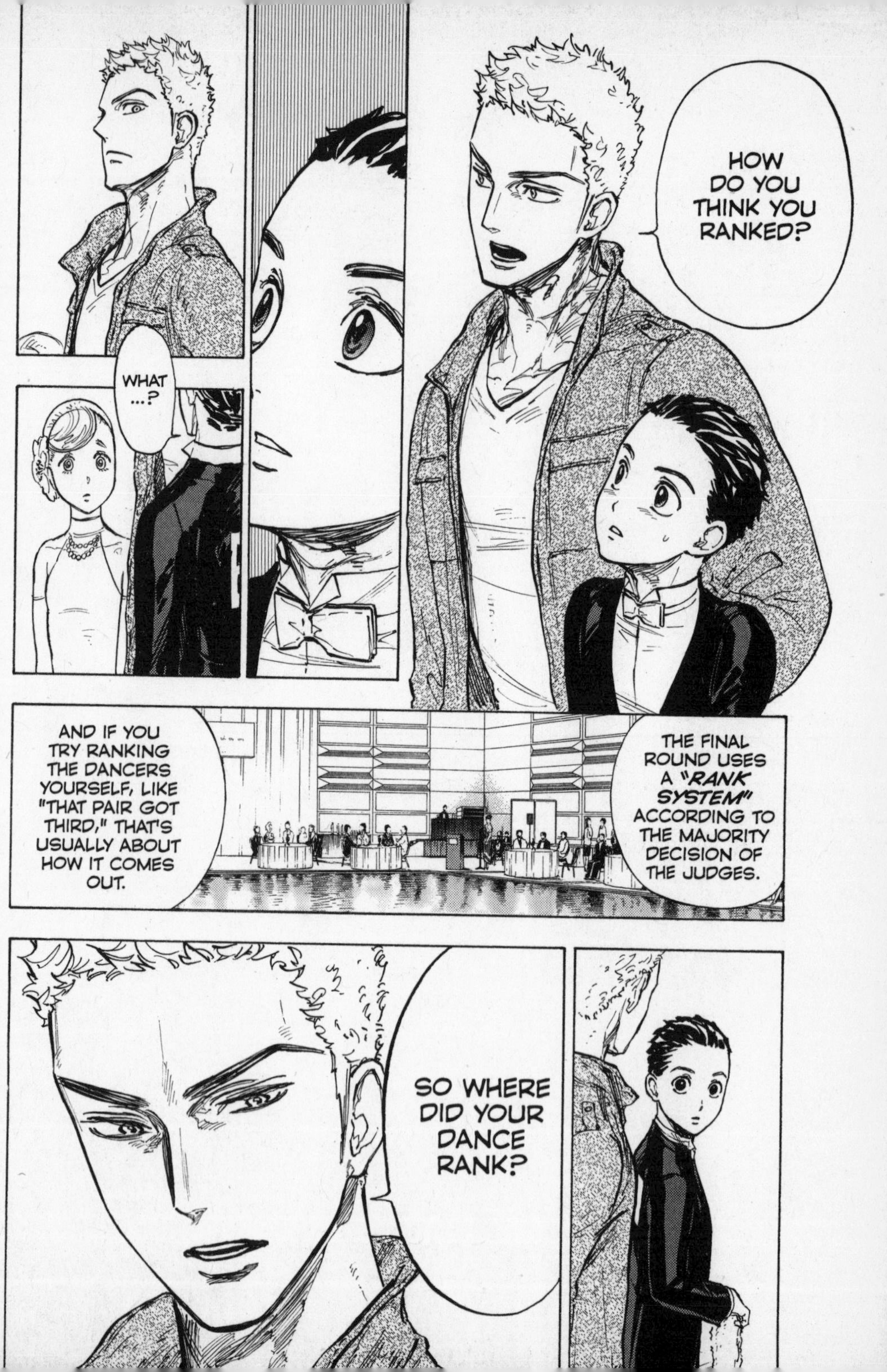
HOW DO YOU THINK YOU RANKED?
WHAT ...?
THE FINAL ROUND USES A "RANK SYSTEM" ACCORDING TO THE MAJORITY DECISION OF THE JUDGES.
AND IF YOU TRY RANKING THE DANCERS YOURSELF, LIKE "THAT PAIR GOT THIRD," THAT'S USUALLY ABOUT HOW IT COMES OUT.
SO WHERE DID YOUR DANCE RANK?

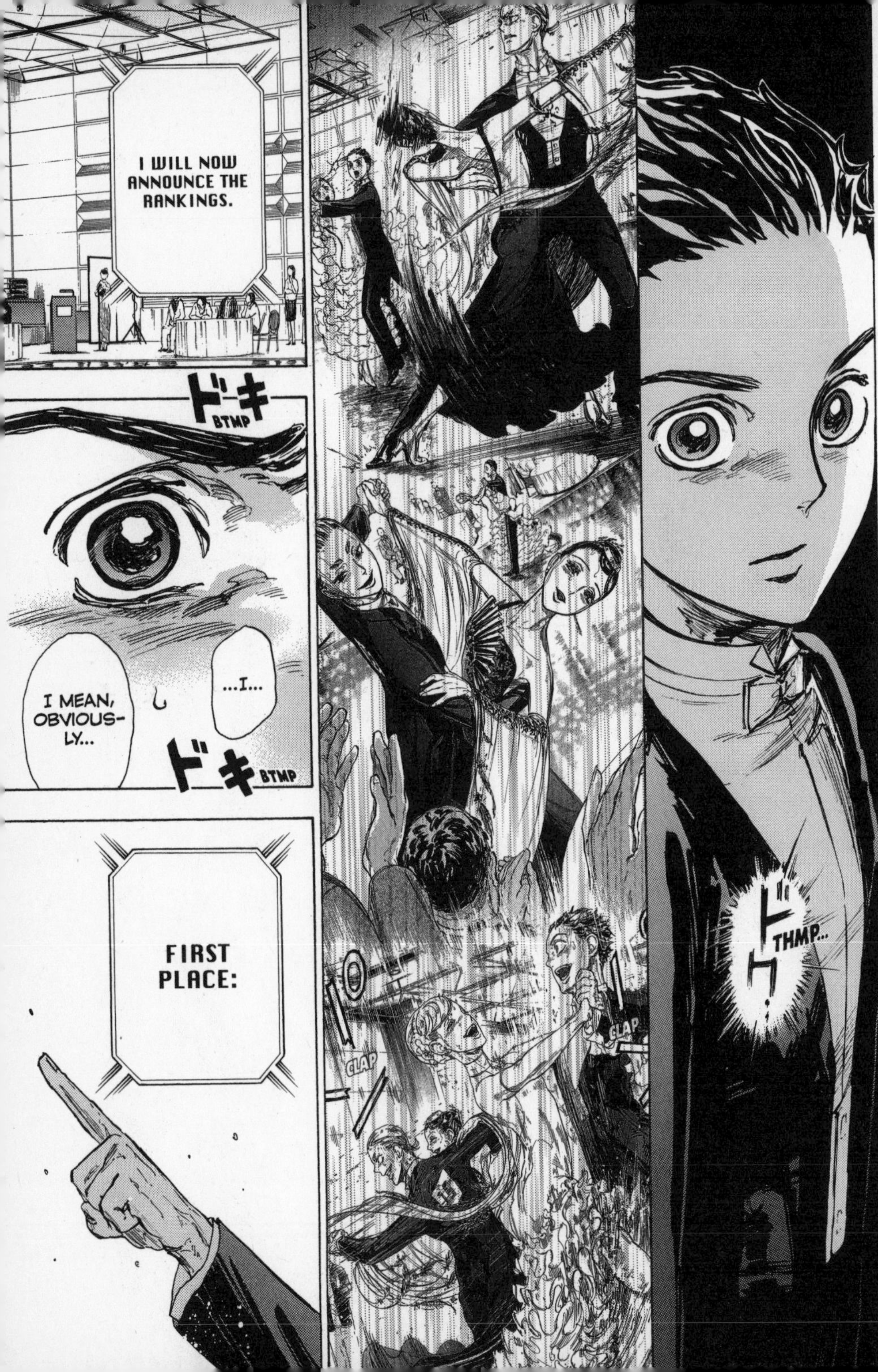
ドッ
THMP...
CLAP
CLAP
I WILL NOW ANNOUNCE THE RANKINGS.
ドキ
BTMP
...I...
I MEAN, OBVIOUSLY...
ドキ
BTMP
FIRST PLACE:

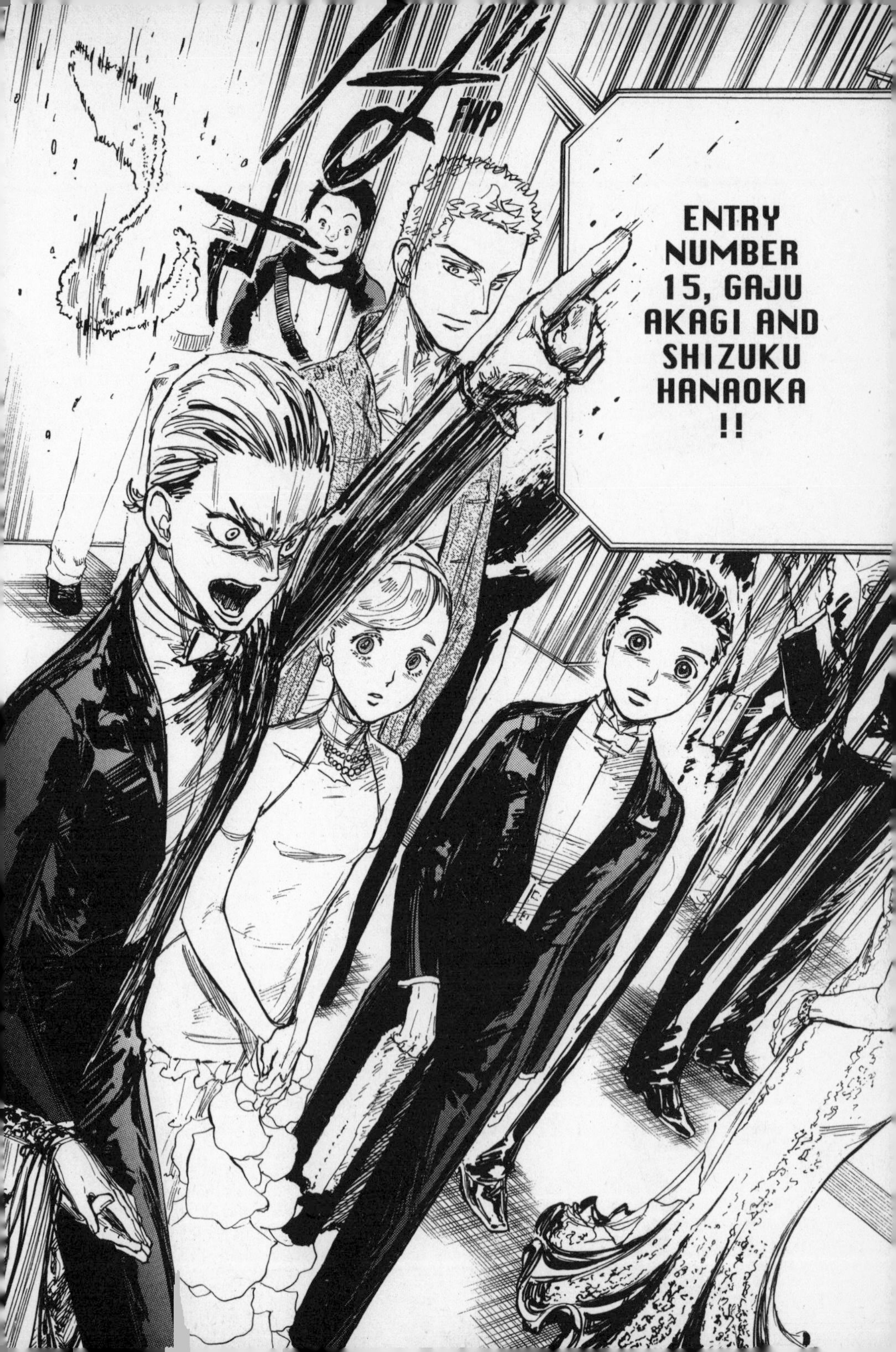

FWP
ENTRY NUMBER 15, GAJU AKAGI AND SHIZUKU HANAOKA !!

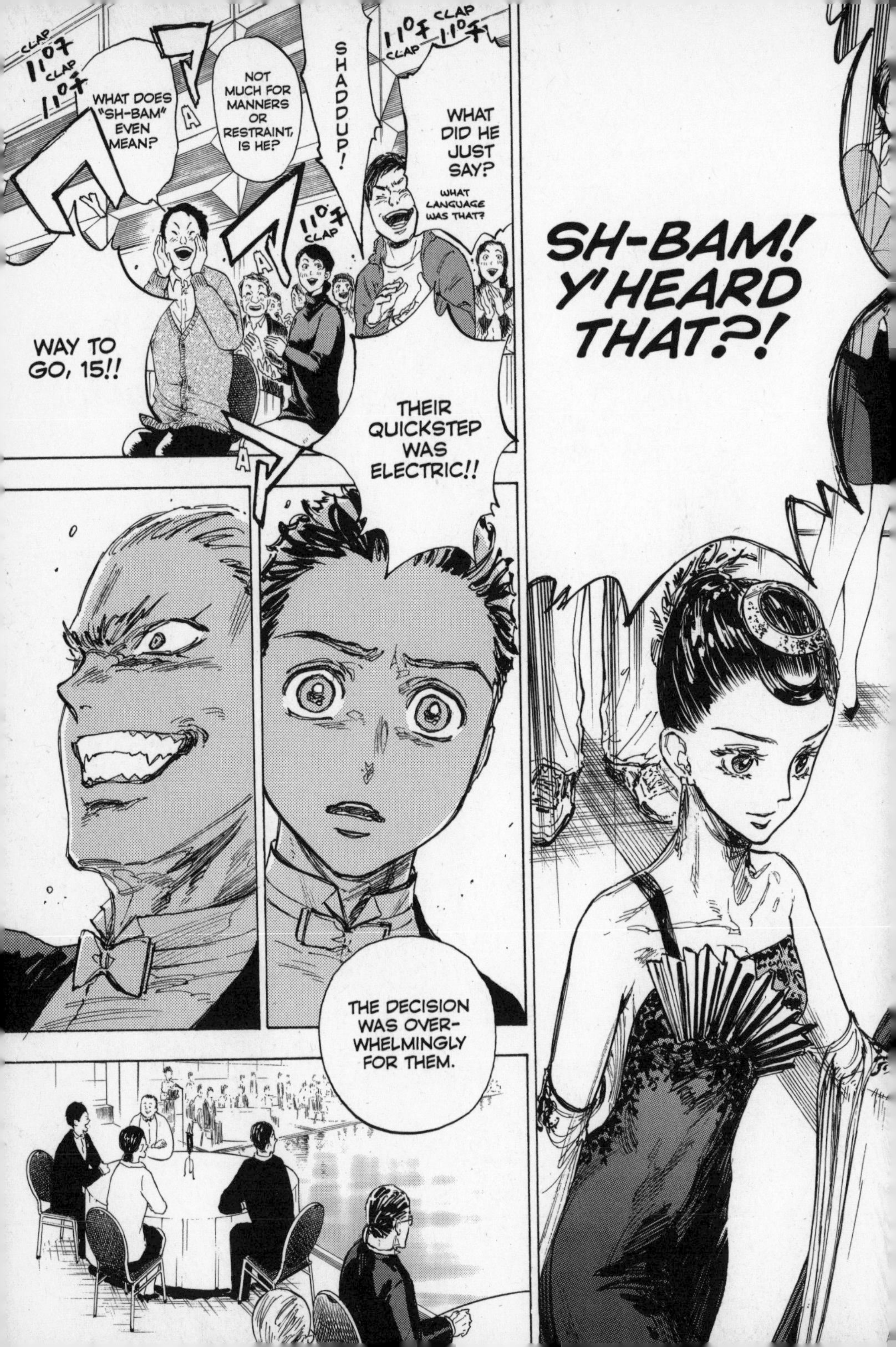
SH-BAM! Y'HEARD THAT?!
パチ CLAP パチ CLAP
WHAT DID HE JUST SAY?
WHAT LANGUAGE WAS THAT?
SHADDUP!
NOT MUCH FOR MANNERS OR RESTRAINT, IS HE?
パチ CLAP
WHAT DOES "SH-BAM" EVEN MEAN?
パチ CLAP パチ CLAP
WAY TO GO, 15!!
THEIR QUICKSTEP WAS ELECTRIC!!
THE DECISION WAS OVER-WHELMINGLY FOR THEM.

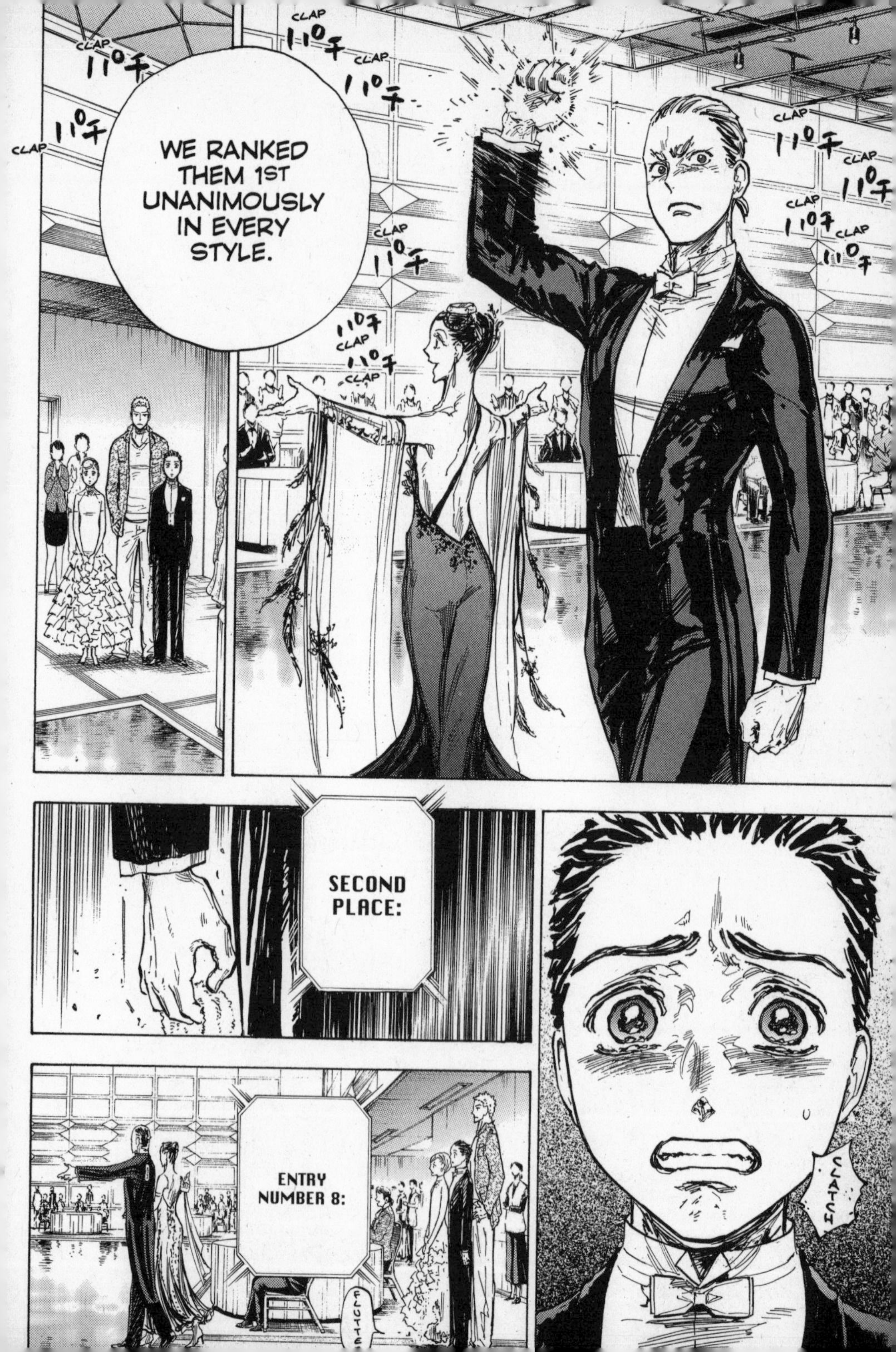
CLAP
CLAP
CLAP
CLAP
CLAP
CLAP
CLAP
CLAP
CLAP
CLAP
CLAP
WE RANKED THEM 1ST UNANIMOUSLY IN EVERY STYLE.
CLATCH
SECOND PLACE:
ENTRY NUMBER 8:
FLUTTE

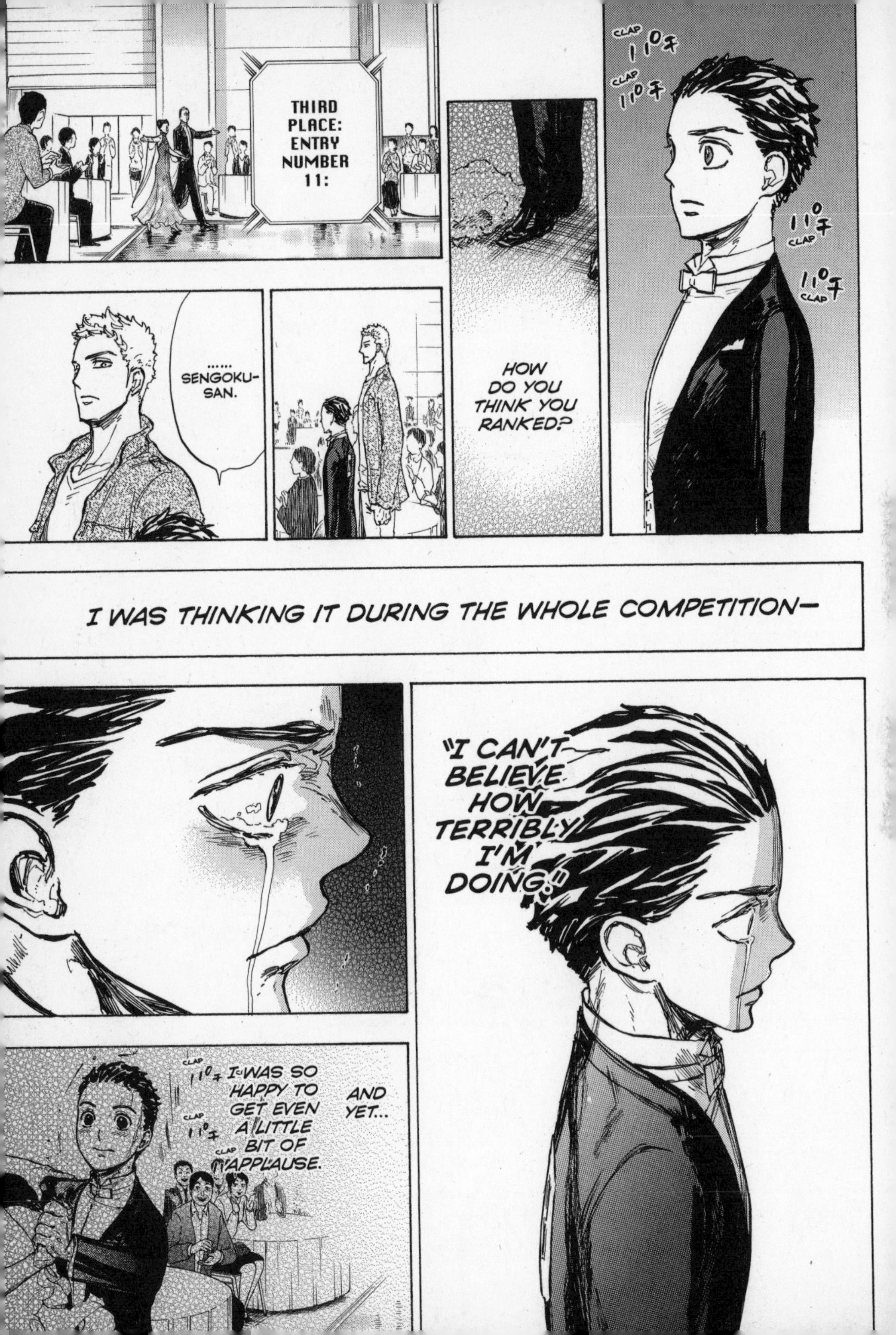
CLAP
CLAP
CLAP
CLAP
HOW DO YOU THINK YOU RANKED?
THIRD PLACE: ENTRY NUMBER 11:
...... SENGOKU-SAN.
I WAS THINKING IT DURING THE WHOLE COMPETITION—
"I CAN'T BELIEVE HOW TERRIBLY I'M DOING."
CLAP
CLAP
CLAP
I WAS SO HAPPY TO GET EVEN A LITTLE BIT OF APPLAUSE.
AND YET...

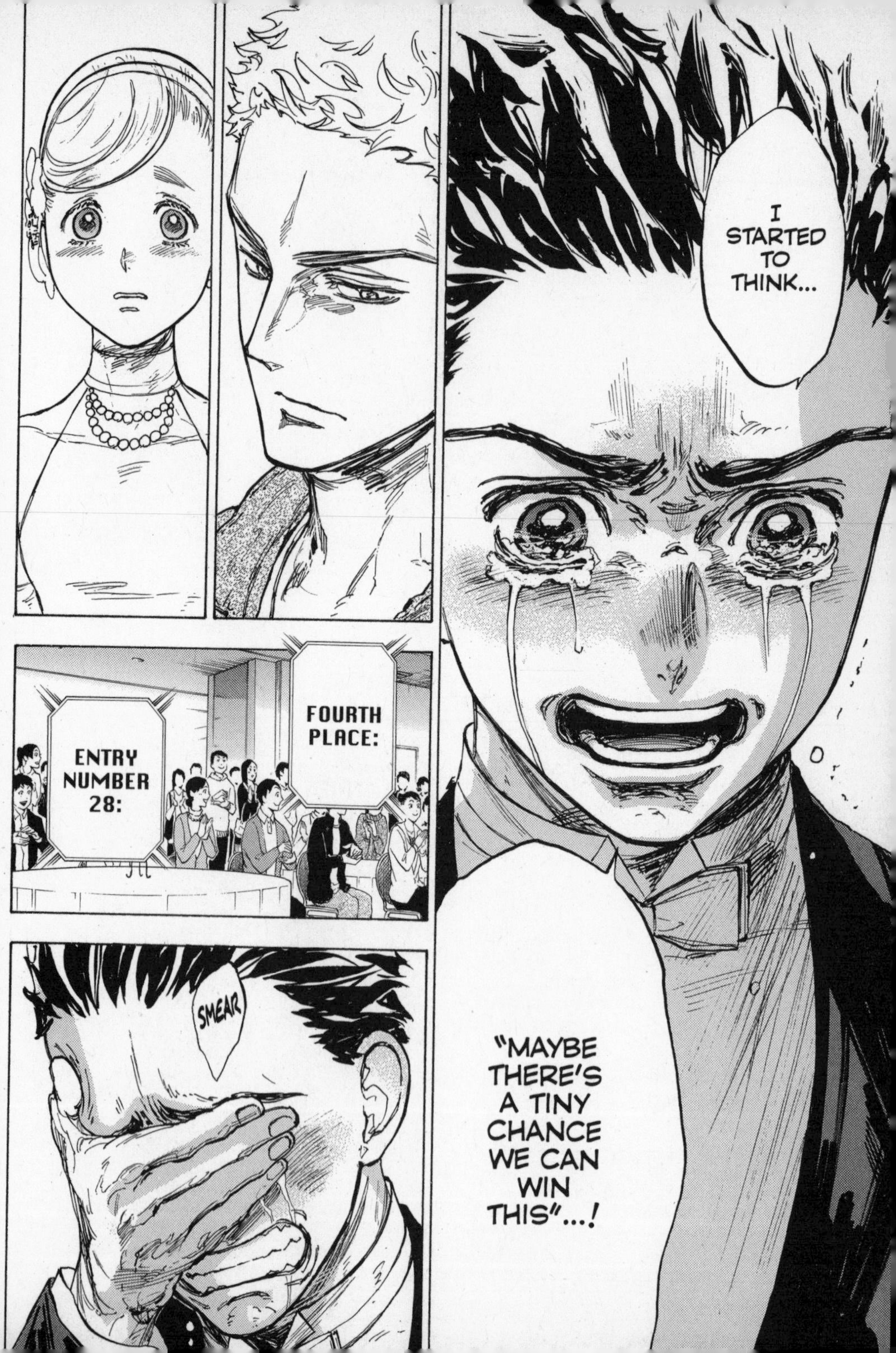
I STARTED TO THINK...
"MAYBE THERE'S A TINY CHANCE WE CAN WIN THIS"...!
FOURTH PLACE:
ENTRY NUMBER 28:
SMEAR

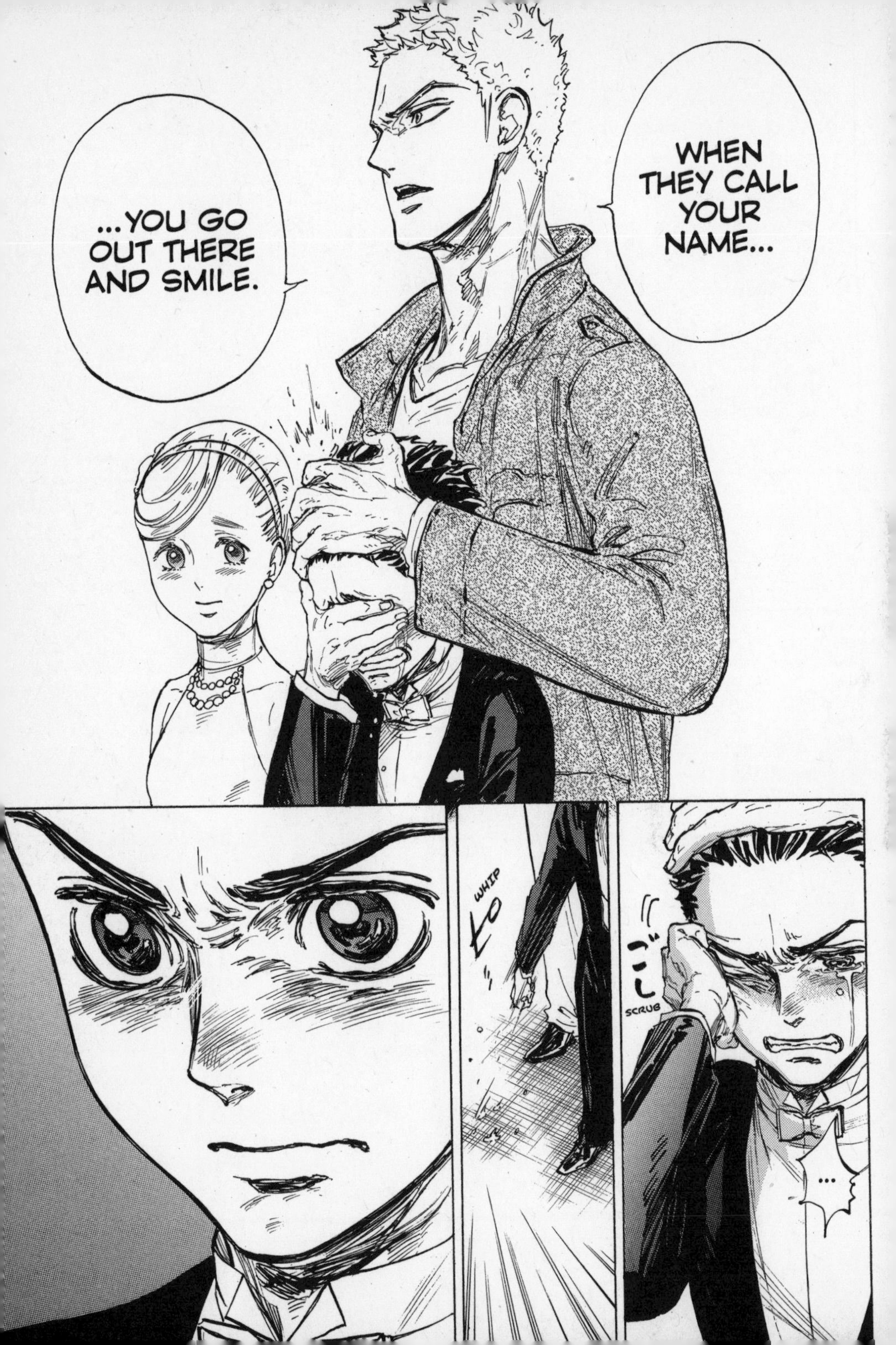
WHEN THEY CALL YOUR NAME...
...YOU GO OUT THERE AND SMILE.
ごし
SCRUB
...
WHIP

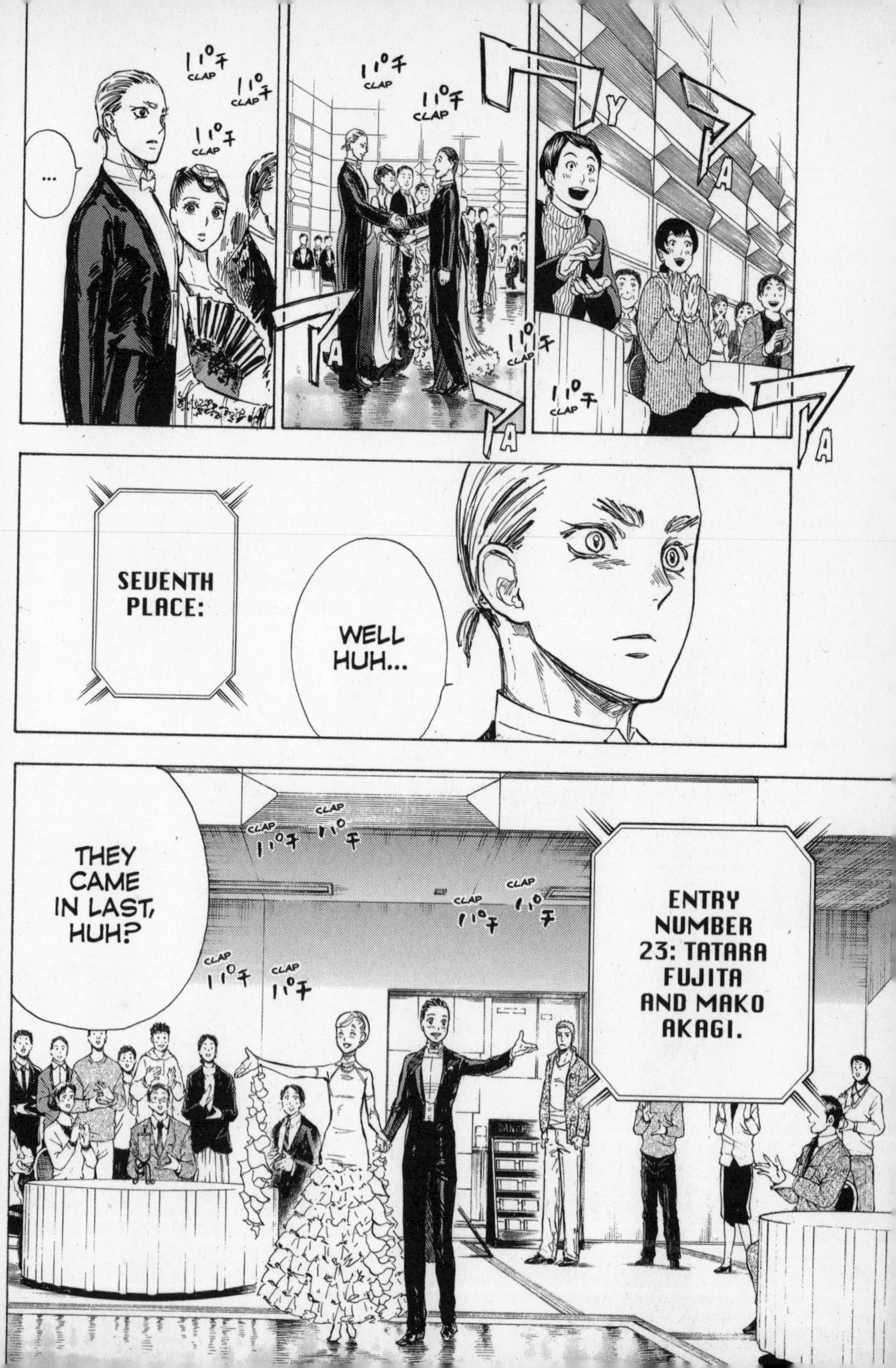
パチ
CLAP
パチ
CLAP
パチ
CLAP
パチ
CLAP
...
パチ
CLAP
WELL HUH...
SEVENTH PLACE:
ENTRY NUMBER 23: TATARA FUJITA AND MAKO AKAGI.
パチ
CLAP
THEY CAME IN LAST, HUH?
パチ
CLAP

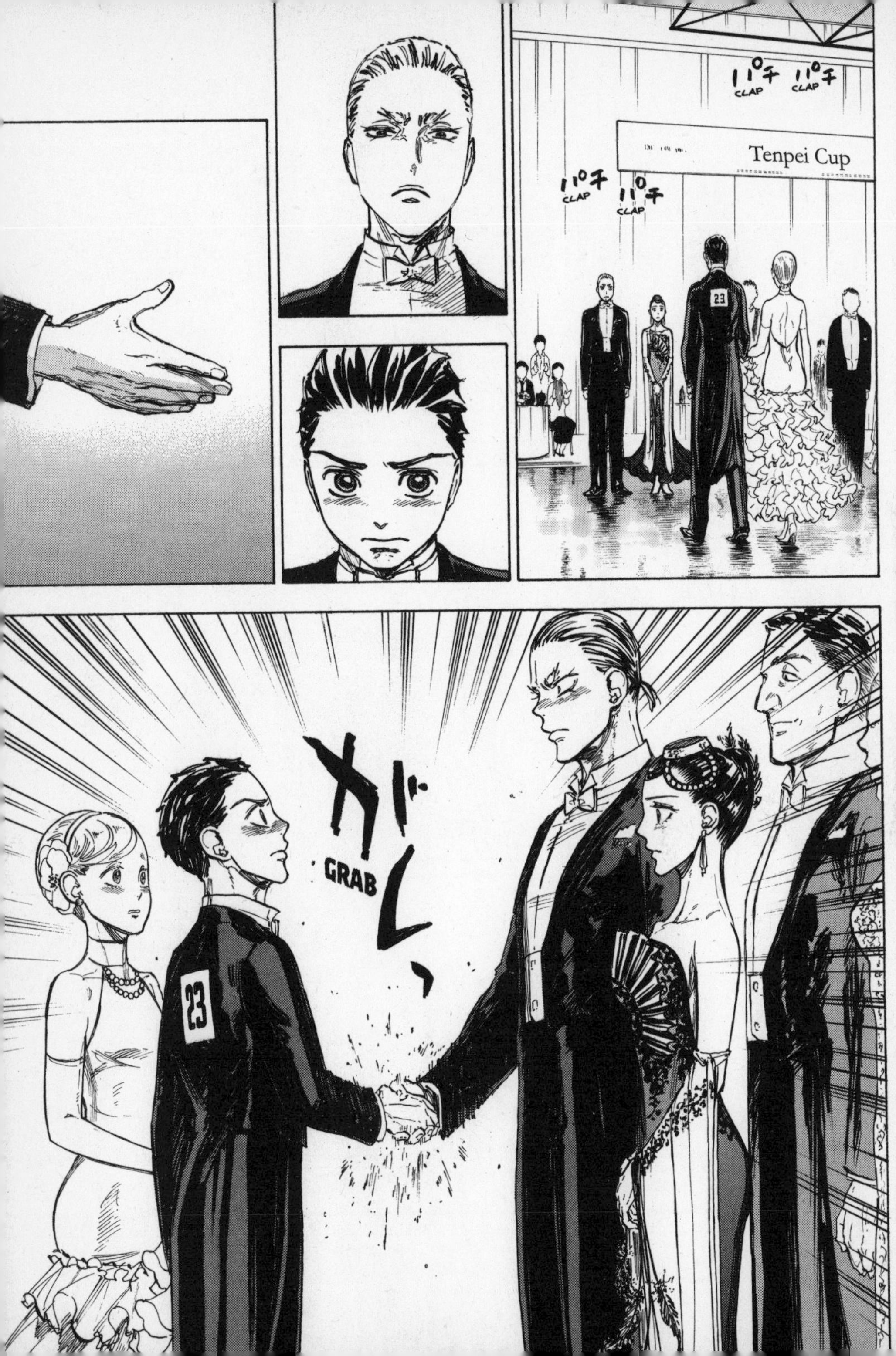
パチ
CLAP
パチ
CLAP
Tenpei Cup
パチ
CLAP
パチ
CLAP
ガシ
GRAB

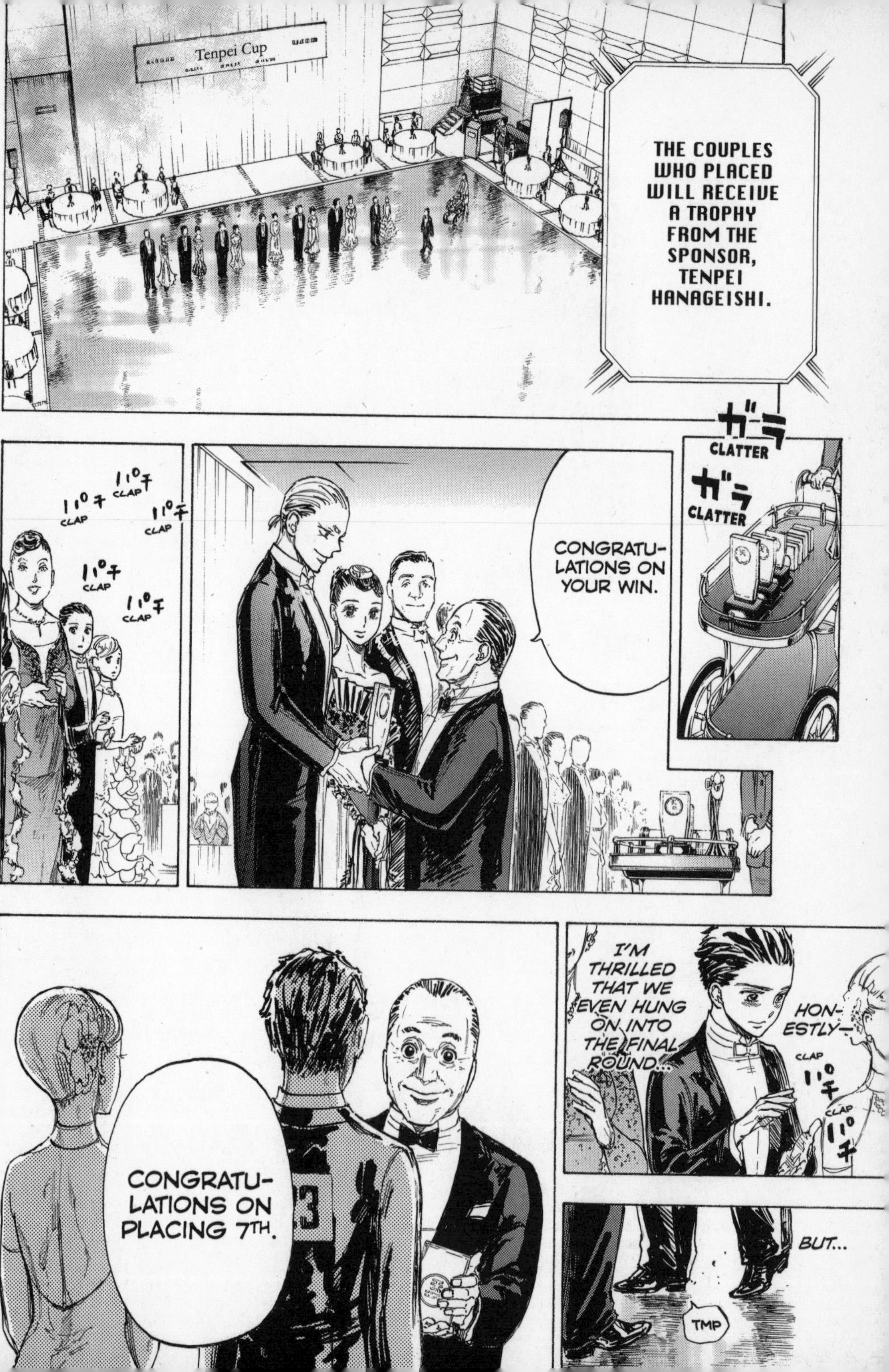
THE COUPLES WHO PLACED WILL RECEIVE A TROPHY FROM THE SPONSOR, TENPEI HANAGEISHI.
Tenpei Cup
ガーラ
CLATTER
ガラ
CLATTER
CONGRATULATIONS ON YOUR WIN.
パチ
CLAP
パチ
CLAP
パチ
CLAP
パチ
CLAP
パチ
CLAP
HONESTLY—
I'M THRILLED THAT WE EVEN HUNG ON INTO THE FINAL ROUND...
CLAP
パチ
CLAP
パチ
BUT...
TMP
CONGRATULATIONS ON PLACING 7TH.

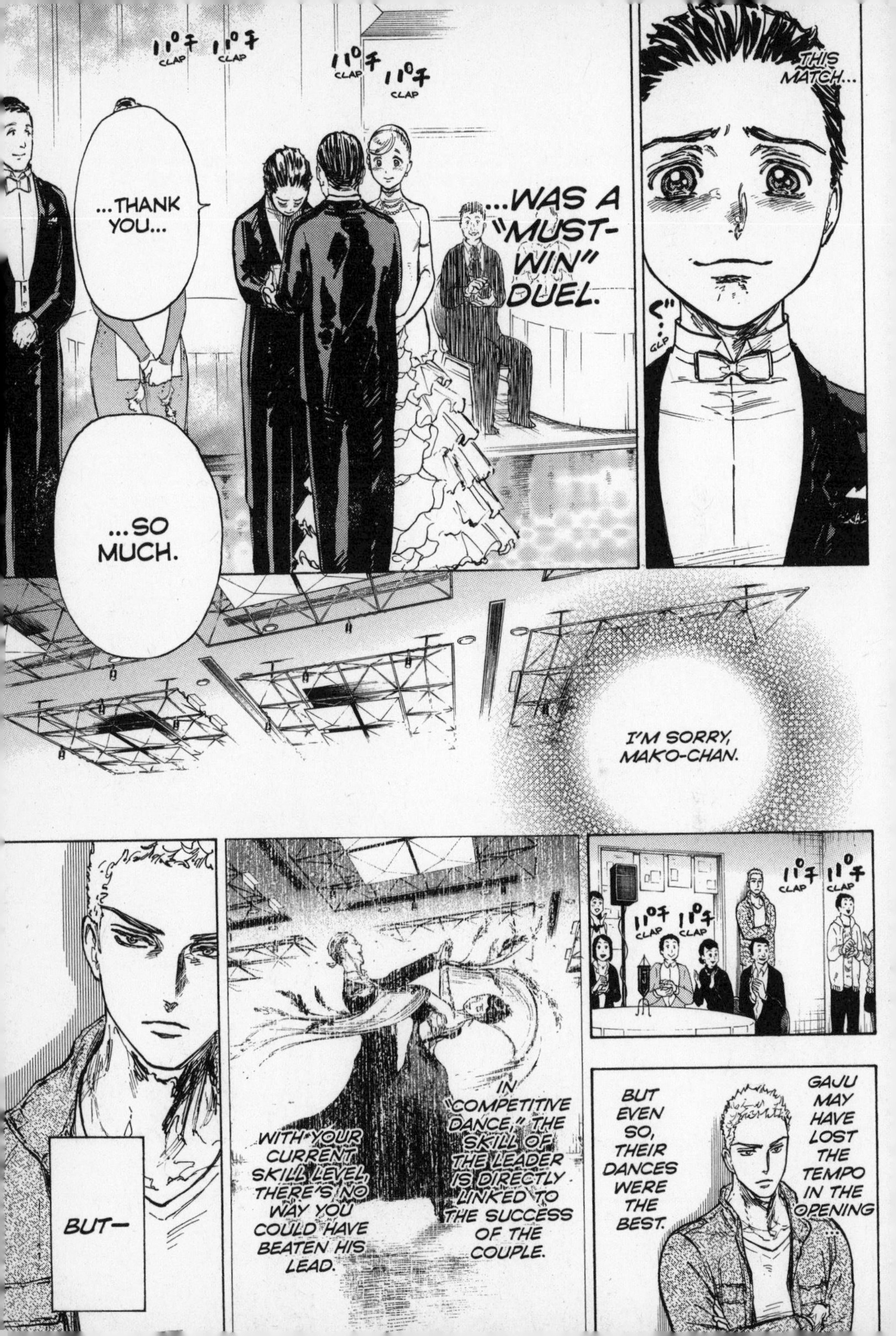
THIS MATCH...
...WAS A "MUST-WIN" DUEL.
ぐ… GLP
パチ CLAP パチ CLAP
パチ CLAP パチ CLAP
...THANK YOU...
...SO MUCH.
I'M SORRY, MAKO-CHAN.
パチ CLAP パチ CLAP
パチ CLAP パチ CLAP
GAJU MAY HAVE LOST THE TEMPO IN THE OPENING...
BUT EVEN SO, THEIR DANCES WERE THE BEST.
IN "COMPETITIVE DANCE," THE SKILL OF THE LEADER IS DIRECTLY LINKED TO THE SUCCESS OF THE COUPLE.
WITH YOUR CURRENT SKILL LEVEL, THERE'S NO WAY YOU COULD HAVE BEATEN HIS LEAD.
BUT—

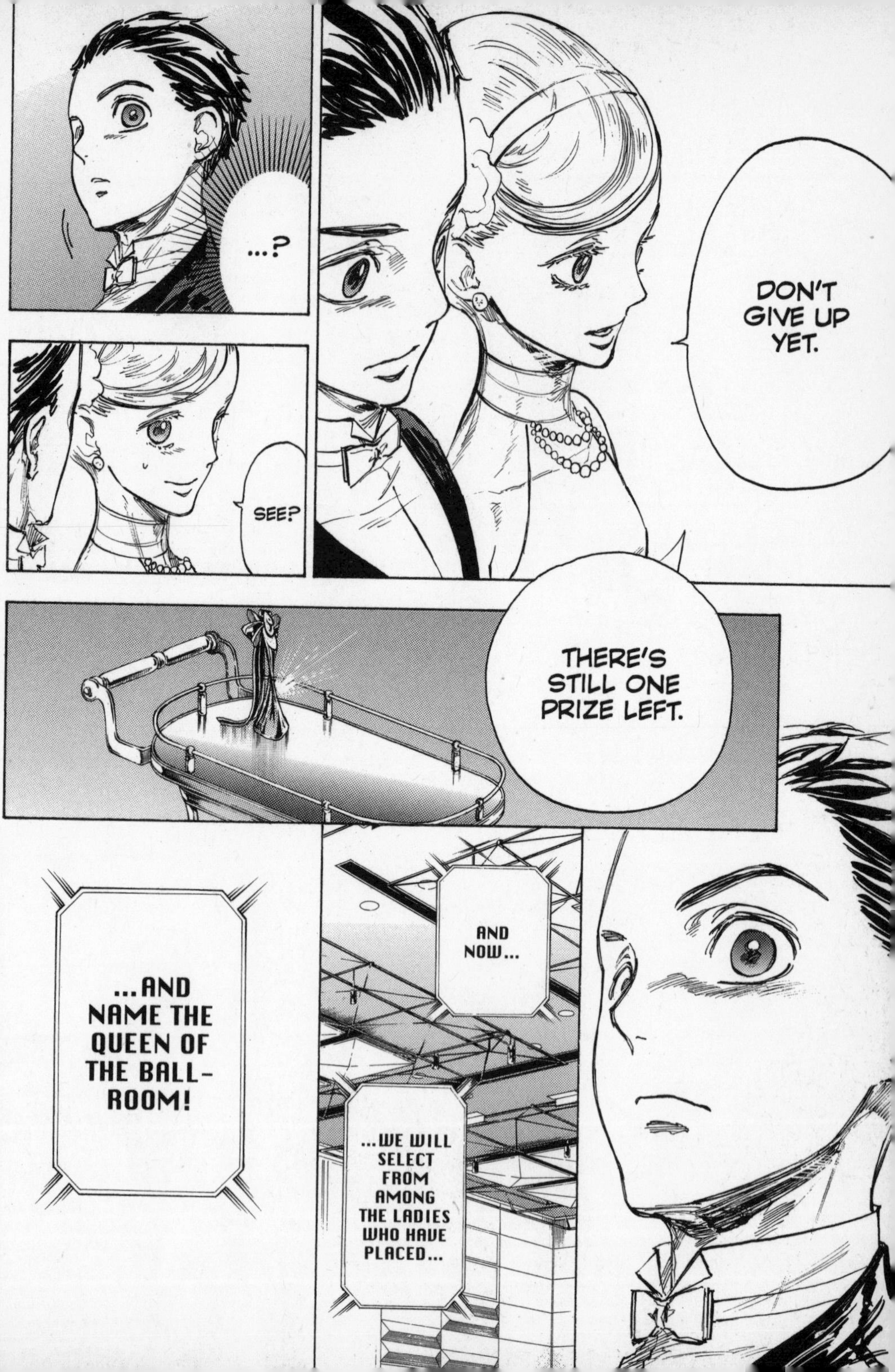
DON'T GIVE UP YET.
...?
SEE?
THERE'S STILL ONE PRIZE LEFT.
AND NOW...
...WE WILL SELECT FROM AMONG THE LADIES WHO HAVE PLACED...
...AND NAME THE QUEEN OF THE BALL-ROOM!

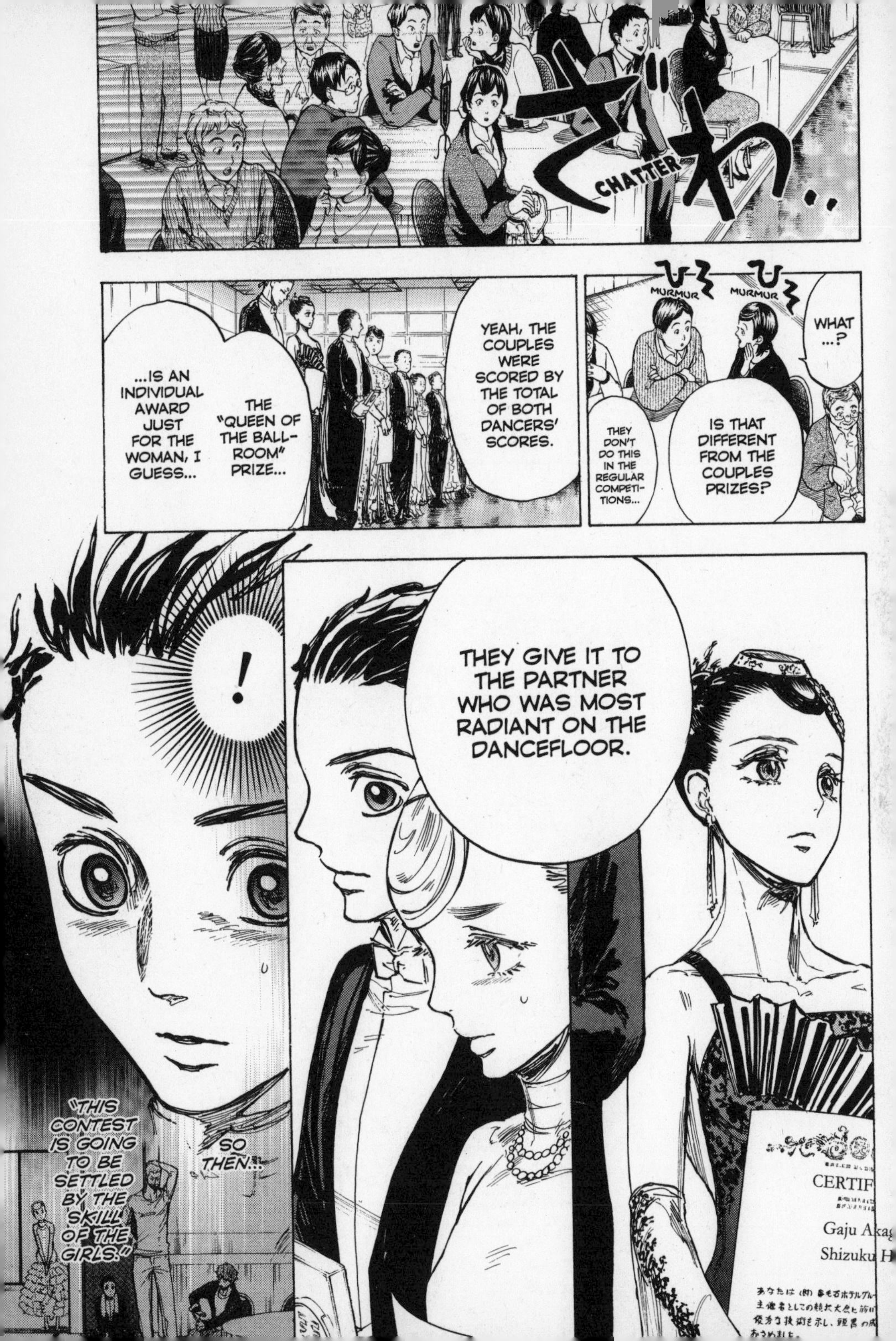
CHATTER
MURMUR
MURMUR
WHAT ...?
IS THAT DIFFERENT FROM THE COUPLES PRIZES?
THEY DON'T DO THIS IN THE REGULAR COMPETI-TIONS...
YEAH, THE COUPLES WERE SCORED BY THE TOTAL OF BOTH DANCERS' SCORES.
THE "QUEEN OF THE BALL-ROOM" PRIZE...
...IS AN INDIVIDUAL AWARD JUST FOR THE WOMAN, I GUESS...
THEY GIVE IT TO THE PARTNER WHO WAS MOST RADIANT ON THE DANCEFLOOR.
!
SO THEN...
"THIS CONTEST IS GOING TO BE SETTLED BY THE SKILL OF THE GIRLS."

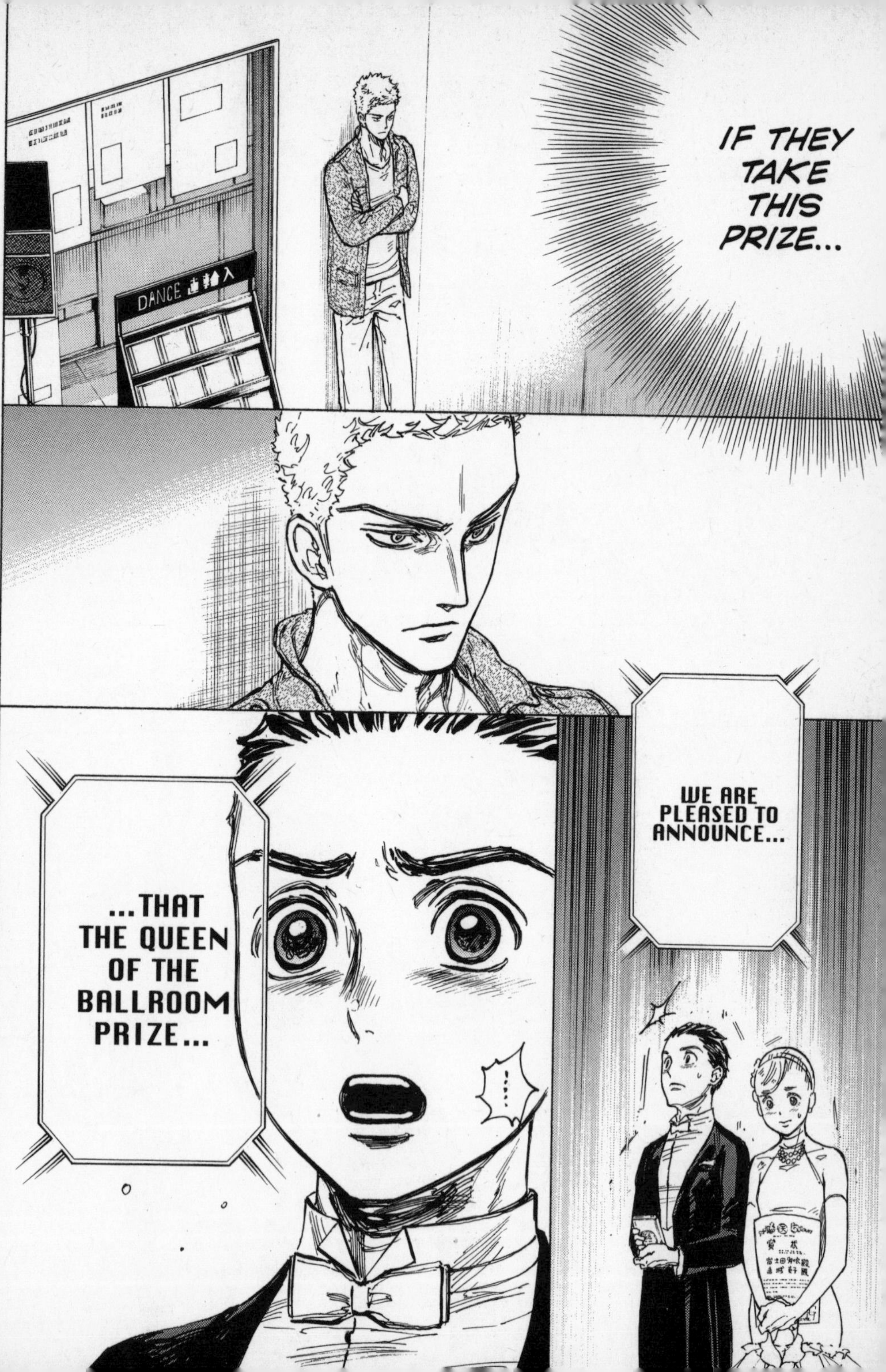
IF THEY TAKE THIS PRIZE...
WE ARE PLEASED TO ANNOUNCE...
...THAT THE QUEEN OF THE BALLROOM PRIZE...
DANCE

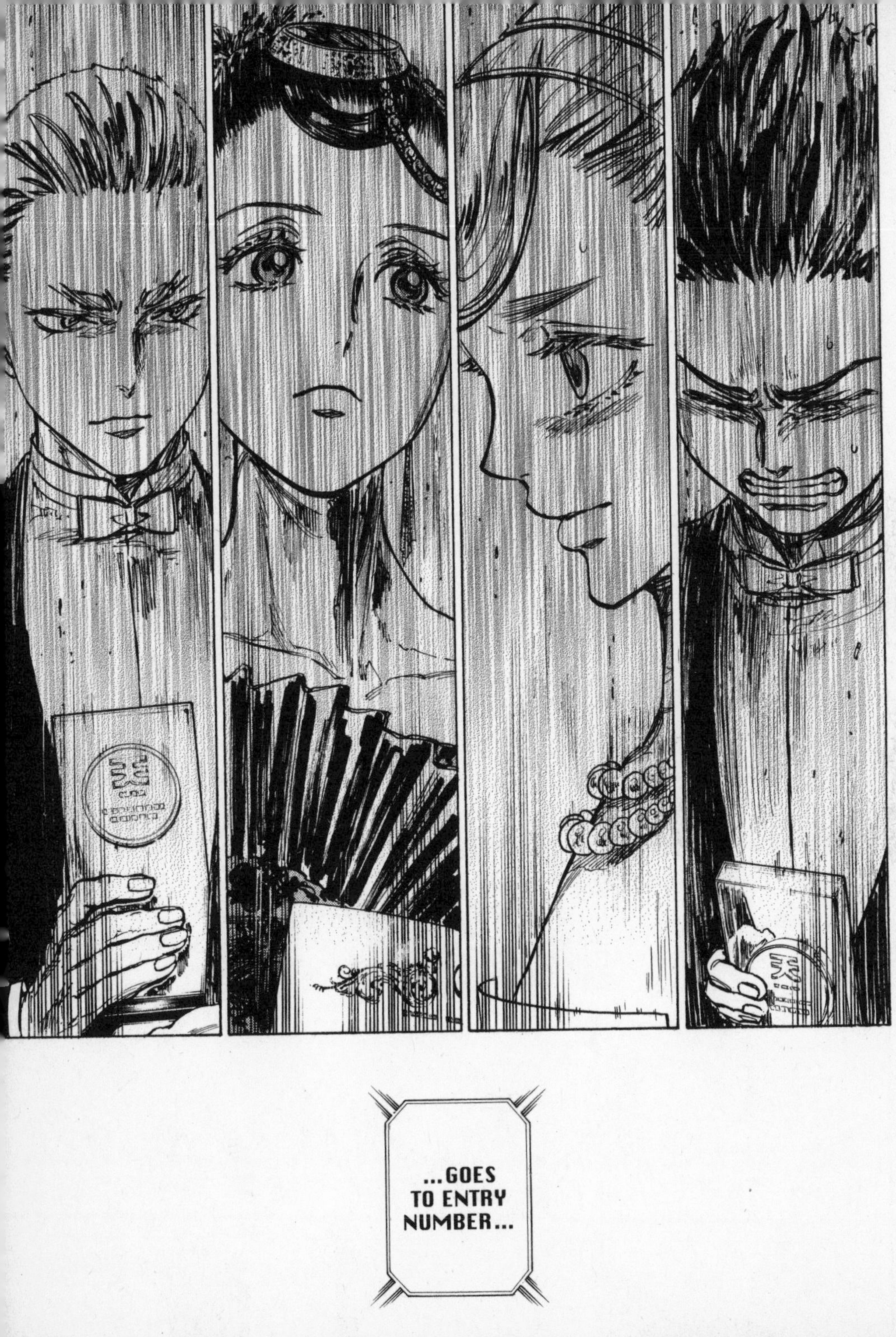
...GOES
TO ENTRY
NUMBER...

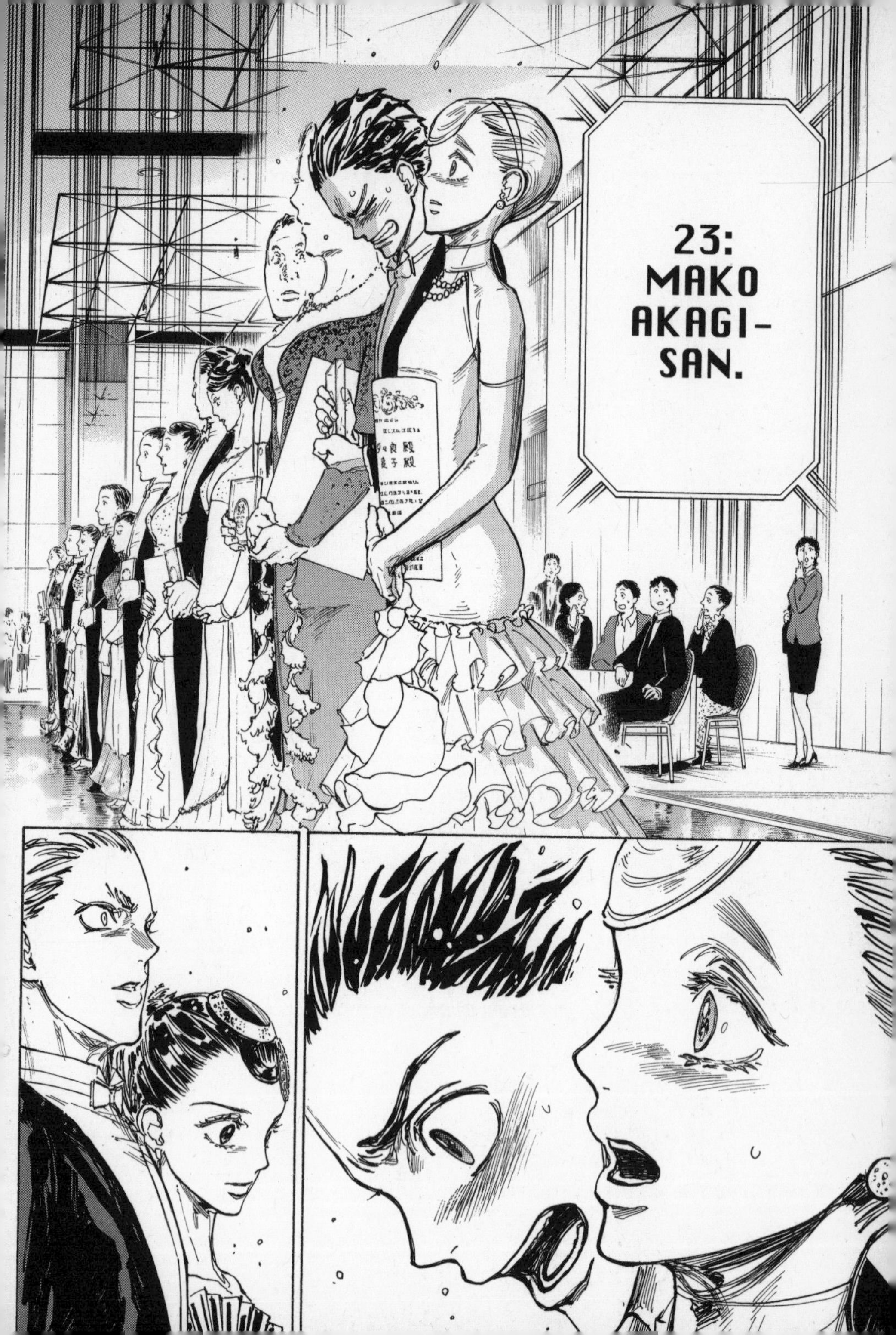
23: MAKO AKAGI-SAN.

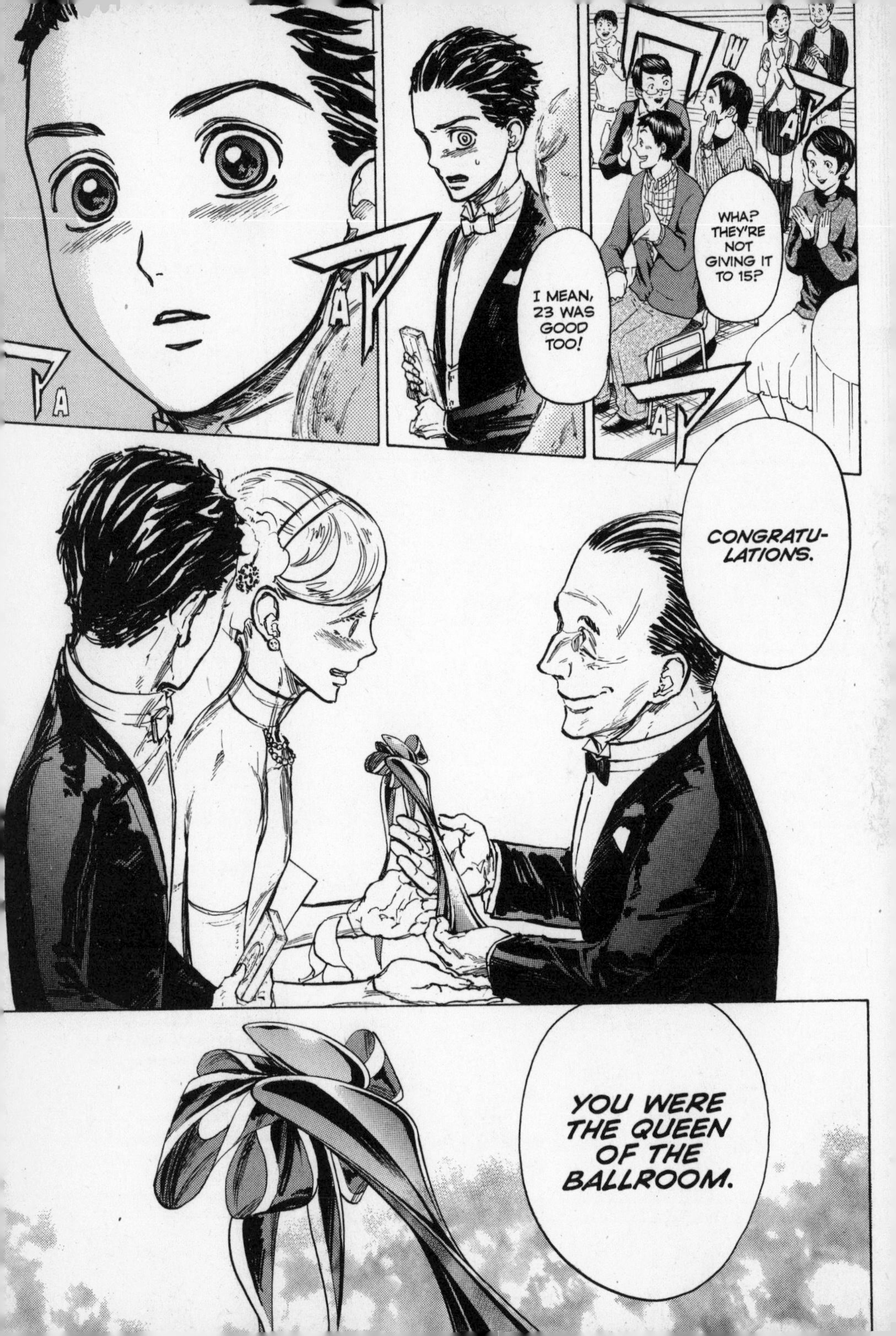
WHA? THEY'RE NOT GIVING IT TO 15?
I MEAN, 23 WAS GOOD TOO!
CONGRATULATIONS.
YOU WERE THE QUEEN OF THE BALLROOM.

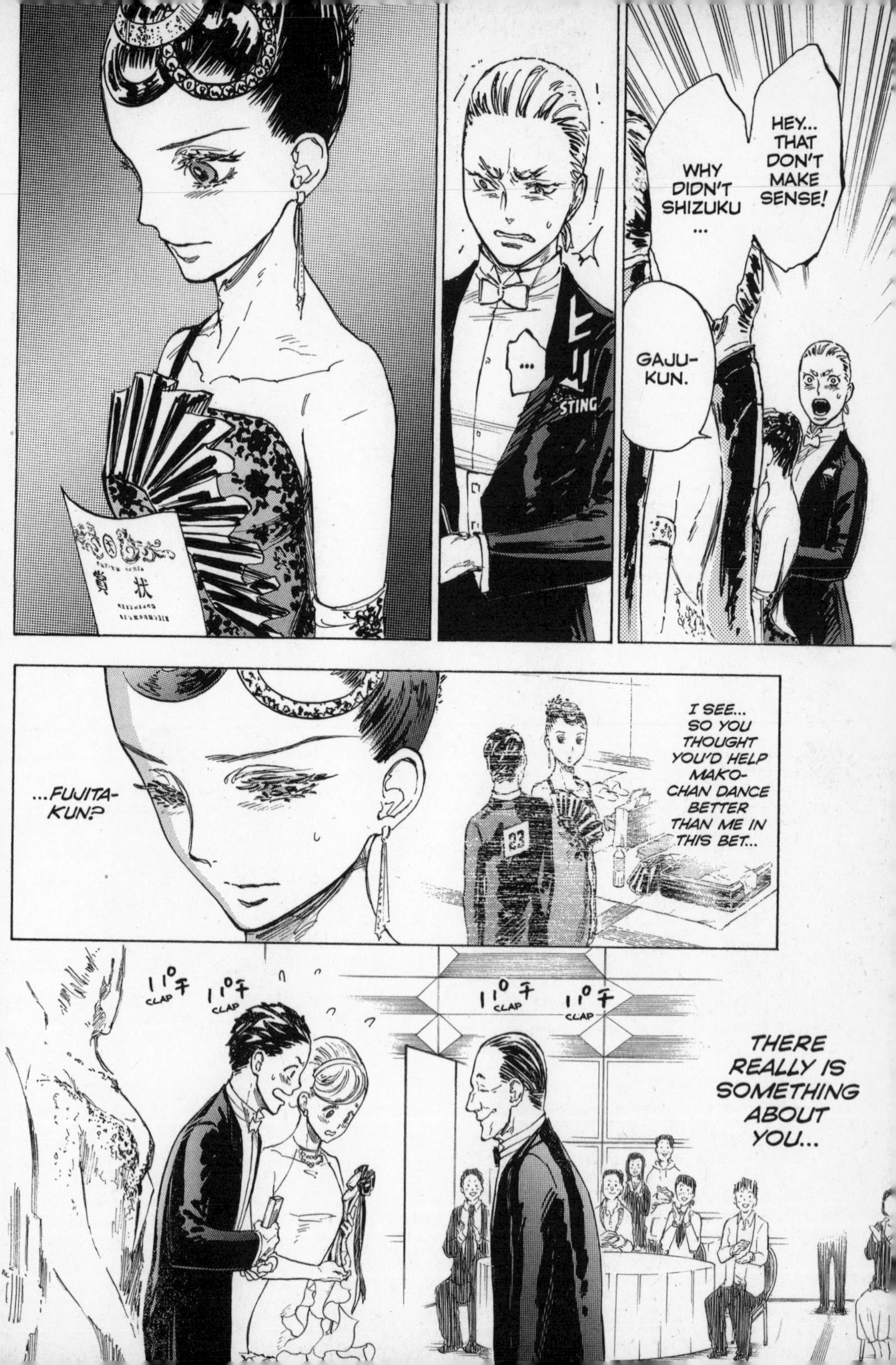
HEY... THAT DON'T MAKE SENSE!
WHY DIDN'T SHIZUKU ...
GAJU-KUN.
...
STING
賞状
I SEE... SO YOU THOUGHT YOU'D HELP MAKO-CHAN DANCE BETTER THAN ME IN THIS BET...
23
...FUJITA-KUN?
THERE REALLY IS SOMETHING ABOUT YOU...
パチ CLAP
パチ CLAP
パチ CLAP
パチ CLAP

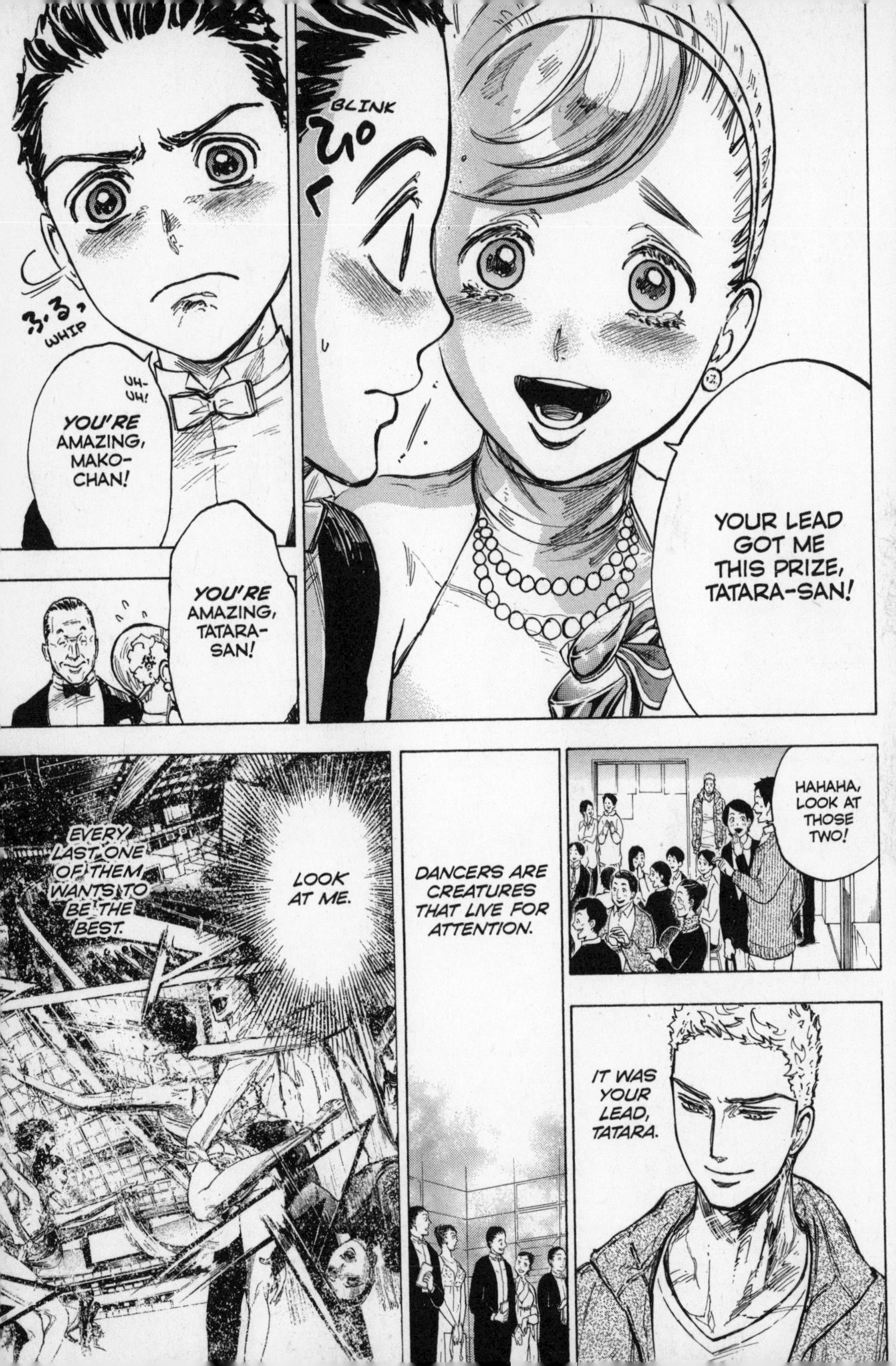
BLINK
YOUR LEAD GOT ME THIS PRIZE, TATARA-SAN!
WHIP
UH-UH!
YOU'RE AMAZING, MAKO-CHAN!
YOU'RE AMAZING, TATARA-SAN!
HAHAHA, LOOK AT THOSE TWO!
IT WAS YOUR LEAD, TATARA.
DANCERS ARE CREATURES THAT LIVE FOR ATTENTION.
LOOK AT ME.
EVERY LAST ONE OF THEM WANTS TO BE THE BEST.

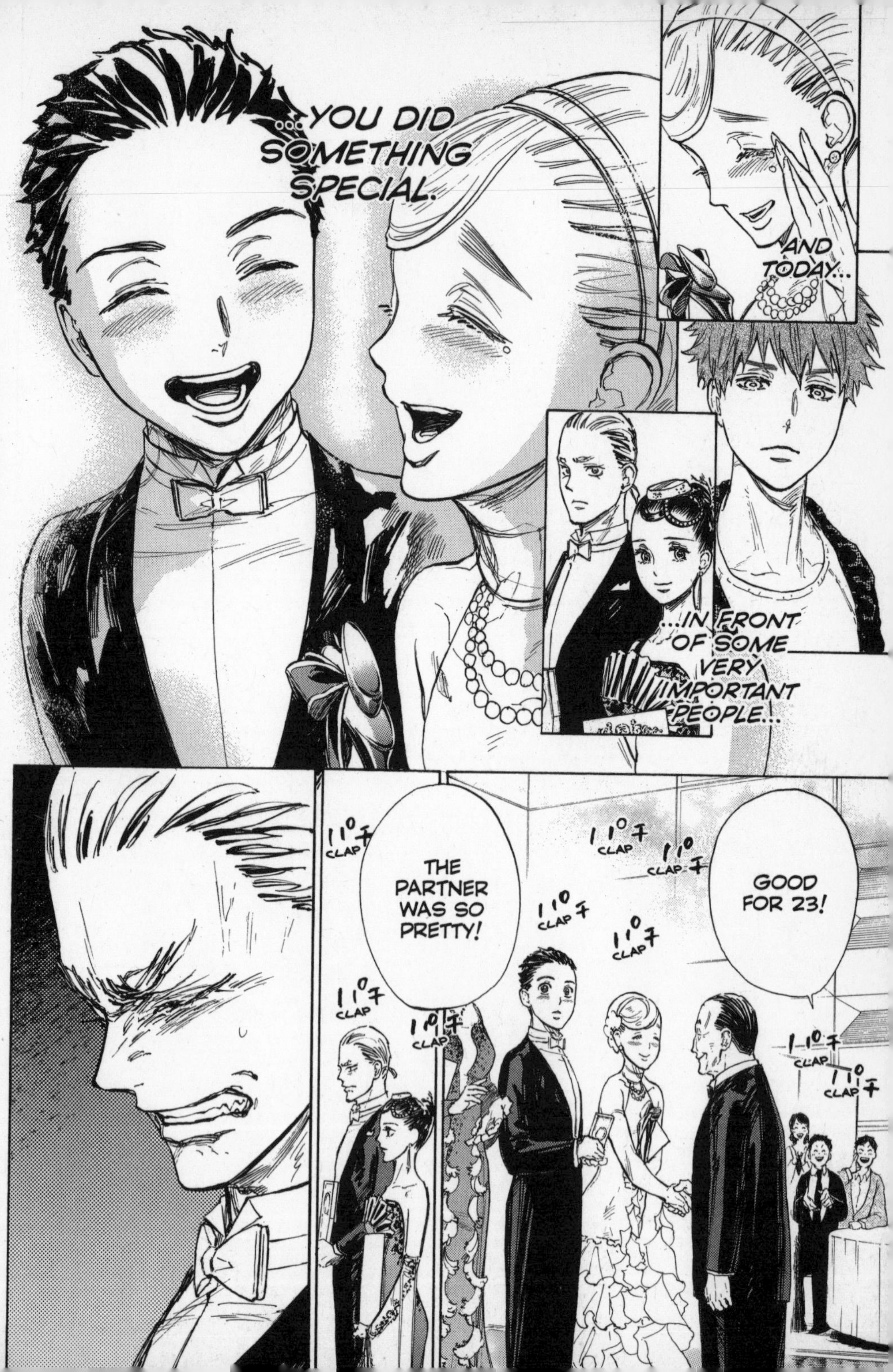
AND TODAY...
...IN FRONT OF SOME VERY IMPORTANT PEOPLE...
...YOU DID SOMETHING SPECIAL.
CLAP
CLAP
GOOD FOR 23!
CLAP
CLAP
CLAP
CLAP
THE PARTNER WAS SO PRETTY!
CLAP
CLAP
CLAP

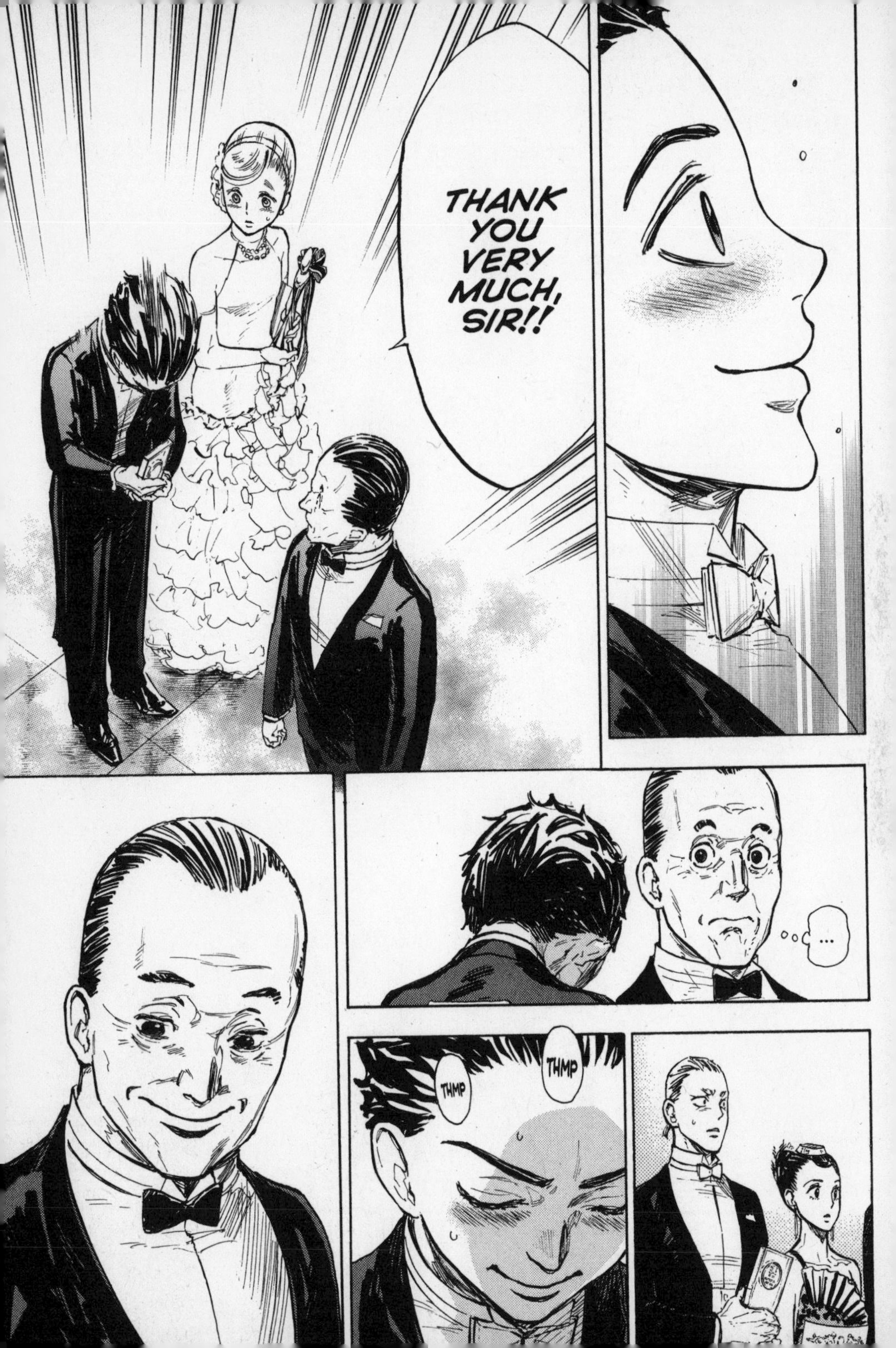
THANK YOU VERY MUCH, SIR!!
...
THMP
THMP

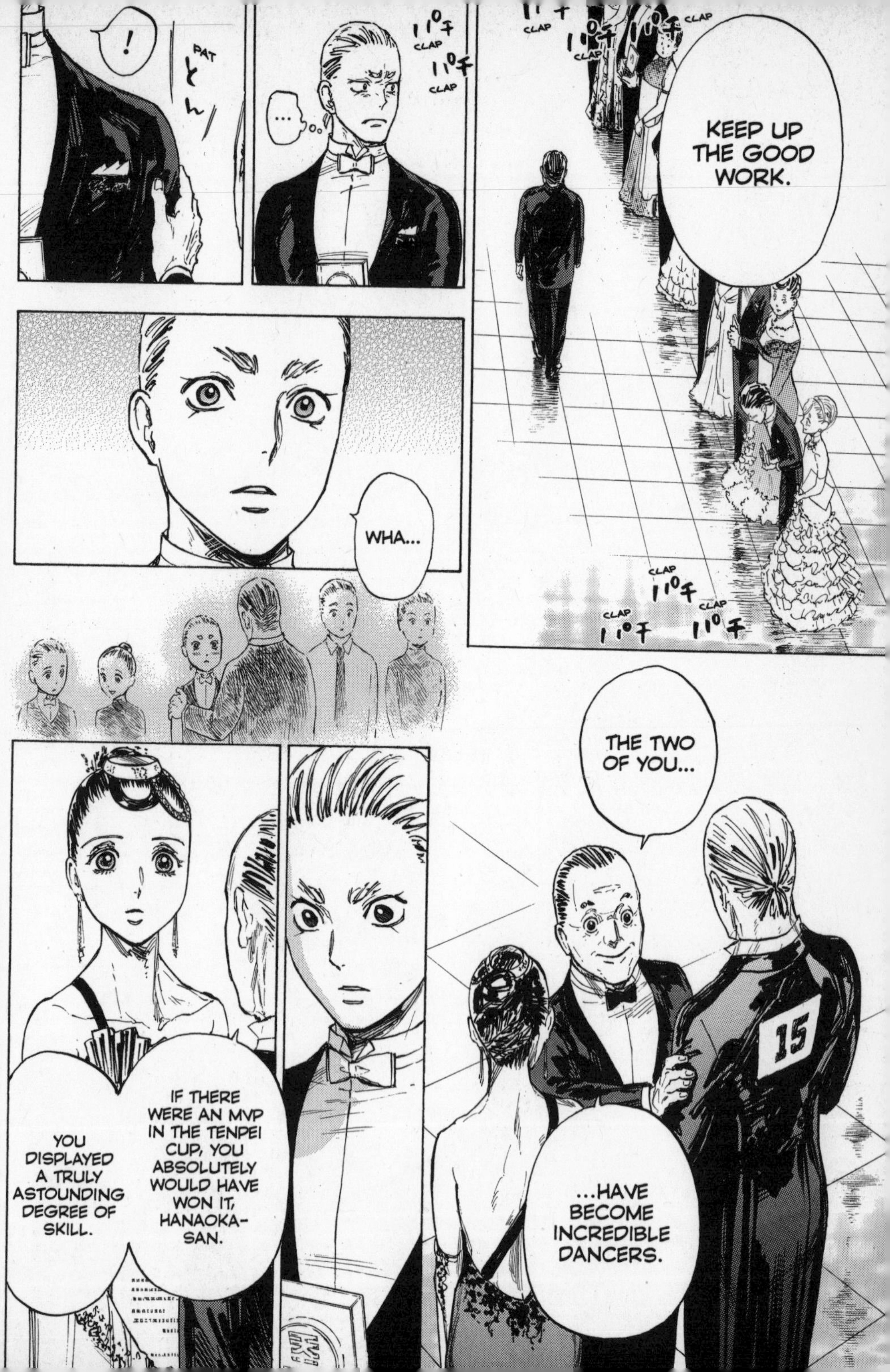

パチ CLAP
パチ CLAP
KEEP UP THE GOOD WORK.
パチ CLAP
パチ CLAP
パチ CLAP
パチ CLAP
...
!
とん PAT
WHA...
THE TWO OF YOU...
...HAVE BECOME INCREDIBLE DANCERS.
IF THERE WERE AN MVP IN THE TENPEI CUP, YOU ABSOLUTELY WOULD HAVE WON IT, HANAOKA-SAN.
YOU DISPLAYED A TRULY ASTOUNDING DEGREE OF SKILL.

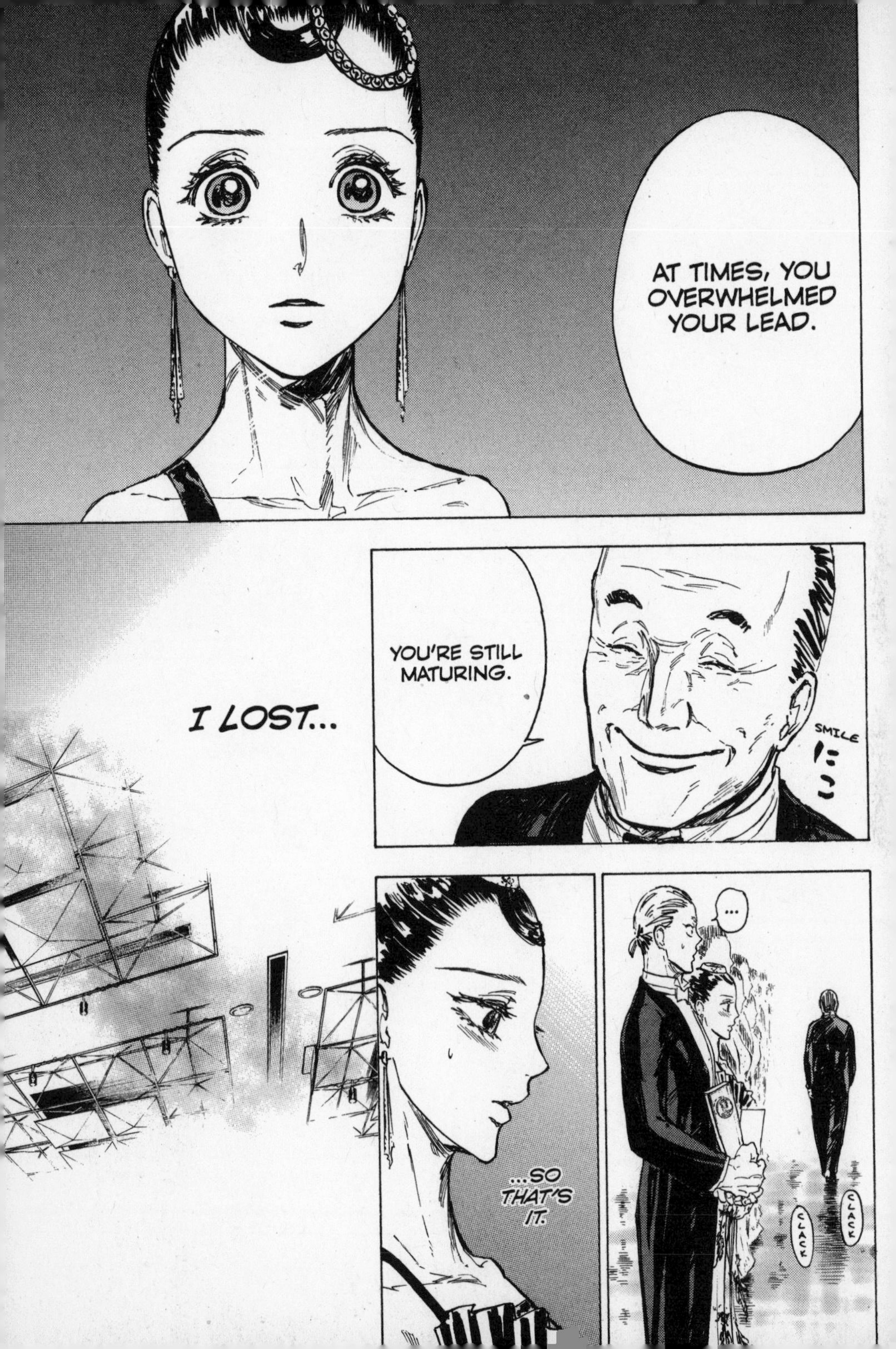
AT TIMES, YOU OVERWHELMED YOUR LEAD.
YOU'RE STILL MATURING.
SMILE
にこ
...
CLACK
CLACK
...SO THAT'S IT.
I LOST...

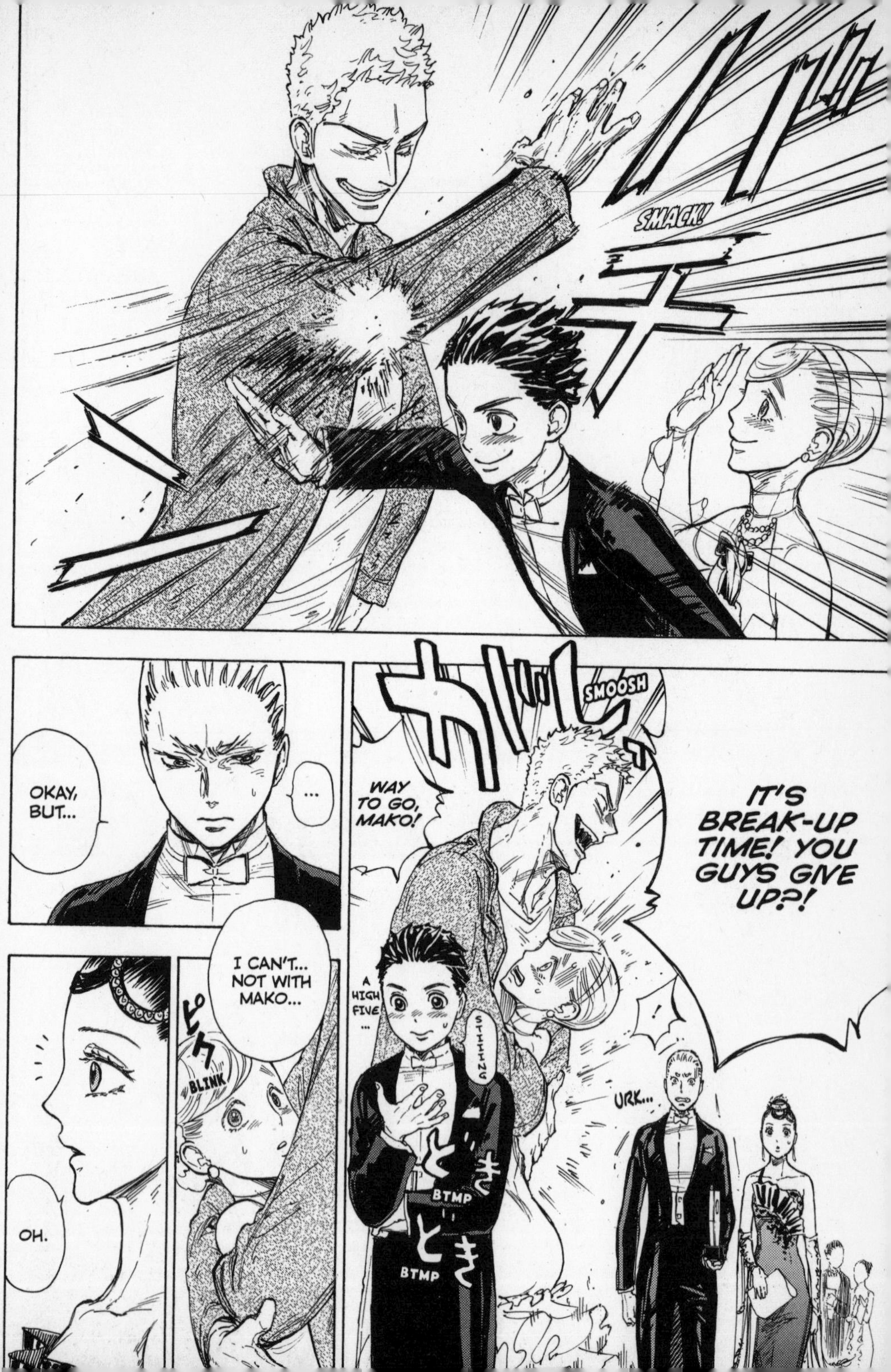
SMACK!
SMOOSH
IT'S BREAK-UP TIME! YOU GUYS GIVE UP?!
WAY TO GO, MAKO!
!
URK...
STIIIING
A HIGH FIVE...
BTMP
BTMP
OKAY, BUT...
...
I CAN'T... NOT WITH MAKO...
BLINK
OH.

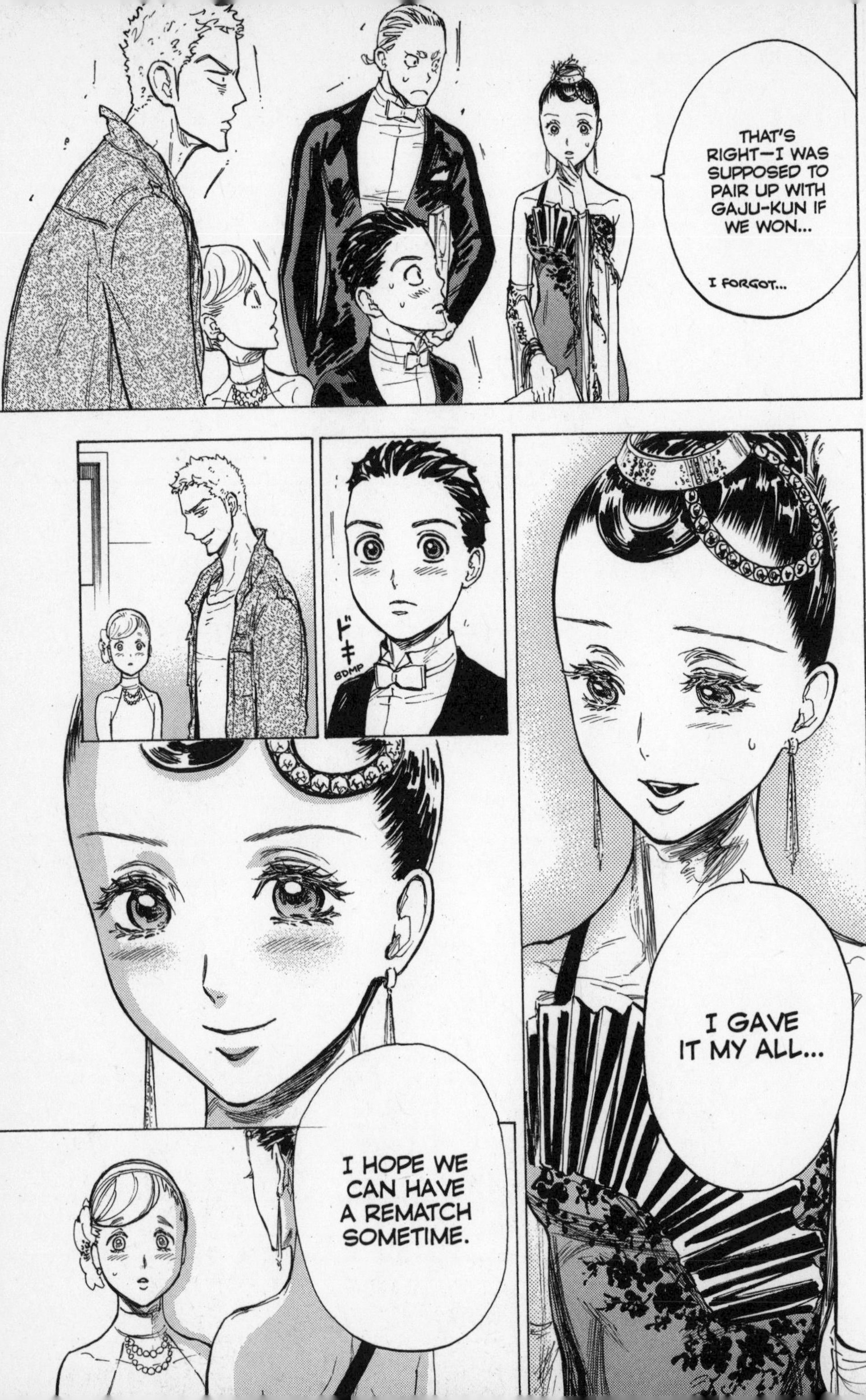
THAT'S RIGHT—I WAS SUPPOSED TO PAIR UP WITH GAJU-KUN IF WE WON...
I FORGOT...
I GAVE IT MY ALL...
ドキ BDMP
I HOPE WE CAN HAVE A REMATCH SOMETIME.

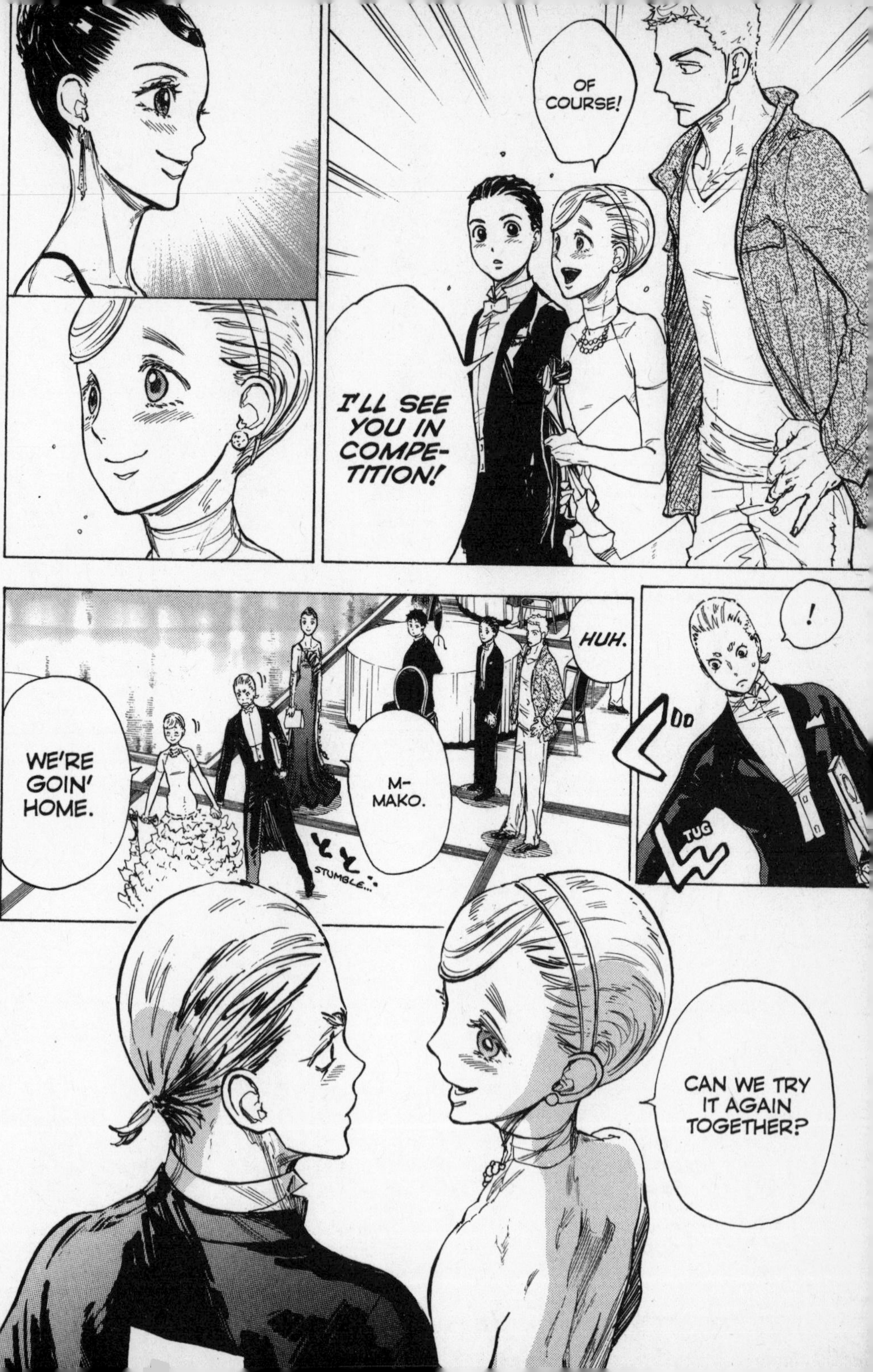
OF COURSE!
I'LL SEE YOU IN COMPE-TITION!
!
DO
TUG
HUH.
M- MAKO.
WE'RE GOIN' HOME.
STUMBLE...
CAN WE TRY IT AGAIN TOGETHER?

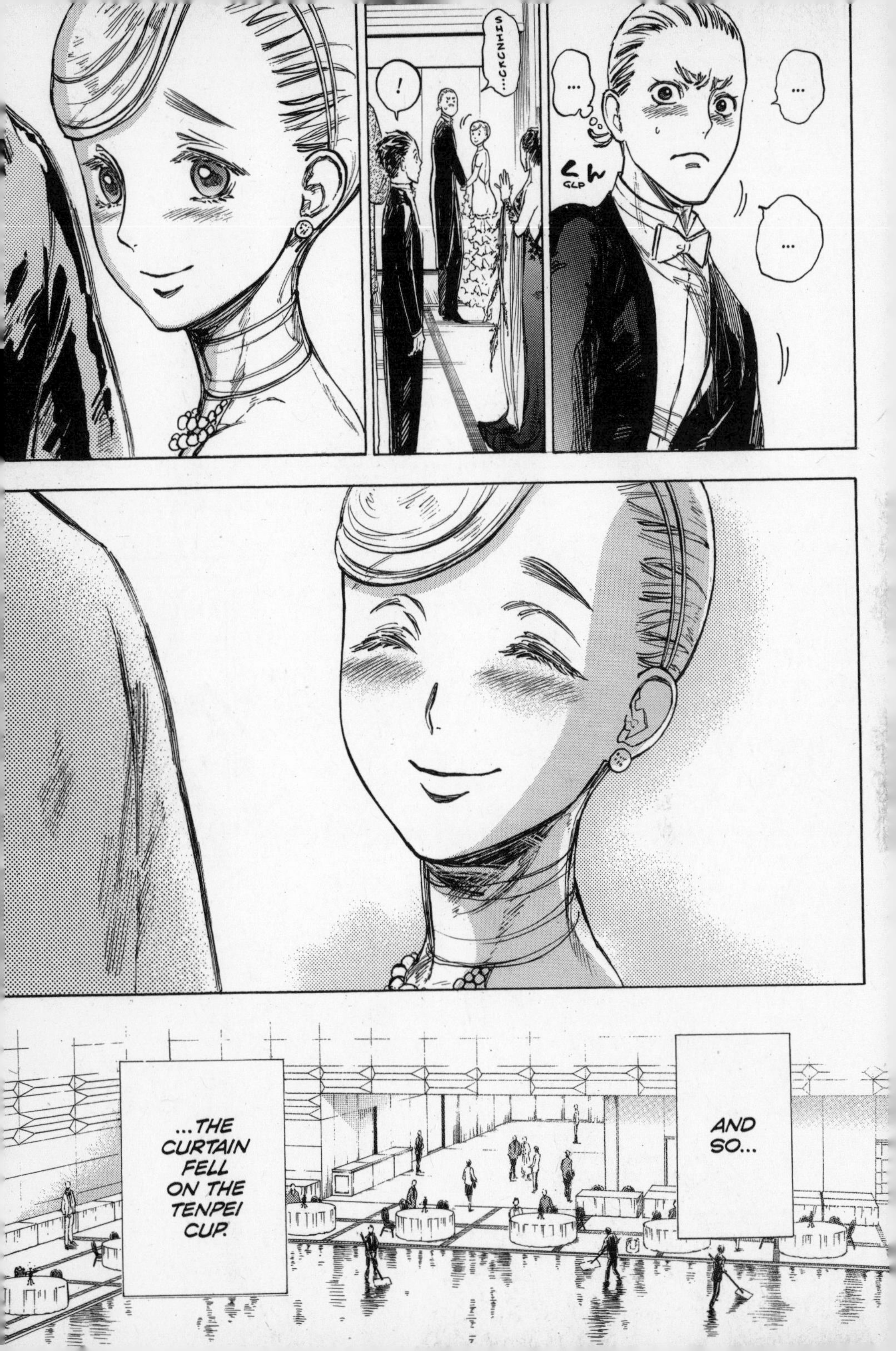
...
...
...
GLP
SHIZUKU...
!
AND SO...
...THE CURTAIN FELL ON THE TENPEI CUP.

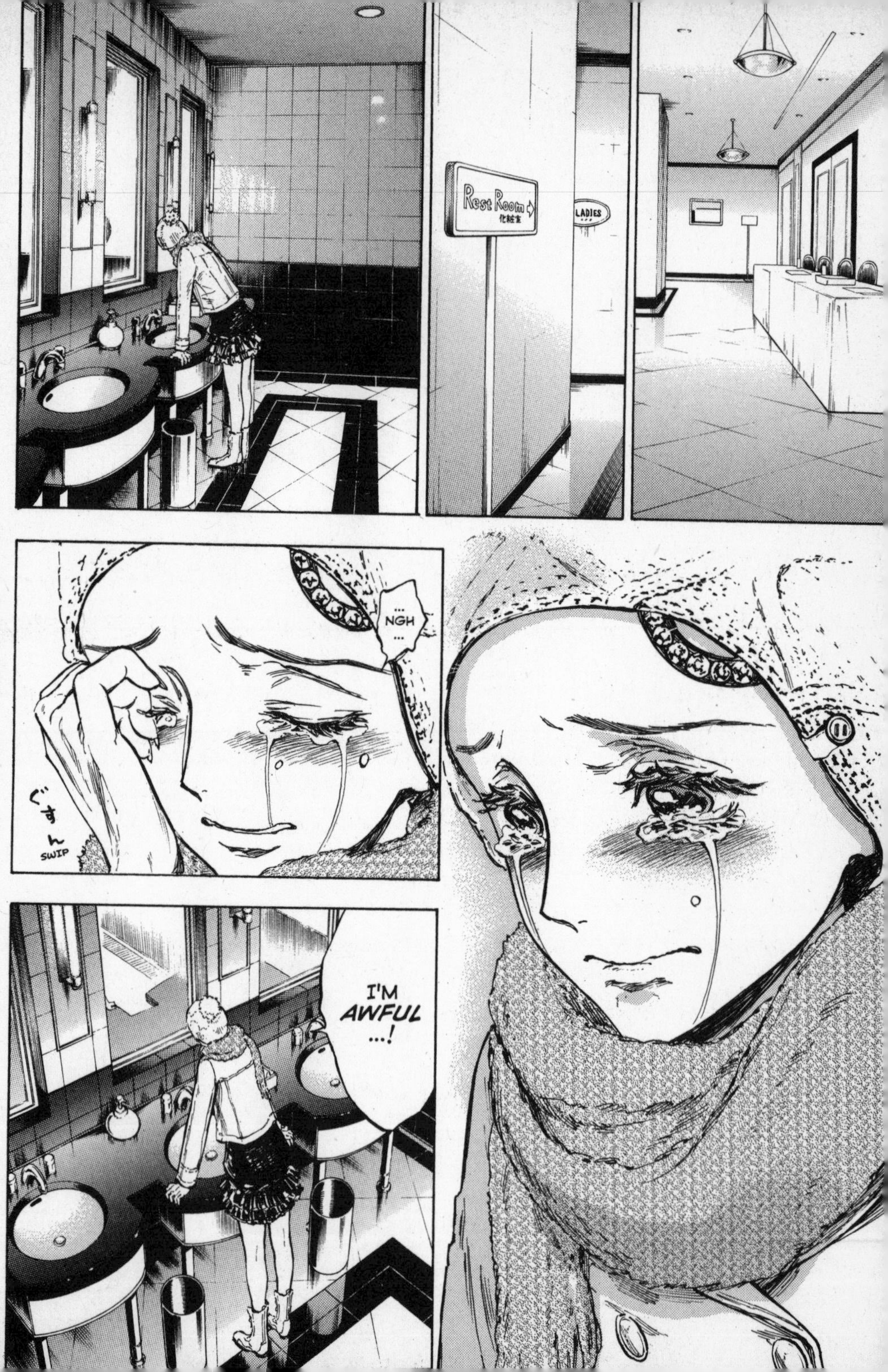
Rest Room
化粧室
LADIES
...NGH...
ぐすん
SWIP
I'M AWFUL ...!

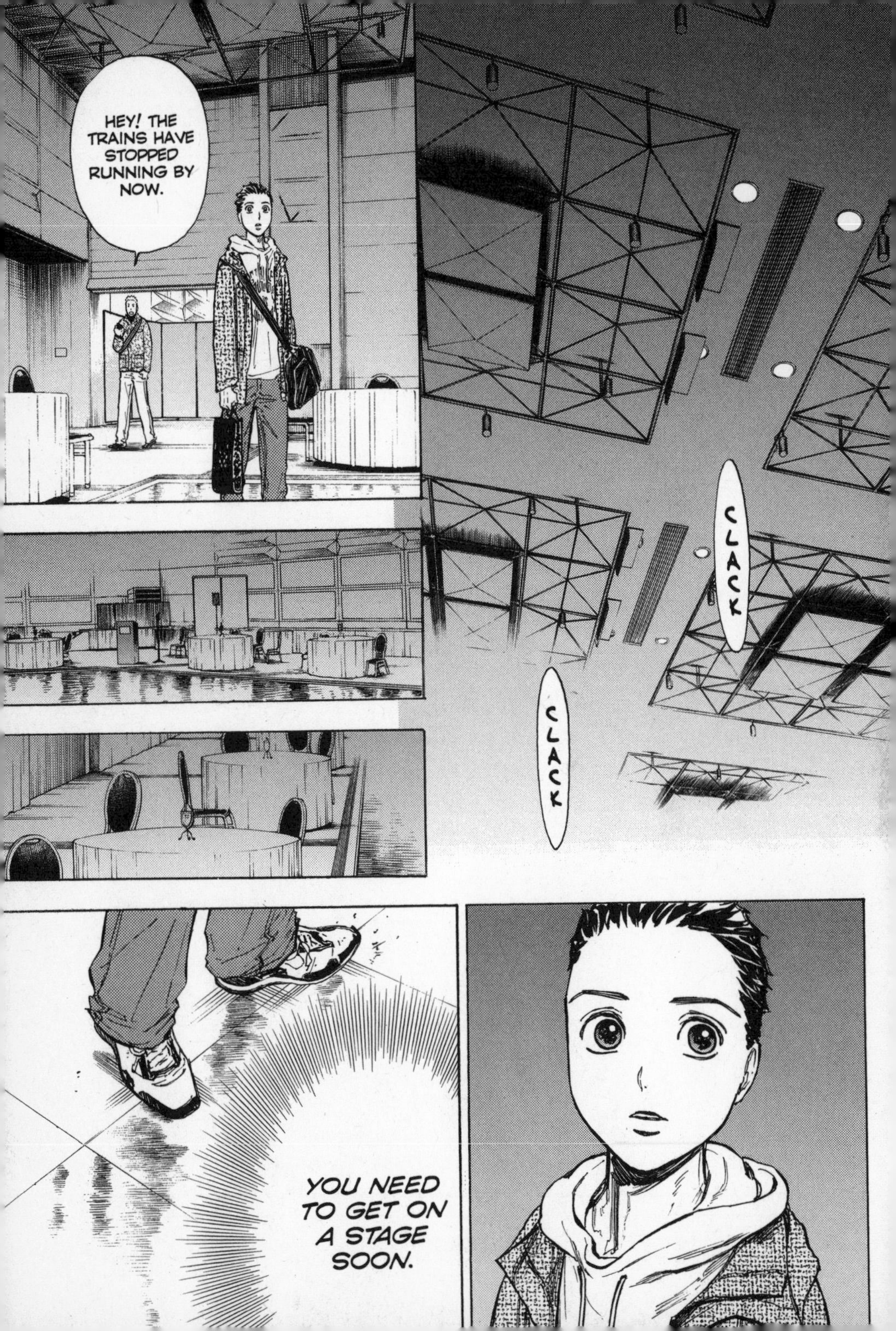
CLACK
CLACK
HEY! THE TRAINS HAVE STOPPED RUNNING BY NOW.
YOU NEED TO GET ON A STAGE SOON.

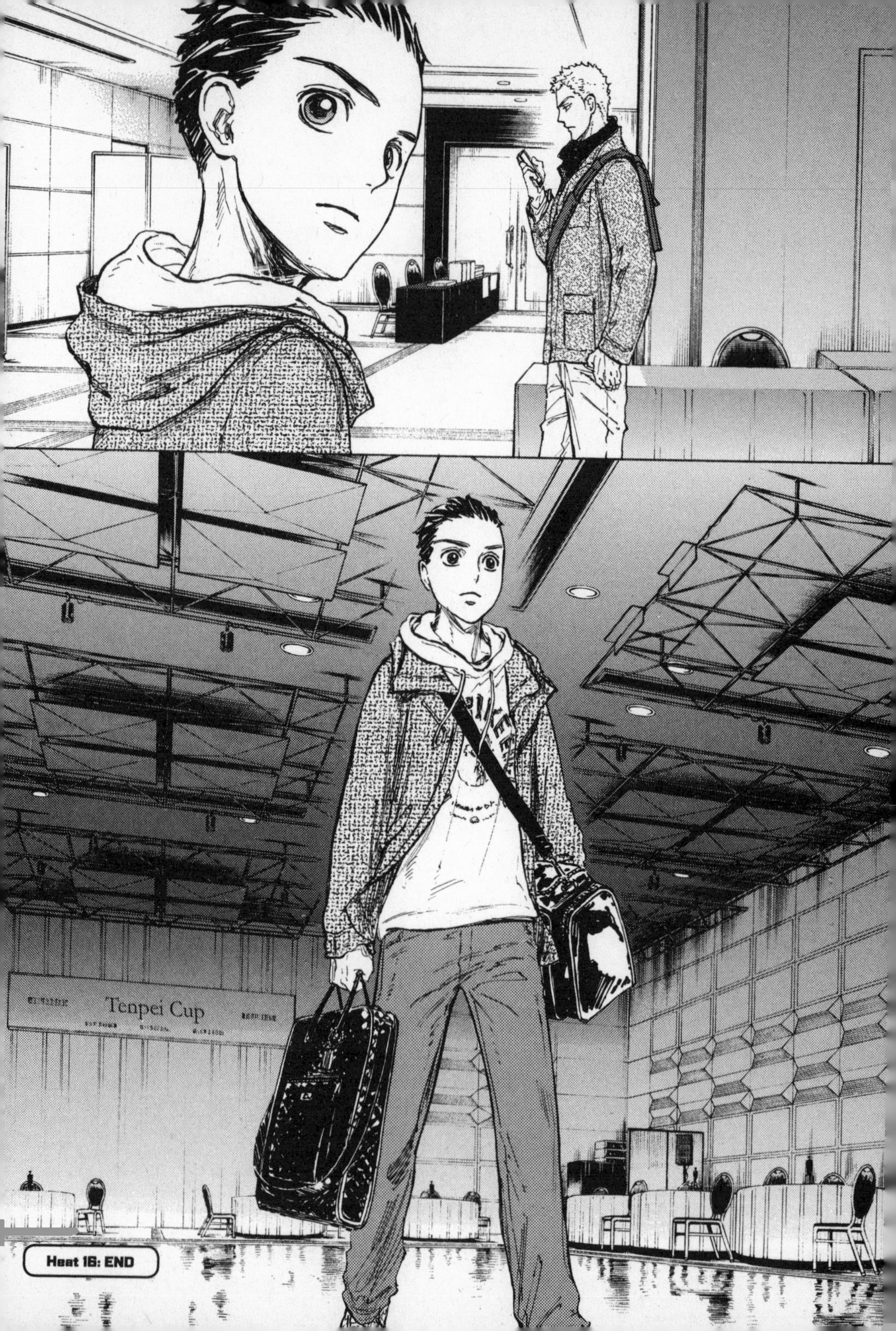
Tenpei Cup
Heat 16: END

# WELCOME TO THE BALLROOM

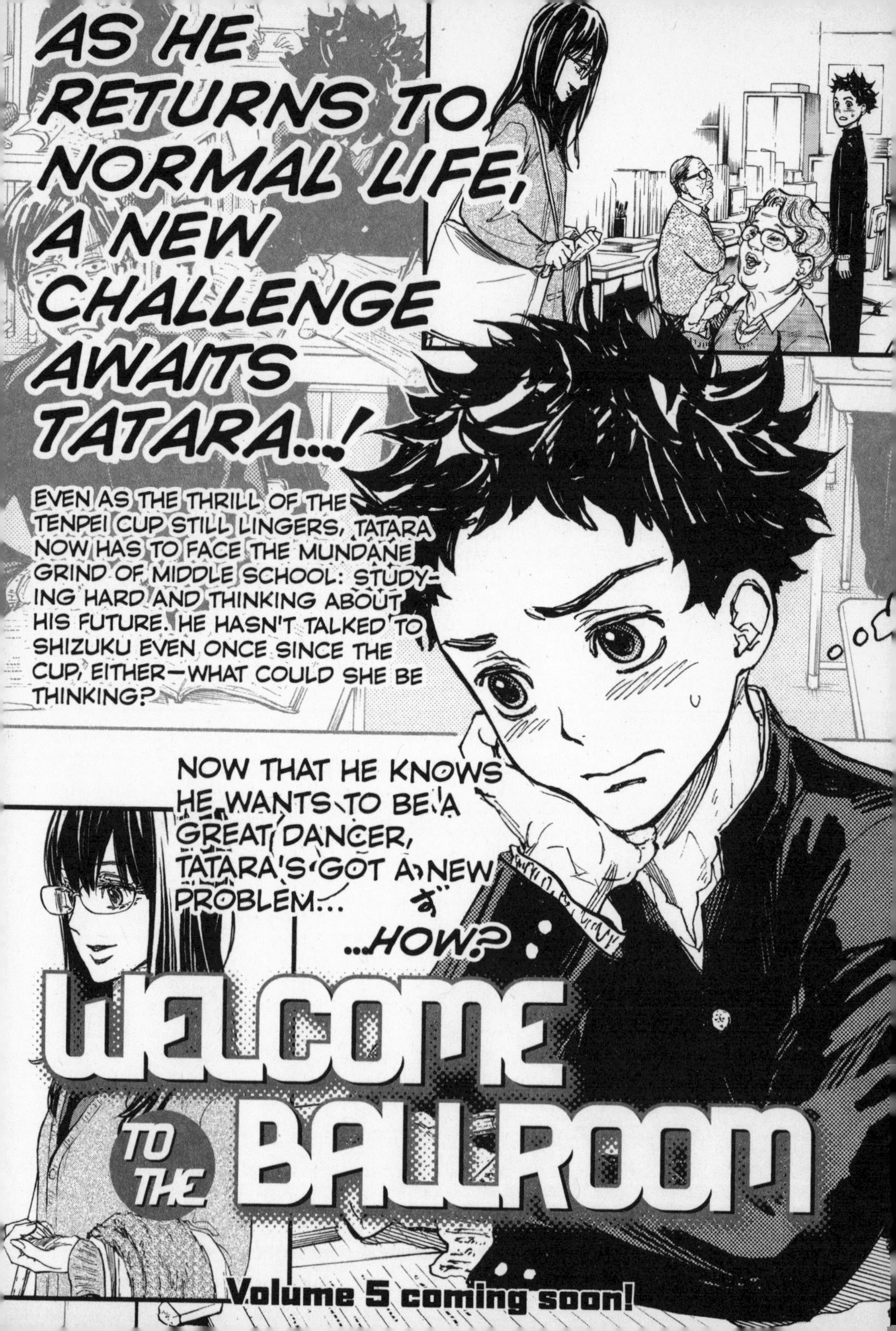

AS HE RETURNS TO NORMAL LIFE, A NEW CHALLENGE AWAITS TATARA...!
EVEN AS THE THRILL OF THE TENPEI CUP STILL LINGERS, TATARA NOW HAS TO FACE THE MUNDANE GRIND OF MIDDLE SCHOOL: STUDYING HARD AND THINKING ABOUT HIS FUTURE. HE HASN'T TALKED TO SHIZUKU EVEN ONCE SINCE THE CUP, EITHER—WHAT COULD SHE BE THINKING?
NOW THAT HE KNOWS HE WANTS TO BE A GREAT DANCER, TATARA'S GOT A NEW PROBLEM...
...HOW?
ず
WELCOME TO THE BALLROOM
Volume 5 coming soon!

Having lost his wife, high school teacher Kohei Inuzuka is doing his best to raise his young daughter Tsumugi on his own. He's a pretty bad cook and doesn't have a big appetite to begin with, but chance brings his little family together with one of his students, the lonely Kotori. The three of them are anything but comfortable in the kitchen, but the healing power of home cooking might just work on their grieving hearts.

"This season's number-one feel-good anime!" —Anime News Network

"A beautifully-drawn story about comfort food and family and grief. Recommended." —Otaku USA Magazine

# sweetness & lightning
### By Gido Amagakure

KC KODANSHA COMICS

© Gido Amagakure/Kodansha Ltd. All rights reserved.

KC
KODANSHA
COMICS

"I'm pleasantly surprised to find modern shojo using cross-dressing as a dramatic device to deliver social commentary... Recommended."

-Otaku USA Magazine

# The prince in his dark days

By **Hico Yamanaka**

A drunkard for a father, a household of poverty... For 17-year-old Atsuko, misfortune is all she knows and believes in. Until one day, a chance encounter with Itaru–the wealthy heir of a huge corporation–changes everything. The two look identical, uncannily so. When Itaru curiously goes missing, Atsuko is roped into being his stand-in. There, in his shoes, Atsuko must parade like a prince in a palace. She encounters many new experiences, but at what cost…?

© Hico Yamanaka/Kodansha Ltd. All rights reserved.

KC KODANSHA COMICS



*New action series from Takei Hiroyuki, creator of the classic shonen franchise Shaman King!*

In medieval Japan, a bell hanging on the collar is a sign that a cat has a master. Norachiyo's bell hangs from his katana sheath, but he is nonetheless a stray — a ronin. This one-eyed cat samurai travels across a dishonest world, cutting through pretense and deception with his blade.

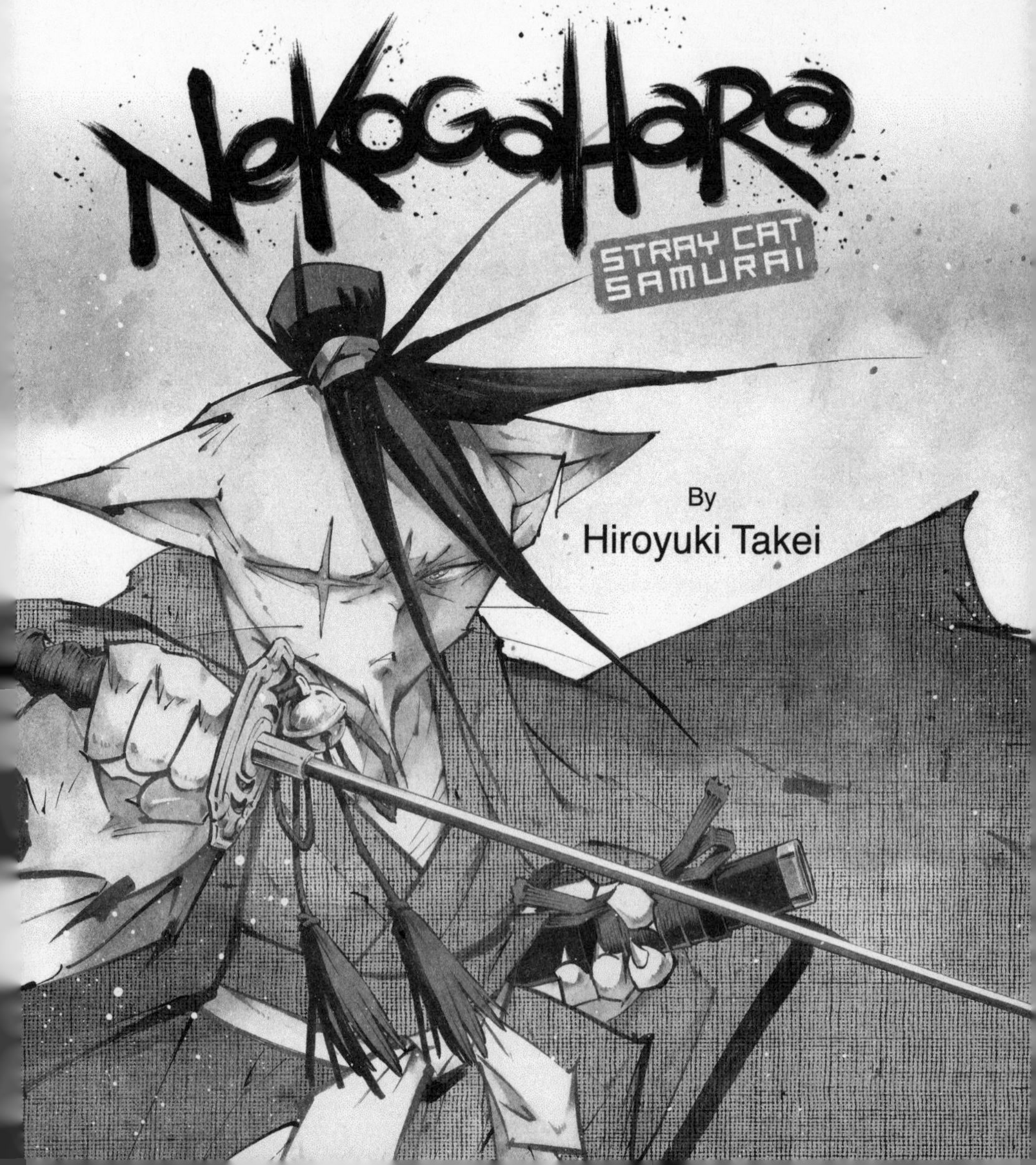
NEKOGAHARA
STRAY CAT SAMURAI
By
Hiroyuki Takei

Japan's most powerful spirit medium delves into the ghost world's greatest mysteries!

Story by Kyo Shiradaira, famed author of mystery fiction and creator of Spiral, Blast of Tempest, and The Record of a Fallen Vampire.

Both touched by spirits called yokai, Kotoko and Kuro have gained unique superhuman powers. But to gain her powers Kotoko has given up an eye and a leg, and Kuro's personal life is in shambles. So when Kotoko suggests they team up to deal with renegades from the spirit world, Kuro doesn't have many other choices, but Kotoko might just have a few ulterior motives...

# IN/SPECTRE

## BY KYO SHIRODAIRA

© Kyo Shirodaira/Kodansha Ltd. All rights reserved.

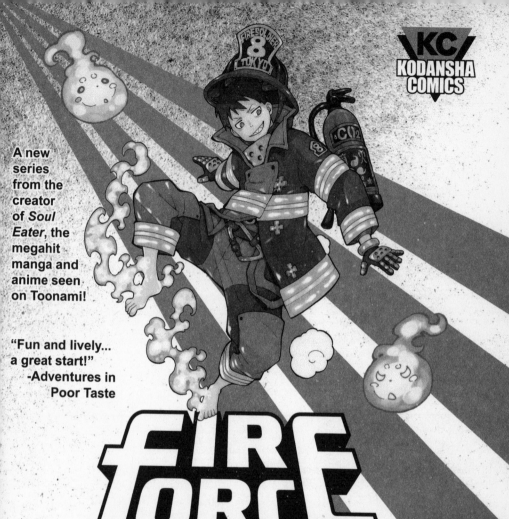

KC
KODANSHA
COMICS

A new series from the creator of *Soul Eater*, the megahit manga and anime seen on Toonami!

"Fun and lively... a great start!"
-Adventures in Poor Taste

# FIRE FORCE

By Atsushi Ohkubo

The city of Tokyo is plagued by a deadly phenomenon: spontaneous human combustion! Luckily, a special team is there to quench the inferno: The Fire Force! The fire soldiers at Special Fire Cathedral 8 are about to get a unique addition. Enter Shinra, a boy who possesses the power to run at the speed of a rocket, leaving behind the famous "devil's footprints" (and destroying his shoes in the process). Can Shinra and his colleagues discover the source of this strange epidemic before the city burns to ashes?

© Atsushi Ohkubo/Kodansha Ltd. All rights reserved.

KC
KODANSHA
COMICS

**The award-winning manga about what happens inside you!**

"Far more entertaining than it ought to be... what kid doesn't want to think that every time they sneeze a torpedo shoots out their nose?"
–Anime News Network

Strep throat! Hay fever! Influenza! The world is a dangerous place for a red blood cell just trying to get her deliveries finished. Fortunately, she's not alone. She's got a whole human body's worth of cells ready to help out! The mysterious white blood cell, the buff and brash killer T cell, the nerdy neuron, even the cute little platelets — everyone's got to come together if they want to keep you healthy!

# Cells at Work!

はたらく細胞

By Akane Shimizu

© Akane Shimizu/Kodansha Ltd. All rights reserved.

*Welcome to the Ballroom* volume 4 is a work of fiction. Names, characters, places, and incidents are the products of the author's imagination or are used ctitiously. Any resemblance to actual events, locales, or persons, living or dead, is entirely coincidental.

A Kodansha Comics Trade Paperback Original.

*Welcome to the Ballroom* volume 4 copyright ©2013 Tomo Takeuchi, English translation copyright ©2017 Tomo Takeuchi

All rights reserved.

Published in the United States by Kodansha Comics, an imprint of Kodansha USA Publishing, LLC, New York.

Publication rights for this English edition arranged through Kodansha Ltd., Tokyo.

First published in Japan in 2013 by Kodansha Ltd., Tokyo, as *Ballroom e Yōkoso* volume 4.

ISBN 978-1-63236-406-7

Printed in the United States of America.

www.kodanshacomics.com

9 8 7 6 5 4 3 2 1

Translation: Karen McGillicuddy
Lettering: Brndn Blakeslee
Editing: Paul Starr

Kodansha Comics edition cover design: Phil Balsman